IRAN AFTER THE REVOLUTION

IRAN AFTER THE REVOLUTION

CRISIS OF AN ISLAMIC STATE

*Edited by Saeed Rahnema
and Sohrab Behdad*

I.B.TAURIS
LONDON · NEW YORK

Published in 1995 by
I.B.Tauris & Co Ltd
45 Bloomsbury Square
London WC1A 2HY

175 Fifth Avenue
New York NY 10010

In the United States of America
and Canada distributed by
St Martin's Press
175 Fifth Avenue
New York NY 10010

A full CIP record for this book is available
from the British Library

ISBN 1 85043 905 2

A full CIP record for this book is available from
the Library of Congress

Library of Congress catalog card number: available

Typeset in Monotype Garamond
by Lucy Morton, London SE12
Printed and bound in Great Britain by WBC Ltd,
Bridgend, Mid Glamorgan

Contents

List of Tables and Figures

Acknowledgements

We are grateful to the institutions and colleagues who assisted us in the preparation of this volume. We acknowledge the support of the Social Sciences and Humanities Research Council of Canada, the School of Policy Studies, Queen's University, its Director Keith Banting, and the Department of Economics at Denison University. We are also indebted to our colleagues Haleh Afshar, Nasrin Rahimieh, Bahram Tavakolian, Dick Davis, Haideh Moghissi and Laura Murray for their helpful advice, and to the anonymous readers for their valuable comments. Thanks are also due to our contributors, who made this collective effort a pleasant and fruitful one. Of course, no book becomes a book without the diligence and patience of the publisher. We are grateful to Anna Enayat and Giles Egginton of I.B. Tauris. All said, no one but us is responsible for any shortcomings that remain.

Foreword

The 1979 Iranian Revolution has been a source of inspiration for the Islamic revivalist movement in many Muslim countries. We believe that the experience of Iran under the rule of the Islamic Republic is also a sobering lesson for those who have placed hopes for liberation of their people in the victory of Islamic revivalism. The specific features of any social movement, including those that are mobilized under the banner of Islam, are determined by the concrete socio-historical circumstances of the society in which these movements take place. It follows that the peculiarities of Iranian society, the rule of the Shah, and Iranian Shi'ism helped to shape the unique features of the Iranian Revolution, the Islamic Republic, and the course of post-revolutionary developments in Iran. We believe, however, that Islamic states, which it is the aim of Islamic movements to establish, share certain universal characteristics defined by the general nature of Islamic revivalism.

In the Introduction we present a framework for the analysis of a revivalist Islamic state. We argue that Islamic revivalism, in essence, is a populist-conservative movement. Its populism resides in its celebration of social justice, benevolence and people's power. It promises to deliver equity and dignity to the underprivileged urban and rural masses, freedom to alienated and suppressed intellectuals, and prosperity to artisans, merchants and industrialists frustrated in their competition with powerful domestic oligopolies and multinational corporations. It promises a utopia wherein everyone imbued with Islamic values will live in peace and affluence on the high plateau of Islamic morality, shepherded by an Islamic state that is guided by no less than the eternal and divine laws of Islam. The conservatism of the movement (the diversity of Islamic interpretations notwithstanding) lies in the fact that Islamic divine law (Shari'a), as expressed by the Quran and by Mohammad, and articulated by fourteen centuries of Islamic jurisprudence, unequivocally defends property rights, gainful activities and the accumulation of wealth. These are the very stuff of a capitalist economy, to which Islamic populism so intensively objects. An

Islamic state, constituted upon the victory of an Islamic revivalist movement, is the arena of contestation between these two tendencies. The
post-victory crisis in an Islamic state is one of self-definition. This, as we
show in the Introduction, entails a long drawn out and painful process of
negation of populism and affirmation of conservatism. Iran's experience
with Islamic revivalism provides, in our view, a hard-learned lesson for all
those who support the struggle for equity, social justice and human dignity
in the Middle East.

We certainly hope to include among our audience the people of the
Middle East – in Algeria, Egypt, Turkey and other countries where Islamic
revivalism is gaining popular support. But more immediately, we aim to
address those Muslim intellectuals, Western liberal Islamicists and Middle
Eastern scholars who have joined in the celebration of Islamic revivalism,
who may see the populist orientation of this movement as a spark of
hope for the liberation of the people of the Middle East. We believe that
the prevailing relativism among postmodernist liberals, who remain deeply
frustrated by the failure of their futile attempt – and that of their disciplines
– only a couple of decades ago to trace the path of modernity by negating
traditionalism, has now come round to negate secularism and the secular
struggle for social liberation in the Middle East. We believe that this new
celebration of revivalism, too, will prove to be a misdirected effort. Of
course, only history can prove the viability of a social theory; although
one should hope that intellectual vigilance may facilitate our understanding
of the course of history. We appreciate the position of the liberal Islamicists
and Middle Eastern scholars in the West: they see themselves and everyone
else (particularly their students) as bombarded by the anti-Islamic propaganda of the defenders of the status quo. They indeed find themselves
between a rock and a hard place. Nevertheless, it is disheartening to
witness the quietism of these liberal scholars in the West in the face of
brutal violations of human dignity and threats to life and freedom in the
Islamic states, as noble as is their fear of transgressing the sanctified walls
of 'otherness', which were erected only to ward off intruders who committed such violations.

The chapters in this book comprise comprehensive studies of several
dimensions of the crisis of a revivalist Islamic state in Iran: its socio-
historical background, its economic turmoil, and its attempt to effect the
ideological reconstruction of Iranian society. These studies, written by
scholars with a first-hand knowledge of Iranian society and its revolution,
are each independent and do not form part of a project aiming to under-
score the crisis of post-revolutionary Iran. In fact, there may or may not
be agreement among the various authors in this volume on the course of
social development in post-revolutionary Iran, or on its various dimensions.

Part I considers three fundamental issues shaping the character of the
Iranian Revolution. Ahmad Ashraf examines the nature of social trans-

formation and class formation in the pre-revolutionary period. He stresses the growth of the well-to-do farmers, and the rise of the new urban middle class, the modern bourgeoisie, and the working class, at the expense of the bazaar merchants and the clergy. He believes that the militant ulema, their bazaari followers and an activist intelligentsia formed the nucleus of a revolutionary coalition that spearheaded the 1979 revolution. Fatemeh E. Moghadam studies the connection between state policy, political stability and the articulation of property rights in Iranian history since the early nineteenth century. The significance of the issue to study of the Iranian Revolution is that, on the one hand, the Shah's land reform and subsequent social policies redefined property relations, and on the other, the definition of private property rights has been one of the major dilemmas facing the Islamic Republic. Ali Rahnema and Farhad Nomani scrutinize the spectrum of ideological and political positions among the various Islamic orientations. They examine the subsystems of Islam articulated by Mortaza Motahhari, Ali Shariati, Navab Safavi and Mehdi Bazargan, and trace the role of Ayatollah Khomeini in the politics of competing subsystems in the post-revolutionary period.

Economics has played a pivotal role in post-revolutionary Iran for two reasons. First, the Islamic revivalist movement and the Islamic Republic proclaimed an Islamic economic system to be an important dimension of the rule of the oppressed (*mostaz'afin*) that it promised to establish in Iran. Second, the post-revolutionary economic crisis has produced one of the most serious dilemmas to face the Islamic Republic. Part II presents studies of various dimensions of the effort toward Islamization of the economy and of the economic crisis in post-revolutionary Iran. Sohrab Behdad examines the course of the economic crisis and its impact on the transformation of politics in Iran. He shows that the inability of the Islamic Republic to define a viable economic system, and the consequent continuation of the economic crisis, have led the regime into a dead end; its only route to survival is thus to negate itself by repudiating its populist policies of the past fifteen years. A study of the development of the industrial structure in the pre-revolutionary decade and the Islamic Republic's subsequent experimentation with various industrial policies is presented by Saeed Rahnema. He argues that after a decade and a half the Islamic Republic has not made any progress toward the creation of a dynamic industrial base in Iran.

Oil revenues and exchange-rate policies are two crucial aspects of the Iranian economy. Djavad Salehi-Isfahani investigates the oil policy of the Islamic Republic in the international and domestic arena, in the context of constraints on oil production, a sluggish international market, and a fast-growing domestic demand for petroleum products. A high rate of population growth, a stagnating domestic economy, and decline in the real value of oil revenues (mainly from exporting crude oil) manifested themselves in a large foreign-exchange gap. Hossein Farzin investigates Iran's attempt to realign its exchange rate in response to the complications resulting from its policy of maintaining exchange control in a system of multiple exchange rates and in the face of social and economic problems confronting the regime following a sharp devaluation of the currency.

Part III is a study of some important aspects of the social policies of the Islamic Republic. Sussan Siavoshi and Asghar Rastegar examine different aspects of the Islamic Republic's education policy. Siavoshi compares the treatment of a number of political and ideological issues in the textbooks of the pre- and post-revolutionary periods, and shows how both regimes have attempted to acquire legitimacy by inculcating their values in the young. Rastegar focuses on health policy and medical education in the Islamic Republic. He shows that the Islamic Republic has attempted to increase its control over the university system by centralizing and politicizing the universities. At the same time, the government made efforts to increase the output at the universities. Rastegar argues, however, that these policies have resulted in substantial deterioration of medical education in Iran.

Shahrzad Mojab and Amir Hassanpour consider the politics of nationality and ethnic diversity by examining the policies of the Islamic Republic toward Iranian Kurdish people. They argue that, although the Islamic leaders denounce nationalism as a Western conspiracy, the Islamic Republic has itself pursued a national chauvinistic policy not unlike that of the Pahlavi regime.

Finally, Haideh Moghissi takes on the controversial issue of women's presence in public life in the Islamic Republic. She investigates policies aimed to restrict the presence of women in the public sphere, and describes the struggle of Iranian women to assert their rights. Moghissi reveals the complex realities and contradictions of sexual politics in Iran and analyses the rise of a Muslim female elite, which was initially mobilized to support the Islamization policies and yet which has come to demand changes in the gender status quo. She argues that the emergence of reformist Muslim women in Iran is a reflection of the contradictions of a society which, although it is well integrated into the world market, persists in preserving an archaic mode of human and social conduct.

Saeed Rahnema and Sohrab Behdad

Introduction:
Crisis of an Islamic State

From Malaysia to Tunisia, Islamic movements are posing a serious challenge to the existing political and social orders. The 1979 revolution in Iran established the viability of Islamic movements in leading a popular revolution. An ayatollah in exile gained the leadership of a victorious revolution against a powerful, and seemingly invulnerable, authoritarian regime. The Shah was ousted, his regime collapsed, and an 'Islamic republic' was erected. *Allah-o Akbar, Khomeini Rahbar!* The force of the masses that shouted this slogan incapacitated the Shah's military machine and drowned out the slogans of the other contenders for political power, from liberal reformers to radical revolutionaries. 'Independence, Liberty, Islamic Republic' became the holy triad of the Iranian revolutionary movement.

The Islamic Republic declared itself the rule of the oppressed (*mostaz'afin*), liberated from 'exploitation and imperialist domination'. Khomeini was hailed as the 'hope of the world's oppressed', and Iran became the Mecca of Muslim activists of the world. To the Afghan Mojahedin, the Shi'is of Kuwait, Lebanon and Iraq, and the opposition forces of Pakistan, Syria, Algeria, Egypt and Malaysia, the Islamic victory in Iran became a source of inspiration and a model for emulation. It appeared that the oppressed people of the world had, at last, found a way to liberation. However, it turned out that the crucible of Iranian revolution produced one of the most disappointing results in the history of revolutionary experimentation.

Meanwhile, the fear of Islamic radicalism incited the reactionary offensive of the status quo everywhere, especially in the West. Their image-making machinery became engaged in a propaganda war, shaping the public consensus in opposition to the revolutionary movements in Muslim countries.[1] After all, the intellectual tradition of the West had already ingrained a deep anti-Islamic and anti-Arab (anti-Middle East) sentiment in the cultural consciousness of its people.[2] Fundamentalism, fanaticism

I

and terrorism became the propagated image of the Islamic movements in the West. The Hezbollah in Lebanon and the bomb planters of the Pan Am airplane over Scotland became the distinguishing symbols of a fanatic Islamic international that is threatening the civilized world. Not surprisingly, the attacks have focused on the struggle of a popular movement, which is revolting against the corruption and oppression of the dictatorial rule, the imperialist domination of the post-colonial powers, and, not least, against the social and economic deprivation of the people of the Middle East. The political essence of this propaganda attack is transparent, in spite of many complexities in its details. This wave of condemnation of the Islamic resurgence has been directed only toward those who are questioning the existing social order. Neither the fundamentalism of Saudi Arabia nor the fanaticism of the 'freedom fighting' Mojahedin of Afghanistan has seemed to be a matter of concern.

Reacting to this anti-Islamic campaign, and in an anti-propaganda effort, a relatively large corps of liberal Islamicists and Middle East scholars have come to defend Islamic movements. They either have declared their support for the 'joyful triumph of the Islamic Ummah [community]',[3] or, at least, have expressed compassion and understanding for the Islamic resurgence, as the rightful struggle of a people to shape their destiny.[4] In *Covering Islam* (1981), Edward Said dispels the Islamophobia projected by the political establishment in the immediate post-1979 revolution in Iran, and in the heat of the US-embassy hostage ordeal. Similarly, John Esposito's *The Islamic Threat: Myth or Reality?* (1992) counters the propaganda offensive of the George Bush administration in the Persian Gulf war of 1991. These works, among others, justifiably and effectively bring to the attention of the public in the West the vengefulness of the conservative and ethnocentric propaganda of politicians, TV commentators, editorial writers, and anti-Islam Islamicists and Orientalists, and try to expose the political bias in the destructive media coverage of the Islamic movement. Islamic revivalism, according to these expositions, is a popular protest against the cultural, political and economic domination of the West, a rediscovery of the 'authentic self' for the oppressed people of the Middle East.

It is a noble deed to deconstruct the destructive, distorted image of a liberation struggle for those in the West who are willing to understand the sounds of fury of the people of a region which has experienced many indignities in recent decades, not to mention past centuries. However, by portraying an idealized cultural–political construct of Islam in the popular movements of the Middle East, the liberal defence of Islamic revivalism follows the blind alley of populism. It fails to understand the limits of the utopian vision of Islamic revivalism, and negates or at least discounts the secular dimensions of the political movement as the ideals of alienated 'Westernized' intellectuals. Thus, this exposition of Islamic revivalism, while it dispels a distorted, hostile image of the Middle East and Islam, replaces it with another distorted, though sympathetic, image. The choice, then, becomes one between two simplified and distorted images, that of a foe or a friend.

This liberal defence of Islamic revivalism is based on two interrelated contemporary intellectual currents: anti-Orientalism and anti-modernization/Westernization. Anti-Orientalism characterizes Orientalism as the European scholarly and artistic search to define and represent the East (Orient) as distinct from, and inferior to, the West (Occident).[5] Orientalism is viewed as the effort of the European nations to discover and learn about peoples and cultures of the colonies, in order to dominate, control and govern these treasures, which they so self-righteously believe belong to them, and whose people are so incapable of ruling themselves that they must be ruled by others.[6] According to the critics, this essentialistic ontological distinction between the 'inferior' Orient and the 'more advanced' and 'civilized' Occident necessarily determines the epistemological and methodological approach of Orientalists.

The intellectuals and scholars of the 'Orient' have long been aware that Orientalists (*mostashreqin*) are the scholarly, artistic and literary soldiers of the colonial structure, fortifying the relationship of domination and exploitation of the East by the West. As Hamid Enayat stated some years before the publication of Said's *Orientalism*, 'although the relations between the various branches of Orientalism and the immediate goals of colonialism may not be readily apparent, the undeniable fact is that Orientalism was largely stimulated by, and in a sense nurtured in the bosom of, colonialism.'[7] The representations of the East by Orientalists such as Comte de Gobineau, Silvestre de Sacy, Ernest Renan, Edward Lane, Lord Curzon, among others in the nineteenth century, are so blatantly racist, and so clearly colonialist, that little is left to imagination or interpretation. Among the contemporaries, such as Sir A.R.H. Gibb, G.E. von Grunebaum and Bernard Lewis, and particularly among the new breed of American 'Orientalists' (for example, Marvin Zonis and Daniel Pipes, albeit that they do not refer to themselves as Orientalists), the overt political and ideological declarations are frequently disguised under the garb of scholarly 'objectivity'. An understanding of the malevolent character of Orientalists has been a part and parcel of the intellectual culture of the Middle East. In the conventional wisdom of the Middle East, every Orientalist is assumed as a functionary of the colonial government, and an ideologue of the West, unless proven otherwise.[8]

Edward Said elaborated this conventional wisdom of the East and brought it to the public of the West in his celebrated *Orientalism* (1978), where he concludes that 'every European in what he could say about the Orient was consequently a racist, an imperialist and almost totally ethnocentric.'[9] But while Said succeeds in demonstrating in many cases the malicious representations of the East, 'the other', by past and contemporary Orientalists, his anti-Orientalism manifesto is a simplification of reality.[10]

Orientalism ignores the contribution of Orientalist studies and their impact in facilitating the reciprocal (albeit asymmetrical) interconnection between the East and the West. It also dismisses the positive influence of the Orientalists on the culture and consciousness of the West, on the understanding of the East by the West, and even on the East's understanding of itself. Raymond Schwab, the French Orientalist of the early twentieth century, argues that the impact of the Orientalist discovery of the East on the European cultural consciousness and philosophical and scientific vision was so impressive that it may be regarded as the second renaissance of Europe.[11] It is interesting to note that only a few years after the publication of *Orientalism*, Said himself praised Raymond Schwab in an introduction to the English translation of Schwab's book. Schwab's study of the Orient is 'so profound and beneficent' to Said that he is even willing to call Schwab an *orienteur* rather than an *orientaliste*.[12] Similarly, one can point to at least some Orientalists who, in spite of their pro-colonial dispositions, have made significant contributions to the understanding of the Orient.[13]

But Said's negation of representations of the Orient by Orientalists has a fundamentally epistemological grounding. His essentialistic perception of the Orient and the Occident leads him to the acceptance of an ontological distinction between the two entities of the Orient and the Occident, and he finds (as al-'Azm points out) that gaining the truth about the culture of 'others' is an impossibility.[14] In Said's words:

> the real issue is whether indeed there can be a true representation of anything, or whether any and all representations, because they *are* representations, are embedded first in language and then in the culture, institutions, and political ambiance of the representer. If the latter is the correct one (which I believe it is), then we must be prepared to accept the fact that a representation is *eo ipso* implicated, intertwined, embedded, interwoven with a great many other things besides the 'truth,' which is itself a representation.[15]

This leads Said to a methodological conclusion that views 'representations ... as a common field of play defined by ... some common history, tradition, universe of discourse'.[16] This conclusion is the basis of an anti-representational approach that declares an uncontested 'ethico-epistemological denial of anyone's right or ability to represent others'.[17] Through this 'possessive exclusiveness', as Said himself calls it, an 'excluding insider' can disqualify an outsider from representation either by 'virtue of experience', or by 'virtue of method'.[18] Therefore it is not only the ideology or methodology of the Orientalists but their 'otherness' that disqualifies them from learning the 'truth' about the reality of the Orient. Separating the East and the West with an essentialistic, ontological divide, as Said does, is no less than 'reversed Orientalism', to borrow a term from al-'Azam.[19]

An important implication of reversed Orientalism is universal relativism. Since the line of 'otherness' is not drawn on continental or national borders, but around cultural distinctions and commonality of historical circumstances, any variations in these cultural or historical experiences would disqualify the 'foreigner' from representing 'the other'. The barrier of discovery is not, then, between the Orient and the Occident, but between any two cultural entities. In this way, one may argue that only the members of a tribe, a religious sect, or even a clan or a family are qualified to represent themselves. In the Middle East, the matter is of grave political importance in the confrontation between the secular and religious social forces. We will return to the issue below. But now let us consider another corollary of reversed Orientalism.

Reversed Orientalism, while it is an effort to dispel the distorted and condescending image of the East as presented by Orientalism, also leads to the idealization and glorification of Eastern traditions. It is true that the culture and rationality of the existence of the East must be understood in its own socio-historical context, which many Orientalists fail to do; but, nevertheless, this context is one of a highly hierarchical, patrimonial, severely repressive social existence with little regard for individual rights and liberties, characteristic of a tributary agrarian society, later dominated by the colonial powers. This is hardly a paradise in which to seek the cultures and values of a liberated humanity. Certainly, one cannot praise the West for attaining such a cultural height, as many Orientalists in fact did. But if the West is at fault for misunderstanding the conditions of existence in the East, we cannot fall off the other edge and idealize the same conditions, ignoring the anguish and wretchedness of life in the East, which is a manifestation of the social relations of production and the existing power structure. Some of the observations and claims of the Orientalists about the Orient, regardless of their intentions, epistemological and methodological perspectives, or policy recommendations, are true reflections of aspects of realities of the Orient, even though Said attempts to dispel them as figments of the Orientalists' 'imagination'.

The anti-Orientalism thesis is consistent with the anti-modernization perspective, which has also become a prevalent current of critique in the West. For several decades in the postwar period, development theorists propagated modernization, that is, Westernization, as the path of salvation for the underdeveloped economies. Based on the Weberian dichotomy of 'traditional' versus 'modern' societies, each with their different behavioural patterns and ethos, and influenced by the behavioural attributes ascribed to these societies by Talcott Parsons, theorists such as Everett Hagen and David McClelland, among others, promoted the idea that prevalent traditions of life and religion among the people of the underdeveloped countries are the main barriers to their economic development.[20] Daniel Lerner heralded the progressive transition to modernity of the Middle East in the early 1950s, in a regularly phased, balanced transformation of 'the demographic, economic, communication and cultural "sectors"' of the society, where not only are 'the modernizing individuals ... considerably less unhappy', but also 'the more rapidly the society around them is modernized the happier they are.'[21] This sociological prophecy, and those of the economists, put into practical and operational planning-policy frameworks by the epicentres of this wave of social reform at Harvard, MIT, the University of Chicago and others, and fuelled by the increasing oil revenues of those who had this heavenly blessing, was transformed into powerful autocratic, bureaucratic, top-down reforms in many Middle East countries. The same took place in the rest of the Third World. It no longer needs much deliberation to observe that this process was neither regularly phased nor balanced. Most importantly, it did not make 'the more modernized' souls any less unhappy than those who were, for one reason or another, left behind. The Iranian Revolution demonstrated the point vividly.[22] The bankruptcy of modernization theory was revealed to whomever bothered to look out from their intellectual tower of illusions.

Understanding of the superficiality and inadequacy of modernization theory soon became an integral part of the anti-establishment intellectual current in the Middle East, as well as in the rest of the Third World. In Iran, Jalal Al-e Ahmad popularized the anti-modernization thesis in the early 1960s, by referring to modernization as *gharbzadegi* (being struck by the West, Occidentosis).[23] The message was clear and simple: modernization is nothing but Westernization of the way of life, which will prolong underdevelopment, aggravate social alienation, and internalize Western domination of the society. The way out of social and economic deprivation is a return to the true 'self', a celebration of traditions and traditional values.

In this sort of critique, Islam is celebrated as the way to the liberation of the 'self' and community in Muslim societies. In the Arab world many Muslim scholars have called for an 'Islamic solution' (*al-hal al-Islami*) to overcome the plight of Muslims.[24] As Yusuf al-Qurdawi suggests, 'Islamic solution means that the entirety of life is molded into a fundamentally Islamic form and character.'[25] This call to return to traditional values, to Islam, had already been made by some Muslim activists, such as Hasan al-Banna, Mowlana Abdul Ala Moududi, and Mojtaba Navab Safavi, and by the organizations that they founded, Ikhwan al Muslimin (Islamic Brotherhood – Egypt, 1920s), Jama'at-e Eslami (Islamic Association – India, 1940s) and Fada'iyan-e Eslam (Crusaders of Islam – Iran, 1950s). The anti-modernization/Westernization current of the 1960s brought some of the more mainstream-minded, already modernized, intellectuals to the path of

Islamic revivalism. In Iran, Ali Shariati and his followers are the prime example of this Islamic intellectual movement. The 1979 popular revolution in Iran, and the spread of Islamic activism to other Muslim countries and communities proved to the world that Islam is, indeed, a doctrine with a mass appeal, and that the march toward change in Muslim societies will be under the green flag of Islam.

Thus, a new mainstream of thought has formed in the study of the Middle East, characterized by what, after the phrase coined by Al-e Ahmad, we call *Sharqzadegi* or Orientitis. By Orientitis we mean glorification and idealization of the values, social institutions, and – as a whole – the traditions of the East. As Islamophobia is a symptom of Occidentosis, Islamophilia is a symptom of Orientitis. Islamophilia is a celebration of the sanctity of popular Islamic beliefs, a rejection of modernization/ Westernization as elitist, domineering and aggressive – and, in any case, unworkable – set in opposition to the Islamophobia of the status quo. Islamophilia is also a rejection of the secularization process in the Muslim countries as the cultural imposition of the West. Hamid Algar's *The Root of the Islamic Revolution* is an example of acute Islamophilia, applauding the 'wave of renewal that has been … inaugurated by the Iranian Islamic Revolution'.[26] Esposito's *The Threat of Islam: Myth or Reality?* is a milder and more representative case. Esposito emphasizes the reality of diversity in contemporary Islam. He argues that the 'secular suppositions' of Western scholarship and 'secular-minded Muslims' have prevented us from realizing the progressiveness of Islam, and from seeing the non-radical, non-fanatical, non-fundamentalist, rational, progressive Muslims and Islamic organizations, whose number surpasses the radical, fanatical, fundamentalist, irrational, retrogressive Muslims and Islamic organizations. Our elitist vision, he asserts, has prevented us from learning about the true nature of Islam and its ulema. Therefore, the argument runs, we have attributed a false rigidity to Islam by emphasizing such irrelevant jurisprudential notions as the closing of the door of *ejtahad*.[27]

Esposito's argument is an extension and elaboration of the view expressed by Said, who maintains that when 'the reforming clergy takes on its (legitimate) role of reformulating Islam in order for it to be able to enter modernity', the Orientalists, with their metaphysical disbelief in the ability of Islam to modernize, label the reformist movement as reactionary, fanatical, and radical.[28] In Said's view, modern Orientalists such as Gibb are 'committed to Islamic orthodoxy' in their 'hostility to modernizing currents in Islam.'[29] Here, Esposito and Said, among many others, express an idealized view of Islam, a faith in the dynamic development of religion, in response to the changes in historical circumstances and the evolution of social consciousness toward social liberation. In theory, such a faith in the evolution of social ideologies and institutions may be based on firm methodological grounds. There is, however, no evidence to suggest, or any reason to believe, that the present Islamic revivalist movement is heading toward an Islamic reformation. Even in Iran, where Islamic resurgence was led from the top, enthusiastically followed by the many strata of society, and was, astonishingly, victorious in capturing the power of the state in a popular revolution, the populist interpretation of Islam soon degenerated to a jurisprudential dispute. This in turn, as the chapters of this book demonstrate, led to a 'pragmatist' redefinition of Islam, in consultation with the International Monetary Fund and the World Bank. If the experience of Iran is any guide, then the defenders of the status quo are foolish to oppose Islam, and the reform-minded Islamophiles err in putting their heart into the Islamic movement in the hope of liberation.

But it is not entirely clear that what the liberal Islamicists are hoping for is the liberation of the Muslim masses. Instead, it appears that the thrust of their argument is that a better understanding of Islam and Muslims by Western policy-makers is a necessary requirement for promoting the interest of their countries in the Middle East.[30] Clearly, the established Islamic states have shown that there is no inconsistency between a 'pragmatic' Islam and the existing world order. Even the ruling clergy in Iran have shown that they can sell oil and buy arms in highly complex international markets, run the satellite communication networks, conduct a modern war, enjoy riding in fine cars, and, above all, seek foreign investments under conditions at least as favourable to the companies as under the Shah's regime. Perhaps these are important facts for the West to digest, and which may encourage it to tone down its hostility toward Islamic revivalism. Yet the compatibility of Islam with modernity at this level had already been shown by such Islamic states as Saudi Arabia, Kuwait and Qatar. The experimentation in Iran proved, in addition, that the ulema are quite capable of taming a revolution, and continuing to ride it. As reassuring as the acceptance of these facts may be for the Western powers, such goals are certainly not what the popular Islamic movements in Algeria, Egypt and Turkey are aiming for. Intellectual sobriety compels us to look beyond the excitements of the popular celebrations.

In our critique of the celebration of Islamic revivalism by liberal Islamicists we make a distinction between Islam at the level of civil society and that of the state. Civil society, being composed of voluntary institutions, may certainly be Islamized or not, as those who take part in these institutions may wish. There is no necessity in a democratic society for uniformity in the ideological orientation and organizational form of such institutions. That is, Islamic revivalism within civil society would involve the removal of barriers that have prevented Muslims from adhering to their Islamic values and from forming social institutions. The corollary of this voluntarism in a democratic society is pluralism. In such a context,

Islamic revivalism could indeed be a struggle for democracy and against the authoritarian regimes that impose constraints on social institutions, Islamic or not. However, in a democratic society such religious freedom cannot imply the imposition of Islamic values, mores and religious practices upon those who do not wish, for religious or other reasons, to practice Islam or follow any particular interpretation of it. Civil society is, among other things, the site of the family. In a pluralistic society the basic rights of all individuals are protected against religious values and practices that question or constrain these rights in the private (family) and public spheres. The issue is of paramount importance with regard to the protection of the fundamental rights of women.

The distinction between civil society and the state is, however, at best blurred in the Islamic revivalist movement. At the base of Islamic belief, a 'truly' Islamic society, as distinct from a 'natural' society (*jahiliyya*, ruled by customs evolved by humans for their own purpose and in ignorance of God), is one which follows the system of morality of Islam, as specified by the divine law (Shari'a). In this context there is an organic relationship between the realm of religion (social norms and values) and political power.[31] In Islam, the totality of society must be organized according to divine law, and political action must have as its objective the execution of God's will. Yet, except for a brief period in the Golden Age of Islam, when Mohammad ruled in Medina (AD 622–32), this organic relation has never been fully established.[32] Faced with secular realities, Muslim leaders throughout the centuries have submitted to the power of the state that they did not consider their own.[33] Meanwhile, as Islam remained mainly in the mosques and in the heart and soul of the people, and the kings and sultans paid occasional homage to the authority of the clergies, the ideal of re-establishing the social order that once existed in the Golden Age has been kept alive. Islamic revivalism aims to transform the Islam of the heart and soul (spiritual Islam) into a political Islam by acquiring political power and establishing an Islamic state.

An Islamic state, by definition, is exclusionary. It is the domination of Islamic precepts through the coercive power of the state over the social, cultural and political life of all segments of society. It marginalizes non-Muslims, Muslims of the sects different from the dominant one (the Shi'i–Sunni differentiation in countries such as Iran, Iraq, Pakistan, Lebanon and Afghanistan is a prime example), and even those in the same sect who adhere to interpretations of Islam in variance with that of the state. Moreover, it eliminates the sphere of secular existence. It is ironic that the secular, anti-Orientalist, liberal scholars of the West, who would regard as reprehensible the possibility of a populist Evangelist government coming to power in any Western society, find it so palatable to prescribe, and even to celebrate, the establishment of religious states for the 'natives' of the Orient.

The struggle to establish a secular, democratic state has been an integral part of the history of many Middle Eastern countries. Iran has been an arena for the secularization debate at least since the 1906–07 Constitutional Revolution.[34] To belittle and downplay the struggle for the secularization of society in the Middle East as a symptom of Occidentosis, and therefore as a non-authentic cultural implant,[35] is at best a rejection of the dynamics of intercultural interactions.[36]

An Islamic state (like any religious state) is undemocratic even for those who are privileged not to be excluded from it. For a state to be Islamic it must be organized, and its affairs be conducted, in accordance with Islamic divine law, the Shari'a, which is most essentially defined by the Quran and the tradition of Mohammad. Islamic jurisprudence (*fiqh*), in various Islamic schools, defines the method of application of the Shari'a to the concrete circumstance. The interpretation of the Shari'a is within the exclusive domain of the ulema (*foqaha*, jurists), the mojtaheds or muftis. In the immediate post-revolutionary Iran, the writing of the constitution was the first step after the declaration of an Islamic Republic. Soon thereafter, Ayatollah Khomeini ordered that plans for the formation of a constitutional assembly be changed to that of an Assembly of Experts (Majles-e Khobregan). Experts in this context meant the mojtaheds. Although non-mojtaheds were allowed to be elected to the Assembly of Experts, Ayatollah Khomeini made it unequivocally clear that the drafting of the constitution in that assembly was the responsibility of Islamic jurists, stating that the 'expression of agreement and disagreement with the precept of Islam is the exclusive right of our reverend jurists.'[37]

Similarly, parliamentary representation is also deemed to play a secondary role to the rulings of the 'experts'. Thus the parliament is a consultative assembly (*showra*). A consultative assembly can raise issues, discuss problems, debate opinions, and even pass laws, but it is not a legislative assembly, for its 'laws' are not enforceable without the approval of the 'reverend jurists'. According to the Constitution of the Islamic Republic of Iran, the laws passed by the Consultative Assembly (Majles) would acquire the force of law only when approved by the Council of Guardians, whose members are mojtaheds and 'Islamic legal experts' (see Appendix). Thus, the legislative assembly is merely consultative in function. The issue is not only the existence of a multilayered legislative structure, which by itself may or may not be democratic. The obstacle to the attainment of a democratic state is that any social and political discourse within the state is limited only to the confines of the Shari'a and subject to the approval of the guardians of the divine law, the mojtaheds. The legitimacy of social policy and legal prescription is sought in the authenticity of interpretations of the irrefutable principles of Islam. In the Islamic Republic, to guarantee that no one will deviate from this narrow path even when popular representation is a reality, the Council of Guardians evaluates candidates for the Majles and approves only those who are 'qualified' Muslims.

It is true that there are various interpretations of the Shari'a, reflecting the differences in social philosophy and political orientation among Muslim individuals or organizations. However, there are clear limits to the scope of variations in interpretation in Islamic jurisprudence. First, these interpretations are in the exclusive domain of the 'learned' jurists. Therefore even the views and interpretations of Shari'a by Islamic political organizations, or politically prominent Muslims, such as Ali Shariati and Mehdi Bazargan in Iran, are viewed as inconsequential or deviationist, or, as in the case of the Mojahedin-e Khalq, heretical. Second, no interpretation may reject the specific pronouncements of the Quran or the tradition of Mohammad. Any such rejection (*naskh*) is also viewed as heretical. Therefore many Islamic precepts, such as those dealing with the position of women in family and public life, the limitation of the rights of non-Muslims, and certain aspects of social life – for example, Islamic forms of punishments (*hodud-shar'ia*) – are explicitly addressed in the Quran or by Mohammad's Tradition, and are therefore irrefutable. On these and similar matters, there is little room for variation in interpretation. Third, interpretations of the Shari'a must be within the bounds of the fundamentals of jurisprudential tradition, established by the grand mojtaheds of the past. Any transgression of these bounds is considered a deviation or revisionism (*bid'a*), which is also heresy. Thus, for the Islamic state, which acquires its legitimacy by expression of its devotion to Islamic divine law, the range of interpretations is confined within the narrow domain of established jurisprudential principles.

In an already established Islamic state, the Islamic opposition may subscribe to a different interpretation of the Shari'a in order to put forth its political platform. As long as the opposition's claims are within the domain of reasonable disagreements, the loyal opposition may conduct its political campaign. However, when the disagreement extends beyond the acceptable range of difference in the jurisprudential tradition, the charge of being deviationist (*monharef*) or hypocritical (*monafeq*) is raised against the opposition Muslim individuals or groups. Such opposition is viewed as refuting the word of God, for which severe reprisals are prescribed.

While a new Islamic state is being established, a period of intense political crisis is to be expected. A crisis of power is a feature of any post-revolutionary state. But Islamic states established by mass movements confront an inherent contradiction which will inevitably lead to a prolonged political and economic crisis. Islamic movements mobilize masses – particularly the urban poor, petty merchants, artisans and peasants – who see no hope for a decent social existence in the prevailing circumstances, under the banner of Islamic social justice, cooperative power and human decency. These movements herald a new social order, an Islamic economy, wherein no one exploits any one and no one is able to amass wealth while others go hungry. They promise a society that has neither the harshness of an unbridled capitalism nor the confinements of an autocratic socialism. The Islamic social order, they pledge, guarantees everyone freedom of enterprise and the means to be enterprising. They promise social welfare and, above all, people's power.

There is no deception, necessarily, at work here. One can surely find reasons to believe that this is what Islam could be. Many passages in the Quran and much of Mohammad's Tradition justify such claims. Any ambitious and socially conscious political activist can find in Islam many streaks of radicalism, from the condemnation of wealth and arrogance to calls for the poor to be the inheritors of the land. Abu Dharr, Mohammad's companion, was one of the earliest defenders of the cause of the oppressed (*mostaz'afin*). He was, however, sent into exile by Uthman, the third caliph of the Muslims, for his disruptive, radical views. For centuries, Abu Dharr's version of Islam, the Islam of the dispossessed, has kindled the hearts of Islamic liberationists, despite recurrent refutation of this interpretation by the Islamic establishment. The 1948 decree of al-Azhar (the authoritative theological centre in Cairo) in support of the caliph Uthman, and Ayatollah Motahhari's condemnation of Ali Shariati for subscribing to an Abu Dharrian interpretation of Islam, are two clear cases in point.[38]

While Islam promises social justice to the poor and destitute, it also makes it clear that the quest for worldly possessions, the accumulation of property and profit, is not only accepted but highly respected. After all, Mohammad called merchants 'God's faithful trustees on Earth' and promised them a special place in heaven.[39] It is not surprising, therefore, that Islam has always had deep roots in the centres of mercantile activity and among the propertied classes, and has always benefited from their generous worldly contributions. The Islamic revivalist movements promise the establishment of a social order that will unite conflicting aims: the welfare of the poor and the security of property. They maintain that once everyone abides by the rules of Islam, when excesses are curtailed and beneficence becomes the social norm, a social balance will be established.

In a new Islamic state, the structure of power that is erected and the social policies that are enacted determine the form of the social order established. The rhetoric of 'togetherness' of the Islamic *omma* notwithstanding, this entails no less than a social conflict and a political confrontation. A populist social force demanding social justice confronts the propertied class defending the existing social order. The populist force relies on the political power of the mass movement, and the conservative force exerts its economic power, and relies on Islamic jurisprudence, which is a strong fortress in defence of property.

Political confrontation in a newly established, post-revolutionary Islamic state entails a process of confining the position of the Islamic political organizations (with their opposing interpretations of Islam, reflecting the conflicting interests of various social groups that they represent) to the domain of acceptability according to Islamic jurisprudence. Thus, political discourse is channelled into the scholastic realm of Islamic jurisprudence, from which not only the non-Muslims and the secular-minded Muslims but also the lay Muslims are excluded, since the matter is defined not in terms of social legitimacy but in terms of the authenticity of the interpretation of the law of God. It is in the arena of public policy that the strict interpretation of Islam, in defence of the propertied class and in support of the conservative political forces, gains the upper hand over any reading of Islam in support of the populist political forces. This confrontation is seen in the experience of the Islamic Republic of Iran, where from the summer of 1980, when the Majles was established, to the end of the third Majles in the summer of 1992, all the main reform laws passed by the populist parliament, such as land redistribution, nationalization of foreign trade, and the labour law, were rejected by the Council of Guardians as being incompatible with Islamic precepts.

The transformation of the Islamic Republic in the course of the post-revolutionary social conflict is a vivid expression of the political crisis of an Islamic state, where, as Fred Halliday suggests, 'internal politics have been more diverse and uncontrollable than those of most other post-revolutionary regimes.'[40] In the early phase of the post-revolutionary period the clerics relied on their closest allies, the religious-minded liberals of the Freedom Movement, and asked its leader, Mehdi Bazargan, to form the Provisional Revolutionary Government. The rule of Bazargan, and subsequently the presidency of Abolhasan Bani-Sadr, the first and the only lay president of Iran, did not last long before being swept away by clerics who established their theocratic state by the deployment of widespread repression and reliance on their populist appeal. By the summer of 1981, all serious contenders for power – mainly non-clerical Muslim organizations and prominent activists – who did not subscribe to *velayat-e faqih* (the rule of the just jurist) were eliminated by the brutal force of state coercion. The Iran–Iraq war (1980–88) provided the Islamic Republic with both a pretext for the repression of internal opposition and the means for an intense ideological mobilization.

Once the *velayat-e faqih* was fully established, the factional confrontations in the Islamic Republic – between the populist forces subscribing to some notion of an Abu Dharrian social order, and the conservative forces reflecting the interests of the propertied class, with strong links to the bazaar merchants – became apparent. While the populists had the majority of seats in the first three parliaments and held on to the position of prime minister for most of this period, the conservatives dominated the Council of Guardians and held some major cabinet posts. Although the

populist faction, relying on the momentum of the revolutionary movement, managed to pursue some of its social welfare policies in de facto,
ad hoc measures, it never succeeded in setting up the policy framework
and the legal structure necessary for establishing a new social order. The
populist faction did not have a clear vision of what this new social order,
the rule of the oppressed, would entail, except inasmuch as it aimed to
restrict private property rights and extend the interventionist power of the
state. Moreover, the vetoing power of the conservative Council of
Guardians over the Majles, always on jurisprudential grounds, frustrated
the efforts of the populists to pass laws. Even the creation of a Council
of Expediency could not resolve factional conflicts. Ad hoc measures,
which were frequently reversed; the economic burdens of the war; the
opposition of the propertied class led by the conservative faction in the
regime; and the international economic pressures accentuated by a glut in
the world oil market – all intensified the economic crisis. Faced with
political and social imperatives, a convergence process began in the Islamic
Republic, bringing the populists close to the conservative position by way
of their acceptance of a pragmatic solution to the crisis. With the death
of Ayatollah Khomeini in June 1989, the pragmatists – a coalition of
conservatives and 'reformed populists' – became dominant. This coalition
has been led by Hashemi Rafsanjani, then the speaker of the Majles, and
now the president of Iran, in his second consecutive term.

This coalition followed a policy of economic liberalization by the decontrolling of prices, privatization of nationalized enterprises, and the
devaluation of the Iranian rial against foreign currencies. The promise of
the rule of the *mostaz'afin*, and the attempt to Islamize the economy are
no longer on the agenda of this dominant coalition. The jurisprudential
debates are now over as the conservatives have succeeded in practically
dispelling the populist interpretation of Islam. Although the remaining
populists in the regime persist in their demands for social justice and the
welfare of the poor, and manage to restrain the pragmatists in their
liberalization effort, the Islamic Republic is in the final phase of its transformation. Although some shifts and shuffling in the regime may be
expected, the Islamic Republic is well set to reconstruct the very economic
and social structure that it initially attempted to replace.

In this process, the Islamic Republic faces some major social obstacles.
In the economic sphere, economic liberalization will lead to a worsening
of the well-being of a wide segment of the population, namely the lower
and lower-middle class urban households. These households have constituted the popular base of the Islamic Republic. Popular opposition to the
Islamic Republic will definitely increase as the liberalization policies reduce
the real purchasing power of the low-income population, without increasing
employment opportunities significantly for the large and growing number
of new entrants to the labour market. Whether the Islamic Republic follows

a stopgap approach, as it has so far, or pursues a crackdown policy, depends on the formation of opposition forces inside and outside the regime. But one thing is clear: the Islamic Republic has been confronted with the limits of its populist policies. This has been a painful realization, which the 'pragmatists' are coming to terms with and the remaining populists resent. Even if the populists within the regime, who have lost their important policy-making and executive positions in the years since the death of Ayatollah Khomeini, manage to recapture their former political domination, it will not take them long to come to many of the same 'pragmatist' solutions.

Moreover, the Islamic Republic is coming to acknowledge its defeat in the cultural arena. The Islamic movement in Iran has aimed to establish traditional Islamic norms of conduct and to impose on the population a totally Islamic cultural milieu. Despite the complete control exercised by the state over the mass media and educational system, and over the shape of social policy (prohibiting what is deemed unacceptable and promoting what is deemed desirable) and the traditional forms of coercion (in addition to an ever-present, vigilant and zealous moral police force) sixteen years after the revolution the Islamic Republic is admitting its failure in the cultural sphere. It has failed to banish secular, non-religious art, literature and popular entertainment. Secular authors, poets and film-makers draw audiences and receive social recognition to the chagrin of the Islamic Republic. Underground video-rental networks distribute what 'a God-fearing Muslim' should never want to watch, satellite dishes are bringing uncensored programmes from MTV and CNN to many urban middle-class apartments, and the BBC remains the main source of news for many Iranians. Above all, the Islamic Republic is losing a hard-fought battle to women who defy its attempt to limit their public presence and their individual liberties. Ironically, it is the younger generation, subject to Islamic ideological propaganda since childhood, which most openly defies the imposed Islamic cultural codes. From job and educational opportunities, to family laws and the dress codes, women have tirelessly fought the Islamic Republic's restrictions in the workplace, on the streets, in the sports arenas, and in general social interaction.

With the defeat of the programme for Islamic social justice, all that is left of Islamic revivalism in Iran is the repressive cultural norms, which the clerics – specially the ultra-conservatives and the remaining populists – view as the only distinction between an Islamic state and the ruling autocratic state in any Third World country. In an ironic way they are right: cultural liberalism added to economic liberalism could be taking the Islamic Republic back to the norms of pre-revolutionary Iran. The wasted constructive potential of a powerful popular revolution; sixteen years (and more) of agony for a nation; and a generation of youth lost to the firing squads, torture chambers, a brutal and senseless war, and a stagnating economy – all these are heavy costs for a social experiment, whose failure anyone with eyes to see should have been able to predict. Those who are enticed by the rhetoric of Islamic revivalism in the Muslim world might do well to look more closely at the Iranian experience.

Notes

1. Said, Edward W., *Covering Islam* (New York: Pantheon Books, 1981); and John L. Esposito, *The Islamic Threat: Myth or Reality?* (New York: Oxford University Press, 1992).

2. Said, Edward W., *Orientalism* (New York: Pantheon Books, 1978), and *Culture and Imperialism* (New York: Alfred A. Knopf, 1994).

3. Algar, Hamid, *The Roots of the Islamic Revolution* (Markham, Ontario: The Open Press, 1983), p 121.

4. See the many books of John L. Esposito, a prolific author and an eloquent representative of this relatively large group of scholars.

5. Said, *Orientalism*, p 2.

6. Ibid., pp 32–3.

7. Enayat, Hamid, 'The politics of Iranology', *Iranian Studies* VI/1 (1973), p 3. For earlier criticism of Orientalism, see Nehru, Jawaharlal, *The Discovery of India* (New York: The John Day Company, 1946) ch 7; and Monteil, Vincent, 'The decolonization of the writing of history', in Wallerstein, Immanuel (ed.), *Social Change; The Colonial Situation* (New York: John Wiley, 1966; this article was originally published in French in *Preuves*, no 142 [1962]).

8. For some accounts of Orientalism by Iranian intellectuals, see Jalili, Abolhasan, 'Sharqshenasi va jahan-e emruz', '*Olum-e Ejtema'i* I/2 (1968); Ashori, Daryosh, 'Iranshenasi chist?' *Barresi-ye Ketab* (1971); Enjavi-Shirazi, Abolqasem, "Ellat-e vojudi-ye esteshraq va mostashreq', *Negin* 8/85 (1972). Citations are from Enayat, *The Politics of Iranology*, p 18.

9. Said, *Orientalism*, p 204.

10. See Rodinson, Maxime, *Europe and the Mystique of Islam* (Seattle: University of Washington Press, 1991), pp 130–1; and Albert Hourani, *Islam in European Thought* (Cambridge: Cambridge University Press, 1991), p 63. While Rodinson and Hourani recognize the 'strength and force' of Said's *Orientalism* with its 'many valuable ideas', which 'is not to be ignored', they both regard his expressions as 'too simple', 'excessive' and near to 'caricature'.

11. Schwab, Raymond, *The Oriental Renaissance: Europe's Rediscovery of India and the East, 1680–1880* (New York: Columbia University Press, 1984; first French publication 1950).

12. Ibid., p ix.

13. For example, Browne, Edward G., *The Literary History of Persia* (1902); Mowlana Jalaloddin Rumi, *Masnavi* (1925) edited by R.A. Nicholson; and Lambton, Ann K.S., *Landlord and Peasant in Persia* (1953) are valuable contributions to the socio-cultural history of Iran by three Orientalists who represent the wide spectrum of Orientalists in terms of their disposition toward the colonial power and the 'otherness' of their subject of study.

14. Al-'Azm, Sadiq Jalal, 'Orientalism and Orientalism in reverse', in John

Rothschild (ed.), *Forbidden Agendas: Intolerance and Defiance in the Middle East* (London: Al-Saqi Books, 1984), p 355.

15. Said, *Orientalism*, p 272.

16. Ibid., pp 272–3.

17. Robbins, Bruce, 'The east is a career: Edward Said and the logics of professionalism', in Michael Sprinkler (ed.), *Edward Said: A Critical Reader* (Oxford: Blackwell, 1992) p 49.

18. Said, Edward W., 'Orientalism reconsidered', in S.K. Farsoun (ed.), *Arab Society: Continuity and Change* (London: Croom Helm, 1985), p 122.

19. Al-'Azm, 'Orientalism and Orientalism in reverse', pp 366–7. See also Moghadam, Val, 'Against Eurocentrism and Nativism', *Socialism and Democracy*, vol 9 (1989), pp 81–104.

20. McClelland, David, *The Achieving Society* (Princeton: D. Van Nostrand, 1961); Hagen, Everett E., *On the Theory of Social Change* (Homewood, IL: Dorsey Press, 1962). Ness, Gayl D., *The Sociology of Economic Development; A Reader* (New York: Harper & Row, 1970) is a compendium of the views of major modernization theorists of the 1950s and 1960s.

21. Lerner, Daniel, *Passing of Traditional Society: Modernizing the Middle East*, (Glencoe, IL: Free Press, 1958), pp 398–401.

22. See Halliday, Fred, *Iran: Dictatorship and Development* (Harmondsworth: Penguin, 1979); and Misagh, Parsa, *Social Origins of the Iranian Revolution* (New Brunswick, NJ: Rutgers University Press, 1989).

23. Al-e Ahmad, Jalal, *Occidentosis; A Plague from the West*, trans. R. Campbell (Berkeley: Mizan Press, 1984).

24. Tibi, Bassam, *The Crisis of Modern Islam: A Preindustrial Culture in the Scientific-Technological Age* (Salt Lake City: University of Utah Press, 1988), p 27.

25. al-Qurdawi, Yusuf, *Al-hal al-Islami, Farida wa Darura* (Beirut, 1974), p 47, quoted in Tibi, *The Crisis of Modern Islam*, p 27.

26. Algar, *The Roots of the Islamic Revolution*, p 9.

27. Esposito, *The Threat of Islam*, pp 200–203. *Ejtehad* means interpretations of Islamic precepts by Muslim jurists (*mojtahed*s). Closing of the door of *ejtehad* is a reference to a jurisprudential view that suggests strict reliance on the rulings of the past *mojtahed*s.

28. Said, *Orientalism*, p 282.

29. Ibid., p 280.

30. See al-'Azm, 'Orientalism and Orientalism in reverse', pp 364–5; and Said, *Orientalism*, p 321.

31. Cudsi, Alexander S. and Ali E. Hillal Dessouki (eds), *Islam and Power* (Baltimore: Johns Hopkins University Press, 1981) pp 7–8.

32. Some Muslims also view the rule of the four Rightly Guided Caliphs, Abu Bakr, Umar, Uthman and Ali (632–61), as a part of the Golden Age of Islam.

33. Enayat, Hamid, *Modern Islamic Political Thought* (London: Macmillan, 1982), p 12.

34. Adamiyat, Fereydon, *Ideolozhi-ye Nehzat-e Mashrutiyat-e Iran* (Tehran: Payam, 1976).

35. Said, *Orientalism*, pp 322–4; Al-e Ahmad, Jalal, *Dar Khedmat va Khiyanat-e Rowshanfekran* (Tehran: n.p., 1958).

36. See Shayegan, Dariush, *Cultural Schizophrenia: Islamic Societies Confronting the*

West (London: Al-Saqi Books, 1992).

37. *Kayhan,* 19 June 1979.

38. See Rodinson, Maxime, *Islam and Capitalism* (Austin: University of Texas Press, 1978), pp 25–6; and Motahhari, Mortaza, *Social and Historical Change: An Islamic Perspective* (Berkeley: Mizan Press, 1986), p 117.

39. Rodinson, *Islam and Capitalism,* pp 16–17.

40. Halliday, Fred, 'An elusive normalization: Western Europe and the Iranian Revolution', *The Middle East Journal,* 48/2 (1994), p 314.

PART I

Ideological and Historical Perspectives

From the White Revolution to the Islamic Revolution

Ahmad Ashraf

Iran's White Revolution of the 1960s, along with its causes, processes and consequences, has been the subject of mounting controversy over the last three decades. The White Revolution and, more specifically, its master project the land-reform programme, have been examined with a view either to praising the Shah's benevolent reforms or to condemning their malevolent motives or harmful consequences. Thus, for example, the left often ascribes the purpose of the White Revolution to an American design to develop dependence on capitalism in the Third World,[1] whereas militant religious circles explain it as a conspiracy on the part of the 'Great Satan' (the United States) to bring on the decline of agricultural production and the dependency of Iran on American grain and foodstuffs.[2] Many believe that the White Revolution and its land-reform programme led to the pauperization of peasants and their exodus to urban areas, factors that in turn contributed to the revolution of 1977–79.[3]

The 'White Revolution of the Shah and the People' was the name for a series of social and economic reform programmes that were initiated by the Shah's regime during the 1960s under increasing exogenous and indigenous pressures for reform. It originally included land reform and five other programmes that were approved in the referendum of 26 January 1963.[4] The land-reform programme, however, was the centrepiece of the White Revolution: the project that gave a revolutionary air to the Shah's reform movement.

Why the White Revolution?[5]

The White Revolution was formulated and implemented from above under pressure from the Kennedy administration. Neither the peasantry nor the bourgeoisie participated at the outset. Its initiation was a political choice originating primarily outside the polity, but its process had not been planned. As a result, its course and outcomes were influenced by the

21

material and non-material interests of the major social forces as well as by domestic and foreign political actors. The principal actors were the Shah; the premier, Ali Amini; the agriculture minister, Hasan Arsanjani; and the Kennedy administration of the USA. A careful examination of the vested interests and the role played by these political actors shows that the direction and implementation of the land-reform programme was influenced primarily by the ideas and personal drive of Hasan Arsanjani, who, exploiting the opportunities of the time, emerged as 'the architect of Persian land-reform'.[6] The driving force behind the land-reform programme originated in two myths. These were the 'impending peasant revolution in Iran' and the 'indispensability of land reform for the development of capitalism'. Belief in these myths was shared by the Kennedy administration and many Iranian Marxists in the early 1960s; and the myth of the indispensability of land reform for the development of capitalism still persists in many Iranian Marxist circles.[7]

During the 1950s and 1960s, the United States had incorporated into its programme of foreign aid a policy of encouraging moderate land reform in less-developed countries in order to bolster their ability to resist the so-called menace of communist encroachment. In conjunction with this policy, the United States badgered the Shah about the necessity for land reform. The Shah then issued a decree calling for the distribution among peasantry of 3000 villages held in crown-land estates. Known as Project Thirty, the crown-land distribution programme received technical and monetary aid from 1952 to 1960.[8] But the 1958 revolutionary coup d'état in neighbouring Iraq and the mounting propaganda campaign from the USSR against the Shah's regime led the American policy-makers to renew pressure on the Shah for a more aggressive reform programme in Iran. In 1959 General Qarani failed in an attempted coup aimed at the installation of an effective reform government in Iran.[9] In 1960, the Shah, under pressure, appointed the reform cabinet of Ali Amini.[10]

The peasant wars of this century, the ascendancy of the peasantry over the proletariat as the driving force in revolutionary theory, the popularity of the theory of 'the guerrilla foco', and the challenges of the Cuban Revolution all spread fear of an 'impending peasant revolution' in the Third World in the early 1960s. In this view of reality, Third World nations were left with two options: land reform from above or peasant revolution from below. Government and revolutionary leaders would compete for the support of the peasantry: 'He who controls the countryside controls the country.'[11] The peasantry could play a highly conservative or highly revolutionary role, depending on its relation to the land: 'No social group is more conservative than a landowning peasantry and none is more revolutionary than a peasantry which owns too little land or pays too high a rental.'[12] This simplistic and short-sighted vision of the world was adopted by the Kennedy administration and served as the focus of the US strategy for 'progress' in the early 1960s.[13] The same image of social reality was held by many Marxist scholars and revolutionaries of those days.[14] The 'necessity' for land reform was predicated upon a number of false assumptions: that a 'revolutionary peasantry' was emerging in Iran; that there was a desperate need for new industries both for cheap rural labour and for the expansion of rural markets; that the development of capitalism required the elimination of the old oligarchy of the landowning class; and that land reform was necessary for the 'primitive accumulation of capital'.[15]

Any evaluation of these assumptions must take into consideration the fact that the Iranian peasantry has shown little inclination for revolution and a low level of participation in the country's major socio-political movements.[16] Iran's 'non-revolutionary peasantry' consisted of three strata: families with small landholdings, sharecroppers, and landless villagers – comprising, respectively, one-fourth, two-fifths and one-third of the rural population. The village class structure prevented the emergence of either a coherent peasant community or a proletarian community, a precondition of peasant or proletarian revolution. The teamwork approach to production in sharecropping villages (the *boneh* system) led to a workable arrangement between landowner and peasant through the mediation of the village head and the heads of work teams. Hence, the extraction of surplus from the peasantry was managed by a group of prominent villagers who served a dual role as trustees of the peasants and appointees of the landowners. The relative power of these prominent farmers and prosperous peasants, along with the weakness of the middle peasantry, diminished the revolutionary potential of the peasantry. The dispersal of the rural population in more than 50,000 small villages (with an average size of 50 households) scattered across a vast and mountainous country inhibited inter-village communication and united action by the peasantry. Moreover, employment opportunities on construction sites and urban labour markets afforded an outlet for the younger generation of villagers, which in turn led to the detachment of many of them from village life and agricultural activities. These circumstantial inhibitions to the revolutionary potential of the peasantry undermined the more pervasive Islamic notion of the sanctity of private property and of sharecropping–tenancy arrangements.

The controversy over the modes of transformation of European societies from feudalism to capitalism has led some observers to approach the Iranian land-reform question primarily from the perspective of a 'labour process', that is, in terms of the internal contradictions of the feudal mode of production as experienced, for example, by England in the course of her capitalist development.[17] But focusing the analysis on the expropriation of peasant holdings as the necessary and sufficient condition for the formation of a free industrial working class and the accumulation of capital places undue emphasis on the role of the land-reform programme of the 1960s in the development of capitalism in Iran.[18] Iran's land reform is equated in this paradigm with the historical process of enclosure in England, an analysis that neglects or underemphasizes a number of factors that influenced the nature and direction of Iran's capitalist development: Iran's specific precapitalist formation and dependent development; the commercialization of agriculture long before land reform; a population explosion; increasing oil revenues; and the technological advances of the latter half of the present century. The population explosion, coupled with the scarcity of arable lands, led to overurbanization and to an oversupply of cheap labour for new industrial enterprises. The major social and economic problem on the eve of land reform was not the scarcity of a labour force but its abundance and the concomitant high rate of unemployment. The oil economy facilitated the accumulation of capital for industrial investments. Thus, there was no need to 'expropriate the peasantry' for the development of capitalism. Furthermore, on the eve of land reform, overurbanization and increasing oil revenues caused urban markets to grow to capacities quite sufficient to absorb the output of the growing number of import-substitution industrial establishments.

Finally, in the early 1960s, the landowning class did not constitute the main obstacle to the development of capitalism in agriculture and industry. The precapitalist arrangement in agriculture was undergoing a gradual change and since the late nineteenth century had adapted itself to some of the requirements of the market economy and the modern state. These changes included the gradual commercialization of agriculture through development of cash crops;[19] the abolition of benefice (*tuyul*) as an intermediary institution between the state and peasantry; the commoditization of agricultural land; the rapid growth of private landownership; and the emergence of extensive commercial agriculture and wage labour. Moreover, many landowners with large and medium-sized holdings showed a genuine interest in commercial farming even before land reform. Hence, had there been no land reform, it is possible that more large landowners would have undertaken commercial farming with wage labour.

Under these circumstances, Hasan Arsanjani, exploiting the opportunities of the time, shaped the course and outcome of the land-reform movement. Arsanjani joined the reformist cabinet of Ali Amini, who enjoyed US support, in May 1961 as minister of agriculture and was entrusted with the implementation of the land-reform programme. The issue of land reform had been part of Amini's campaign against Dr Manuchehr Eqbal's cabinet and his ruling Melliyun Party in the 1960 Majles election. Amini believed in a gradual land-reform programme, spread over ten to fifteen years, including a ceiling on the amount of large-scale absentee landownership, improvement of farmers' managerial skills, and better economic productivity.[20] This approach to land reform was generally attractive to both the Shah and the Kennedy administration. The Shah was interested in land reform not only to appease the Kennedy administration and normalize his relations with the United States, but also to dismantle the power base of the landowning classes and to gain the support of the peasantry for his regime as well as to overshadow and confuse the urban opposition forces of the liberal nationalist and leftist groups. The Kennedy administration favoured Amini's programme of land reform primarily because it offered to forestall a peasant revolution.[21] Arsanjani's conception of land reform was, however, fundamentally different.

Influenced by the peasant wars of the twentieth century, Arsanjani advocated a version of peasant socialism and peasant power. He secured decrees, regulations and a referendum to implement an original strategy for Iran's land-reform programme. He believed in the necessity of eliminating feudalism and landlord–peasant relations in the means of production (*nezam-e arbab-ru'yati*) and in creating a self-reliant peasantry through a cooperative movement. He often criticized the idea of a revolutionary proletariat in Iran, an idea cherished by the orthodox Marxists. 'Not the industrial working class but the peasantry is the genuine revolutionary driving force in Iran', he said.[22] His lifelong ambition and dream was to mobilize and lead a peasant movement and to use it as a power base from which to seize leadership of the state. He opposed such American methods of land reform as those employed in the crown-land distribution programme of the 1950s, that is, gradual land distribution through cadastral surveys and mapping. He argued for a practical form of implementation.

Arsanjani had been nurtured in a farmer–bazaar milieu – his father and elder brother were farmers and his mother came from a bazaar merchant family – where he developed a hatred for feudalism and an admiration for the middle peasantry. As a rural cooperative officer in 1940–41, he surveyed a number of villages and established cooperative societies in Damavand, Saveh and Najafabad. He continued to fight for the cause of the peasantry in the 1940s and 1950s in articles published in *Darya* and in his relationship with the Ahmad Qavam and Haji Ali Razm-Ara cabinets. When he became the minister of agriculture in 1961, Arsanjani proved to be a tough and well-experienced campaigner with clear, workable ideas. The secret to the success of his reform programme lay in a simple method of land distribution that used the traditional order of landholding (*nasaq*) as its basis. In the first stage of this land reform the maximum allowable ownership of land was one village; thus, it covered only about 20 per cent of the villages. However, Arsanjani's tactics led to a mass mobilization of the peasants throughout the countryside. He often incited the peasants by attacking feudalism, criticizing the landlord–peasant relationship and referring to the 'criminal landowners' and the 'dearest peasants' in his fiery speeches to the nation.[23]

Arsanjani's shock tactics alarmed the United States, the Shah and Amini. An American Iranist and CIA consultant reports that he 'kept asking [Arsanjani] why there was such urgency to the land reform programme?'

Arsanjani replied, 'The nature of the sickness required a quick solution. Why? A proper cadastral survey would have taken ten years. To break the opposition I have to destroy the power of the 100 great landowners very quickly.' He scoffed at the suggestion that the Americans were responsible for the land reform programme: 'The first thing I did was to get rid of all the American agricultural advisors to the Ministry of Agriculture.'[24] The Shah was also alarmed by the accelerated pace of reform and 'resented and feared the power that Arsanjani was collecting independently of the throne, based on peasants and urban liberals.[25] Like the Shah and the Americans, Amini viewed Arsanjani as suspect, dangerous and extremely ambitious and was critical of his 'urgency' in the implementation of the distribution; he ordered the minister of information to censor Arsanjani's powerful and arousing radio speeches.[26] Arsanjani successfully organized the Congress of Rural Cooperatives in January 1963, when some 4700 delegates gathered in Tehran. He was also instrumental in the referendum of 26 January 1963 in support of land reform, in which the peasants actively participated. But shortly after these events he was forced to resign.

Arsanjani has been described as 'a tough crusader who, in his own words, pushed the land reform programme "not as Minister of Agriculture but as a *rahbar* (leader)"'.[27] He was considered the 'architect of land reform' who formulated and implemented 'Persia's original strategy'.[28] His effective reform measures were irreversible, and as he prophesied after his dismissal, there would be no regression: 'I have hammered in the last nail of both feudalism's (*nezam-e arbab ru'yati*) and the Shah's coffins', he said.[29]

The land-reform programme had three stages. The first, under Arsanjani's leadership, was a quasi-revolutionary movement. The second, with Arsanjani out of the picture, was appropriately labelled counter-revolutionary.[30] The agenda, at this stage, was suppression of the peasantry, establishment of 'law and order', and protection of medium-sized and small landholdings.[31] The third stage, however, was a moderate reform from above in which the state ceded ownership of holdings under share-cropping and tenancy (rental) agreements to the peasant occupants. The broader state agrarian policies and strategies in the course of the White Revolution took shape, in their turn, in two consecutive phases: the land-reform programme of the 1960s and the agrarian programmes of the 1970s. The implementation of these programmes, along with rapid population growth and urban economic development, led to substantial changes in rural class structure and agrarian relations.

The White Revolution and the Rural Social Classes[32]

Iran's agrarian classes underwent a relatively slow period of change from 1925 to 1960, followed by a period of relatively rapid transformation in the 1960s and 1970s. In the first period the traditional agrarian relations of *arbab-ru'yati* continued, with some modifications, whereas in the second period traditional bonds were abolished and the new agrarian relations emerged. As will be discussed in Chapter 2, between the 1920s and the 1950s Iran experienced an expansion and consolidation of private land-ownership (*arbabi*), for which a modern legal foundation was established by the land-registration law of 17 March 1932.[33] Furthermore, in this period, the commoditization of land and commercialization of agriculture, which had begun in the late nineteenth century, continued at a more rapid pace.[34]

Although the period of the 1930s marked a decline in the political and social status of the landowning class as a whole, the large landowners reasserted themselves in the following two decades as major players on the political scene. The landowners themselves and others who came from landowning families constituted about two-thirds of the Majles deputies in the period between 1920 and 1950.[35] These representatives repeatedly rejected or emasculated legislation dealing with income tax, land tax, rural development, universal literacy and land reform; they also succeeded in rejecting the credentials of the deputies who opposed the *arbab-ru'yati* relations.[36] A study of Iran's political elites in the 1960s found that 56 per cent of the fathers of the national elite were landowners.[37] The land-owning class possessed even more political power at the local level; the provincial and district governors and other officials, as well as the rural police, were often heavily influenced by local landowners.[38]

The rural population, constituting about two-thirds of Iran's total population at the beginning of the 1960s, could be divided into three classes: (1) peasant proprietors and petty landowners; (2) sharecroppers and small, single-family tenants (*ru'yat*, in its more specific connotation); and (3) landless villagers known as *khoshneshins*, most of whom were at the bottom rung of the village class structure. In the early 1960s, these strata comprised, respectively, 25 per cent, 40 per cent and 35 per cent of the country's rural population.[39]

The land-reform programme of the 1960s overhauled the traditional ties of *arbab-ru'yati* and introduced to rural Iran new modes of agrarian relations. It led to the sale of either whole plots or a portion of the plot to the occupant sharecroppers according to the traditional practice of crop division.[40] Thus, land reform transferred the ownership of some six to seven million hectares of agricultural land (about 52 to 62 per cent of the total) to the occupant sharecroppers and tenant farmers.[41] After the implementation of land reform the social distinctions, though not the maldistribution of income, among sharecroppers, peasant-owners, and small landowners was effectively eliminated, and thus small landowners and peasant proprietors formed nearly two-thirds of the rural population.[42] The remaining one-third consisted of landless villagers (*khoshneshins*).

In the meantime, the Agricultural Development Bank of Iran, which provided large amounts of subsidized credit, was the main vehicle for the rapid growth of commercial agriculture in the private sector. From 1969 to 1980, the bank granted more than three thousand low-interest loans (from 4 to 12 per cent), together with its grants to large- and medium-scale agricultural enterprises. These bank loans amounted to $1.6 billion. The bank also participated in establishing six regional development banks and investment firms with a registered capital of $400 million. In the same period, it undertook joint projects with 46 large agricultural firms registering a capital of $360 million.[43] To promote commercial agriculture in the public sector, the government established eight large agricultural enterprises with 155,000 hectares of valuable farm land and an annual budget of $200 million.[44] Furthermore, it established 93 farm corporations with 315,000 hectares of land and 39 production cooperatives with 100,000 hectares. These quasi-public enterprises were created and managed by government agents with minimum participation by peasant shareholders. Government policies aimed at developing commercial farming and initiatives taken by prosperous peasants and commercial farmers helped bring some 4.3 million hectares of new land under cultivation from 1960 to 1975, of which 84 per cent consisted of holdings with more than ten hectares. As a result, the total amount of arable land increased from 11.4 to 15.7 million hectares, and the number of holdings from 1.9 to 2.5 million units.[45]

Commercial farmers included 25,000 mechanized farmers, livestock farmers and poultry farmers; at the top of the pyramid were the owners of 100 agro-industries and very large farms established in the 1960s and 1970s.[46] Commercial farmers were often traditional landowners, traders or entrepreneurs from the top echelons of the state bureaucracy. They formed an influential core of individuals at both the national and local level.[47] A study of a representative sample of 651 commercial farmers carried out in five provinces in the mid-1970s indicates that among the large-scale farmers (those with an average of 364 hectares of land), 69 per cent had inherited the land that they farmed and the rest had purchased their lands, whereas other farmers had inherited about half the land that they cultivated and had purchased the other half.[48]

The prosperous peasantry and upper-echelon villagers included several groups with different relations to rural life: the village small landowners and prosperous peasants, the village traders and owners of small capital, and the public servants. The first group came from the old small landowners, former well-to-do sharecroppers and village traders.[49] The land reform of the 1960s, with its recognition of the property rights of small landowners and its sale of non-mechanized lands to occupant sharecroppers, led to the expansion of these groups. In addition, many people with a small amount of capital gradually acquired some land, either from the landowners or from the pauperized small landowners through moneylending and the pre-harvest purchase of crops, thus joining the ranks of the small landowners.[50] In 1974, for example, there were 120,000 units of agricultural production with less than 50 hectares of land that were worked primarily by wage labour. These units also sold more than half their products to the market.[51] Prosperous peasants and small commercial farmers owned most of the 400,000 units of 10 to 50 hectares (45 per cent of the total arable lands) in the mid-1970s. The village traders, moneylenders, and renters of agricultural implements (for example, oxen, tractors and mills) constituted the second component of the village upper class. In 1976, there were 81,000 working proprietors in the wholesale and retail trade, and 17,000 trade managers and travelling salesmen in the rural areas.[52] The prosperous members of this stratum 'control[led] the major portion of rural capital and credit and thus exercise[d] an influence upon the whole production system'.[53] Ranked next to the traditional landowners and their bailiffs, prosperous villagers were located at the middle level of the village hierarchy in the pre-land-reform era. However, after land reform, these people moved into the upper level of the village social structure. They were able to consolidate their position by establishing a working relationship with government agents and by joining the boards of such state-initiated rural organizations as village councils, cooperative societies, houses of justice (*khaneh-ha-ye ensaf*), cultural houses and political party cells.[54]

The middle peasantry came mainly from the old sharecroppers, tenant farmers, and family landholders and peasant farmers of the pre-land-reform era. The land-reform programme of the 1960s led to a substantial increase in the number of family landholders and middle peasantry. In the mid-1970s, 930,000 holders of plots of from 2 to 10 hectares, who owned about 28 per cent of the total arable lands, formed the main core of the middle peasantry in Iran.[55] Most members of this stratum also earned additional income from seasonal work in the cities.

The lower peasantry consisted of peasants holding undersized plots of land and landless villagers. In the mid-1970s, over one million holdings, constituting 45 per cent of the total number, were less than 2 hectares, making up merely 5 per cent of the total agricultural land.[56] In the majority of cases, the size of a holding was less than the subsistence size, that is, less than a plot of land sufficient to provide a living for a peasant family. This subsistence size was differentially determined by the availability of water, type of crops and the technique of agricultural production.[57] Landless villagers were primarily the product of rapid population growth between the 1940s and the 1970s. In 1976, there were 1.1 million landless agricultural workers and 1.3 million workers in industry and services, for a total of approximately 2.4 million employed individuals in rural areas, of whom about half a million were unpaid family workers.[58]

Peasants of the middle and lower echelons as well as landless villagers benefited from the economic boom of the mid-1960s to the late 1970s, and their income level and living standard improved substantially. The annual expenditure in rural households, in constant dollars, increased from about $1000 in 1965 to about $2000 in 1975.[59] A study of the changes in two villages in the Qazvin area over a 30-year period shows that one was transformed into a modern commercial centre and the other (with a population of about 700) became a community of small landowners. In the latter case, the villagers' per-capita income of $1000 came from the following sources: 21 per cent from agriculture, 22 per cent from animal husbandry, 34 per cent from work in neighbouring factories and farms, and 22 per cent from a combination of labour and small capital.[60] Another village, located in one of Iran's more backward regions, experienced both social change and economic growth in the 15 years before the revolution of 1977–79.

> By the time of the revolution, payments to the landlord, as well as his license to extort whatever he wanted, were matters of the past. The peasants were masters of their own land. Even more important, a stream of wages and salaries was transforming the village. About a quarter of the married men earned either a salary or a regular income from an enterprise, craft, or trade. The remainder of the men still pursued their peasant activities, and in addition, more than half of them earned wages from seasonal work in the cities, and many more did so from work in the village itself; also an unmarried son or daughter might contribute a wage or salary. Overall, there was hardly a household in the village which did not benefit from at least one salary or seasonal wage.[61]

Still another survey of five rural areas (Saveh, Tavalesh, Taleqan, Sari and Karaj/Rudehin), conducted shortly after the revolution in 1979, revealed that the majority of the peasants surveyed were fairly satisfied with their living conditions, and that many of them were hostile to the revolution.[62]

The villagers, about half the country's population on the eve of the revolution, remained indifferent to the uprisings. Of 2483 demonstrations in support of the revolution, only 2 per cent occurred in rural areas. Some peasants took part in counter-revolutionary demonstrations such as those in which anti-regime demonstrators were attacked with clubs; and the bazaars, local offices of the Ministry of Education and homes of revolutionary activists were pillaged.[63]

Many contend that the land reform of the 1960s led to the failure of agriculture in general, and of agricultural production in particular – thus causing Iran's dependency upon imported foodstuffs – and the pauperization of the peasantry, which led to increasing rural-to-urban migration.[64] Both views are wrong. The population explosion – increasing from approximately 19 million in 1956 to more than 34 million in 1976 – was the major cause in both cases. The rapid population growth combined with rising incomes led to an increased demand for foodstuffs, a demand that outpaced the rate of increase in agricultural products from 7 to 19 million tonnes in the period 1960–75. In the same period, agricultural land increased from 11.4 to 15.7 million hectares.[65] As a result, the volume of imported foodstuffs leapt from less than 0.5 to over 2.5 million tonnes during the same period.[66] The rapid population growth, combined with urban-pull factors and rural-push elements, also encouraged a mass migration of villagers to the cities. Located for the most part in arid, semi-arid and mountainous areas, Iran's agrarian sector was not able to support the increasing number of villagers. Considerable rural-to-urban migration had already begun in the 1940s and 1950s. Thus, for example, the population of Tehran increased from 0.5 million in 1940 to 1.5 million in 1956 and 3 million in 1966 – in a period when land reform had not yet made its impact upon rural Iran. One factor that had made an impact, however, was the urban bias of government agencies, which, by pricing agricultural produce below its real market value, imposed prices that lagged far behind the rapidly increasing prices of industrial products and wages, thus thwarting investment in the agricultural sector. Another 'bourgeois bias' of the government agencies was the provision of a large amount of financial aid for commercial farmers, coupled with the relative neglect of the middle and lower peasantry. The 1960s land reform is also blamed for dismantling the grassroots work-team organization known as *boneh*. However, the *boneh* system was a component of the old *arbab-ru'yati* mode of production in the arid and semi-arid areas in which wheat culture predominated. With the abolition of the *arbab-ru'yati*, the *boneh* system, which had been initiated and safeguarded by the old landowning class, disappeared.

The White Revolution and Urban Social Classes[67]

During the 1960s and 1970s public bureaucracies grew rapidly; the number of public-sector wage- and salary-earners in urban areas rose from approximately 0.5 million, or one-fifth of the economically active urban workforce in 1956, to nearly 1.5 million, or over one-third in 1976.[68] The average share of the state in total consumption leapt from 10 per cent in 1959 to 35 per cent in the mid-1970s. The average share of the public sector in capital formation increased from 36 to 54 per cent in the same period.[69] As a result, in the mid-1970s, over 50 per cent of the GDP was created in the public sector and a substantial portion of the remainder came from trade, construction activities and other services that were generated mainly by the state's expenditure of oil revenues. The state emerged as the largest capitalist in this period and owned all heavy industries, many other large industrial concerns (see also Chapter 5), all major transportation networks and agro-industries, and tightly controlled the banking system. It developed into a rentier capitalist state, controlling the emerging social classes.

The bureaucratic elite

With the unprecedented expansion of bureaucratic agencies and public enterprises during the 1960s and 1970s, a group of young professionals – a bureaucratic elite of state managers – rose to prominence. Taking key positions within the powerful modern state with its increasing financial resources, this new bureaucratic elite played a pivotal role in Iran's economic and social development in this period. The state bureaucracy strongly favoured the graduates of foreign universities, placing them in or quickly promoting them to such high posts as managers of state-owned enterprises, department heads, vice-ministers, and so forth. Thus, the period of the White Revolution was marked by a shift of power from the old landed gentry to the rising bureaucratic and professional elements.

The new middle class

The growth of bureaucracy, increasing demands by the public and private sectors for technicians and managers, and the rapid expansion of a Western-style educational system resulted in the rise of a non-entrepreneurial modern middle class, including independent professionals, civil servants, military personnel, white-collar employees, technicians in private enterprise and an intelligentsia. A dramatic expansion took place in the size of the civil bureaucracy and in the technical competence of its middle and upper echelons in the period 1956–76. In 1956 there were 200,000 professional, technical and clerical workers in Iran; by 1976 there were nearly a million, two-thirds of whom worked for the state.[70] Between 1960 and 1976, the number of students enrolled at the senior high-school level rose from 250,000 to over 900,000, while the number of students in post-secondary schools increased from about 20,000 to over 150,000. The number of Iranian students studying abroad (mostly in Europe and the United States) increased from 15,000 in 1960 to over 70,000 in 1976.[71]

Although earlier generations of the new middle class had retained a connection with Iran's traditional culture, the generation of the White Revolution became increasingly Westernized and isolated from the country's indigenous popular culture and from Islamic values and modes of behaviour. It was only in the mid-1960s that large numbers of intellectuals, particularly those from lower-middle-class and rural backgrounds, began adopting militant Islamic ideologies (see Chapter 3). This trend was especially evident in the mid-1970s among university students, about one-third of whom came from the bazaar and rural backgrounds.[72]

After the 1953 coup d'état, the Pahlavi state continued to have difficulty in rallying the support of the new middle class. Most intellectuals, barred from freedom of political activity, remained sympathetic toward the remnants of the National Front or the non-Tudeh left. Many writers, teachers, lawyers, physicians, engineers and students were opposed to or highly ambivalent about the regime.[73] The rapid growth in the number of students coincided with a worldwide trend toward the radicalization of youth. Following an abortive attempt at liberalization in the early 1960s, many Iranian students adopted leftist and revolutionary ideas and formed numerous political, revolutionary or guerrilla organizations, waiting for an opportunity to strike against the regime.[74]

The modern bourgeoisie

A sustained period of growth for the Iranian bourgeoisie began in the late 1950s, when the government started providing low-interest loans. Subsidized loans were at first provided by the state-owned Industrial Credit Bank, established in 1956, and the Revaluation Loan Fund administered by the National Bank from 1957 on. In the first three years of its operation, the Industrial Credit Bank extended 82 loans totalling $10.5 million to 70 projects. The Revaluation Loan Fund was much larger, providing 64 million dollars in 1541 loans over a three-and-a-half year period. Later, in the 1960s and 1970s, the dramatic increases in oil income led to further capital accumulation by the private sector in at least two ways: first, the state provided credit to business magnates at favourable rates;[75] second, inflation created windfall profits from land speculation and real-estate development. State incentives to substitute domestic products for imports led many importers of industrial goods to establish factories. Such factories increased the contribution of the private sector to capital acquisition in machinery and construction from $750 million in 1959 to $6.7 billion in 1977. The number of factories employing ten or more workers rose from 1400 units, with nearly 100,000 workers in 1960, to 5400 units – 96 per cent of which were in private hands – with nearly 400,000 workers in 1976.[76] Huge state construction projects, an expansion of internal markets, rapid population growth and a growing rate of urbanization allowed hundreds of merchants, industrialists, import traders, contractors, consulting engineers, commercial farmers and others to make fortunes. The most effective mechanism for ensuring the profitability of a venture was protection from imports under exclusive licensing, which in effect created monopolies or oligopolies. Furthermore, the industrial and commercial elite expanded their traditional presence in urban real estate, but still, at this stage, more as investors than as developers.[77]

The bazaar merchants suffered a relative loss in trade as the process of import substitution eliminated the import trade in many goods. In addition, the import of raw materials for industry became increasingly concentrated in the industrial firms or their associated companies. The rapid rise in the import of capital goods led to further expansion of the modern commercial sector, yet the volume of imports rose so much – from $514 in

1963 to $2570 million in 1972 – that even the traditional bazaar merchants made profits. Domestic trade expanded and despite the emergence of the rudiments of a modern distribution system, controlled by the manufacturers and large importers, the bazaar maintained its presence in the distribution network of the country. Many wholesalers prospered by becoming the link between the manufacturing establishments and the retailers, especially in the provinces.[78]

By the early 1970s a prosperous modern bourgeoisie had been formed in Iran. This group, however, was not allowed to participate in politics or to organize autonomous organizations. After 1962, despite the growth in the size and financial resources of the entrepreneurial elite, the autonomy of their organizations declined as they came increasingly under state control. In this period, the old Chamber of Commerce and the newly formed Chamber of Industries and Mines, presided over by a former minister of industries and mines, were merged to facilitate the work of the Ministry of Economy and other state agencies in their dealings with the big merchants and industrialists. The state's motive was not so much economic as political. The chamber, on the other hand, functioned as an institution for articulating the narrow interests of its constituent groups – primarily specialized trade or industry syndicates – but refrained from involvement in any broad policy issues. For example, it had absolutely no input into the planning process and the economic strategy of the government. Individual members believed that election to the board of the chamber enhanced their access to the bureaucracy and that with such access they could make their own personal deals. The regime's relationship to the entrepreneurial group was that of patron to client.[79]

Despite the much closer economic links among the upper bourgeoisie, and between them and the state sector, and despite their growing size and financial resources, they gained little political power, not because they did not aspire to acquire it and to protect their interest collectively, but rather because they had not been allowed since the early 1960s to establish autonomous associations, to voice their concerns through their representatives in parliament, or to publicize their views through independent media. For example, when a number of interest groups were allowed by the government to participate in elections in the mid-1970s, several leading industrial entrepreneurs entered the campaign as candidates for the Senate and the Majles. The well-financed and highly publicized campaign of these industrialists irritated the Shah, who bitterly warned that 'the affluent candidates who have somehow managed to get elected to the Majles and the Senate are by no means allowed to misuse their political office in order to protect the interest of capitalists and plunder the people'.[80] Of the seven programmes of the White Revolution announced during 1975, three were directed against the bourgeoisie. These were: the extension of industrial ownership, the anti-profiteering campaign, and the fight against land and housing speculation. The policy that frightened and humiliated the bourgeoisie as a whole was the anti-profiteering campaign of 1975. To launch the campaign, the state mobilized several agencies under a special task force headed by the minister of commerce. Some 2000 students were recruited to monitor prices and bring the violators before a special tribunal. Many industrial and commercial establishments, including scores of major industrial units, were harassed. A number of leading businessmen were arrested, heavily fined and exiled to remote locations. Neither the Chamber of Commerce nor the bourgeois representatives in parliament, who held over 10 per cent of the seats, made the slightest protest. Although many businessmen had the attention of powerful figures in the court, they could not convince the court to change the policies until economic realities forced the issue.[81]

The religious groups

The White Revolution began when the Grand Ayatollah Sayyed Hosein Borujerdi, the powerful, conservative and accommodating leader of the Shi'ite community, died in 1961. In the years after his death, the clerical establishment became more open to new ideas and leadership and was divided into three main factions. The largest segment, including most high-ranking ulema, continued the accommodating stance of their predecessors. A second group of the ulema collaborated with the Pahlavi regime. Some members of this group were appointed by the Shah as leaders of Friday prayers in Tehran and other major cities; others were attached to the state-controlled distribution of religious endowments; and still others served as advisers and officials of the Religious Corps Organization which was founded as part of the White Revolution.[82] These clerics were often denounced by Ayatollah Khomeini and his circle as 'clerics of the palace'.[83] Beginning in the early 1960s, a small group of militant clerics started a third grouping within the Qom religious establishment. Capitalizing on the resentment of the ulema over such issues as land reform, women's suffrage, and the extension of diplomatic immunity to American military advisers in Persia in the early 1960s, this group rallied around the charismatic Ayatollah Khomeini, who soon emerged as a new object of emulation with the title of the Grand Ayatollah.[84] Meanwhile, the religious hierarchy made the necessary doctrinal and organizational adaptations to the country's new economic, political and cultural environment. Using modern means of communication, as well as its own informal networks, the Qom centre improved its capacity for collecting and distributing religious taxes and used its resources for educational, charitable and political purposes. It attracted hundreds of new students from many parts of the country on a full-time or seasonal basis, thus guaranteeing the expansion of its influence throughout the country. Finally, in an attempt to counter the encroachment of Western culture and secularism even more actively, in the 1960s a small segment of Khomeini's followers began to address the social and political concerns of the urban middle classes, especially the young intelligentsia, in a new Islamic language of protest.[85] Khomeini's young, politically active companions and disciples had often been critical of the apolitical stance of the religious leaders at Qom and Najaf and were referred to, pejoratively by the more conservative ulema, as political clerics.[86] Furthermore, the radical ideas of Ali Shariati, who adored Khomeini's revolutionary stance while preaching 'Islam without clerics', were appealing to college students. Khomeini's charismatic leadership and Shariati's radical ideas successfully attracted a large group within the intelligentsia who opposed the Shah's regime as well as the collaborationist and accommodating ulema.

The working class

Between 1956 and 1976, with the soaring pace of industrialization, the number of industrial workers employed at large establishments increased dramatically, from 70,000 to 400,000. By 1976, there were roughly 1,250,000 wage earners in production and related activities, including 750,000 in industries, mines and related occupations, and 500,000 in construction.[87] On top of the labour pyramid, in terms of social status, job security and wage levels, were workers in over 800 large-scale (that is, with 100 or more workers) modern urban industrial establishments in the oil industry, petrochemicals, steel, machine tools, various import-substitution industries and transportation enterprises. Members of this labour aristocracy, constituting as much as one-third of the urban manufacturing labour force by 1976, received wages and fringe benefits that were five times more than those of the lower-salaried industrial workers.[88] By 1976, real wages were double their 1969 level, and by 1978 workers' purchasing power in the larger manufacturing establishments was 50 per cent higher than in 1974. The remaining two-thirds of the labour force consisted of semi-skilled and unskilled workers in construction, mining, small-scale industries and services in the urban areas. 'Taken in money terms [construction workers'] wages had gone up tenfold in these two decades [1959–78]; but even allowing for stagnation up to 1976, their real wages in 1978 were three times better than in 1959.'[89] To the lower echelons of the labour force, one must add over half a million impoverished self-employed in the so-called informal sector and those in low-paid services, many of whom lived in the slums and margins of the cities along with poor rural migrants.[90]

From the 1953 coup d'état to the 1979 revolution, workers were prevented from organizing independent trade unions. After a 1963 government decision to allow the formation of trade unions under the control of the Ministry of Labour, the number rose from 16 in 1964 to

519 in 1972. To control these syndicates, the government established an umbrella organization, the Workers' Organization of Iran, in 1967. The leftist groups in the meantime continued to be active – though at a much curtailed level – among industrial workers, with the pace and scale of these activities intensifying in the 1970s.[91] Of some 140 strikes in the 1970–77 period, 83 per cent took place in industrial establishments with 100 or more workers. Of these, over two-thirds (70 per cent) were peaceful; in over half of the cases the workers' demands were met.[92] In the course of the revolution, the industrial proletariat, especially those working in public enterprises, entered upon the revolutionary stage at about the same time as white-collar state employees. They often went on strike along with the white-collar workers in the same industry, making their protests more effective and enabling them to close down many essential services and industries. Industrial workers in the private sector, however, remained relatively inactive in the course of the revolution.[93]

Conclusions

The ideological guideline of the Shah's White Revolution was the old Iranian and Islamic concept of 'organic benevolent statism': at its economic base were the increasing oil revenues and expanding public enterprises; its political and coercive power base was the rapidly expanding public and military bureaucracies; and its social base was built upon the manoeuvrings and mediations among conflicting forces in society. The accumulation of vast political and economic resources within the public domain made the state the supreme social mediator among the major social forces, including the dominant classes of the public and private sectors, the modern and traditional middle classes, and such popular classes as peasant proprietors, privileged workers in the modern industrial sector, and urban poor and rural migrants. Under these circumstances the state acquired great bargaining power and relative autonomy vis-à-vis the society, thus subordinating all social forces to its selective and often arbitrary development policies and strategies.

The process of intellectual divergence and cultural alienation reached its climax in the 1960s with the emergence of a new Westernized intelligentsia that boasted about its contempt for and ignorance of religion and traditional Persian culture. A segment of this group, many of whom were educated at Western universities, replaced the old-guard political elites in the course of the White Revolution. Meanwhile, the religious establishment at Qom showed resilience and experienced a drastic intellectual change, which paved the way for its appeal to the young intelligentsia and the impending rise to power of its militant and politicizing segment.

Under these circumstances, the main societal role of the state became that of an uncomfortable mediator among major conflicting forces in society. The selective mode of the state's social mediation – with its strong statist and bourgeois-capitalist biases – led to increasing grievances on the part of the urban middle and lower middle classes against the state. The state managers were bitterly critical of the windfall capital accumulation by the private-sector magnates and influence peddlers manoeuvring around the royal court. The entrepreneurs and the *nouveau riches* of the private sector were discontented with their powerlessness vis-à-vis the arbitrary decision-making of the state, with the authorities' support of privileged labour, with the competition of state-owned enterprises, and with the lack of political power and an autonomous organizational base. The rapidly growing intelligentsia, though it had acquired a handsome share of the petrol pie, was discontented with its political powerlessness and the repression of human rights. The members of the bazaar–mosque alliance were dissatisfied with the state's increasing interventionist policies (including state-owned and operated chain stores, rising taxes, and the campaign against price gouging) as well as with the encroachment of a Western mode of life, which was considered a threat to their traditional urban Islamic lifestyle. The rising expectations of fixed-income wage- and salary-earners, including industrial workers and government employees, led them to increase their demands for higher salaries and fringe benefits.[94] Yet the state's clear objective was to prevent the transformation of the class conflict from a covert to an overt one. To this end, it relied on benevolent distributive policies as well as on repressive measures and prevention of the formation of autonomous class-based organizations, including those of the *grande bourgeoisie*, intelligentsia and the industrial proletariat.

Iran's regime in this period may be characterized as a neopatrimonial authority, under the command of the Shah, that was imposed upon a rentier state. The Shah proved himself to be, time and again in periods of political strife, an incompetent autocratic ruler. Such a regime was susceptible to challenge and collapse in times of crisis. There were a number of reasons for this. In general, rentier states tend to be vulnerable because they are the centre of resources and thus monopolize the mechanisms of economic development with ever more paternalistic, distributive, accumulative and extractive policies. In Iran, these circumstances led the state to assume excessive responsibilities, thus encouraging if not forcing the privileged classes to retreat from responsibility, weakening the internal cohesion of the dominant classes and the invisible links between the rulers and major social classes and groups in society.

With the regime organized around a network of patronage relations, the dominant classes became 'politically immature'. The political culture of the power elite, top bureaucrats, army commanders, state managers, *grande bourgeoisie*, as well as of intellectuals and the new middle classes, was essentially a culture of idleness. As individuals, they were given an opportunity for social mobility and for promotion of their own material interests, but as a group they were systematically denied the opportunity to protect their class interests through organized and independent political action. They were ignorant of Iranian culture as well as the living conditions of the traditional strata of the masses of villagers, urban poor and rural migrants. As a result, the Shah's patronage system constantly weakened the ability of the leading elites to forge alliances among themselves or to guide, mobilize and control the contenders for state power in times of political turmoil. The political and mobilizational feebleness of the bureaucratic/military elites and entrepreneurial classes, their low level of symbolic and institutional autonomy, and their low level of political maturity were all detrimental to the regime at the time of trouble.

The White Revolution eliminated the traditional foundation of patrimonial authority – the ulema, the bazaaris, and the landowning classes – which had maintained linkages among the old oligarchy as well as between them and the masses of urban, rural and tribal communities. They were replaced by new classes and groups – the newly-created *grande bourgeoisie*, the young Western-educated bureaucratic elites, and the new middle classes who had weak links among themselves and were unable to or incapable of developing a strong connection with the core of the state or with the intelligentsia and other key elements in urban society. The new elite's lack of an independent political base often meant that they did not have any significant input into major economic and policy decisions, whereas the old elite, by virtue of its traditional patron–client relations with the local populations, had provided a point of articulation between the state and the urban society. Because of the Shah's fear of independent power centres, members of the new power elite and the *grande bourgeoisie* were denied the opportunity to organize themselves into effective political groupings.

In the 1970s, the nucleus of a revolutionary coalition was formed from a small group of militant ulema, their bazaari followers and activist intelligentsia who together had ready access to the extensive human, financial and spatial resources of the bazaar, the mosque and the school–university networks. A crack in the regime, in conjunction with pre-existing organizational networks and solidarity groups in the urban society, was needed as a catalyst for the mobilization of an effective protest movement.

Finally, the character of the ruler in 'autocratic rentier states' is an important factor in crisis management. A ruler's lack of a will for power at a time of crisis would, of course, be detrimental to the system as a whole. A combination of these factors was present in the mid-1970s. The Shah began to lose his will to fight, especially after the victory of Jimmy Carter in the American presidential race of November 1976 and the ensuing pressure of human-rights issues by the new Democratic administration in Washington. These political pressures to accord human rights gave the revolutionary coalition opportunities for mass mobilization. When the political upheavals of 1977–79 came, the feeble character of the Shah, combined with the political immaturity and structural weaknesses of the newly dominant middle classes, led to the collapse of the Pahlavi regime.

Notes

1. See, for example, Nika'in, Amir, *Rusta-ye Iran dar Entezar-e Tahavvol*, (Tehran: Hezb-e Tudeh-ye Iran, 1981).

2. See Khomeini, Ruhollah, *Sahifeh-ye Nur*, 18 vols (Tehran: Vezarat-e Ershad-e Eslami, 1983): Vol I, pp 264–5; Vol IV, p 24; Vol V, pp 23, 39, 136; Vol VI, p 181.

3. Hooglund, Eric, 'Rural participation in the revolution', *MERIP Reports* 87 (May 1980), pp 3–6.

4. The original programmes of the White Revolution included the land-reform programme to redistribute the holdings of major landlords among the landless peasants who worked the land, nationalization of forests, sale of state-owned enterprises to the public, workers' profit-sharing in 20 per cent of net corporate earnings, voting and political rights for women and the literacy corps. Thirteen more programmes were presented from January 1964 to late December 1975, including the health corps, the reconstruction and development corps, the houses of equity, nationalization of water resources, urban and rural reconstruction, administrative revolution, a scheme for employee and public ownership, price stabilization and a campaign against profiteering, free education and daily free meals for students from kindergarten to grade eight, free nutrition for infants up to the age of two, nationwide social security, a campaign against land and housing speculation, and a fight against corruption.

5. This part of the chapter is drawn from a section in Ashraf, Ahmad, 'State and agrarian relations before and after the Iranian Revolution, 1960–1990,' in Farhad Kazemi and John Waterbury (eds), *Peasant Politics in the Modern Middle East* (Gainsville: Florida International University Press, 1991), pp 277–84.

6. Warriner, Doreen, *Land Reform in Principle and Practice* (Oxford: Clarendon Press, 1969), pp 109–35.

7. See, for example, Najmabadi, Afsaneh, *Land Reform and Social Change in Iran* (Salt Lake City: Utah University Press, 1987), pp 3–42; Tabari, Azar, 'Land, politics, and capital accumulation,' *MERIP Reports* (March–April 1983), pp 26–30; Bizhan, Jazani, *Capitalism and Revolution in Iran* (London: Zed Books, 1982) pp 50–53; Momeni, Baqer, *Eslahat-e Arzi va Jang-e Tabaqati dar Iran* (Tehran: Entesharat-e Peyvand, 1980), pp 161–221; Sudagar, M., *Barrasi-ye Eslahat-e Arzi, 1340–1350* (Tehran: Pazand, 1979), pp 7–38; Sazman-e Feda'i-ye Khalq-e Iran, *Darbareh-ye Eslahat-e Arzi va Natayej-e Mostaqim-e an* (Tehran, clandestine, 1975), pp 3–21.

8. See Warne, William, *Mission for Peace: Point 4 in Iran* (Indianapolis: Merrill, 1956), pp 190–204.

9. Cottam, Richard, *Iran and the United States: A Cold War Case Study* (Pittsburgh: Pittsburgh University Press, 1988), p 128.

10. Pahlavi, Mohammad Reza, *Answer to History* (New York: Stein and Day, 1980), pp 22–23; Cottam, *Iran and the United States*, pp 128–9; Bill, James, *The Eagle and the Lion: The Tragedy of American–Iranian Relations* (Newhaven: Yale University Press, 1988), pp 142–4.

11. Huntington, Samuel, *Political Order in Changing Societies* (New Haven: Yale University Press, 1968), p 292.

12. Ibid., p 375.

13. See, for example, Humphrey, Hubert, *Alliance for Progress: A Firsthand Report from Latin America* (Washington DC: The Sidney Hillman Lectures, 1963), pp 5–28; Packenham, Robert, *Liberal America and the Third World* (Princeton: University Press, 1973), pp 59–69.

14. Roxborough, Ian, *Theories of Underdevelopment* (London: Macmillan, 1979), pp 29–32.

15. Ashraf, 'State and agrarian relations'.

16. See, for example, Kazemi, Farhad and Abrahamian, Ervand, 'The non-revolutionary peasantry of modern Iran,' *Iranian Studies* XI (1978), pp 259–308.

17. Roxborough, *Theories of Underdevelopment*, pp 1–12.

18. Najmabadi, *Land Reform*, pp 33–42; Momeni, *Eslahat-e Arzi*.

19. Nowshirvani, Vahid, 'The beginnings of commercialized agriculture in Iran', in A.L. Udovitch (ed.), *The Islamic Middle East, 700–1900: Studies in Economic and Social History* (Princeton: Darwin Press, 1981), pp 547–91.

20. Amini, Ali, 'An interview with Dr Ali Amini on land reform in Iran', conducted by Hormoz Hekmat (Paris, 1986), author's personal file.

21. Amini, 'An interview'; Hooglund, Eric, *Land and Revolution in Iran* (Austin: University of Texas Press, 1982), p 44; Hughes, T., 'Land reform in Iran, implications for the Shah's White Revolution', research memorandum, US Department of State, Director of Intelligence and Research, 8 February 1965, pp 1–4; Cottam, *Iran and the United States*, p 128.

22. Arsanjani, Hasan, *Mosahebeha-ye Radiyo'i-ye Doktor Arsanjani* (Tehran: Ministry of Agriculture, 1962), pp 233–8.

23. Ibid.

24. Wilber, Donald, 'Memorandum of conversation: Dr. Hasan Arsanjani, Minister of Agriculture', (10 November 1962), author's personal file.

25. Zonis, Marvin, *The Political Elite of Iran* (Princeton: Princeton University Press, 1971), p 60.

26. Amini, 'An interview'.

27. Bill, James, *The Politics of Iran: Groups, Classes and Modernization* (Columbus: Merrill, 1972), p 143f.

28. Warriner, *Land Reform*, pp 109–35.

29. Amini, 'An interview'.

30. Mahdavi, Hossein, 'The coming crisis in Iran', *Foreign Affairs* 44 (October 1965), pp 134–46.

31. Lambton, Ann K.S., *The Persian Land Reform, 1962–1966* (Oxford: Clarendon Press, 1969), pp 194–256.

32. This part of the chapter is drawn from a section in Ashraf, 'State and agrarian relations', pp 284–90.

33. Lambton, Ann K.S., *Landlord and Peasant in Persia* (London: Oxford University Press, 1953), pp 182–9.

34. Nowshirvani, 'The beginnings of commercialized agriculture', pp 547–91.

35. Shaji'i, Zahra, *Namayandegan-e Majles-e Showra-ye Melli dar 21 Dowre-ye Qanungozari* (Tehran: Institute for Social Research, 1965), pp 179, 249.

36. See, for example, the cases of Sayyed Ja'far Pishevari, Haji Rahim Kho'i, and Sayyed Hasan Arsanjani in the 14th and 15th sessions of the Majles.

37. Zonis, *Political Elite*, p 158.

38. Lambton, *Landlord and Peasant*, pp 268–74; Arsanjani, *Mosabebeh-ha*, pp 150–77.

39. Estimates from the Statistical Centre of Iran, *First National Census of Agriculture* (Tehran, 1962), Table 10.

40. Ashraf, Ahmad, and Ali Banuazizi, 'Policies and Strategies of Land Reform in Iran', in Inayatullah (ed.), *Land Reform: Some Asian Experiences* (Kuala Lumpur: APDAC, 1980), pp 33–5.

41. Estimated from Statistical Centre of Iran: *First National Census of Agriculture*, Table 101; Khosrow Khosrovi, *Barrasi-ye Amari-ye Vaz'iyyat-e Arzi-ye Iran dar Shesh Ostan* (Tehran: Markaz-e Nashr-e Daneshgahi, 1988), pp 6–8, 63–66, 98–100, 142–5, 162–4, 189–91.

42. Azimi, Hosein, 'Towzi'-e zamin va daramad dar astana-ye eslahat-e arzi', in *Ketab-e Agah: Masa'el-e Arzi va Dehqani* (Tehran, 1982), pp 75–94.

43. Agricultural Development Bank of Iran, Bureau of Economic Studies, unpublished material (Tehran, 1981).

44. Plan and Budget Organization, *Budjeh-ye Koll-e Keshvar* (Tehran, 1979).

45. *Ketab-e Agah*, pp 161–3.

46. Ajami, Ismail, 'Land reform and modernization of the farming structure in Iran', *Oxford Agrarian Studies* 11 (1973), pp 1–12; Okazaki, Shoko, *The Development of Large-Scale Farming in Iran: The Case of the Province of Gorgan* (Tokyo: The Institute of Asian Economic Affairs, 1968).

47. Ashraf, Ahmad, 'Dehqanan, zamin va enqelab', *Ketab-e Agah*, pp 15–17.

48. See Qahraman, Babak, 'Dow yaddasht', *Ketab-e Agah*, p 139.

49. Lambton, *Landlord and Peasant*, pp 275–82.

50. Keddie, Nikkie, 'Stratification, social control and capitalism in Iranian villages before and after land reform', in Richard Antoun (ed.), *Rural Politics and Social Change in the Middle East* (Bloomington: Indiana University Press, 1972), pp 383–8.

51. *Ketab-e Agah*, p 185.

52. Statistical Centre of Iran, *National Census of Population and Housing, November 1976, Total Country* (Tehran, 1981), pp 112–13.

53. Hooglund, Eric, 'Khwushnishin population of Iran', *Iranian Studies* (August 1973), p 232.

54. Keshavarz, Hushang, *Barresi-ye Eqtesadi va Ejtema'i-ye Sherkat-e Sahami-ye Zera'i-ye Reza Pahlavi* (Tehran: Institute for Social Research, 1970), p 118; Ashraf, Ahmad, The Role of Rural Orgnaizations in Rural Development: The Case of Iran', in Inayatullah, *Rural Organizations*, pp 138–46.

55. *Ketab-e Agah*, p 180.

56. Ibid.

57. The subsistence size in most cases varied from 2 to 10 hectares.

58. Statistical Centre of Iran: *National Census of Population*, p 88.

59. See *Ketab-e Agah*, p 186.

60. Mahdavi, Hosein, 'Tahavvolat-e si saleh-ye yak deh dar dasht-e Qazvin', *Ketab-e Agah*, pp 59–64.

61. Anonymous, 'Current political attitudes in an Iranian village', *Iranian Studies* 16/1–2 (1983), p 5.

62. Dowlat, Manizheh, Bernard Hourcade and Odil Puech, 'Les paysans et la revolution Iranienne', *Peuples Mediterranéens* 19 (January–March 1980), pp 19–42.

63. Ashraf, Ahmad, and Ali Banuazizi, 'The state, classes, and modes of

mobilization in the Iranian revolution', *International Journal of State, Culture and Society* 1/3 (1985), pp 23–5.

64. See, for example, Khomeini, *Sahifa-ye Nur*, Vol I, pp 264–5; Vol IV, p 24; Vol V, pp 23, 39, 136; Vol VI, p 181; Dana, F.R., *Amperializm va Forupashi-ye Keshavarzi dar Iran* (Tehran: Naqsh-e Jahan, 1979); Rouleau, Eric, 'Khomeini's Iran', *Foreign Affairs* 59 (1980), pp 1–20; MacLachlan, Keith, *The Neglected Garden: The Politics and Ecology of Agriculture in Iran* (London: I.B. Tauris, 1988); Majd, Mohammad Qoli, 'The political economy of land reform in Iran', in *Land Use Policy* (January 1991), pp 69–76; Karshenas, Massoud, *Oil, State and Industrialization in Iran* (Cambridge: Cambridge University Press, 1990).

65. *Ketab-e Agah*, p 182.

66. Statistical Centre of Iran, *Statistical Year Book , 1966* (Tehran, 1967) p 101; *Statistical Year Book, 1981* (Tehran, 1981), p 670.

67. This section is drawn from the following two articles: Ashraf, Ahmad and Ali Banuazizi, 'Class System vi. Classes in the Pahlavi Period', *Encyclopaedia Iranica* V (1992), pp 677–91; Nowshirvani, Vahid, and Ahmad Ashraf, 'Iran's rentier state and the development of its entrepreneurial elite: 1950s–1970s,' paper prepared for the Conference on Middle Classes and Entrepreneurial Elites of the Middle East, Berkeley, 9–12 May 1991.

68. Public Statistics of Iran, *National Census of Population and Housing, 1956*, I, p 283; Statistical Centre of Iran: *National Census of Population, 1976*.

69. Bank Markazi, *National Accounts of Iran 1959–1976*, in Persian, (Tehran, 1981) pp 126–7, 406, 416–19, 422–4.

70. Public Statistics of Iran, *National Census of Population*, 1956, I, p 283; Statistical Centre of Iran: *National Census of Population, 1976*, pp 61, 64, 67.

71. Statistical Center of Iran, *Bayan-e Amari-ye Tahavvolat-e Eqtesadi va Ejtema'i-ye Iran dar Dowran-e Por-eftekhar-e Dudman-e Pahlavi* (Tehran, 1976), pp 41, 51; *Statistical Year Book, 1968*, p 75.

72. Nasafat, Mortaza, *Sanjesh-e Afkar-e Daneshjuyan-e Keshvar* (Tehran: Institute for Psychological Research, 1975) p 91.

73. Ashraf and Banuazizi, 'The state, classes', pp 25–9, Bill, *Politics*, pp 73–102; Herz, Martin, 'Some intangible factors in Iranian politics', from American Embassy, Tehran to Department of State, Washington (A-702, 15 June 1964), pp 4–12.

74. See, for example, Haqshenas, Torab, 'Communism iii. In Persia after 1953', in *Encyclopaedia Iranica* VI (1993), pp 105–12; Matin-Asgari, Afshin, 'Confederation of Iranian students', in *Encyclopaedia Iranica* VI (1993), pp 122–5.

75. Salehi-Isfahani, Djavad, 'The Political Economy of Credit Subsidy in Iran, 1973–1978', *International Journal of Middle East Studies* 21/3 (1989), pp 359–79.

76. Bank Markazi, *National Accounts*, pp 408–9; Statistical Centre of Iran: *Bayan-e Amari*, p 131; *Statistical Year Book, 1981*, pp 433–86.

77. Nowshirvani and Ashraf, 'Iran's rentier state'.

78. See, Ashraf, 'Bazar iii. Socio-economic and political role of the bazar', in *Encyclopaedia Iranica* IV (1990), pp 30–44.

79. Ashraf, 'Bazar iii'; and 'Chamber of Commerce, Industries, and Mines of Persia', in *Encyclopaedia Iranica* V (1992), pp 354–8.

80. *Rastakhiz*, 23 June 1975, pp 1–2.

81. Nowshirvani and Ashraf, 'Iran's rentier state'.

82. Akhavi, Shahrugh, *Religion and Politics in Contemporary Iran* (Albany: Suny Press,

1980), pp 129–43.

83. Khomeini, Ruhollah, *Velayat-e Faqih, Hokumat-e Eslami* (Tehran, 1978), pp 199–204.

84. Rafsanjani, Ali Akbar Hashemi, *Enqelab ya Be'that-e Jadid* (Qom, 1980), p 19.

85. Rohani, Sayyed Hamid, *Barrasi va Tahlili az Nahzat-e Emam Khomeini dar Iran* (Qom: Entesharat-e Dar al-Fekr, 1979), I, pp 623–4; Ashraf, Ahmad, 'Theocracy and charisma: new men of power in Iran', *International Journal of Politics, Culture and Society* 4/1 (1990), pp 113–21.

86. Ashraf, 'Theocracy and Charisma,' pp 120–21.

87. Statistical Centre of Iran, *National Census of Population, 1976*, pp 68, 85. These figures do not include workers in the service sector and self-employed artisans and shopkeepers.

88. Halliday, Fred, *Iran: Dictatorship and Development* (Harmondsworth: Penguin, 1979) pp 189–90.

89. Hakimian, Hassan, 'Industrialization and the standard of living of the working class in Iran, 1960–79', *Development and Change* 19 (1988), p 13.

90. See, for example, Kazemi, Farhad, *Poverty and Revolution in Iran* (New York: State University of New York Press, 1980), pp 46–67.

91. Keyhan, Mehdi, *Haftad Sal Jonbesh-e Sandika'i dar Iran* (Tehran, 1980), pp 28–32.

92. See Ashraf and Banuazizi, 'The State, classes', p 685.

93. Sazman-e Cherikha-ye Feda'iyan-e Khalq Iran, *Jonbesh-e Khalq va Tabaqe-ye Kargar* (reprinted by CISNU, West Berlin 1978) p 7. For the statement by the Fada'is concerning the apathy of the working class, see Ashraf and Banuazizi, 'The State, classes', pp 33–4.

94. The heightened awareness of welfare issues during the revolutionary mobilization in October–November 1978 was primarily due to the reading of the human-rights document (*hoquq-e bashar*) by government employees and blue-collar workers, which they measured in terms of 'human salaries'. This experience resulted from a significant misunderstanding of the Persian term *hoquq* which means 'salary' or 'an obscure notion of rights'.

2

State, Political Stability and Property Rights

Fatemeh E. Moghadam

Introduction

In the course of the twentieth century Iran has experienced two major revolutions: the Constitutional Revolution (1906–07) and the Islamic Revolution (1978–79). Unlike other major twentieth-century revolutions such as the Russian, the Chinese and the Cuban, the Iranian revolutions did not have a socialist ideology. Furthermore, in both revolutions a segment of the wealthy bazaar merchants, the elite members of the ulema, as well as other wealthy groups, participated. The Constitutional Revolution resulted in the consolidation of private property rights. In the case of the Islamic Revolution, there were instances of confiscation and disruption of large-scale industrial and landed property rights. However, these disruptions were not systematic, many wealthy individuals maintained their wealth, and others were able to reclaim it. Furthermore, the ownership rights of the smaller agricultural and industrial producers did not become subject to disruption. In spite of some irregularity and arbitrariness in the treatment of large-scale wealth, the institution of private property has not been challenged by the state. I will argue that the existing stage of the development of property rights and the relationship between the propertied groups and the state have been important factors contributing to the treatment of private property in the twentieth-century revolutions in Iran.

In order to substantiate my argument, I will examine the evolution of property rights in land since the nineteenth century and will extend the analysis to the post-revolutionary period. I will demonstrate that the development of private-property land rights has been discontinuous with setbacks and retrogressions, and that there has been persistent competition between the state and private owners over these rights. Even in its recent history, the land reform (1962–67) can be cited as another example of the ability of the state to reverse private rights. The post-revolutionary period was also marked by disruptions in private-land-ownership rights, although on a relatively small scale. I will argue, however, that the general tendency has been toward development and clarification of private rights, and that

45

the developments have resulted in structural changes in the property rights system. I will also argue that protest against the ability of the state to challenge property rights has been an important component of both revolutions.

It has been argued that the development of property rights is evolutionary. The adjustments in property rights need not be the result of a conscious endeavour and may be the outcome of gradual changes in social mores and traditions.[1] These tendencies, however, can be disrupted through arbitrary attempts to negate the rights. In Iran from about the eleventh to the nineteenth century nearly all ruling dynasties came from a nomadic tribal origin. I have elsewhere argued that the recurrence of nomadic dynasties was accompanied by periodic negation of the existing rights, and was an important impediment to the evolution of landownership rights in Iran.[2] The assumption of power by the Qajars (1785) represented the last example of the rise of a new nomadic dynasty. Thus the evolution of property rights during the period being studied was not disrupted by another nomadic conquest.

Demsetz has argued that changes and developments in property rights result from changes in technology and economic institutions. New technologies bring about new cost efficiencies and contribute to the emergence of new property rights.[3] Here I will argue that the transportation, communication and other technological developments of the nineteenth and twentieth centuries contributed to the growing integration of Iran into the world market economy, and induced market, political and other institutional developments. These changes contributed to the development of private property rights in land, and resulted in a departure from the historical pattern.

As this study traces the long-term development of property rights, we need appropriate criteria with which to evaluate the relative development or the regression of these rights. I will make a distinction between the factors that determine clarity or precision and those that involve ambiguity and imprecision, and between those that explain arbitrariness – sudden and unlawful disruptions – and those that ensure order and security in the rights. Where land has been acquired through voluntary exchange or other undisputable private means, and where its proceeds are used for purely private purposes, the type of ownership is private. By contrast, where political power is the basis of ownership, land is controlled by state institutions, and its proceeds are used for public purposes, the category is state ownership. For undeveloped rights, however, a clear distinction between the two may not always be possible. While the central government may not be the source of an individual's or a group's control over land, local political power may be. The number of competing parties that have proprietorship claims on land can be used as another criterion of clarity.[4] Where a single proprietor has full claim and control over a piece of land, and workers are only wage-earners without any holding rights, the claim is clear. If there exists a hierarchical set of competing claimants each may try to attenuate and/or undermine the rights of others. The reduction in the number of competing claimants contributes to the clarity of the rights. Any category of property rights requires a set of systematic rules defining privileges, limitations and mechanisms of transfer. To the extent that a legal system or tradition specifies the rights, it contributes to clarity of these rights.

If the basis of transfer is political power, it would be coercive and would undermine private rights. By contrast voluntary sales are a by-product of private rights. However, the ruling elite may use coercion to force owners to sell. Nevertheless, the adherence to the mechanism of sale indicates a degree of recognition of the owner's rights, and may be considered less arbitrary than outright confiscation. Another mechanism would be transformation of state lands into private ownership through usurpation.

Background: The Sociopolitical and Economic System

Many writers have considered the nineteenth century as the beginning of the modern era in Iran.[5] It coincides with the penetration of Western European influence and the growing participation of Iran in world markets. It can be viewed as the beginning of the disintegration of Iran's earlier political system that had been a succession of nomadic dynasties. During the nineteenth century, the main impetus of change was the gradual integration of Iran into the world economy. The rapidity of change was more apparent during the second half of the century; and the fragmented economy of Iran, which had relatively little exchange activity, became internally as well as internationally integrated. Since these developments took place under the commercial impact of the industrial powers, the internal development did not mean a parallel expansion in both industry and agriculture. The expansion of exports was mainly in agricultural products.[6]

A study of factors that gave rise to the Constitutional Revolution are beyond the scope of this chapter and have been more thoroughly examined by other writers.[7] I will mention some of the factors only briefly. Although the Qajar rulers maintained absolute and arbitrary power for the most part, they were unable to realize the traditional ideal of central adminis-tration. This allowed the traditional communal groups such as tribes and the ulema to enjoy a considerable autonomy, while at the same time providing an opportunity for the newly rising interest groups to attain power. The commercial developments of the nineteenth century gave rise to the growth of an indigenous group of merchants who were interested in a less arbitrary form of government and a stronger legal system, and had the means to finance the movement. Contact with the West and the introduction of modern education created an intelligentsia interested in a Western constitutional style of government. The infrastructural developments allowed for greater communication and the possibility of a more orchestrated form of protest in the major cities. Nationalism, and the feeling that the arbitrary nature of the rule was the main reason for the foreign concessions, also contributed to the movement. At the turn of the century, Iran officially adopted a system of constitutional monarchy.

The constitutional government did not have a well-developed and institutionalized professional army, and tribal militarism continued to be the most important form of military power. The rise of Reza Shah (1925), who set up the first non-tribal dynasty in Iran, was a significant change. In some ways Reza Shah realized the ideals of the constitutionalists. His coming to power and the reorganization of the army and central bureaucracy were interwoven. His rule was accompanied by considerable economic development and modernization. At the same time, Reza Shah's rise to power may be viewed as a negation of the democratic ideal of the constitutional movement, and a return to autocratic administration, as he tried to reduce the power of the parliament. Reza Shah founded a centrally administered form of government that contained a curious combination of modernism and traditional absolutism.

An important development in the twentieth century for Iran was the discovery and extraction of oil; it became Iran's single most important export commodity and source of foreign exchange earnings. Oil was discovered around 1900 and extractions began in 1908. According to a concession granted by the Qajar rulers, the British Petroleum Company had monopoly control over the southern Iranian oil fields. The growing importance of oil in international markets and the view that the concessionary agreement was an exploitation of Iranian natural resources dominated twentieth-century Anglo-Iranian relations as well as Iranian politics. During the period of social uprisings (1941–53) that followed Reza Shah's abdication, the issue of the nationalization of oil became dominant in Iranian politics. It became the central focus of the struggle of nationalist liberals to rejuvenate the constitutional power of the parliament. The rise and fall of the nationalist government of Mosaddeq (1951–53) was directly linked to the politics of oil. In August 1953, a CIA-staged coup overthrew the nationalist government and brought Mohammad Reza Shah (1941–79) back to power.

The period 1953–79 witnessed the consolidation and the rise of quasi-absolute power and the ultimate demise of Mohammad Reza Shah. The Shah succeeded in reducing the power of the parliament and in enhancing his own. An important characteristic of the period was the continual increase in oil prices and in Iran's share of the oil revenues, culminating in the OPEC oil price increase of 1973. This was also a period of rapid industrialization, urbanization and the development of infrastructure. The Iranian economy and society underwent major structural changes during this period.

Property relations in land: 1000–1800

Throughout the period, there were many instances of disruption and reversion of private proprietorship claims and rights by the state. However, there was considerable variation in the extent and scope of the disruptions. They varied from outright plunder, causing loss of land-ownership for those with full, legitimate claims, to forced sales and a reclamation of state lands that had been privatized through usurpation; the scope varied from a substantial portion of landed property in the country to small-scale confiscations. There was also considerable ambiguity and imprecision in the rights. The distinction between state and private properties for those holding power was not always clear. The simultaneous existence of different layers of competing claimants on land – land-grantee, landowner and peasant – created ambiguity in these rights. Throughout this period, land was used for revenue administration. However, land assignment was not the only mechanism of legitimization of tenure: sales and usurpations also occurred.[8]

The superimposition of nomadic dynasties was the most important contributor to arbitrariness and ambiguity in property rights. An important objective of the conquerors was to redistribute wealth in their favour by means of force. As conquests recurred, the retrogression and reversion of property rights also recurred periodically. At the inception of a dynasty the nomadic influence was stronger, and there was greater arbitrariness and ambiguity in the rights. Arbitrary property relations persisted throughout each dynasty,[9] but on a relatively smaller scale with the passage of time. Under each dynasty, the composition of the ruling elite remained relatively stable, and land remained within the families. Political stability also allowed a greater role for the market mechanism and the fairly clear and non-arbitrary Islamic legal system.

The system of land-revenue administration underwent a marked change under the Safavids. The state bureaucracy was on the whole capable of maintaining control over the two major categories of state lands, *khaleseh* (crown land) and *tuyul* (land grant). Invariably, the grants were in return for service, the discontinuity of which resulted in the discontinuity of the grant,[10] and the distinction between private and state lands became clearer. Private property rights tended to evolve. The privately owned, *melki*, lands comprised an important category of the holdings.[11] They were not subject to the superimposition of a grantee, and the prevalence of relative order suggests a decline in arbitrariness. Charitable religious, *vaqf*, lands had existed since the inception of Islam, but the highly religious character of the Safavid dynasty, together with the general trend of the period toward development and clarification of property rights, allowed this category to assume much greater significance and more security.[12] The subsequent invasions and civil wars disrupted these developments, but there were some lasting impacts as later rulers resorted to some Safavid practices. However, in many instances, the Qajars did revert to the pre-Safavid tradition of superimposition of a grantee, *tuyuldar*, on both landowners and peasants.

Peasants lived in village communities and shared the produce with the landlords according to the Islamic rules of *moqasemeh*. The landlord could be the *tuyuldar*, *khalesehdar* or *malek*; the ulema as the trustees and beneficiaries of the *vaqf* shared the produce with the peasants on these lands. Sometimes peasants had to share the produce with both the private landholder and the land-grantee. The rights of peasants over the land and the produce also varied with the extent of political stability.

Evolution of Land Ownership: 1800–1953

In the course of the nineteenth century, there was no change in the ruling dynasties in Iran, and no massive confiscation and reallocation of landed property. In general, property rights in land tended to evolve and clarify, but there were setbacks and retrogressions.[13] The state's objective to develop a modern professional army increased the need for income; the share of the crown lands, *khaleseh*, was increased through confiscation and forced sales. At the same time, land-grantees also privatized state lands through usurpation and purchase; and the general inability of the rulers to establish a strong system of central administration contributed to the privatization process. New developments were taking place, however. From the middle of the nineteenth century there was growing commercialization of agriculture and increased development of internal markets. The development of a quasi-modern bureaucracy and banking system undermined the need for the use of land for revenue administration; monetization of the economy increased commercialization of land.[14] These developments were conducive to the evolution of private property rights.

The early Qajar period is marked by an increase in *khaleseh* lands. Throughout the Qajar rule, sporadic attempts were made by the rulers to convert private or quasi-private lands into *khaleseh*.[15] More frequently, however, the tendency was for the *khaleseh* lands to become private property. In order to raise revenues, the Qajaras sold *khaleseh* lands. As many of these lands were in a state of ruin, and as it was believed that private ownership was likely to improve cultivation and increase output, the lands were sometimes given to cultivators.[16]

The Qajars made land grants, *tuyuls*. The term *tuyul* covered a variety of grants. Some were grants on the revenue attached to certain offices.

Others were grants of *khaleseh* land in lieu of salary. In tribal areas, the holder was under an obligation to provide military contingents. Sometimes the *tuyul* was a grant of the right to collect the taxes of an area, or merely immunity from taxation. The dominant category was the grant of *khaleseh*.[17] As *tuyul* was often hereditary, the tendency for the holders of *khaleseh* lands was to treat them as private property through usurpation; and for the holders of other categories to claim quasi-autonomy from the central government. Although many features of communal land use persisted in tribal areas, the tendency was toward privatization of these lands; and for the tribal chiefs to claim both land proprietorship and autonomy. The state in general tended to lose control, and the grantees tended to increase their claims over these lands.

Under the Qajars, *vaqf* lands continued to be an important category of holdings, although to a lesser extent than in the Safavid period. During the later Qajar period there was considerable conversion of *vaqf* into private property, mostly by the members of the religious community. The ulema continued to be an important propertied group as the trustees of *vaqf* and as private owners.[18]

Monetization of the economy, growing commercialization of agriculture, and the development of a quasi-modern bureaucracy that reduced the need to use land as a means of revenue administration, all contributed to the growing commercialization of land. These developments in turn gave rise to a new landowning class. Because of the profitability of agriculture, merchants began investing in land.[19] During the reigns of both Nasereddin Shah and his successor, merchants with funds managed to purchase *khaleseh* lands at bargain prices. Land was also acquired as a result of extending loans to landlords who could not repay in cash. But these merchants did not join the ranks of the large landlords until the twentieth century.[20] Possession of land conferred a considerable politico-economic benefit upon the holder. Large landholders often kept a body of armed retainers. This was specially acute in the case of the tribal khans. Throughout the Qajar period landholders were the most powerful group in the country.[21]

The growing power of landholders, together with the persistence of arbitrariness in the treatment of private property, can be cited as a major contributor to the Constitutional Revolution. One of the leading revolutionary newspapers, *Qanun*, viewed the establishment of a non-arbitrary legal system as the most pressing issue. It argued that the legal system, among others, should set up laws to protect private property and to prevent the state from arbitrary confiscations. The newspaper was consistently pro-monarchy and was only against absolutism.[22] It can be argued that because of historical precedence, the propertied groups viewed any major change in the composition of the ruling elite as a prelude to arbitrariness and confiscation of private property. They only sought to reform and constitutionalize the existing monarchy. Although many powerful land-holding tribal khans were opposed to the general ideals of the revolution – and some writers have referred to the tribal anarchism that followed the revolution as a traditional counter-revolution[23] – the autonomy of many large landholders in the tribal areas and elsewhere contributed to the weakness of the Qajars and as such aided the constitutionalists.

The Constitutional Law of 1907 officially abolished *tuyul*. Many *tuyul* and *khaleseh* lands became private properties (*mulk*) of their holders. The Civil Code was specially strong and developed a body of laws concerning private property in land. However, the Civil Code was silent about other land categories such as *vaqf* and *khaleseh*, which can be interpreted as being indifferent, or even non-supportive toward these categories of ownership.[24] Shortly after the constitution was granted, a Department of Owqaf (religious endowments) was set up in order to control the *vaqf* lands.[25] In the case of tribal lands, the law recognized them as the private properties of the tribal khans. In 1922, the Department of Land Regis-tration was established. The long-lasting historical tradition of the use of land for revenue administration came to an end.

The rise of Reza Shah accompanied new and somewhat contradictory developments. During the early years of his reign considerable areas of land were confiscated by the state from tribal and other large landowners. In many instances *khaleseh* lands located in areas outside the zones of influence of these tribal leaders and the local influentials were transferred to them. This policy was intended to break the political power and autonomy of these large landlords.[26] In the 1930s, Reza Shah also pursued policies of forced sedentarization and peasantization of nomads. Tribal lands were parcelled and allocated to individual tribal households. From a production viewpoint the policy proved to be highly unsuccessful and was in many instances abandoned. However, it did result in considerable parcelling of land and in depropertization of tribal khans. In order to reduce the economic autonomy of the ulema, among other policies, Reza Shah set up a government organization to control *vaqf* lands, but did not challenge the essence of the ulema's right to these lands. They remained the legal beneficiaries of *vaqf*.

Reza Shah's threat to landownership was accentuated by the appetite of the monarch and his functionaries for landed property. Most of his personal estates, *amlak-e saltanati*, however, were acquired through pur-chases (though often at nominal and unjust prices and forced sales), and there was no pretence at revenue administration. Lands held by the monarch as well as those of his functionaries were viewed as private property, and were administered separately from the *khaleseh* that was generally regarded as state land.[27]

There were also positive developments in private-property rights. Being the largest landowner, Reza Shah was interested in passing laws that strengthened landlordism. The parliament, dominated by landlords, passed laws – especially the Civil Code of 1929 – to consolidate these rights.[28] The general establishment of law and order, economic development, growing commercialization and integration of the economy all contributed to the growing commercialization of land. Economic development and the establishment of a centralized bureaucracy reduced the state's dependency on land. For both political and economic reasons, the state gave up *khaleseh* lands. In addition to allocating *khaleseh* in exchange for other lands, there were sales of *khaleseh*. In general, the relative share of *khaleseh* declined, and that of private property rose.

In summary, under Reza Shah certain historical patterns in land proprietorship persisted, but there were also new and evolutionary developments. The rise of a new dynasty disrupted some of the existing landownership rights, and created a new landowning aristocracy. Access to political power continued to be an important prerequisite for land proprietorship, and return to quasi-absolutism posed a potential threat to private landowners. However, the overall trend under Reza Shah was that of market integration, growing commercialization of land, and development of private property. When aggressive confiscation was pursued by Reza Shah, the policy was aimed at destroying proprietorship claims of a more traditional and political type, one that had evolved primarily as a result of non-market military and political forces, and one that was viewed as an obstacle to the political unification of the country. In general, land proprietorship policies contributed to the political integration of the country and did not create conditions that could generate long-term decentralizing tendencies.

After the abdication of Reza Shah in 1941, once again the landlord-dominated parliament was strengthened. An important feature of the period was the landlords' attempt to reclaim the lands that had been taken away by Reza Shah. The parliament made provisions for partial return of these lands to their original holders. By a royal decree in 1941, the personal estates of Reza Shah, known as the Ceded Properties, were to be returned to the state. In 1942 a law was passed calling for the return of some specified categories of these estates to their original owners. As a result of this and a subsequent law (1949), some of the Ceded Properties were returned to the original owners. Some of these properties became a *vaqf* for the Pahlavi family with its income devoted to charitable purposes. Another portion was returned to the reigning shah.[29]

Although some of the measures by Reza Shah were reversed, these policies together with the development of markets and commercialization of land created a tendency toward the establishment of relatively smaller landownerships, and a reduction in the size of the area held by very large and politico-militarily powerful landlords.[30] By the 1950s, new and relatively smaller-sized land proprietorships had emerged in the tribal areas.

Depending on the historical background of a tribal region, Reza Shah's denomadization policies gave rise to the emergence of a variety of new production organizations. For example, in Larestan, prior to government intervention, the society had been vigorously egalitarian, without a persistent wealth differentiation among commoners. The tribal leaders did not enjoy great socio-economic power. However, the forced sedentarization policies of the 1930s, and the subsequent changes of the 1940s, resulted in growing wealth differentiation and the emergence of a group of agro-pastoral owners who entered into a sharecropping relationship with the remaining population. In the first years of sedentarization, land began to replace flocks as a standard of wealth. Competition for the more fertile tracts of crop land was so keen that the ability to obtain and keep them became a benchmark of political status. Those lineages who procured the most productive fields in the first instance usually came to control a larger area than they could themselves cultivate. Consequently, they entered sharecropping agreements with others. They became the owners of the new agro-pastoral combines.[31]

Similar developments of a relatively smaller-sized landlord-type private ownership are likely to have emerged elsewhere in the tribal areas. As the historical patterns of land ownership and tribal hierarchies were different and more complex in other areas, they gave rise to more complex outcomes. For example, in Kurdestan a new and smaller-sized tenant farming, where the land belonged to an absentee landowner, emerged. finally, in some parts of Kurdestan as well as Fars many tribal confederacies were preserved, and large tracts of land continued to belong to the khans.[32] Even in these cases, there is a likelihood of reduction in the area held by the khans. Comprehensive data concerning the reduction in the area held by large and politically powerful landowners is not available, but examples can be cited. During the reign of Nasereddin Shah, the largest landlord (Zellol-Soltan) allegedly owned two thousand villages, with a population of half a million. At the time of land reform in 1962, the largest landlord owned only two hundred villages.[33]

By the 1950s, there had also been a significant development of large-scale capitalist-type landownership with wage labour. The most widespread geographic area was in Gorgan. Examples could also be found elsewhere, especially around Tehran, though in the latter case often many share-cropping labour relations persisted. The growing monetization and integration of the economy had ignited the disintegration of the traditional sharecropping relations. Mechanization of agriculture in the period after the Second World War accelerated this process.[34] At the time of the implementation of land reform in 1962, a significant portion of holding areas – about 7 per cent of the holding areas (according to rough estimates) – were mechanized and depended heavily on wage labour.[35]

It can be argued that an important contributor to the downfall of

Mosaddeq in 1953 was the state of existing property relations. In the political turmoil of these years the landlord-dominated parliament tried to undermine the arbitrary power of the monarch, and weaken his confiscatory power. In this respect, different propertied groups, such as land-holding aristocracy, merchants who owned merchant and industrial capital in addition to land, and the ulema were allies. Once the nationalist government assumed a more radical anti-monarch position, fear of the collapse of law and order and of the possible confiscation of private property prevailed. This fear had historic roots and was compounded by the existing inequalities and the active presence of the pro-Soviet communist Tudeh party. Even the traditional bazaar merchants and their religious allies were not willing to trade off greater insecurity in private property for oil nationalization, and they turned against the nationalist movement.

Direct Producers' Property Rights

At the beginning of the nineteenth century, peasants were in a position similar to those in the earlier dynastic changes. Wars, tribal competitions, and the rise of a new dynasty contributed to abuse and destruction in the countryside. Plunder and violence, partially or totally, deprived peasants of their traditional rights over the produce. Over time, however, the prevalence of relative order and stabilization of landlords' property rights resulted in relative stabilization of the traditional peasant sharecrops. Commercialization of agriculture during the second half of the century is likely to have further contributed to the stabilization and clarification of the producers' conventional land rights, as well as increased economic stratification among peasants in the more commercialized rural areas. The evidence suggests strengthening of the permanent holding, *nasaq* rights, differentiation in the size of *nasaq*s, and development of wage-labour in the more commercialized areas. There is also evidence of direct contact between merchants and cash-crop-producing peasants.[36] However, peasant land rights remained primarily based on tradition.

The legal developments of the Constitutional Revolution affected landlords only; the relationship between landlord and peasant continued to be regulated by custom.[37] However, the abolition of *tuyul* was accompanied by the presence of government officials in the rural areas. As many local landowners had considerable control over these representatives, the initial impact of this presence was insignificant. In the long run, however, these measures resulted in a decline in the relative power of the landlords, increased power and presence of the central government in the rural areas, and a decline in the relative dependence of peasants on landlords.[38]

As stated earlier, the first half of the twentieth century was accompanied by the development of landlords' property rights. However, there are also indications that the legitimacy of the institution of landlordism was being challenged. At the turn of the century, the aborted leftist Jangali and Khiabani movements both had land-reform programmes. The pro-Soviet Democratic League, which had controlled Azarbaijan during 1945–46, redistributed land to peasants. Although during 1941–53 the landlord-dominated parliament tried to strengthen the position of landowners, voices supporting peasant proprietorship were also heard. For example, the small minority representation of the Tudeh party in parliament was vocal in its advocacy against the system of landlordism, which was viewed as backward and unjust.

Reza Shah's detribalization policies had some impact on the development of direct producers' landownership rights. The nomads were either ordered to elect a place of residence on lands traditionally recognized as belonging to their tribe, or they were given *khaleseh* lands on which to build houses and to improvise the techniques of intensive farming.[39] Because of its negative impact on production, forced sedentarization failed as a policy even before the abdication in 1941. Nomads did not possess the technical skills necessary for their transformation into successful farmers. Their agricultural lands were generally of low quality, and pasturage within a restricted radius meant a reduction in pasture and deprivation of the milk products provided by their flocks.[40] Data on the relative share and type of proprietorships that emerged as a result of detribalization policies is not available. Even before Reza Shah's abdication, in many tribal areas government allowed limited migration. As discussed earlier, in many areas denomadization did not result in the rise of peasant proprietorship, but in relatively smaller landlord proprietorships. Nevertheless, the policy is likely to have had some positive impact on the development of peasant proprietorships. For example, in Kurdestan two types of peasant proprietorships emerged: one in which the farmers owned the land themselves, the other which gave right over land that theoretically belonged to the government.[41]

There were also minor attempts to redistribute land to peasants. According to a decree issued in 1946, some *khaleseh* lands were to be sold to peasants. The implementation of this policy was unsuccessful, however, and did not bring a significant change in peasant proprietorship.[42] In spite of their inadequacies, these policies are likely to have had some impact on peasant proprietorship. In addition, the growing integration of markets and commercialization of agriculture may have had some positive impact on peasant proprietorship. According to rough estimates, in 1934 only between 2 and 5 per cent of peasants were proprietors.[43] In 1960, 26 per cent of agricultural lands were reported to be owned by cultivators.[44] In 1960, a significant portion of peasant proprietors are likely to have received land as a result of the distribution of *khaleseh* lands that began in 1958 and was a prelude to land reform. Nevertheless the change in the relative proportion of peasant proprietors is sufficiently large to suggest positive changes in peasant proprietorship during the first half of the twentieth century.

Property Relations: 1953–79

After 1953, the Shah had to cope with two categories of opponent: landlords, who challenged his arbitrary power through their parliamentary representation; and the leftist opposition, who promised land to peasants. The parliamentary representation of landlords was dependent on their peasant and tribal votes. Depriving landlords of their lands would weaken their relationship with their voters and undermine their ability to obtain votes. The successful implementation of land reform could also deprive the left of a major source of propaganda. The growing oil revenues and other sources of industrial capital had undermined the importance of land as a source of wealth for the royal family. Also, the Kennedy administration pressured the Iranian government to implement reforms.

A series of reforms called the White Revolution were implemented, and land reform was the most important component. The government, like its liberal and leftist opposition, argued that landlordism was backward and unjust and had to be eradicated. In 1958, the crown lands were distributed, and in 1962–66 a massive land reform undermined the traditional institution of landlordism. These two reforms combined probably redistributed more than 35 per cent of the total agricultural lands, representing one of the most massive redistributions of landed property in Iranian history.[45]

Land reform was implemented about a century and a half after the ownership rights of landlords had begun to undergo considerable evolution. The reform was a reversal of this evolutionary trend. Although not a direct confiscation, it meant forced sales at government-assessed prices and terms. As the sales were non-voluntary, the landlords viewed them as yet another confiscation and redistribution of landed property by a despotic state. The reform created a strong antagonism among the landowning groups. It included the redistribution of *vaqf* lands, a major source of income for the ulema. The latter, too, was antagonized. In 1963 there was a major uprising in which the ulema and the landlords as well as many other opposition groups participated. The most fierce opposition came from religious groups led by Ayatollah Khomeini. The uprising was unsuccessful, the Shah was able to suppress it, and Khomeini was sent into exile.

Prior to the implementation of reform, various land-reform bills that had been introduced or passed were opposed by the ulema. In 1960 Ayatollah Borujerdi, the leading mojtahed and Source of Imitation of the time, addressed a letter to the parliament opposing the passage of a moderate land-reform bill that limited the size of landed estates. He argued that the bill was in conflict with the Islamic law, Shari'a.[46] The passage of the land reform law of 1962 was followed by a protest from a number of the leading ulema on the grounds that they should have been consulted in the formulation of the law. No doubt the clear lack of conformity with the Shari'a had been a factor in the ulema's opposition to reform. Along with many sweeping secularization policies, the passage of the land-reform law without their consultation was another challenge to the traditional role of the ulema as law-makers. The state thus took another step in excluding them from sharing power. It is also plausible to argue that a segment of the clergy may have favoured a moderate land-reform law in which land forcefully and illegally taken from the peasants would be returned to them. However, conformity with the Shari'a implied that those who had legally purchased, inherited, or become owners through legal usurpation could not be forced to sell their lands; and *vaqf* lands could not become subject to forced redistribution.

Land reform eliminated the rights of landlords, and redistributed land in favour of peasants. While a violation of the private rights of landlords, it reduced the number of competing claimants on land to only one. Therefore, it was a clarification of ownership rights. Historically in Iran, the peasants' right to land was often expressed as a share of the total village holdings without identification of the exact plot of land, *mosha'*. By allocating exact plots, *mafruz*, to individual households, land reform undermined the communal aspects of peasant ownership, by emphasizing their private rights. Historically, two categories of peasants worked in a village: those with permanent holding rights, *nasaq dars*, and those without, *khoshneshins*. The *nasaq dars* were the beneficiaries of land reform. Thus, the reform further increased social stratification within the rural areas.

An important objective of the reform was to undermine the remnants of tribal autonomy and militancy. Land reform, with its emphasis on the creation of peasant proprietorship, broke up the common tribal lands and allocated the plots to individual tribal households. The reform was a major blow to the tribal social organization of production, which was based on communal use of the land. Giving land to tribesmen accelerated the process of detribalization. This process was compounded by the law for nationalization of pastures, which prevented the use of common pastures by both tribal and settled village communities. This was an unpopular law in the rural areas and was viewed as an arbitrary intrusion of the state into communal proprietorship rights.

In the post-land-reform period, other policies were implemented to change the structure of landownership. It was argued that the existing production units were inherently inefficient. The policy recommendation was to introduce large-scale farms, irrigated by river dams or deep wells, and managed by a modern corporate system. This policy proposed integrating agriculture and industry on the farm level. Initially, the advocates of this policy suggested a comprehensive coverage throughout most rural areas. The implementation of the policy in the case of the so-called agri-businesses meant that peasants would sell their lands to the government, who would then lease them to a large agri-business corporation. In the case of 'farm corporations', the peasants would give up their individual rights to a specific plot of land and would become shareholders in the corporation. As a result of this policy, rural households came into direct confrontation with the confiscatory power of the state. By 1976, less than 2.25 per cent of the total holdings were held by these large-scale farms, most of which suffered from high costs and low productivity.[47] Serious discussions were held within administrative circles about breaking up the farms and turning them over to small-scale producers. Even though the implementation of the policy was slowed down and gradually abandoned, there was no explicit statement of policy change. Consequently, insecurity of landownership continued to persist in the rural areas. The post-land-reform policies of structural change in property relations did not allow the Shah to gain the support of the direct beneficiaries of land reform.

Land reform and other state interventions in property rights were interpreted by the propertied groups to mean that should the Shah find it desirable for his own purposes, he would not refrain from redistributing private industrial and merchant capital. Thus, policies concerning rural landownership were a decisive blow to the uneasy alliance between the landlords, bazaar merchants, the ulema, and the monarchy. The binding holding this otherwise competitive and challenging political relationship together was the assumption that political stability would contribute to security of private property. The changes in property relations refuted this theory. It is fair to argue that the existing state of property relations was an important contributor to the uncompromising opposition of these privileged groups to the Shah. The impact of land reform on the rural population was also uneven. It did not create strong rural support. Many rural migrants who came to the cities were from the dissatisfied groups, and, among other grievances, objected to the policies of state intervention in rural private and communal property relations.

Land reform disrupted the evolution of the property rights of landlords. However, it reduced the number of competing claimants for lands from two – landlord and peasant – to one, thus contributing to the clarification of rights. Furthermore, by providing legal legitimacy to the private rights of the direct producers, land reform accelerated the evolution of these rights. The disruption of the rights of landlords antagonized this group, and created a general sense of insecurity concerning large-wealth owner-ship. The evolution of the direct producers' rights was not complete; the state continued to intervene in the land tenure system, and was perceived as a competitor. The reform, however, contributed to the perception that all direct producers had a legitimate right to own land, although those who had been excluded were antagonized. Once again, structural changes in property rights contributed to social tension. The clergy was able to capitalize on this tension. Because of a long tradition of Islamic Shari'a, in protecting private property rights, as well as the clergy's initial opposition to land reform, they were able to attract support among the wealthy. However, Ayatollah Khomeini called himself a supporter of the oppressed, *mostaz'afin*, and an opponent of the oppressors, the *mostakberin*. The poor could interpret this statement as Khomeini's intention to redistribute wealth in their favour. In the course of the revolution, however, no clear definition of the relationship between wealth ownership and being *mostakber* was given, and this ambiguity prevented many wealthy individuals from participating in the revolution.

After the revolution there were widespread land seizures. The Provisional Government and the 'revolutionary prosecutor' expropriated the property of prominent individuals associated with the Pahlavi regime. Widespread seizures of land were also initiated by the villagers, often encouraged or led by left-wing political groups. In some instances landlords sought to recover the land they had lost under the Shah's land reform, and registered in their own names disputed land and land in the public domain. According to a decree in September 1980, the cultivation of disputed lands was left in the hands of those who had cultivated the land in the previous year, pending a final settlement. These lands came to be known as temporary cultivation lands.[48]

There were heated debates in the Iranian parliament concerning the final settlement of these lands. The conservatives argued that the Islamic law, Shari'a, does not permit the confiscation of legitimately owned private property. By contrast, the populists used the Islamic doctrine of *zarurat*, which holds that the primary rulings of Islam may be temporarily waived in emergencies or conditions of overriding necessity. They argued that 120,000 farmers and their families were living on these lands and they could not be made landless. Finally, a law passed in 1986 provided that those lands, which as of 20 March 1981 were in the hands of non-owner cultivators, would be transferred to them permanently, provided they were landless or land-poor, lacked any other adequate source of income, and were residents in the locality. Landowners who were needy and lacked other sources of income were entitled to keep up to three times the amount of land that was considered necessary in each locality for the maintenance of a rural family. Cultivators dispossessed to provide for needy landowners were to be given land elsewhere, and dispossessed landowners were to be paid the 'fair value' for their land.[49] In spite of the passage of this law, however, the position of a significant portion of these temporary cultivations remained unresolved.

It can be argued that arbitrariness in landownership and confiscation of land belonging to the elite of the former regime conforms to the historical pattern of the changes in dynastic rule. In comparison with the historical precedent, however, the total land that became subject to potential owner-ship change was small – roughly 5 per cent of the total arable land in the country.[50] Furthermore, the structural changes in landownership were in general conformity with those of the earlier land reform. Thus they represented another stage toward the evolution of the direct producers' rights. In many instances, the initial land seizures were arbitrary, however; the settlement of the issue was subject to parliamentary debates and to new interpretations of the Islamic law. Thus, in many ways the post-revolutionary changes in landownership were less arbitrary than those of the earlier periods, and they are a continuation of the trend toward clarifi-cation and development of the direct producers' rights.

Conclusion

The pre-nineteenth-century private property rights exhibited two un-developed characteristics: often the rights were imprecise and ambiguous, and there were many instances of disruptions and reversions of the rights. From the beginning of the nineteenth to the mid-twentieth century, there was a general tendency toward clarification of private property land rights. The use of land for revenue administration was abolished, the distinction between state and private lands became more clear, and there was a general decline in the relative share of state lands and an increase in that of the private. The number of competing claimants for land was reduced to two, and in some cases to only one – peasant proprietorship, or landowners using wage labour. The constitutional and other legal reforms resulted in the clarification and strengthening of the rights of private landlords.

The developments of the 1960s and 1970s, however, were a reversal of the general trend of consolidation and development of the rights of land-lords. The rise of a strong monarch with aspirations to increase his political power and undermine the sources of political challenge contributed to a massive change in the distribution of landownership, and thus contained an element of arbitrariness. However, the changes in property relations reduced the number of competing claimants for land to one, and there-fore contributed to the clarity of the rights. Furthermore, the reforms undermined communal aspects of landownership and strengthened pri-vate-property rights. As traditional communal rights tend to be somewhat vague, the changes created more clarity. Finally, the inability of the state to reverse the rights of the cultivators and to create large-scale farms was another indication of consolidation of the private rights of the cultivators.

In the post-revolutionary period, once more, the change in ruling elite resulted in arbitrariness and confiscation of private landed property. However, the share of the land that became subject to potential owner-ship change was relatively small, and the changes contributed to the development of direct producers' land rights, and can be viewed as another stage in the development of these rights.

In summary, since the nineteenth century the trend in the development and clarification of the rights of direct producers has been consistently positive and evolutionary. However, the private rights of large landowners have been subject to major setbacks and retrogressions due to state intervention.

Notes

1. Demsetz, Harold, 'Toward a theory of property rights', *The American Economic Review: Papers and Proceedings* LVII/2, (1967), p 350; North, Douglas C., and Robert P. Thomas, *The Rise of The Western World* (Cambridge: Cambridge University Press, 1973), pp 389–412.

2. Moghadam, Fatemeh, 'An historical interpretation of the Iranian Revolution', *Cambridge Journal of Economics* 12 (1988), pp 401–18.

3. Demsetz: 'Toward a theory', p 350.

4. Kumar, Dharma, 'Private property in Asia: The case of medieval South India', *Comparative Studies in Society and History* XXVII/2 (1985), pp 340–66; Mendelsohn, O., 'Pathology of the Indian legal system', *Modern Asian Studies* XV/4 (1981), pp 840–42.

5. Abrahamian, Ervand, *Iran Between Two Revolutions* (Princeton: Princeton University Press, 1981); Issawi, Charles (ed.), *The Economic History of Iran* (Chicago: The University of Chicago Press, 1971); Keddie, Nikki, *Roots of Revolution* (New Haven: Yale University Press, 1981).

6. Nowshirvani, Vahid, 'The beginnings of commercialized agriculture in Iran', in A.L. Udovitch (ed.), *The Islamic Middle East, 700–1900* (Princeton: Princeton University Press, 1981), p 547.

7. Arjomand, Said Amir, *The Turban for the Crown* (New York: Oxford University Press, 1988), pp 35–59; Abrahamian, Ervand, *Iran Between Two Revolutions*; Katouzian, Homa, *The Political Economy of Modern Iran*, (New York: New York University Press, 1981).

8. Moghadam, Fatemeh, 'Property rights and Islamic revolution in Iran', in Haleh Esfandiari and A.L. Udovitch (eds), *The Economic Dimensions of Middle Eastern History: Essays in Honor of Charles Issawi* (Princeton: Darwin Press, 1990).

9. Bastani Parizi, M.E., *Siyasat va Eqtesad-e Asr-e Safavi* (Tehran: Safi Ali Shah, 1978), pp 80–89; Fragner, Bert, 'Social and internal economic affairs', in Peter Jackson and Lawrence Lockhart (eds), *The Cambridge History of Iran* Vol 6 (Cambridge: University Press, 1986) pp 499–524; Lambton, Ann K.S., 'The internal structure of the Saljuq empire', in J.A. Boyle (ed.), *The Cambridge History of Iran* Vol 5 (Cambridge: Cambridge University Press, 1968), pp 251–65; Fazlollah, Rashid al-Din, *Jame' al-Tavarikh*, two vols, Karimi (ed), (Tehran: Iqbal, 1959), pp 9, 777–88, 825.

10. Minorsky, V. (ed.), *Tazkirat al-Muluk* (Cambridge: Heffer and Sons, 1956), pp 3–90; Bastani Parizi, *Siyasat va Eqtesad*, pp 61–77.

11. Ibid.

12. Lambton, Ann K.S., *Landlord and Peasant in Persia* (Oxford: Oxford University

Press, 1953); Moghadam, 'Property rights and Islamic revolution'.

13. Issawi: *The Economic History*, pp 208, 219–21.

14. Ibid., pp 206–12; Nowshirvani, 'Commercialized agriculture', pp 247–91.

15. Lambton, *Landlord and Peasant*, pp 148, 152–4.

16. Ibid.

17. Ibid., p 139.

18. Ibid., pp 153–5.

19. Nowshirvani, 'Commercialized agriculture', p 561.

20. Ibid., pp 578–9.

21. Lambton, *Landlord and Peasant*, p 140.

22. Khan, Mirza Malkom, *Ruz-nameh Qanun*, Nateq, Homa (ed.), (Tehran: Sepehr Publishers, 1976).

23. Arjomand, *The Turban for The Crown*, pp 48–57.

24. Lambton, *Landlord and Peasant*, pp 178–9.

25. Ibid., pp 231–2.

26. Ibid., pp 241–2.

27. Ibid., p 260.

28. Abrahamian, *Iran Between Two Revolutions*, pp 137, 149–50; Issawi, *The Economic History*, pp 206–12.

29. Lambton, *Landlord and Peasant*, pp 256–7.

30. Ibid.

31. Black-Michaud, Jacob, *Sheep and Land* (Cambridge: Cambridge University Press, 1986), pp 87–9.

32. Ibid., p 2; Barth, Fredrick, 'The land use pattern of migratory tribes of south Persia', *Norsk Geografisk Tidsskrift* XVII/ 1–4 (1959), pp 1–11, 21.

33. Khosrovi, Khosrow, *Jame'eh Shenasi-ye Rusta'i dar Iran* (Tehran: Tehran University Press, 1972), p 25.

34. Okazaki, S., *The Development of Large-Scale Farming in Iran: The Case of the Province of Gorgan* (Tokyo: The Institute of Asian Economic Affairs, 1968), pp 8–9.

35. Moghadam, Fatemeh, 'The effects of farm size and management system on agricultural production in Iran' (unpublished D.Phil. dissertation, Oxford University, 1978).

36. Nowshirvani, 'Commercialized agriculture', pp 572–4.

37. Lambton, *Landlord and Peasant*, p 195.

38. Ibid., p 179.

39. Black-Michaud, *Sheep and Land*, pp 84–5.

40. Lambton, *Landlord and peasant*, pp 258; Black-Michaud, *Sheep and Land*, p 85.

41. Barth, 'The land use pattern', p 21.

42. Lambton, *Landlord and Peasant*, pp 243–4.

43. Sandjabi, Karim, *Essai sur l'economie rurale et le regime agraire de la Perse* (Paris, 1934), pp 117, 127, 138, cited in Keddie: *Roots of Revolution*, pp 103, 284.

44. Ministry of Agriculture, *Survey of Agriculture: 1960* (in Persian) Vol 15, (Tehran, 1961), p 14.

45. Moghadam, 'An historical interpretation', p 408.

46. Lambton, 'The internal structure', p 56.

47. Moghadam, Fatemeh, 'An evaluation of the productive performance of agribusinesses: an Iranian case study', *Economic Development and Cultural Change*, XXXIII/4 (1985), pp 755–76.

48. Bakhash, Shaul, *Reign of the Ayatollahs: Iran and the Islamic Revolution* (New York: Basic Books, 1984), pp 195–216.

49. Bakhash, Shaul, 'The politics of land, law, and social justice in Iran', *Middle East Journal* XXXXIII/ 2 (1989), pp 190–99.

50. Ibid., p 187.

3

Competing Shi'i Subsystems in Contemporary Iran

Ali Rahnema and Farhad Nomani

Introduction

Secular ideologies which have left a significant imprint on the modality of thought, behaviour and life of twentieth-century citizens are generally distinguishable by clearly delineated political and economic systems specific to them. Islam as an ideology does, however, allow for the inference and deduction of different subsystems, each categorized on the basis of its particular discourse on political economy and eventually its own distinguished social system. The object of this paper is to distinguish, categorize and analyse Shi'i subsystems in the context of post-revolutionary Iran. In this process, a preliminary discussion of the roots of emerging Islamic subsystems will be presented. Our analysis is conducted within the framework of the hypothesis that the existence of a multiplicity of Islamic subsystems, Shi'i or Sunni, under the umbrella of Islam provides a potent political rallying force for Islamic movements in opposition, while the existence of these same subsystems constitutes a destabilizing element once political power has been won in the name of an all-encompassing Islam.

Roots of Islamic Subsystems

The divine foundation of the Islamic system imposes a set of fixed and immutable obligations, as well as laws, concerning what is permissible and what is prohibited. These are considered as applicable and appropriate for all times, places and people; and essentially pertain to the regulation of the individual's relation with God. Islam is categorical and unswerving about obligations incumbent on the believer. These fundamentals include faith in the unity of God, the prophethood of Mohammad, and the day of resurrection. The Shi'is consider *emamat*, or the belief in the Twelve Imams, and *'adl*, or justice, also as fundamentals of the faith. Islam is also clear on those required religious practices (*'ebadat*) which are proof of the believer's truly submissive nature toward God.

Again, in terms of required religious duties, all Muslims, irrespective of their particular subsystem, are obliged to fast, go on pilgrimage, pay the Islamic tax and wage holy war, under the particular conditions articulated by the faith. Even though nuances do exist in the modality, the circumstances and the appropriate conditions for performing the latter duties, all subsystems are equally committed to absolute allegiance to these fundamental principles of the faith. Islamic subsystems share the same fundamental basis of the Islamic system and thereby obtain their legitimacy and authority. They are the natural consequence of the process of adaptation of Islam, as an eternal religion, to the changing conditions and pressing circumstances that emerged in different geographical parts of the Islamic empire.

As long as the Prophet was alive, he was responsible for leading Muslims towards the objective of becoming worthy of God's vicegerency on earth. His essential tool of educating the people to that end was the Quran, and, most important of all, the correct interpretation of its text in terms of content, form, essence and spirit.[1] As both the spiritual and temporal leader of the Muslim community (*ommat*), he dealt with the elaboration and at times modification of fixed issues pertaining to religious duties and practices, as well as worldly and thus generally flexible issues such as the modality of operation of the Islamic economy, which fell under the rubric of transactions (*mo'amelat*). Thus the divine texts were protected from misinterpretations and a multitude of different and at times conflicting interpretations.

Since the death of the Prophet, Islamic jurists have used four major sources on which they base, and from which they derive, their Islamic judgement on emerging problems. These are the primary sources composed of the Quran and the Sunna (the Tradition of the Prophet), and the secondary sources of consensus (*ejma'*) and analogy (*qiyas*) for the Sunnis, and consensus and reason (*'aql*) for the Shi'is. The use of tertiary sources, where jurists make pronouncements on the basis of what they subjectively consider to be in accordance with the real spirit of Islam, also became prevalent after the death of the Prophet. Tertiary sources such as juristic preference on the basis of equity (*estehsan*), and rulings based on public convenience (*al-masalah al-morsalah*) or public welfare (*esteslah*), implicitly constituted a fifth source of Islamic jurisprudence, even though they are generally considered as a variant of analogy or independent judgement (*ejtehad*). Apprehension on considering them as an independent source of law is rooted in the fact that tertiary sources are essentially delinked from explicit texts in the primary sources. The major Islamic Sunni subsystems, namely the Hanafis, Malekis, Shafe'is and Hanbalis, as well as the Usulis among the Shi'is, use variations of such sources as the basis of their rulings. Shi'is have argued that religious law (*shar'*) commands to what is commanded by reason and that the requirements of religious law are those of reason.[2] The acceptance of tertiary sources as a basis of Islamic law paved the way for the increasing application of human reason within the general framework of the spirit of Islam.

The explanation of why different subsystems branched out from the main body of Islam can be provided through an answer to the following question: How can Muslims, believing in the same Prophet and sharing the same fixed fundamental nucleus of principles and religious duties articulated in the Quran, and the same four sources and references for solving their emerging problems, differ on appropriate Islamic solutions to various worldly problems to the extent that they should feel compelled to organize themselves into different Islamic subsystems?

On the issue of price regulation in an Islamic society, for example, Islamic subsystems have pronounced different views, as different versions of an authentic and clear Tradition of the Prophet exist on the issue.[3] Both Shi'is and Sunnis accept and refer to this Tradition according to which, in response to the request of a man who asked the Prophet to set price controls on hoarded goods, the Prophet refused and emphasized that prices were set by God and He raised and lowered them as He willed. This clear statement of the Prophet in favour of the freedom of the market to set prices without government intervention has, however, given rise to numerous different positions.

The followers of Abu Hanifa's subsystem accept price controls when 'outrageously inflated prices of the food merchants' threaten to cause injury to the rights and interests of the Islamic public.[4] The Malekis hold that merchants should be restrained from selling at a higher price when the market price is already high.[5] Malek, however, opposed the extremist position of certain jurists who ruled that even under normal circumstances price ceilings had to be applied to protect consumers.[6] Imam Shafe'i rejected any interference with the forces of the market on the basis of the argument that people are entitled to dispose of their wealth as they see fit and that no one can force them to part with it against their will.[7] The Hanbali position is close to that of the Shafe'is, yet some of their jurists have ruled for the application of price control in emergencies or for basic necessities such as food, clothing and housing.[8] The positions articulated by various Shi'i subsystems in Iran fall within the same spectrum, varying from complete non-intervention to permanent control and even the replacement of market prices with administrative prices.

Four apparent causes can be identified to explain why Islam as a monolithic universal ideology has bred different branches of different shapes in the form of Islamic subsystems. It is argued that the branches are of different shapes because they resemble different temporal economic systems, sometimes compatible and sometimes not with their respective political systems. The four causes listed below clearly do not constitute an exhaustive list.[9]

First, a significant factor can be attributed to the inconsistencies among different jurists in their interpretation of the primary sources. Why should inconsistencies and differences occur among the rulings of equally learned men of Islamic jurisprudence who share the same religious principles and are supposed to have had the same education and depend on the same references? In an enlightening article, Mohammad Mojtahed-e Shabestari emphasizes the role of subjectivity and plays down the role of the 'true content' of the explicit primary texts in determining the ruling or opinion of jurists. He argues that it is impossible to derive the Islamic concepts of ownership, work, distribution of wealth and justice from the primary sources without social, philosophical or scientific preconceptions and prejudices.[10] In short, it is the jurists' subjective analyses of primary sources that lead to different interpretations, represented in different subsystems.

Second, the disparity of injunctions that exist in the primary sources on particular issues, generally concerned with worldly affairs, can constitute another factor. Despite the divinely inspired revelations that have abrogated and altered certain earlier revealed texts, the Quran includes certain important statements on issues pertaining to political economics that seem contradictory even to learned Islamic jurists.[11] The Islamic status of wealth, its approved source of generation and accumulation, its permissible amount, and even its authorized method of disposition, constitute important sources of complications. Two opposing positions, one in support of a quantitatively unregulated amassing of wealth and another in favour of a perfectly equal distribution of income, can be found and upheld on the basis of different Quranic verses and different interpretations of the same verse.[12] Historically the emergence of subsystems can be traced back to Abu Dharr Gifari's dispute with the third Caliph, Uthman, and Mu'awiya, his governor of Damascus, over the extent of permissible wealth in Islam.[13]

Third, the plethora of as many as forty thousand acts, injunctions and statements that are attributed to the Prophet and known as the Tradition of the Prophet constitute another factor in the emergence of different rulings organized in different subsystems. Considering that the Prophet had discouraged the Companions from writing his Traditions (Sunna), his death allowed for the mushrooming of his orally reported pronouncements and acts, as a legal basis for judgement. The authenticity of a large number of the reported Traditions could not be proven by tracing them back, through the chain of transmitters, to the Prophet. The significance of the Sunna in rulings and what constitutes a reliable and authentic report of the Prophet's Tradition is by itself a source of disagreement among competing Islamic subsystems. While Imam Abu-Hanifa (d. 767), the founder of the Hanafi subsystem of Islamic jurisprudence, is reported to have accepted the authenticity of only 17 reports of the Prophets' Traditions, Imam Ahmad-ibn Hanbal (d. 857), of the Hanbali school, accepted more than thirty thousand reports of Traditions.[14]

The Hanbali jurists placed such great emphasis on Traditions as the principal source of their rulings that they even chose to use un-authenticated Traditions (*morsal*). Other jurists of the Hanafi, Maleki and Shafe'i subsystems of the Sunni school refused to accept unauthorized Traditions. The fact that the Shi'is add the tradition of the infallible Shi'i Imams to that of the Prophet increases the pool of available Traditions and consequently the possibility of emerging inconsistencies. Once again, various Traditions concerning important socioeconomic issues – such as the extent of private ownership, the distribution of wealth, the legality of landownership beyond what can be cultivated by the owner, sharecropping and rent in agriculture, and hiring of labour in the process of production – allows for the construction of different discourses.[15]

Fourth, the prevalence of different tertiary sources of Islamic juris-prudence, which allows jurists to base their deductions on the implicit meaning of primary texts (*ta'wil*), in reality permits them to rely primarily on their own reason and discretion. The use of different tertiary sources, each emphasizing different aspects of the spirit of Islam, has also contrib-uted to the birth of different subsystems. There is, however, consensus among jurists that independent judgements have to be firmly rooted in the primary sources and therefore in harmony with them. Yet it is argued that due to his employment of the tertiary source of juristic preference on the basis of equity (*estehsan*), Abu-Hanifa rejected and opposed as many as four hundred of the Prophet's established Traditions.[16] The use of tertiary sources provides individual jurists with a great degree of flexibility and discretion, paving the way for competing subsystems. Khomeini's invo-cation of the primacy of the overriding interests of the Islamic state even at the cost of sacrificing the principles of '*ebadat* has taken the application of tertiary sources to the limit of suspending obligatory religious practices at the discretion and behest of the governing absolutist jurisconsult. The diversity of rulings by Islamic jurists has led some to argue that there is an absence of ideological consensus among Islamic jurists or the *foqaha*.[17]

Shi'i Subsystems: The Centripetal Force of the Revolution

The victory of the Iranian Revolution demonstrated the efficiency of different Shi'i subsystems in uniting a socially stratified and class-ridden society under the banner of Islam. Any one particular ideology appealing to one specific class or class alliance would have antagonized or threatened the excluded classes, preventing the formation of the broad popular front that overthrew the Shah's regime. The diverse Shi'i subsystems, which were given a free reign before and shortly after the revolution, presented different ideologies based on the fixed principles and bases of Islam. All subsystems shared the basic tenets of Shi'i Islam, and derived their ideal models implicitly or explicitly from the same four sources of jurisprudence, namely the Quran, the Sunna, reason through *ejtehad*, and consensus. Each, however, adopted different and at times opposing positions on issues relating to political philosophy, economics, sociology and civil law. Therefore each appealed to one or more social groups by presenting a different kind of ideal life and society. The social groups repelled by one subsystem were attracted by another. Consequently a very large majority of Iranians were attracted to one or another subsystem, all united under the general umbrella of Islam.[18]

Once in power, the clerical leadership drew upon the specific jargon and particular economic, political and social tools of the different subsystems that had brought it to power. According to changing circumstances and political moods, the leadership employed a different discourse and subsequently different policy tools belonging to different subsystems to ride over emerging national problems. As expediency dictated, different but legitimate policies were adopted, since they all remained within the general framework of the Islamic system. During the decade of Khomeini's leadership, four important, yet by no means exclusive, subsystems based on the works and/or activities of Motahhari, Shariati, Navab-Safavi and Bazargan shaped the domestic and foreign policy of Iran.

The theoretical formulation and development of each subsystem has to be understood, appreciated and analysed within the prevailing sociopolitical circumstances of their time. Navab-Safavi's subsystem reflects his concern and anxiety with the onslaught of modernization and its 'corrupting' side effects, the spread of which he believed eroded the convictions of the true believers, ultimately uprooting traditional religious values. So, Navab-Safavi's subsystem was born out of an Islamic reaction to the essentially moral consequences of modernization. In this sense it can be considered an anti-modernization discourse.

The three other subsystems of Motahhari, Shariati and Bazargan, provided in one way or another an Islamic response to the spread of communism in Muslim Iran. All three men, active in and familiar with Iran's university environment, were witness to the ascent of Marxist-Leninist thought in Iranian intellectual circles since 1963. In the 1960s, one of the greatest appeals of Marxism-Leninism to Third World intellectuals was its convenience as an internally consistent 'package-solution kit'. By embracing communism, intellectuals had access to a coherent and interrelated body of theory that had prescriptions for all types of problems: philosophical, economic, social, political, historical and even psychological. As a powerful tool for social analysis and a catalyst for social change, revolutionary communism attracted increasing numbers of Iranian youth, eclipsing the appeal of nationalism, Islam and the conservative communism of the Tudeh party, which had each played an instrumental role in politicizing Iranians between 1945 and 1963.

While Ali Shariati's subsystem was an attempt at accommodating, co-opting and eventually dissolving Marxism-Leninism in Islam, Motahhari's and Bazargan's subsystems were non-accommodating, confrontationist and therefore counter-Marxist-Leninist. Motahhari and Bazargan tried very hard to distinguish, wherever possible, between the real or imaginary similarities of Islam and Marxism. Shariati, however, sought such similarities and tried to prove Islam's superiority by demonstrating that Islamic solutions for social, political and economic injustice predate the solutions of Marx and Lenin. Shariati hoped to convince his large audience of Iranian youth that Marxism was only a fake replica of Islam. Motahhari and Bazargan, however, sought to prove that, in its superiority, Islam had nothing in common with communism.

Motahhari's subsystem

Motahhari's subsystem is the reflection of an Islamic jurist's attempt to revive Islam as a potent ideology capable of redressing the social, political, economic and cultural ills of Iran. It demonstrates his anxiety and disconcertedness at the absence of a holistic Islamic discourse capable of countering Marxism and winning back the misguided youth. Motahhari's approach to attracting the youth was through invitation and intellectual persuasion. As such, his subsystem was reformist rather than revolutionary. Motahhari sought to present an Islam that was free of superstition, parochialism and conservatism; yet he was intent on purifying Islam of what he believed to be the deviationist innovations of Shariati's school.

Motahhari refused to accept the notion propagated by radical Muslims that piety and righteousness were the monopoly of the oppressed and the disinherited (*mostaz'afin*).[19] He argued that, on the contrary, believers and the pious could be found among all classes, and that on numerous occasions the Quran referred to groups of the disinherited and exploited as infidels and disbelievers. Thus, Motahhari sought to demonstrate that the essentially Marxist notion of social polarization on the basis of the exploited and the exploiters was alien to Islam, which believed in differentiating between people on the basis of their piety.[20]

In his subsystem, Motahhari tried to demonstrate that according to Islam an individual was not judged or determined by his class position, but by his resistance to the temptations of Satan and his devotion to the fulfilment of his religious obligations.[21] Writing against the radical Muslims, Motahhari concluded that Islam did not conceive of the disinherited as the sole class that actively participated in social movements, and that therefore their condition did not constitute the only concern of the revolution. In Motahhari's subsystem, contrary to that of Shariati and the

Mojahedin's, the Quran does not state that the object of historical development or evolution is the imposition of the hegemony of the disinherited class.[22]

It would be safe to say that, after the two men fell out with one another, Motahhari was equally, if not more, apprehensive about the influence of Shariati's radical subsystem than that of the communists. Motahhari believed that Islam had to be guarded against what he called the 'eclectic school', which in his opinion combined certain principles of communism with some aspects of existentialism and had mixed the combination with Islamic concepts and jargons. Such a discourse, according to Motahhari, was not Islamic; and further, it was incapable of presenting an independent school which would return to the Muslims their lost sense of identity.[23]

On freedom, Motahhari was attracted to the modern notions of freedom of thought and expression, yet he was effectively constrained by the limits that a clerical reading of the Shari'a provided. On the one hand, Motahhari argued that freedom of thought was the prerequisite for the development and evolution of mankind. He was persistent in reminding all that 'in the Islamic Republic, there will be no limitation on the freedom of thought and all should be free to present their authentic ideas.'[24] On the other hand, he warned against conspiracy, wrong ideas and opinions harmful to both the individual and society.[25] Motahhari was critical of political democracy, since it elevated the will of the majority to a position above that of God. He regarded the replacement of divine law by man-made laws as a modern-day aberration which he believed to have disastrous consequences for the Islamic community.[26] According to Motahhari, Islamic freedom and democracy has to assure the humane development of mankind.[27] Since Islam is considered to have established the goal of attaining God's vicegerency, which implies the highest possible level of humane development as man's ultimate objective, and has clearly indicated the means of achieving that aim, it follows that the pursuit of the Islamic path would satisfy the ultimate goals of freedom and democracy.

In Motahhari's subsystem, the position of leadership and decision-making is reserved for the clergy. He argues that only those who are thoroughly familiar with the Quran, the Sunna, Islamic jurisprudence and Islamic epistemology can occupy positions of leadership.[28] Motahhari's emphasis on the role and significance of the clergy is a response to Shariati's anti-clerical subsystem.

The issue of social justice is of great importance in Motahhari's subsystem. He rejects the radical position of Shariati that Islamic social justice expresses equality in income or wealth. In his view, Islam assures equal opportunity for all. On this basis, differences in human capability, effort, aptitude, dexterity, work habit and entrepreneurship should be rewarded accordingly, and consequently they should be different. Motahhari's view that the neoclassical notion of differences in rewards on the basis of different contributions is non-discriminatory and just is based on the argument that in the act of creation God willed such differences.[29] Targeting the Shariati subsystem, and the radical Muslims of the early days of the revolution, Motahhari attacks those who maintain that Islamic social justice implies absolute equality in consumption, and that such a condition could only be established through strict rationing.[30] Rewarding different contributions equally is viewed by Motahhari as the antithesis of justice.

The Islamic economic system according to Motahhari's subsystem is characterized by (1) the acceptance of private property up to an (undefined) acceptable amount; (2) the rejection of the notion that any type of property is the result of exploitation; (3) the belief in the principle that from each according to his ability and to each according to his need does not constitute justice but injustice; (4) the belief in the notion that the fruits of a person's labour belong only to him and may not be expropriated, since such an act would be the essence of injustice; (5) the rejection of a perfectly equal distribution of income; (6) the conviction that solidarity with the dispossessed and a tendency toward a more equitable distribution of income can only be secured once the rich, based on Islamic spirituality, voluntarily participate in helping the poor; (7) the rejection of statism, whereby the government takes from individuals and spends on others as it sees fit; (8) the notion that poverty is not a 'bad' condition, since it can lead to well-being.[31]

After Motahhari's death, his economic notes were compiled and published in a book called *A Look at the Islamic Economic System*. A large portion of the book is on the analysis and critique of secondary sources of Marxian and sometimes capitalist economics. In the relatively limited space allotted to Islamic economics, Motahhari's notes, which were probably never intended for publication but reflected his own personal grapplings and speculations with economic themes, raise certain controversial issues. Reference to these notes are only interesting from an academic point of view, since the established market-oriented view of Motahhari's economic position is summarized in the six points presented above. In his notes, Motahhari argues that machinery and not handtools used in the process of production 'manifest social progress', and that it is not the indirect product of the capitalists but that of the intelligence and genius of the inventors or society. Thus, the products of collective intelligence and genius cannot become the private property of individuals and must therefore become the collective property of the Muslim community.[32] Having said this, Motahhari emphasizes that his position does not 'negate individual or private ownership, but [recognizes] collective ownership in specific cases'.[33]

In his analysis of Marx's concept of surplus value, Motahhari argues that contrary to Marx's view, for whom the profit of the capitalist derived from the ownership of machines is unjust, there is no reason why the machine that has been bought by the religiously legitimate (*mashru'*) money of a wealthy person should be expropriated from him and converted into public property.[34] Having vindicated and legitimized private ownership of what he calls machines, he reaches a diametrically opposite conclusion in his definition of an Islamic concept of surplus value. Motahhari identifies three sources of surplus value: 'unjust wages, exploitation of consumers and machinery (or industrial capital)'.[35] According to his notes, machines create surplus value and this feature, more than any other one, renders 'new capitalism' illegitimate.

Motahhari's confusing and contradictory remarks should be viewed in terms of (1) his attempt to familiarize himself with economic issues; (2) his measurement and contrasting of different concepts in light of Islamic precepts and the spirit of Islam; (3) the absence of clearly Islamic formulations on such themes; (4) the significant influence of Marxist thought in the intellectual circles of Iran, and Motahhari's original attempt perhaps to incorporate radical policies and jargons, an approach that he later rejects.

During and after the revolution, Motahhari's market-oriented subsystem was embraced not only by the traditional commercial bourgeoisie, who had historical and strong ties with the clergy, but by different types of property-owning groups which had decided to stay in Iran and continue with their activities in the Islamic Republic, and also a very large section of the economically conservative yet prominent clerical figures who did not wish to see radical socioeconomic changes as a result of the revolution. From the point of view of this latter group, the Islamic revolution's objective was to impose the Shari'a under the leadership of the clergy. On this point, too, there was a perfect coincidence of views between them and Motahhari, whose authority had been greatly enhanced by Khomeini's unreserved support for him as the Islamic Republic's leading theoretician.

Ali Shariati's subsystem

Shariati's subsystem is an attempt at fusing together the themes and ideas of all those Western and Eastern seminal theoreticians that Shariati believed had shaped the world outlook of modern Western intellectuals. During his stay in Paris, Shariati was greatly influenced by themes such as anti-colonialism, anti-imperialism, anti-capitalism, anti-despotism, humanism, social democracy and social justice, which constituted the building blocks of the dominant ideology of Western intellectuals in the post-Second World War decades. Shariati believed that intellectuals, and not the backward masses, were the catalysts of social change. Iranian intellectuals, who constituted his major target and audience, had to be politicized in order to carry out their liberating historical duty.[36] To reach and touch them with his words, Shariati sought to incorporate and present the prevalent revolutionary themes of his generation, the efficacy of which had been proven in the course of all successful anti-colonial and anti-imperialist wars, in the language of Islam. The popularity of Shariati's subsystem among the youth and the intellectuals was based on his utilization of Islam as an effective and familiar medium of communicating an essentially Western-inspired set of ideas. By accommodating and incorporating the essence of their appealing message, Shariati's Islamic subsystem broke the ideological monopoly of Marxist-Leninist intellectuals who claimed to possess the only consistent, progressive, revolutionary and historically applicable world outlook. To those university students who had come from mainly traditional families in which it was natural to be a believer, and who had also been exposed to the 'package-solution kit' of the left, Shariati's subsystem provided an ideal and an identity that they could be proud of and defend. It combined Islam with the progressive concerns of an intellectual in the 1970s.[37]

In his presentations Shariati enumerated the significance and the contributions of such Western luminaries as Pascal, Marx and Sartre in order to assist man to become liberated. Then he proceeded to explain that to become liberated, Iranian Shi'i intellectuals did not have to follow the works and paths of each of these different Western giants, since the sum total of their merits and contributions could be easily found in one man, Imam Ali.[38] Thus for Shariati, the Islam of Imam Ali represented the quintessence of all the progressive schools of thought of the West which were concerned with social justice, liberation and humanism.

Shariati was not a *mojtahed*. He based his Islamic interpretations and judgements on what he had learnt from his father and his own studies in the field. His major sources were the Quran, and the Sunna, with an emphasis on the tradition of Imam Ali and Imam Hosein. In cases where Shariati interpreted Quranic verses and deduced references to modern concepts such as the working class and class struggle, he was clearly relying on his independent reasoning, based on what he considered to be the spirit, objective and correct direction of Islam. Less than a year before his death, while discussing Islam in a conversation with Ayatollah Motahhari and Ayatollah Khamene'i, the present spiritual leader of the Islamic Republic, Shariati referred to the fact that Islam, the Quran and the Sunna were used and invoked in Saudi Arabia to further the interests of Aramco Oil Company and King Faisal's family. Shariati concluded that 'we witness the fact that the Quran devoid of its specific direction becomes meaningless, so does the Sunna and even the unity of God (*towhid*). *Emamat* means direction.... Go in this direction and if you look back, the Quran and the Sunna will lead you astray.'[39]

According to Shariati, the Islam of Imam Ali, which reflected a polarized view of society based on struggling classes, represented Islam's correct vision of society. Subsequently, Shariati argued that the pursuit of the correct direction of Islam culminated in the transformation of prevalent class and power structures and the imposition of the economic, political and social power of the oppressed and dispossessed (*mostaz'afin*) over the proprietors and the oppressors (*mostakberin*). Imam Ali had accepted the Caliphate to restore social justice and equality, which had been the prime objective of Islam during the leadership of the first and second Caliphs, but had been neglected and grossly violated during the rule of the third Caliph, Uthman.[40]

In Shariati's subsystem, class struggle has found its manifestation in the historical struggle between the two antagonistic discourses of monotheistic and polytheistic Islam. Thus, twentieth-century Islam is not viewed as a monolithic paragon of virtue, but is believed to be divided into two opposing camps of good and evil. Polytheistic Islam, however, also fights under the same green flag of 'There is but only one God', and thus sows the seeds of confusion among the believers as to what is right and wrong. The Islam that Shariati supports is the one that follows the path of Imam Ali, *Eslam-e 'Alavi*. This he calls monotheistic Islam. This revolutionary Islamic view has the following attributes: (1) belief in the creation of a new social order based on the Shi'i principals of egalitarian justice (*'adl*) and the revolutionary leadership and guidance of the 12 Imams (*emamat*); (2) belief in human free will and one's ability to choose; (3) belief in human collective responsibility to challenge and resist oppression and to struggle for the realization of an ideal classless monotheistic Islam; (4) belief in moral and collective incentives and the rejection of material incentives; (5) belief in the primacy of praxis for its members, who are not only believers but have to prove their faith through social and political activism; (6) belief in revolutionary justice, one that is retroactive, when injustice has been committed; (7) belief in the benevolent dictatorship of a saintly figure who has the right attributes of a just Imam; (8) belief in the incompatibility of political democracy with capitalism and, therefore, the impossibility of achieving democracy as long as capitalism flourishes; (9) belief in the struggle against capitalism, exploitation and private property as the economic manifestations of class-oriented polytheistic Islam; (10) belief in the implementation of equality in the distribution of income and consumption; (11) belief in an Islamic reformation or Protestantism which would once and for all prevent the emergence of a 'religious and clerical despotism'; (12) belief in the struggle against those ossified members of the clergy who justify a pacifist view of Islam in the face of social injustice and inequality; and (13) belief in the struggle against colonialism and imperialism.

According to Shariati, polytheistic Islam is one that remains passive and submissive to class oppression and repression, injustice and economic inequality. This counter-revolutionary and conservative Islam is argued to have emerged during the Safavid period, when the Safavid monarchs,

especially Shah Soltan Hosein, embraced Shi'i Islam, propagated super-
ficial and formalistic aspects of the faith, and denuded it of its singular
pillars of justice and revolutionary leadership. Polytheistic Islam is argued
to be the doctrine of those who wish to pacify Islam in order to justify
and legitimize the oppressive and unjust class rule of the property-owning
classes against the impoverished and the oppressed masses. *Eslam-e Safavi*
is the Islam of those who coexist with and support the status quo.[41]
Shariati believed that polytheistic Islam was rooted in the property ownership of a minority and the lack of property ownership of a majority.[42] The
real danger of this brand of Islam, according to Shariati, lay in its claim
to the mantle of Islam, since by inviting the people to engage in individual
religious practices (*'ebadat*), and invoking the cause of Islam, it undermined the essential social, political and economic message of the faith.
Reducing Islam to the practice of prayers, fasting, going on pilgrimage,
and even waging holy war, depoliticized the people and diverted their
energy from establishing the new Islamic social order.[43]

The marked and deep-rooted influence of Shariati's subsystem on
modern Islamic thought in Iran is undeniable. From 1969, when he started
to propagate widely the contents of his revolutionary subsystem through
his popular lectures at the Hoseiniyeh Ershad, and even after his death
through his books, Shariati succeeded in converting a whole generation of
Muslim high-school and university students to his view of Islam. After
the Islamic revolution, some of these young Muslims rejected the ideology of the clerical leadership, which they identified as polytheistic Islam.
Those who heeded the invitation of the 'great teacher' to oppose actively
what was considered *Eslam-e Safavi*, joined the Organization of the People's
Mojahedin, and some formed smaller groups under the name of Forqan,
Arman-e Mostaz'afin, and Kanun-e Nashr-e Andishehha-ye Shariati. A
considerable number, however, found Ayatollah Khomeini's Islamic
discourse compatible with *Islam-e 'Alavi*, which Shariati had upheld as the
authentic Islamic model. Many chose to support and work for the Islamic
Republic.

The existence of a tendency within the state apparatus, and even at the
highest ruling echelons of the Islamic Republic, espousing and even
militating for the implementation of certain objectives of the Shariati subsystem became ever more apparent after Khomeini's radical proclamation
and *prise de position* on the occasion of the inauguration of the third Islamic
parliament, in April 1988. In a curiously similar language to that of Shariati,
Khomeini spoke of two distinct types of Islam. He defended the Pure
Mohammaden Islam. He described it as the Islam which 'in theory and
practice belongs to, defends and is in the service of the impoverished of
this world, the *mostaz'afin*, those who have been oppressed throughout
history and the mystical militants'. Opposed to the Pure Mohammaden
Islam is the American Islam, which 'belongs to, defends and is in the

service of, the capitalists, the *mostakberin*, the oppressors, the care-free, well-to-do, the opportunists, the hypocrites and the fortune-seekers'.[44] What Shariati termed monotheistic Islam or the Islam of Ali (*'Alavi*) was now dubbed the 'Pure Mohammaden Islam', while Khomeini renamed what Shariati termed polytheistic Islam or the Islam of the Safavids the 'American Islam'.

After the Islamic Republic's repression of Islamic opposition, parties and groups that looked up to Shariati as their spiritual ideologue became suspect. In 1983, the Association of the Instructors of the Qom Seminary Schools, which is a powerful religio-political organization, published a book on Motahhari's defence of Islam against Shariati's 'conspiracy' against the faith. Shariati was portrayed as 'a poisonous deviationist' whose ideas, according to Motahhari, were based more on socialism, communism, historical materialism and existentialism than on Islam.[45] The condemnation of Shariati's views, through the words of no less than Motahhari, came to be considered the Islamic Republic's official line on Shariati.

After Khomeini's death and the outbreak of an open clash between the two subsystems in the leadership for the attainment of absolute political power, key members of the Militant Clerics effectively rehabilitated their ideological godfather. By referring to the validity of Shariati's socioeconomic thoughts and by publicly claiming allegiance to certain aspects of his views, Shariati's subsystem once again became the source of inspiration for young egalitarian Islamic revolutionaries in power, who wished to save Islam from the ossified conservative old guard. On the occasion of a seminar on 'Shariati and the Renaissance of Islamic Thought' at Tehran University, Hadi Khamene'i (Ayatollah Khamene'i's brother), Abolhasan Haerizadeh, Asadollah Bayat and Asgharzadeh, all members of the parliament at the time and strong supporters of the Militant Clerics, supported Shariati's thoughts as completely compatible and in accordance with Khomeini's on crucial socioeconomic and political themes. Bayat said: 'Had our great Imam not distinguished between the Pure Mohammaden Islam and the American Islam' some of Shariati's writings would not have been properly understood.'[46] *Resalat*, the newspaper reflecting the anti-Shariati views of the Qom Seminary instructors, retaliated against rehabilitation of Shariati's ideas by reminding its readers that (1) Shariati had committed numerous technical errors on Islamic issues; (2) he had made unpardonable attacks on Shi'i dignitaries such as 'Allameh Majlesi; (3) those (that is, the Militant Clerics) who maintain that the Imam's analysis of two different types of Islam is the same as that which Shariati had outlined before were belittling the Imam; (4) Shariati's philosophy, according to Motahhari, was not based on Islam, but on socialism, existentialism and historical materialism; (5) Khomeini had always remained silent on Shariati, and had he viewed his own thoughts as compatible with Shariati's he would have said so! In reality,

however, Khomeini had referred to Ali Shariati as a divisive phenom-
enon, the introduction of whose ideas is alluded to as a pre-planned
Satanic plot aimed at breaking up the unity and common cause of the
Muslims, thus sapping their energy.[47]

Navab-Safavi's subsystem

The rise, development and significance of Navab-Safavi's subsystem should
be understood in the historical context of Iran between 1924 and 1956.
Navab-Safavi was born in 1924. This was a critical period in Iran's history.
Reza Khan, the powerful minister of war, who had been dissuaded by the
clergy from proclaiming a republic in Iran, was preparing the ground for
the establishment of the Pahlavi dynasty. Reza Khan became Reza Shah
in 1925. In his quest for power, Reza Khan had been careful to secure the
support of the clergy by promising to propagate and defend the cause of
orthodox Shi'i Islam, as had been the practice of all Iranian kings since
the Safavid dynasty. The role of the kings as the defenders of the faith
was a crucial legitimizing factor in view of the fact that all of them were
autocratic rulers. Therefore, Reza Khan's pretence to piety by participating in all traditional religious rituals and ceremonies was a necessary
gesture in the process of fulfilling all the requirements for becoming king.

Within the span of ten years, by emulating Mustafa Kemal Ataturk –
his role model – Reza Shah had become convinced that his country could
be relieved of backwardness and inferiority in comparison to the advanced
industrial countries of the world by following their paths and implementing
their policies. Industrialization and modernization were believed to be the
cure of all ills. Western monopoly over both resulted in an infatuation
with Westernization. The rapid imposition of modernization and Westernization from above implied a rupture with traditional Islamic mores and
values. In the process of his Westernization drive, Reza Shah did not
hesitate to repress any opposition. Insulting the deep religious sentiments
of the people and its possible social consequences were of no significant
concern to him. On 20 and 21 August 1935, Reza Shah ordered an assault
on the Gowharshad Mosque in Mashhad, where public feelings were being
roused against his policy of imposing a national dress code, part of which
was the de-veiling of Iranian women. The unprecedented act of attacking
and causing bloodshed in a mosque by the so-called defender of the faith
was a clear signal that the dictator intended to uproot Islam, as Ataturk
had attempted to do, if it became an obstacle to modernization.

The power vacuum that resulted from the banishment of Reza Shah in
1941 created a conducive atmosphere for the rapid growth and propagation of the different social, political, philosophical and religious outlooks
which had been suppressed during his reign. A wide spectrum of political
parties and organizations from the left to the right were formed and

became immediately active. Among these organizations – the majority of which represented one or another of the secular Western ideologies – the Fada'iyan-e Eslam (the Devotees of Islam) were founded by Navab-Safavi to push back the tide of de-Islamization or apostasy that had been ushered in by Reza Shah.

The central concern of Navab-Safavi's subsystem was to restore the supreme Islamic values that had dominated all aspects of life before Reza Shah's modernization drive. The morally neutral state, which reflected the victory of laicity over religion and the secular over divinely-inspired laws, was clearly an anathema to orthodox Shi'is. Shariati and Bazargan had adopted values and ideas relevant and pertinent to the needs of the twentieth century from other ideologies, sought and found implicitly compatible or similar themes in the body of primary and secondary Islamic sources, and had then proceeded to present a concept not specifically Islamic. Navab-Safavi's subsystem, however, was purely doctrinaire and completely immune to principles and concepts exogenous to traditional mainstream Shi'i Islam. In his testament before facing a military firing squad in 1956, he explained the objective of his subsystem. He wrote, 'in the pursuit of His cause, I tried to impose the reality of Islam on the whole world and to free Islam and all Muslims from the clutches of ignorance, lust and oppression. I tried to implement the enlightened rules and edicts of Islam, to disseminate Islamic culture and knowledge and to bring life to today's dead souls.'[48]

The Navab-Safavi subsystem is characterized by the belief in (1) the administration of society according to the Islamic laws, an important aspect of which is the application of Islamic punishments; (2) the incapability of secular laws to direct individuals toward felicity and salvation; (3) the abolition of all un-Islamic laws; (4) the compatibility of the monarchy with Islam; (5) the institution of martyrdom as a necessary act for the defence of Islam; (6) the primacy of combating all foreign influences, ideas and tendencies which are deemed to be corrupting and deviationist; (7) minimizing contact and interaction between Muslims and foreigners, and rupturing all political and military ties with countries such as the United Kingdom, the United States and the Soviet Union, since they are all believed to be controlled and conditioned by lust and worldliness; (8) a military alliance among all Islamic states; (9) the revolutionary execution of all those who are disrespectful toward Islam or oppose the Islamization of society; (10) the construction of a mosque in every governmental office, factory and school, where prayers should he held regularly; (11) sexual segregation in schools and workplaces and even on buses; (12) the strict observation of the Islamic dress code for women; (13) the prohibition of alcoholic beverages, cigarettes, gambling, prostitution, nightclubs, modern music, films (with two exceptions), poetry and novels; and (14) a thoroughly Islamic educational system.[49]

It could be argued that Navab-Safavi would have been perfectly content with what Shariati called Islam-e Safavi. His subsystem is essentially concerned with the social enforcement of Islamic morality, values and customs, as was prevalent in Iran between the Safavid and Pahlavi dynasty. The Islamic institution of temporary marriage is applauded as the most suitable means for satisfying man's sexual desires, but men and women are prohibited from working in the same factory since the mixing of the sexes is believed to lead to immorality and lustfulness. In Navab-Safavi's ideal Islamic society, life is divided between work, which is intermittently interrupted by the performance of religious duties; attending to the family, a part of which is providing religious education to the young at home; and the performance of religious obligations. In this subsystem, a lifestyle that leaves extra time for leisure is potentially dangerous. Leisure time frees the imagination and allows individuals to speculate, question and pose problems.

Navab-Safavi's subsystem could be imposed on any economic system, with the one condition that interest is forbidden. Navab-Safavi believed that the Islamic state was responsible for the provision of basic needs for the unemployed and the impoverished. In a truly Islamic state, he believed, Muslims would automatically and without any coercion accept the voluntary and obligatory financial commitments that Islam prescribes. This would generate the funds to enable the state to carry out its social responsibilities. On the issue of non-Islamic governmental revenues, Navab-Safavi believed that the modern coercive tax system had to be replaced with the Islamic taxes of *zakat* (income tax, wealth tax or both), *kharaj* (land tax), and *jaziyeh* (a poll tax on non-Muslims).[50]

Navab-Safavi did not have a very high opinion of economics and economists. He believed that 'the science of economics, seven year plans and foreign financial advisers were a hoax to deceive and rob the people.'[51] For him, the small-scale petty grocer had far greater economic abilities than all the highly educated university graduates. The emulation of the petty grocers' business customs and policies were believed to pave the way to economic growth and national prosperity. The petty grocers were even believed to be more honest and less corrupt than merchants. In his subsystem, the private accumulation of capital as practised by small shopkeepers is viewed as necessary for society. As long as capital remained in circulation through investment or trade, the profit accrued from it was justified and legitimate.[52] He exalted the money-making mentality of small shopkeepers to the extent that he suggested that the economy would do much better if a small shopkeeper were to become the Minister of Finance, and that the frugal manner in which grocers managed their stores and accumulated capital should subsequently become a model for Iran's Minister of Economy to emulate.

Navab-Safavi and three other key figures of the Fada'iyan-e Eslam were executed on charges of assassination and conspiracy on 17 January 1956. Ayatollah Borujerdi, the highest Islamic authority in Iran, who could have intervened and pleaded for a royal pardon to spare Navab-Safavi, showed his dislike for Fada'ian-e Eslam by keeping silent, implicitly condoning their death.

A number of Navab-Safavi's followers later organized themselves into Hey'at-ha-ye Mo'talefeh-ye Eslami, or the Islamic Coalition of Mourning Groups (ICMG). The ICMG was created under the direct recommendation of Khomeini in the Spring of 1963.[53] It was made up of three different religious groups. Two were affiliated to different mosques in Tehran and one was affiliated to the bazaar. All three groups included old members or sympathizers of the Fada'ian-e Eslam in their ranks and their leadership.[54] The majority of the 12 men of the Central Committee of the ICMG were also veterans of Navab-Safavi's organization. The ICMG operated under a five-man Clerical Council, the most influential member of which was Motahhari. The organization, however, operated under the influence of Navab-Safavi's value system.[55]

On 21 January 1965, in the tradition of the Fada'ian-e Eslam, Mohammad Bokhara'i, a member of the ICMG, assassinated Prime Minister Hasan-Ali Mansur for betraying Iran in the interest of United States' imperialism and for banishing Ayatollah Khomeini. After Khomeini was sent into exile, the ICMG became convinced of the necessity for armed struggle and the creation of a nationwide Islamic organization. For this purpose a new party called Hezb-e Mellal Eslami (Party of Islamic Nations) was born out of the ICMG. The activities of this new organization were short-lived since, after the assassination of Mansour, more than one hundred members of the ICMG – its prominent lay members and Moheyedin Anvari, one of the five members of the Clerical Council – were arrested on 16 October 1965. Four members, including Bokhara'i, directly involved with the assassination were executed. The rest were given prison sentences. The organized political activities of the ICMG came to a halt until the revolution.

After the revolution, the ICMG became active again, and the majority of its members became closely associated with and vocally supported the Militant Clergy of Tehran, the ideology of which combined elements of Motahhari's and Navab-Safavi's subsystems. The compatibility and congruence of the Motahhari and the Navab-Safavi subsystems had already been demonstrated in the practical organizational structure of the ICMG, in which the clerical leadership came from Motahhari and the practical tasks were performed by members who had been steeped in the Fada'ian-e Eslam school of thought. Even though the Navab-Safavi and the Shariati subsystems are less compatible, certain staunch partisans of the radical Militant Clerics of Tehran (the political and ideological rival of the Militant Clergy of Tehran), such as Sadeq Khalkhali, are also ardent supporters of the Navab-Safavi subsystem. Both Islamic radicals and conservatives (on socioeconomic issues) admire the Navab-Safavi subsystem for its firm position on the implementation of Islamic laws down to the last detail; its intolerance for and violence against opposition to a subjective concept of Islamic activities; its inflexible position on the total Islamization and homogenization of society through the forceful imposition of Islamic values, customs and mores; and its unswerving intention to eradicate all that is subjectively considered to be non-Islamic.

Bazargan's subsystem

Bazargan, like Shariati, is not mojtahed or a cleric. It is said, however, that he does not need to follow the directions and suggestions of a *marja'-e taqlid* (a supreme authority on religious laws) in the practice of his religious duties since he practices *ehtiyat* or caution. This implies that, on the basis of a thorough knowledge of Islamic rules, practices and edicts, he takes such extreme precautions in performing his religious duties down to the letter that he does not need to follow a *marja'-e taqlid*. Bazargan's subsystem is unique in the sense that, based on the Quran, it tries to present Islam as a non-coercive and tolerant religion compatible with liberalism and political democracy.

Unlike the three other subsystems – according to which proximity to God and salvation was determined by (1) following the directives and leading role of the clergy (Motahhari's); (2) class struggle to impose the power of the disinherited on the property-owning classes (Shariati's); and (3) Islamization of society through its incessant and violent purification of un-Islamic values, practices and individuals (Navab-Safavi's) – Bazargan views Islam as a non-discriminatory religion in which the most rewarding act in the eyes of God is to serve the people whom He has created. Bazargan's Islam is one of non-exclusion in which the 'other' – the anti-clerical intellectuals, the capitalists or the unveiled women – are neither castigated nor viewed as 'corrupters on earth'. By including the 'other' in God's family, Bazargan singles out tolerance as the cornerstone of Islam.[56]

The Bazargan subsystem is distinguished by the following particular features. First, the observation and implementation of Islamic ordinances are considered to be private matters left to the discretion of individuals. It is argued that God has willed individuals to be free in their judgements and decisions. Freedom of choice is thus identified as the coordinating mechanism of the relation between God and individuals.[57] Once God is argued to have given individuals the freedom of choice, forced compliance with Islamic edicts becomes meaningless and coercion as a mechanism to ensure Islamization loses validity and justification.[58] Bazargan's subsystem is similar to the other subsystems in that the implementation of the Shari'a constitutes its principal objective. Yet only a society that has consciously and freely chosen the Shari'a as its guide can be truly considered an Islamic society. According to Bazargan's subsystem, God does not wish to impose His view of what is good on individuals, since coercion would negate their God-given freedom of choice. Even if individuals choose not to perform their obligatory religious duties, such as fasting and prayers, they may still be considered as Muslims. As long as monotheism is not negated, individuals cannot be branded as apostates since the Quran commands that 'there can be no coercion in religion'.[59]

Second, according to Bazargan's subsystem, Islam has provided ordinances that restrain individuals from committing forbidden acts. Ordinances dealing with punishments and retributions have been formulated to control humankind's wrath and vengefulness. Bazargan argues that this disincentive system exists to prevent cruelty, not to cause and perpetrate it.[60] The imposition of such penalties is limited by the fact that 'God's mercy and blessing belong more to those who are charitable than to those who resort to the use of retribution.'[61] Furthermore, the individual is the only one allowed and invited to impose limitations on himself. The individual's relation to himself is argued to be organized around a personal sense of his growing awareness.[62]

Third, Bazargan argues that even though God foregoes His own rights in relation to individuals by giving them the freedom of choice, He will not allow the rights of any one individual to be violated by another. No one may commit injustice, cheat, deceive, exploit, oppress or violate the rights and freedoms of others. The Islamic principle that 'no one can do damage or harm to any other person and no one can be subjected to damage or harm by any other person' is invoked as the basis on which individual relations in society are coordinated.[63] Bazargan's use of this principle is an Islamic application of Pareto-optimality, where an act that improves the condition or welfare of one person or group at the cost of worsening the position or welfare of another is viewed as unacceptable.

Fourth, Bazargan argues that as soon as the Prophet was appointed to govern the people, God ordered him to 'consult with the people on issues and policies' that concerned their lives.[64] An Islamic government necessitates consultation with the people, and political democracy is argued to constitute the cornerstone of Islamic political thought. Using the practice of the Prophet as his model of Islamic government, Bazargan argues that 'one thousand years before the emergence of the concept of democracy in the West, the government of the people by the people was practised in the days of the Prophet.'[65] In Bazargan's subsystem, blind obedience and the imposition of a religio-political monolith is a clear violation of Islamic precepts. He rejects the forced imposition of religious or political instructions, even by a *marja'-e taqlid*, since it tampers with the principle of man's freedom and responsibility.

Fifth, Bazargan's subsystem is based on a mixed economy, in which the sanctity of property and contract are respected, and the market with its price mechanism coordinates demand and supply. As long as capital and wealth are accumulated legally and legitimately, according to Islamic yard-sticks, Bazargan maintains that the rewards belong to the owner of the capital.[66] In Bazargan's subsystem, the *mostaz'afin* or the disinherited, whose welfare should be guaranteed in an Islamic state, do not only constitute the workers and the peasants but also 'the clerical workers, the small shopkeepers, the bazaaris, the members of the private sector and the students'.[67] The combination of wage labour and the means of production in the process of factory production is viewed as a successful and happy marriage which leads to the implementation of democracy and the develop-ment of freedom, equality and social justice.[68] The existence of wide income disparities and social extremities is also viewed as deplorable from an Islamic perspective. Bazargan charges the government, which he considers to be the protector of national and not class interests, to defend the rights of consumers in the face of hoarding and excessive-profit-seeking merchants. He argues that the peasantry should also be defended against the illegal incursions of landowners, who have obtained their land through their contact with the Pahlavi court.[69] In Bazargan's Islamic mixed economy, the government is further responsible for ironing out the problems that the private sector cannot cope with – the provision of public services and securing public welfare – without ever becoming too self-indulgent. Bazargan accepts economic equity and justice as a desirable Islamic objective, because in such circumstances the socioeconomic position of individuals would depend only upon their labour.[70] However, he points out that 'one should not expect the easy victory of justice and equity over oppression and tyranny before the appearance of the hidden Imam, but neither should one give up hope.'[71]

In Bazargan's subsystem there is no Islamic justification for the govern-ment of the jurisconsult (*velayat-e faqih*) if it is understood as a position of unlimited power with no accountability to the people. Khomeini's edict of 6 January 1988 proclaimed the absolutist government of the jurisconsult (*velayat-e motlaqeh-ye faqih*) and gave absolute legal power to the jurisconsult. This edict provoked the reaction of the Freedom Movement of Iran (FMI), Bazargan's political organization, which declared 'from a sociopolitical point of view, the absolutist government of the jurisconsult is nothing other than religious and state despotism and dictatorship, resulting in the dis-appearance of freedom, independence and identity.'[72]

According to Bazargan's subsystem the total monopolization of power in the hands of the governing jurisconsult is an unprecedented religious innovation that is neither rooted in the Quran and the Sunna, nor reflects the democratic Quranic principle that 'affairs of the people should be conducted on the basis of mutual consultation'.[73] Its purpose is, in fact, to silence all voices of opposition. The FMI pointed out that the absolute power of the jurisconsult subjects religion to political imperatives, while the distinguishing feature of an Islamic state is that religion would be in command and politics would be a dependent function of it. Therefore, it argued, Khomeini's edict is contrary to the Quran and the Sunna, since it equates the powers of the governing jurisconsult with that of God.[74] Ever since the first presidential election in the Islamic Republic, candidates were closely screened and excluded on the basis of Islamic beliefs. As long as this type of discrimination is applied against the left, the Mojahedin, or Bazargan's FMI, the clerical forces in power justify and condone the practice. They argue that in an Islamic state only those who were qualified or dedicated Muslims could run for political positions. In the summer of 1985, during the third presidential elections, the Council of Guardians excluded, from a total of 50 presidential candidates, Mehdi Bazargan, the first prime minister of the Islamic Republic, and 46 others on the grounds that they did not possess the required Islamic qualifications.

Ironically, the cause of political democracy, democratic rights and procedures, along with the people's participation in determining their own affairs, have been championed after Khomeini's death by the Militant Clerics of Tehran, which espouses Shariati's subsystem. Faced with the powerful thrust of the Motahhari- and Navab-Safavi-oriented Militant Clergy of Tehran, aimed at barring them from political representation of any sort, the Militant Clerics suddenly realized the merits of political democracy, as all embattled political forces contending for power do. The Council of Guardians, dominated by those closely affiliated to Motahhari's and Navab-Safavi's subsystems, is entitled to reject the Islamic credentials of applicants for public office. It excluded the non-clerical forces that were approved in the first years of the revolution. During the elections to the Second Assembly of Experts and the Fourth Parliament, prominent clerical candidates who were on the Militant Cleric's list were also disqualified.

Bazargan's political concern for pluralism, freedom of speech and assembly, and the freedom to run for public office, was always derided and ridiculed as a perverse Western infatuation with liberalism by the Students Following the Imam's Path (SFIP), who took over the American embassy in 1979. Pragmatism and political survival have forced the anti-Bazargan proponents of Shariati's subsystem to become good parliamentarians ardently defending the most fundamental political aspect of Bazargan's subsystem – political democracy. On 16 October 1990, Asgharzadeh, an anti-liberal militant of the SFIP, a radical member of the Third Parliament, and closely affiliated with the Militant Clerics, defended Western democracy and attacked 'the dark reactionary forces which did not believe in the determining role of the people and the bottom-up process of government, but believed that the people should be led from above and that the parliament was a joke'.[75]

Shi'i Subsystems in Post-Revolutionary Iran

The very recent history of Iran has demonstrated that as soon as the revolution was won all the major participating organizations and groups began to show signs of dissent and divergence on several issues. Factions within each group claimed to be of pivotal significance to the ideology they espoused. The major surprise, for those who were not familiar with the historical intricacies of the Islamic movement, came with the realization that the mainstream Islamic movement, which seemed homogeneous, united and tenacious, was also plagued with internal division and rivalry.

The process of purifying the mainstream Islamic opposition movement had started as early as 1972. During that year and again in 1974, Ayatollah Khomeini met with a delegation of the Organization of the People's Mojahedin in Najaf.[76] Suspicious of their brand of Islam and the recurrent use of Marxist themes in their theoretical analysis of socioeconomic topics, Khomeini refused to give them his public blessing or his financial support. He even refused to speak about them publicly or refer to them in his writings or declarations. His snub came at a time when the prestige of the Mojahedin as the Islamic vanguard of the armed resistance movement in Iran was in the ascendant. Ahmad Khomeini recalls that at the time his father had said 'I read their books, they were deviationist and non-Islamic, therefore I did not endorse them.'[77] The claim to be Islamic, to maintain allegiance to the fixed principles of the faith and even the conscious choice of martyrdom in the spirit of Imam Hosein, which proved their practical devotion to the cause of holy war (*jehad*), qualified the Mojahedin as an Islamic subsystem. Yet Khomeini's steadfast position reflected his understanding of the reality that to endorse the Mojahedin would be an important religious concession to a potential political rival. While the Mojahedin's political integrity during their opposition to the Shah was beyond doubt, their religious interpretations and qualifications were made suspect by the objections of the traditional clergy.

Khomeini's attempt to isolate the Mojahedin fits well into the logic of competing Islamic subsystems, vying for public recognition as an essential prerequisite for political power. However, even though both sides looked upon the other with suspicion and distrust, neither the Mojahedin nor Khomeini publicly denounced or antagonized the other until after the revolution. The semblance of unity was maintained in the name of Islam. The process of marginalization that Khomeini initiated against the Mojahedin in 1972 entered into its final and effective physical stage with the Mojahedin's declaration of war on the Islamic Republic and the subsequent annihilation of their military power. The potential political threat of their legacy at home also vanished once they embraced the cause of Iran's adversary in the Iran–Iraq war.

During the first post-revolutionary years, the seemingly united main-stream forces under Khomeini's leadership invoked a simple argument in justifying their political and armed struggle against antagonistic Islamic subsystems. They maintained that 'no group or party could propagate social, economic or political ideas that were shrouded in Islamic terms, but were constructed on a non-Islamic substructure or foundation.'[78] This type of analysis justified the politically sensitive point that the leadership represented the only authentic Islamic discourse, and any deviation from it could therefore be viewed as un-Islamic and potentially heretical. The position that hammers at a single possible Islamic system conveys the idea that the proper use of Islam's fixed and immutable principles could only result in an undifferentiated and uniform social, economic and political position. As much as this harmonious position reflected the wishful think-ing of the ruling mainstream clerics, in the course of time it proved to be far from reality. The Islamic subsystems of Bazargan, Bani-Sadr, Shariatmadari and the Mojahedin were based on the immutable funda-mental principles of Islam; and that is why, even though their political position was derided as liberal, pro-American, capitalist or hypocritical, no serious theoretical effort was made to prove that they were un-Islamic.

Shortly after the defeat of all politically antagonistic subsystems and the full monopolization of power, the seemingly unified leadership found itself divided and split into warring subsystems. The ripple effects of such subsystem rivalries crippled the proper functioning of the polity and the economy. For example, during different periods the relationships between the Council of Guardians and the parliament, the president and his prime minister, the prime minister and a group of his ministers, the head of the Supreme Judiciary Council and a number of his judges, the minister of trade and the bazaar, the Islamic jurists who were proponents of traditional Islamic jurisprudence (*fiqh-e sonnati*) and the jurists supporting the dynamic brand of Islamic jurisprudence (*fiqh-e poya*), became tense if not hostile.

The Islamic Republic's attempt to hide from the public the widening differences and growing rivalries within the leadership failed. The disso-lution of the so-called monolithic Islamic Republic Party, which was to symbolize the unity of all Islamic subsystems, on 1 June 1987 clearly reflected the problem. When such rivalries found an echo in the armed forces and the Revolutionary Guards, Khomeini threatened the subsystems with reprisals. Finally, the leadership, plagued by division and factionalism, conceded that differences could emerge among true believers as long as they remained loyal followers of Imam Khomeini – a concession that the already vanquished subsystems had not been willing to make.

The dissolution of the Islamic Republic Party forced the competing forces to find a different medium of expression for their disagreements. The theatre of confrontation was thus shifted to its real ideological source. On 20 March 1988, a group of prominent Islamic jurists, led by Mehdi

Karobi and Musavi Kho'iniha, left their traditional and prestigious strong-
hold of the Association of Militant Clergy of Tehran (Jame'eh-yeh
Rowhaniyat-e Mobarez-e Tehran) and established the Assembly of Militant Clerics of Tehran (Majma'-ye Rowhaniyun Mobarez-e Tehran) under
the auspices of Khomeini.[79] This long-existent, but newly formalized faction was composed of clerics generally known for their anti-Western and
especially anti-American foreign policy, egalitarian social outlook, statist
and anti-capitalist economic policies and, finally, stoical and puritanical
view of life. The timing of the announcement of this new political force
was chosen because of the upcoming parliamentary elections. The third
parliamentary elections of the Islamic Republic led to the defeat of the
Militant Clergy representing Motahhari's and Navab-Safavi's subsystem,
and the victory of the Militant Clerics, representing Shariati's.

In an important message, which acknowledged the ideological conflict
between the Shariati-inspired Militant Clerics and the Motahhari/Navab-
Safavi-inspired Militant Clergy, Khomeini endorsed both subsystems. In
his arguments, Khomeini provided a clear exposition of his interpretation
of the theory of Islamic subsystems. In his address, which has come to
be known as the 'Covenant of Brotherhood' (Manshur-e Baradari), he
argued that since the door of *ejtehad* was open, differences of opinion
among the *foqaha* on a list of issues was permissible. This long list included controversial worldly topics such as the problem of ownership and
its limitations; the issues of land, taxation, domestic and foreign trade;
mozara'a (sharecropping); *mozaraba* (silent partnership) and rent; banking
and foreign exchange; cultural issues; and limits to individual and social
freedoms. Khomeini even included Islamic punishments (*hodud*) and blood-
money (*diyat*) as topics open to differences of opinion on the basis of
ejtehad. Khomeini, however, cautioned:

> You have to realize that as long as your differences and positions are within the
> framework of the issues referred to, the revolution would not be threatened. But
> if differences become substructural and revolve around principles, the system
> would become weakened and fragile. It is clear that if disagreements occur
> among those who are loyal to the revolution, their differences would be solely
> political, even though they may take on an ideological form. This is because they
> all share the same bases and principles, and that is why I endorse them all. They
> are all loyal to Islam, the Quran and the revolution.[80]

Justifying his endorsement of the newly formed Militant Clerics which
had the full support of his son, Khomeini added that 'it is on this basis
that I have said that constructive criticism does not mean disagreement
and the new organization does not imply discord. Constructive and
appropriate criticism leads to the growth of society, and if it is well founded
it would guide and lead both tendencies.'[81]

Khomeini's understanding of Islamic subsystems differs from ours in that he considers loyalty to the revolution – which means allegiance to the governing jurisconsult or Ayatollah Rohullah Khomeini – as a fixed component of the fundamental bases and principles of the faith. For Khomeini, an Islamic discourse which did not believe in the policies and positions of the Islamic Republic's leadership, irrespective of its Islamic credentials, did not constitute an Islamic subsystem. The Islamic characteristic of subsystems was thus dependent on Islam, the Quran and allegiance to Khomeini as the embodiment of the revolution.

The death of the Imam created a religio-political authority vacuum. The combined position of the palm-bearer of the revolution, the highest religious source of imitation, and the absolutist governing jurisconsult, allegiance to whom legitimized an Islamic subsystem, was left effectively unoccupied, even though Ayatollah Khamene'i was immediately chosen as the governing jurisconsult by the Assembly of Experts. Khomeini had attained uncontested political power and unchallenged spiritual authority through a long process of struggle, before and after the revolution. Only his unique characteristics gave him the power to encourage, reprimand, balance and ultimately use the competing subsystems for what he believed to be the benefit of Islam and then the Republic. Khomeini's will was their command.

The process of moving rapidly from a multiplicity of Shi'i subsystems at the beginning of the revolution to a single hegemonic one was successfully accomplished through Khomeini's effective use of his political and religious authority to impose a permissible frame of operation. Once the veritable law-maker in the land and the guardian of an artificial unity among incompatible ideologies died, the rivalry of the subsystems for control of the fate of the Republic came out into the open. Before the elections to the Fourth Parliament, in April 1992, the two major tolerated Islamic forces clarified their positions on domestic, economic and foreign policy through speeches made by their highly placed government functionaries, members of parliament and publications (*Resalat* representing the views of Militant Clergy; and *Salam*, *Jahan-e Eslam* and *Bayan* voicing the opinion of Militant Clerics). In this process, each subsystem championed the economic interests of one social group or class. The crushing parliamentary victory of the Militant Clergy allowed them and their supporters to occupy all sensitive political, judicial and military positions. Had not the Council of Guardians intervened in favour of the Militant Clergy, one could have deduced certain instructive conclusions on the state of socioeconomic and political development in Iran. The political hegemony of one or a combination of subsystems in a truly democratic election process would in one way or another reflect the relation of power among different classes in Iran, which is itself to a large extent a reflection of Iran's level of economic development.

Notes

1. Abdullah, Yusuf Ali, *The Holy Quran, Translation and Commentary* (Maryland: Amana Corporation, 1989).

2. Motahhari, Mortaza, *Bist Goftar* (Tehran: Sherkat-e Offset, 1982), p 28.

3. Khorasani, M., Va'ezzadeh, *Majmu'eh-ye Maqalat-e Farsi-ye Avvalin Majma'-e Eqtesad-e Eslami* (Tehran: Entesharat-e Astan-e Qods-e Razavi, 1990), pp 109–10; Ahmad Ibn Taymiya, *The Institution of the Hisbah* (Leicester: The Islamic Foundation, 1985)), pp 49–50.

4. Ibn Taymiya, *The Institution of the Hisbah*, p 55.

5. Ibid., p 47.

6. Islahi, Abdul Azim, *Economic Concepts of Ibn Taimiyah* (Leicester: The Islamic Foundation, 1988), p 95.

7. Ibn Taymiya, *The Institution of the Hisbah*, p 48.

8. Islahi, *Economic Concepts of Ibn Taimiyah*, pp 96–8.

9. Jenati, 'Taqrib-e Manabe' va Mabani-e Fiqh-e Ejtehadi Beyn Mazaheb-e Eslami', *Taqrib Beyn-e Mazaheb-e Eslami*, 1 (September/October 1980).

10. Khorasani, *Majmu'eh-ye Maqalat*, pp 165–7.

11. Ibid., pp 20–23.

12. The Quran, 9:35, 7:31.

13. Cameron, A.J., *Hazrat Abu Dharr al-Ghifari* (Lahore: Islamic Publishers, 1982).

14. Mashkour, M.J., *Dictionary of Islamic Sects* (Mashhad: Astan-e Qods-e Razavi, 1989), pp 168, 170.

15. Afzal-ur-Rahman, *Economic Doctrines of Islam* (Lahore: Islamic Publications, 1980), vol 1, pp 48, 222; vol 2, pp 168, 186–8.

16. 'Azadi-e Tafakor', *Howzeh* 27 (August/September 1988).

17. 'Fiqh va Eqtesad-e Eslami-e Salem', *Howzeh* 25 (March/April 1988).

18. Rahnema, Ali, and Farhad Nomani, *The Secular Miracle: Religion, Politics and Economic Policy in Iran* (London: Zed Books, 1990), pp 19–36.

19. Motahhari, Mortaza, *Naqdi bar Marxism* (Tehran: Entesharat-e Sadra, 1984), p 124.

20. Rahnema and Nomani, *The Secular Miracle*, p 42.

21. Motahhari, Mortaza, *'Adl-e Elahi* (Tehran: Entesharat-e Sadra, n.d.), p 81.

22. Motahhari, Mortaza, *Jame'eh va Tarikh* (Tehran: Entesharat-e Sadr, n.d.), pp 162–70.

23. Motahhari, Mortaza, *Piramun-e Enqelab-e Eslami* (Tehran: Entesharat-e Sadra, n.d.), pp 14–15 and 162–3.

24. Motahhari, *Piramun-e Enqelab*, p 11.

25. Rahnema and Nomani, *The Secular Miracle*, p 43.

26. Motahhari, *Piramun-e Enqelab*, p 102.

27. Ibid., p 104.

28. Motahhari, Mortaza, *Nehzat-ha-ye Eslami dar Sad Saleh Akher* (Tehran: Entesharat-e Sadra, n.d.), p 71.

29. Motahhari, *'Adl-e Elahi*, p 115.

30. Motahhari, *Piramun-e Enqelab*, p 149.

31. Ibid., pp 151–2; and Motahhari, *'Adl-e Elahi*, p 185.

32. Motahhari, Mortaza, *Nazari beh Nezam-e Eqtesadi-ye Eslam* (Tehran: Entesharat-e Sadra, 1989), pp 58, 146.

33. Ibid., p 56.
34. Ibid., p 145.
35. Ibid., p 133.
36. Shariati, Ali, *Khod Sazi-ye Enqelabi* (Tehran: Hoseiniyeh Ershad, 1977), p 158.
37. Rahnema and Nomani, *The Secular Miracle*, p 54.
38. Shariati, *Khod Sazi*, pp 142–4.
39. Ibid., pp 38–9.
40. Shariati: *Khod Sazi*, p 144.
41. Shariati, Ali, *Tarikh-e Adyan* (n.pub., n.d.), pp 320–25.
42. Shariati, Ali, *Mazhab 'Aleyh-e Mazhab*. (n.p., n.d.), p 18.
43. Ibid., p 42.
44. *Kayhan*, 31 March 1988.
45. Abolhasani, Ali, *Shahid Motahhari; Efshagar-e Towte'eh* (Tehran: Daftar-e Entesharat-e Eslami, 1984), pp 236, 417.
46. *Resalat*, 18 June 1990.
47. Khomeini, Ruhollah, *Sahifeh-ye Nur* Vol 2 (Tehran: Markaz-e Madarek-e Farhanghi-ye Enqelab-e Eslami, 1983), p 250.
48. Khoshneiyat, Sayyed Hosein, *Sayyed Mojtaba Navab-Safavi* (Tehran: Entesharat-e Manshur-e Baradari, 1981), p 202.
49. Rahnema and Nomani, *The Secular Miracle*, pp 73–96.
50. Navab-Safavi, Mojtaba, *Barnameh-ye Enqelabi-ye Fada'iyan-e Eslam* (Tehran: n.p., n.d.), p 34.
51. Ibid., p 34.
52. Khoshneiyat, *Sayyed Mojtaba Navab-Safavi*, pp 237–8; and Navab-Safavi, *Barnameh-ye Enqelabi*, p 34.
53. Badamchian and Bana'i, *Heyatha-ye Mo'talefeh-e Eslami* (Tehran: Entesharat-e Owj, 1983), p 34.
54. Ibid., pp 127–128.
55. Madani, Sayyed Jalaledeen, *Tarikh-e Siyasi-e Mo'aser-e Iran* Vol 2 (Qom: Daftar-e Entesharat-e Eslami, 1983), p 101.
56. Rahnema and Nomani, *The Secular Miracle*, p 104.
57. Bazargan, Mehdi, *Bazyabi-ye Arzesh-ha* (Tehran: n.p., 1983), Vol 1, p 132; Vol 2, p. 109.
58. Ibid., Vol 3, p 78.
59. Ibid., Vol 1, p 78.
60. Rahnema and Nomani, *The Secular Miracle*, p 105.
61. Bazargan, *Bazyabi-ye Arzesh-ha* Vol 2, p 25.
62. Ibid., p 118.
63. Ibid., p 113.
64. Ibid., Vol 3, p 12.
65. Ibid., Vol 1, p 117.
66. Bazargan, Mehdi, *Moshkelat va Masa'el-e Avvalin Sal-e Enqelab* (Tehran: n.p., 1983), p 201.
67. Ibid., p 119.
68. Bazargan, Mehdi, *Kar Dar Islam* (Houston: Book Distribution Center, 1978), p 29.
69. Bazargan, *Moshkelat va Masa'el-e*, pp 119–20.
70. Bazargan, *Kar Dar Islam*, p 38.

71. Bazargan, *Bazyabi-ye Arzesh-ha,* Vol 2, p 228.

72. Nehzat-e Azadi-ye Iran, *Tafsil va Tahlil-e Velayat-e Motlaqeh-ye Faqih* (Tehran: Nehzat-e Azadi Iran, 1988), p 150.

73. The Quran, 42:38.

74. Nehzat-e Azadi-ye Iran, *Tafsil va Tahlil,* pp 97, 118.

75. *Resalat,* 17 October 1990.

76. Abrahamian, Ervand, *Radical Islam: The Iranian Mojahedin* (London: I.B. Tauris, 1989), p 148.

77. 'Mavaze'-e Emam dar barabar-e Monafeqin', *Pasdar-e Eslam* (July/August 1982).

78. 'Eslam va avamel-e jenah-bandi', *Pasdar-e Eslam* 24 (November/December 1983).

79. *Kayhan,* 26 March 1988.

80. 'Payam-e Hazrat-e Emam', *Pasdar-e Eslam* 84 (November/December 1988).

81. Ibid.

PART II

State and Economy

4

The Post-Revolutionary Economic Crisis

Sohrab Behdad

Since the 1979 revolution, Iran has been plagued by an economic crisis of the post-revolutionary type.[1] Other Third World countries, in spite of many differences in the character of their revolutions and their geopolitical and socioeconomic conditions, have suffered from a similar type of economic crisis in their post-revolutionary periods.[2] Iran's post-revolutionary economic crisis has been aggravated by disputes among proponents of various interpretations of Islamic jurisprudence, the war with Iraq, and frequent gluts in the international oil market. In this chapter I will study the general characteristic of the economic crisis and the transformation of politics in post-revolutionary Iran.

A post-revolutionary economic crisis is the outcome of open social confrontations. It is the economic manifestation of what Theda Skocpol calls a post-revolutionary structural crisis.[3] Revolutionary conditions jeopardize the security of capital and paralyse the state in its functions to protect property and to facilitate the production process. These problems interrupt the production process and result in an economic crisis. The more advanced the capitalist development of the economy, the more intense and extensive will be the post-revolutionary economic crisis. The crisis will be intensified by disruptions in the linkages with the world economy. The economic crisis will be contained when the new regime can establish a new economic order and the production process can be resumed undisturbed. The definition and the establishment of a new economic order in a post-revolutionary society is, however, the subject of an intense political struggle. This political struggle reflects, on the one hand, the conflict of interest among various social classes and groups that the regime claims to represent, and on the other, the effort of the regime to eliminate the economic power of those loyal to the *ancien régime* by restructuring the economy. The path of resolution of these conflicts and the eventual orientation of the new regime (if it does not collapse in the process) will depend on the course of development of the political struggle in the post-revolutionary period. It is in this context that the political and economic crises in post-revolutionary conditions may be examined.

The prolonged post-revolutionary economic crisis in Iran and its specific features may be further explained by a number of factors peculiar to Iranian society and revolution. They are: (1) the remarkably popular character of the revolutionary movement in the polarized socio-economic structure of Iran; and (2) the unarticulated expression of class interest and revolutionary objectives and programme. On the one hand, the mass of the Iranian population, the urban poor, the working class, civil servants and intellectuals, proprietors and the bourgeoisie (except its top stratum), with obviously varying interests, were mobilized to overthrow the Shah's regime.[4] The rural workers and small farmers joined the revolutionary movement in its final moments. Yet, the movement lacked any specific programme or clearly defined objective except to demand the end of the Shah's regime and the 'ills' that it had caused. Economic objectives were expressed as political slogans only spontaneously in mass demonstrations and, after the uprising, by various rival political groups. These slogans were acted upon by mass movements, or by the government and its 'revolutionary organs', in an effort to pre-empt rival political groups. In short, the question of determining the objectives of the revolution was postponed to the post-revolutionary period, and then the ruling regime did not possess a programme of action.

Furthermore, (3) the ambiguities in Islamic ideology and jurisprudence promoted a range of interpretations about the organization of the economy in an Islamic society (see Introduction and Chapter 3). These interpretations are reflected in the vast literature that has become known as 'Islamic economics'.[5] Formulation of a model by Iranian Muslim intellectuals and theoreticians for the organization of an Islamic economy, and therefore the debate about various interpretations of Islam on the economic question, did not begin much earlier than the final phase of the revolutionary movement.[6] The core of the debate in Islamic economics is about the role of the state in the economy and the limits of private property rights.[7] As long as the state is not Islamic, the controversy is an inconsequential intellectual debate. The problem, however, becomes a highly critical political issue when, as in Iran, the establishment of a new Islamic state is the outcome of a popular revolution under the egalitarian banner of Islamic ideology. In the absence of an economic programme, the post-revolutionary economic reconstruction has to await formulation of a model by the regime for the organization of the economy. This is clearly a political issue reflecting the relative power of various social groups and the general disposition of the regime toward these social groups. In an Islamic state, however, the resolution of this conflict must take place in the context of Islamic jurisprudence.

Finally, (4) given the hierarchy of jurisprudential authority (*ejtehad*) in

Shiʻism, and that the Islamic Republic failed to incorporate this hierarchy fully in the formal structure of the state, a dual structure of authority developed in post-revolutionary Iran.[8] Factional confrontations could not be resolved through the conflict-resolution process devised by the formal structure of the state. Deadlocks developed on economic policy issues in spite of ad hoc changes in the hierarchy of legal authority in the Islamic Republic.

These factors, specific to the Iranian Revolution, have prolonged the post-revolutionary economic crisis. The Islamic Republic has not been able to provide its model for the post-revolutionary reconstruction of the economy, nor has it been successful in providing the necessary social and legal institutions required for an undisturbed production process to go on. The war with Iraq and the glut in the international oil market, from 1985 to 1989, and since 1993, aggravated the economic crisis. When, after the death of Ayatollah Khomeini in 1989, the dominant faction in the Islamic Republic abandoned its revolutionary claims for economic restructuring and set itself up to reconstruct a liberal economic order under the auspices of the World Bank and the International Monetary Fund, it confronted a crippling opposition from both inside and outside the regime. The crisis continues as the Islamic Republic remains incapable of deciding a path of economic recovery for Iran.

The Economic Dimensions of the Revolution

In the revolutionary movement the Islamic leadership gained the support of the widest possible social spectrum. The urban and rural poor supported the commitment toward social justice. In a society where the rural per-capita income was less than one-half of that in the urban economy, where the wealthiest 10 per cent of the urban households received about 40 cents of every dollar of the urban income while the bottom 10 per cent of households received only 1.2 cents, and the wealthy demonstrated their wealth in the most obnoxious and arrogant forms of conspicuous consumption, the rule of Islamic economic justice, whatever that might be, was attractive to a large mass of the population.[9] Also, in an economy where only a small circle of companies had access to the means of accumulation and the association with international capital to establish local oligopolies (see Chapter 5), and in which small and ʻless privileged' firms faced insurmountable barriers, the latter quite naturally felt oppressed and deprived of their fair share. The largest segment of these ʻoppressed' capitalists were the bazaar merchants, who were frustrated in their efforts to move to modern manufacturing, banking and other highly profitable and oligopolistic activities. They, too, found the Islamic movement appealing, especially since they traditionally had close ties with the Islamic clergy. In addition, large numbers of urban and rural small proprietors, shopkeepers and crafts workers found themselves threatened by the ever-expanding oligopolistic networks and thus felt that the slogan of Islamic economic justice was appealing and reassuring.

The Resolution of the Ashura march (11 December 1978) may serve as a reflection of the economic orientation of the revolutionary movement. This resolution was read on the second day of the largest mass demonstration, which has been viewed by Ayatollah Khomeini and other leaders of the Islamic Republic as the referendum against the Shah's rule. After demanding the establishment of the Government of Islamic Justice, the resolution asked for 'the guarantee of the right of workers and peasants to the full benefit from the product of their labour', an end to 'the exploitation of man by man', and elimination of 'exploitive profiteering and economic domination which will result in accumulation of great wealth, on the one hand, and deprivation and poverty, on the other'. The resolution demanded 'honorable economic independence, rejuvenation of agriculture and independent development of industries to the limits of self-sufficiency and liberation from dependence from foreign domination, and an end to exploitation and colonialization of, and dependence on, imperialism of East and West'.[10]

These objectives represented a negotiated summation of the demands of various political groups whose representatives met in the Centre for Defence of Human Rights just before the march. Although Marxist groups and organizations were not represented in these meetings, their main demands were reflected in this resolution. They wanted to abolish exploitation and 'economic dependency' through promotion of economic equality and elimination of 'dependent capitalist' relations and the monopolistic power of the 'dependent capitalists'.[11] 'Dependency', 'dependent capitalism' and 'dependent capitalists' became the revolutionary shibboleths in the general discourse of Islamic propagandists and public officials.

In the months that followed, the slogans in the mass demonstrations and the resolutions of striking workers and various newly formed organizations expressed more specific demands.[12] These demands included the nationalization and expropriation of large industries, banks, mines, large land holdings and real estate. Many of these demands were formulated spontaneously,[13] and in numerous cases they were acted upon without the political sanction of the 'leadership of the revolution', and at times – after the February uprising – in spite of the official decrees of the revolutionary government. When the Provisional Revolutionary Government came to power in February 1979, the newly formed workers' councils had already taken over most of the large enterprises.[14] Banks had been attacked and burned since November 1978. Owners of many large enterprises had fled the country.

The waves of revolutionary upheaval had washed away the sanctity of property ownership. As Moghadam points out in Chapter 2, Iranian history has witnessed many occasions of destabilization of property relations. In the 1979 revolution, however, the legitimacy of property as 'excessive wealth', the source of economic power of the Iranian oligarchy, and in the form of foreign capital came under attack. Thus, in the revolutionary movement, largeness, ties to the Shah's regime, and foreign affiliation were generally the criteria for the de facto takeovers and official expropriations. With no clear definition, these criteria could simply become relative measures, and they did. For example, in a small provincial town a car dealership could be viewed as a large imperialist outpost, the owner of 50 hectares of land a despicable landlord, and a retired major a close associate of the Shah. Takeovers and expropriations were widespread during the height of the revolutionary period.

Bazargan's government, which as a matter of principle opposed nationalization, found the nationalization of banks and large manufacturing enterprises unavoidable as they were mostly financially bankrupt and abandoned by their owners and managers, who had fled the country. In the summer of 1979, the Provisional Revolutionary Government declared all private banks, insurance companies and many manufacturing enterprises nationalized.

Moreover, the Revolutionary Islamic Courts expropriated the wealth of those who were considered 'corrupt on earth'. Hence, many large non-bank, non-industrial holdings, including service enterprises and real estate were also expropriated. The extent of the nationalization and expropriation may be shown by the following figures: the 28 banks that were nationalized held 43.9 per cent of all bank assets in Iran; and by 1982, 14.2 per cent of all manufacturing enterprises with ten or more workers (excluding the nationalized oil industry), employing 68.1 per cent of manufacturing workers and producing 70.9 per cent of value-added, were under public management.[15] In 1976 only 3.5 per cent of these enterprises were under government or mixed ownership.[16] In the rural sector the peasants confiscated and held onto 800,000 hectares of prime agricultural land. This is about 6 per cent of the total agricultural land in Iran. The confiscated wealth by the Revolutionary Islamic Courts was transferred to the Foundation for the Oppressed (Bonyad-e Mostaz'afin). These holdings, by 1982, included 203 mining and manufacturing enterprises, 472 commercial farms, 101 construction companies, 238 trading and other service enterprises, and 2786 real-estate properties.[17] Subsequently, some of these enterprises and real estate properties, plus some of the other enterprises that were confiscated later, were transferred to other foundations, such as the Martyr's Foundation (Bonyad-e Shahid) and the Fifteenth Khordad Foundation.

Expropriation and nationalization, shortages of imported goods (to which the US and European trade embargo contributed),[18] the disputes between workers' councils and management in large enterprises, and the

Table 4.1 Value-added Index in Major Economic Activities 1977–1992[a]

| | Total value-added index (%) | | | | | | | | | Per-capita value added (%) | |
| | war and the oil glut | | | | economic liberalization | | | | | | |
	1977	1980	1984	1988	1989	1990	1991	1992	change[b] 1977–92	index 1992	change[b] 1977–92
Agriculture	100	117	143	161	167	181	190	204	(4.9)	123	(1.4)
Industry	100	80	101	85	91	103	120	126	(1.5)	76	(-1.8)
Services	100	102	116	89	91	97	108	117	(1.0)	70	(-2.4)
Non-oil GDP	100	99	117	102	106	115	127	136	(2.1)	82	(-1.3)
GNP (at market prices)	100	84	106	83	86	97	109	124	(1.5)	75	(-1.9)

Notes: [a] in 1982 prices. [b] Average annual rate of growth.

Source: Bank Markazi: *National Accounts of Iran (1974–1987)* (in Persian, Tehran, 1991); *National Accounts of Iran (1988–1990)* (in Persian, Tehran, 1992); and *Economic Report and Balance Sheet* (in Persian), various issues.

delays in carrying out government projects, all contributed to the decline of output and employment. Between 1978 and 1980, the economy suffered a decline. Value-added in industry (including mining and construction) in 1980 (in 1982 prices) was 80 per cent of the 1977 level (see Table 4.1).[19] As the salaries of government employees increased substantially in these years, value-added in public services (accounting for about one-third of value-added in all service activities) increased by 19 per cent, while value-added in trade had declined by 21 per cent and that of financial services by 14 per cent. Agriculture, however, managed to increase its value-added above the pre-revolutionary level by 17 per cent, in spite of the takeover movement in the rural economy. (Peasants brought their newly acquired land under cultivation immediately to prove their ownership.) The effect of disruption on economic activities is best reflected by the decline in the level of investment. By 1980, gross domestic fixed-capital formation (investment) was only 57 per cent of its 1977 value. Investment in machinery, a more accurate indicator of industrial investment, had declined to only 36 per cent of the level in 1977 (see Table 4.2).

In the midst of the general economic decline, the relative income share of the poor and the middle-income households in the urban and the rural economy increased significantly. Redistribution of income-earning assets, the interruptions in the production process – which had a more adverse effect on income from profit, interest and rent – and the redistributive income policies of the government, all contributed to the narrowing of the inequality gap in these years. Even more interesting is the fact that in this period the share of poor and middle-income households in the declining urban economy increased, relatively and absolutely. Clearly the wealthy lost and the poor and the middle class gained from the immediate effects of the revolution.[20]

Islamization of the Economy: The Unresolved Dilemma

The issue of Islamization of the economy was raised only in the last days of the revolutionary movement. The Marxist and radical non-Marxist organizations (most significantly the Fada'iyan-e Khalq and the Mojahedin-e Khalq) had acquired a high degree of visibility. Their young activists in the factories, farms, universities and street marches were successful in publicizing their anti-capitalist, anti-dependency slogans. The basic epistemological and methodological differences between Marxism and Islam aside, there was little difference between the concrete economic proposals of the Marxists and those of the radical Islamic intelligentsia following the thoughts of Shariati and Taleqani.

From the early post-revolutionary days the economic question became the focal point, and two tendencies were formed within the regime. Prime Minister Bazargan and his Freedom Movement of Iran (Nehzat-e Azadi-

Table 4.2 Gross Domestic Fixed Capital Formation (Investment) 1977–1992[a]

| | Investment index (%) | | | | | | | | change[b] 1977–91 | Average annual investment 1978–91 as % of 1977 |
| | *war and the oil glut* | | | *economic liberalization* | | | | | | |
	1977	1980	1984	1988	1989	1990	1991	1992		
Private	100	68	102	47	52	52	78	86	-1.7	67
Machinery	100	23	74	23	38	45	95	na	-0.4	36
Construction	100	93	118	60	59	57	69	na	-2.6	84
Government	100	48	61	26	26	34	45	47	-5.5	49
Machinery	100	51	95	28	33	49	61	na	-3.4	64
Construction	100	48	48	26	24	29	40	na	-6.4	44
Machinery, total	100	36	84	25	36	47	79	na	-1.7	49
Construction, total	100	66	77	40	39	41	52	na	-4.6	60
Total	100	57	79	35	38	43	60	64	-3.6	57

Notes: [a] in 1982 prices. [b] Average annual rate of growth.

Sources: Bank Markazi: *National Accounts of Iran (1974–1987)* (in Persian, Tehran, 1991); *National Accounts of Iran (1988–1990)* (in Persian, Tehran, 1992); and *Economic Report and Balance Sheet* (in Persian), various issues.

ye Iran) promoted only moderate reforms for the economy. They maintained that private-property rights were to be respected and protected,
and that nationalization must be limited only to those cases in which the
national interest was involved, or when the original owners had fled the
country. In their view, the main role of the state in the economy was to
provide the proper atmosphere for the private sector. When the clergy
took complete control of the political regime by purging Bani-Sadr from
the presidency in the summer of 1981, this point of view was represented
by a powerful minority of conservative clergy within the regime, who
vehemently opposed the interventionist policies of the Islamic Republic
and promoted the post-revolutionary reconstruction of a *laissez faire* market
economy. This conservative tendency received the support of the major
Sources of Imitation (*maraje'-e taqlid*), except Ayatollah Khomeini, who
seldom confronted them on matters that did not directly affect the security
of the state.[21] Since the laws and policies of the state in the Islamic Republic
must be in accordance with Islamic law, and since the high ranking
ayatollahs are the indisputable authorities on Islamic jurisprudence, their
opposition was a serious challenge to the interventionist policies of the
Islamic Republic.[22]

The dominant tendency in the Islamic Republic, however, followed a
populist-statist orientation. It emphasized the rule of the *mostaz'afin* (the
oppressed) and perceived the Islamic Republic as an interventionist state
that would impose extensive limitations on private-property rights. This
tendency was a strong agitation in the early post-revolutionary expropriation movement and in opposition to Bazargan's Provisional Revolutionary
Government, and later to Bani-Sadr's presidency. Moreover, this faction
of the Islamic Republic supported the establishment of various revolutionary foundations in an attempt to create grassroots support for an
Islamic regime and to confront the radical opposition to the Islamic
Republic.

The influence of this faction is seen in the economic dimensions of
the Constitution of the Islamic Republic. The constitution regards the
Iranian Revolution as a movement aimed at the triumph of the oppressed
and deprived over the oppressor. The most controversial aspects of the
constitution regarding economic issues are Articles 44 and 49. According
to Article 44, the economy is to consist of state, cooperative and private
sectors, in that order. The state sector is to include, most importantly, 'all
the large-scale and major industries, foreign trade, major mineral resources,
banking, insurance, [and] energy'. The domain of the private sector,
according to the constitution, is limited to those activities that 'supplement
the economic activities of the state and cooperative sectors'.[23]

Limits may be imposed on wealth based on the legitimacy of its source.
According to Article 47 of the Constitution, 'private ownership, legitimately acquired, is to be respected. The relevant criteria are determined

by law.' Article 49 defines illegitimate sources of ownership. In addition to usury, bribery, theft and illicit sources, they include the usurping and misuse of endowments (*moqofat*).[24] These criteria under the Islamic Republic could be (and have been) interpreted very widely – from acceptance of the status quo to Proudhon's notion that property is theft.

The critical area of conflict between the conservative and the populist-statist tendencies was in the legislative process for developing the new legal structure of the regime. Each group, no less fundamentalist than the other, sought to provide legitimization for its demands in Islamic jurisprudence. The Sources of Imitation, however, stayed away from the formal structure of the government. Ayatollah Khomeini, in an attempt to avoid a confrontation on the terrain of Islamic jurisprudence outside the governmental structure, selected the majority of jurists in the Council of Guardians from among those who represented the conservative view. According to Article 96 of the constitution, any bills passed by the Majles must be approved by the Council of Guardians for compatibility with the 'ordinance of Islam' and the constitution before becoming a law. Thus, by placing the conservative jurists in the Council of Guardians, Ayatollah Khomeini brought the jurisprudential conflict within the structure of the state and the political arena, which he had under his control.

In the first post-revolutionary decade, in the 1980s, the Majles passed a number of controversial bills on economic matters, and the Council of the Guardians persistently rejected them as un-Islamic. The disagreements were over urban land ownership, mineral rights, confiscation of the property of those who have fled the country and, most importantly, rural land redistribution, nationalization of foreign trade, and the labour law.

The conflict surfaced in August 1981, when the Majles passed a bill nationalizing the *mawat* and *bayer* urban land. Although *mawat* means lands that have never been reclaimed, and *bayer* means reclaimed lands that have been left unused, in the urban settings the reference was to valuable vacant land parcels, generally kept for speculative purposes. Immediately after the revolution, the Islamic Republic declared its commitment to provide housing for the poor. Urban land appeared as the most significant limitation in the implementation of this policy. The bill restricted the amount of vacant urban land that one could hold and nullified the ownership of 'excess' lands. The Council of Guardians rejected the bill. The thrust of its argument was a verse from the Quran requiring believers to 'traffic and trade by mutual consent',[25] a saying of Mohammad to the same effect, and the 'established principle' that 'people have control over their possessions'.[26] Hashemi Rafsanjani, then the Speaker of the Majles, and a number of prominent members of the Islamic Republic appealed to Ayatollah Khomeini. In a letter to the Majles on 11 October 1981, Ayatollah Khomeini invoked the principle of 'secondary rulings' (*ahkam-e sanaviyyeh*) under conditions of 'urgency' (*zororat*), and gave the Majles the authority to decide the urgency of matters. That is, the Majles was empowered to pass laws that were inconsistent with the primary rulings of Islam (*ahkam-e avvaliyyeh*) if the passage of these laws were necessary for the preservation of the Muslim society. The Majles declared 'urgency' and forwarded the law to the Council of Guardians, which approved it in March 1982, under the principle of 'secondary rulings'; but only for five years and with the proviso that the state must compensate the owners of *bayer* and *dayer* (reclaimed and in-use) lands.[27] The Council of Guardians, however, refused to approve several versions of the law concerned with the redistribution of agricultural land (even under the 'secondary rulings' principle) and nationalization of foreign trade (even though explicitly mentioned in the constitution). It also refused to approve the labour law and the extension of the urban land law.[28]

The position of the Council of Guardians was supported by the bazaar merchants, the industrialists and the proprietors, who considered the domination of the state over the economy a serious restraint on their activities. This idea – associated with Bazargan's Freedom Movement in the early post-revolutionary period – was successfully championed by a growing vocal and powerful faction of the clergy with strong Islamic revolutionary credentials, and with overwhelming justification in the tradition of Islamic jurisprudence. This faction also opposed the usual government controls found in the modern developed and underdeveloped capitalist economies.

An important example of this is the Council of Guardians' objection to the labour law that was passed after much debate by the Majles in November 1988. The Council's objections were based on the jurisprudential interpretation that a wage contract is a private matter between employer and employee, and the state cannot compel either party to accept any conditions or limitations. The Council believed that all restrictions on the wage rate, other compensation for workers, child labour and maximum hours of work were un-Islamic.[29] Furthermore, in a confrontation between the export merchants and the Bank Markazi Iran, the merchants argued that the state had no legal right according to Islamic jurisprudence to require them to surrender their exchange earnings to the Bank Markazi at the official exchange rate. With the backing of the Grand Ayatollahs, the merchants succeeded in 1983 to convince the Bank Markazi to limit its exchange-control policy to the state's earnings from the export of oil.[30]

The confrontation gave rise to a controversy of traditional-versus-dynamic jurisprudence (*fiqh-e sonnati va fiqh-e poya*). The populist-statist ideas were stated by Muhammad Baqir Sadr, a Shi'i jurist from Iraq, and Mortaza Motahhari, a prominent theoretician of the Islamic Republic, who maintained that the precepts of Islam must be interpreted in the light of the modern conditions in a capitalist society.[31] Sadr and Motahhari argued that what was permissible at the time of Mohammad may not be so now because market relations have changed. They prescribe a role that allows the state to intervene in the economy in order to maintain the Islamic 'social balance according to Sadar'. Opponents, however, rely on a strict traditional interpretation of Islamic jurisprudence. But the issue could not be settled by political debate, and the opposing Grand Ayatollahs were not willing to budge. In fact, Motahhari's book on Islamic economics was banned after pressure from Qom.[32] The debate over the definition of an Islamic economic system was never resolved during Ayatollah Khomeini's lifetime.

The War and the Normalization Process

The economic imperatives in maintaining and consolidating political power, especially in the context of war mobilization, forced the regime into ad hoc reactions in order to mitigate the social manifestations of the economic crisis. This resulted in an iterative process of adjustment toward normalization of the production process within the existing structure of the Iranian economy.[33] The process has been marked by the regime's acceptance of pragmatic economic solutions, abatement of its initial populist-utopian claims for restructuring the economy, and the convergence of the main factions within the regime.

Beginning in 1981 and following the consolidation of power in the Islamic Republic and in response to the war mobilization effort, property rights were substantially restored as nationalization and official expropriation subsided and takeovers were no longer tolerated. Militant workers' councils were replaced by compliant Islamic workers' councils, causing many agreements with transnational corporations to be reinstated or renewed. Between 1981 and 1984, the economy expanded (see Tables 4.1 and 4.2). By 1984, value-added in industry (in 1982 prices) reached the 1977 level, value-added in manufacturing was 14 per cent above that of 1977, but value-added in construction had declined by 17 per cent. Government investment in construction in 1984 was less than one-half of the 1977 level, while that of the private sector had increased by 18 per cent (mainly as the result of the increase in construction of low-income houses, followed by redistribution and the takeover of urban land and general disregard for the zoning laws). Compared to 1977, non-oil GDP had increased by 17 per cent and investment had increased considerably since 1980, although it was still less than in 1977 (see Tables 4.1 and 4.2).

In the 1981–84 recovery the inequality gap began to widen. The ratio of the expenditures of the wealthiest to that of the poorest 20 per cent of urban households, which had declined from 14.7 in 1977 to 9.1 in 1980, increased to 11.4 in 1984. The change in the ratio of the top 10 per cent to the bottom 10 per cent of urban households was more remarkable: the wealthiest 10 per cent consumed 31 times as much as the poorest 10 per cent in 1977; this ratio declined to 17.9 in 1980 but returned to the pre-revolutionary level by 1983. A similar pattern occurred in the rural inequality gap between 1979 and 1984.[34]

The populist-statist faction, unable to get its economic bills through the Council of Guardians, managed to take advantage of the mobilization for war to increase the state's control of the war economy by several measures such as price control and rationing. Implementation of these measures, however, confronted the resistance of the private sector and the political opposition of the conservative faction. Meanwhile, black markets were thriving, and benefits from government licensing of activities and outright corruption were increasing.

Intensification of the Economic Crisis and the Rise of Pragmatism

Significant instruments of economic control have been the allocation of exchange earnings from oil exports, import licensing, and the management of the nationalized sector of the economy. The legitimacy of the government's power to exercise control over the economy by these and other means was repeatedly questioned by the conservatives. The decline in oil revenues, which began in 1984, intensified their attack and diminished the financial resources of the government.

The Iranian economy is highly dependent on oil revenues. In the early 1980s these accounted for 95 per cent of exchange earnings. With the decline of oil revenues, the economy and the government confronted a serious constraint. More than 80 per cent of Iranian imports are intermediate products and capital goods, most of which are used in Iranian manufacturing industry. In 1983, over one-half of the total value of primary and intermediate inputs into Iranian industries were imported products. In 1979–84 for every 1000 rials of value-added in manufacturing, $5.38 of imported inputs were needed.[35] In 1984, oil revenues began to decline sharply, from $21 billion in 1983 to less than $14 billion in 1985, and to only $6 billion in 1986 (see Table 4.3). Between 1981 and 1984, as production was resumed through the war mobilization effort, Iran imported, on average, $16 billion a year. From 1985 to 1988, however, Iran could not import any more than $10 to $12 billion a year. Even with this decline in imports, the current-account balance showed a large deficit amounting to $5 billion in 1986.[36] Iran had to rely on its foreign-exchange reserves, and began using short-term credit to finance its current-account deficit. Iran's imports of capital goods declined from about $4 billion in 1983 and 1984 to about $2 billion a year between 1985 and 1988. Similarly, annual imports of intermediate products decreased from about $8 billion a year in the early post-revolutionary years to about $5 billion in 1986–88.[37]

The decline in imports resulted in a contraction in industries, and a decline in output and employment throughout the economy (see Tables

Table 4.3 Balance of Payments 1977–1992 (US$ million)

	1977	1980	1984	1985	1986	1987	1988	1989	1990	1991	1992
Exports, merchandise	21,521	12,338	17,087	14,175	7171	11,916	10,709	13,081	19,305	18,415	19,279
Oil and gas	20,926	11,693	16,726	13,710	6255	10,755	9673	12,037	17,993	15,802	16,343
Non-oil products	595	645	361	465	916	1161	1036	1044	1312	2613	2936
Imports, merchandise	−17,968	−10,888	−14,494	−12,006	−10,585	−12,005	−10,608	−13,448	−18,330	−23,941	−21,150
Intermediate and capital goods (%)	(82)	(73)	(84)	(86)	(82)	(82)	(82)	(82)	(87)	(88)	(na)
Trade balance	3553	1450	2593	2169	−3414	−89	101	−367	975	−5526	−1871
Current-account balance	1293	−2434	1924	−476	−5156	−2090	−1869	−191	327	−7826	−4651

Source: Bankl Markazi, *Economic Report and Balance Sheet,* various issues.

4.1 and 4.2). Between 1984 and 1988 all major economic activities, except agriculture, continued to decline. Non-oil GDP, in 1982 prices, declined by 8.2 per cent in 1986, 4.1 per cent in 1987, and 7.8 per cent in 1988.[38] In total, between 1985 and 1988 the economy shrank by 19 per cent.[39] Since the agricultural sector grew during this period, albeit at the rate of about 1 per cent a year, most of the economic contraction was experienced in the urban economy. Large manufacturing enterprises (those with more than 50 workers), which relied heavily on imported intermediate products, suffered the sharpest decline (see Chapter 5). Between 1984 and 1988 their output decreased by 32 per cent, and their productivity by 30 per cent.[40] Investments during this period declined even more sharply – to less than half the 1988 rate. This sharp decline was even more pronounced in investments in machinery since most of these investments are spent on imported capital goods (see Table 4.2).

In addition to the decline in output and investment, imports of consumer goods – which the regime relied on to remedy domestic shortages and to provide some politically sensitive items of mass consumption – had to be curtailed from $2.9 billion in 1983 to $1.5 billion in 1988. As a result, the rations for many essential consumer products were reduced or discontinued, and prices continued to rise. According to official estimates, the price index for consumer goods and services in urban areas more than doubled between 1984 and 1988 in spite of the strict price-control measures in effect.[41]

The fall in oil revenues caused an increase in the budget deficit. Import-tax revenues, accounting for one-quarter of the total tax revenues, also declined by about 50 per cent as a result of the fall in imports. Other taxes had to be increased in the government budget to supplement the decline in oil revenues. Consumption taxes remained an important source of revenue (about 16 to 20 per cent of all tax revenues in these years). For example, taxes on soft drinks more than tripled between 1984 and 1988, reaching 29.1 billion rials, while real-estate taxes amounted to only 14.5 billion rials. Taxes on cigarettes increased to 92.8 billion rials, exceeding the revenue from proprietors' income taxes (86.5 billion rials). Nevertheless, the budget deficit increased from 639 billion rials in 1984 to 2125 billion rials in 1988 – about half of all government expenditures.[42] This large budget deficit had to be financed entirely by increased liquidity, which has a highly inflationary effect. (Sales of bonds to the public have never been used for deficit financing in the Iranian economy.) The economic toll of the war and the costs of not having an integrated and consistent economic policy became apparent after 1985 when the decline in the oil revenue reduced the ability of the government to manoeuvre out of its immediate economic problems. Thus, the unpopularity of the war and opposition to the government's economic policies increased.

The burden of the foreign-exchange gap was not evenly distributed through the economy. The allocation for war expenses was left almost intact. The industries under government control, and the industrialists and merchants with closer ties to the regime, received favourable quotas. The struggle for foreign-exchange quotas became a matter of survival in the marketplace, a battle to be fought in the government bureaucracy and in the political arena. The clamour for denationalization of industries and reduction of government intervention in the economy became more intense in the bazaar and other business circles, in *Resalat*, the vocal fundamentalist opposition newspaper, and even among the deputies in the Majles. The unrealistically ambitious economic plan, which took three years to be debated by the two factions in the High Economic Council and the cabinet and was held up for another two and half years in the Planning Committee of the Majles, was finally scrapped in 1986. In its place a more pragmatic plan, utilizing available capacities within the existing economic structure, was passed by the Majles on 31 January 1990.[43]

Frustrated in its effort to get its reform bills passed and to exert control over the private sector, the populist-statist faction began to see pragmatism as a means for survival. That is, the dominant faction in the Islamic Republic began to work within existing circumstances in order to maintain the state's position in the economy, to preserve the institutions established since the revolution, and to confront the most conservative opposition elements.

The first step was to end the war with Iraq. Hashemi Rafsanjani outlined the Islamic Republic's acceptance of the cease-fire. In his Friday prayer sermon in August 1991, he said:

> We had serious difficulties in the economic aspects of the war. I still cannot tell you everything. I will tell you some and history will tell you the rest.... We had a letter from the Minister of Economy and others who were responsible for the economy. We discussed it in the cabinet and took it to Imam [Khomeini].... The letter said that we had reached the red line in the use of our economic resources and budget. It said we had gone even below the red line, and people can't take it any more. We could not tell you that then, but I can say it now that the Governor of Bank Markazi wrote to us saying that although foreigners do not lend to us and we do not borrow from them, we have $12 billion in debts that we have to pay.[44]

On 20 July 1988, Ayatollah Khomeini drank his 'cup of hemlock', and accepted the UN cease-fire Resolution 598.[45]

In its transformation toward pragmatism, the populist-statist faction began to abandon its commitment to economic restructuring and reform. The original orientation within the populist-statist philosophy, nevertheless, still remained a strong – although diminishing – force within the government. It was particularly strong in the same institutions that had contributed the most to the political survival of the regime in the earlier years

– the 'revolutionary foundation' and the state-run media. Radical Muslim intellectuals managed to maintain their strength in the 1988 parliamentary elections. They were able to acquire *fatwas* from Ayatollah Khomeini in 1987, legitimizing, on jurisdictional grounds, certain types of intervention in the economy by the state. They were able to subject the decisions of the Council of the Guardians to the ruling of a newly devised higher authority (not foreseen in the constitution), the Council of Expediency (Showra-ye Maslahat). Thus the populist-statists succeeded in passing the controversial labour law in spite of the opposition of the Council of Guardians. They also succeeded in disrupting the efforts of the Islamic Republic to acquire foreign loans and investment from European concerns by instigating the Salman Rushdie affair in the spring of 1989. But they were not successful in implementing any major policies, and economic circumstances clearly favoured the tide of pragmatism. Increasing employment and output, and reconstruction of war damage, had become immediate tasks that the Islamic Republic had to accomplish in the face of increasing mass dissatisfaction.

Corruption, clientalism and the war economy accelerated the accumulation process in certain activities in spite of the general contraction of the economy in the post-revolutionary years. The lion's share of the benefits had been acquired by those who had enjoyed close ties with the regime. The bourgeoisie as a whole, which felt deprived of its 'fair share' prior to the revolution, attempted to block the rapid oligopolization of the market by the more privileged segments of its ranks, who clustered around a number of seemingly 'non-profit' giant conglomerates.[46] The bourgeoisie wanted to increase its own growth by demanding denationalization of industries and a major reduction in government control.

Such demands were particularly appealing to the urban population, disenchanted with revolutionary rhetoric and ineffective short-term economic policies. They were eager to see some prosperity and were tired of waiting in long lines for food rations. At the aggregate level, the problem can be seen by looking at some vital statistics reflecting the decline in living standards in the post-revolutionary years (see Table 4.4). In 1977, national income per capita (in 1982 prices) was 292,000 rials; in 1989 it was only 150,800 rials. Since the rate of inflation was higher than the official rate, the decline was even sharper. This setback was experienced in an economy where a decade earlier, thanks to the oil revenues, national income per capita, in real terms, had almost quadrupled and private consumption expenditure had more than doubled. Between 1977 and 1988, per-capita private consumption in the urban economy fell by 30 per cent, and in the rural economy by 19 per cent. Meanwhile, urban unemployment increased from 4.4 per cent in 1977 to 13.4 per cent in 1984 and 18.9 per cent in 1988. The disenfranchised as well as the underprivileged and the households in the lowest 10 percentile by income suffered. The size of

Table 4.4 A Profile of Changes 1965–1991

	1965	1977	1988	1991
Population (million)	25.1	34.7	52.7	55.8
Oil revenue per capita (current US$)	24	602	203	283
National income per capita				
(1974 IR)	26,800	105,700	–	–
(1982 IR)	–	292,000	190,800	190,800
Private consumption expenditure per capita				
(1974 IR)	19,300	48,900	–	–
(1982 IR)	–	151,700	177,200	148,300
Urban (1982 IR)	–	207,200	143,600	166,700[a]
Rural (1982 IR)	–	100,200	81,500	102,400[a]
Unemployment				
Urban (%)	–	4.4	18.9	20.6[b]
Rural (%)	–	13.4	9.2	6.3[b]

Notes: [a] 1990 figures. [b] 1990 estimates according to Bank Markazi, *Economic Report and Balance Sheet* (1990), p. 86. In *Economic Report and Balance Sheet* (1991), p. 84, these numbers are changed to 11.4% (urban) and 12.3% (rural).

Source: Bank Markazi, *Economic Report and Balance Sheet*, various issues.

the decline in consumption and the rate of unemployment was so large that a broad segment of the urban population was affected. The gains in the pre-revolutionary decade of prosperity were eroded, especially for urban households. The effect of the economic crisis on the rural population, however, was not so adverse. This was partly due to the agricultural sector, which had managed to expand when other sectors had stagnated or declined. Moreover, the high rate of rural-to-urban migration has shifted some of the rural poverty and unemployment to the urban centres.

The fall in per-capita national income is sharper than in per-capita personal consumption, partly because the value of social services and public goods decreased more than personal consumption. Government expenditures (in 1982 prices) declined by 40 per cent between 1977 and 1988, in spite of the added cost of the war with Iraq.[47]

Complete normalization of the production process in Iran hinges upon the availability of imported industrial inputs. The postwar reconstruction effort magnified the foreign-exchange gap. By 1988, it became clear to the Islamic Republic that external financing was unavoidable, especially as long as the glut on the oil market continued. Foreign borrowing was still viewed as 'selling the country to foreigners' by many in the Islamic Republic.[48] According to the First Economic Plan, Iran was expected to rely on $28 billion external financing over the duration of the plan (1989–93).[49] This estimate was based on the projection that the non-oil exports of Iran would be about $17.8 billion in the five years of the plan.[50] In spite of many generous export-promotion schemes, however, in the first four years of the plan the value of non-oil exports totalled only $7.9 billion (see Table 4.3). It must be noted that the non-oil exports of Iran have a high import content. According to a report by the Ministry of Agriculture, for example, foreign-exchange requirements for producing a tonne of apples is $460, for oil seeds $319, and for almonds $981.[51] Production and exports of these goods are profitable because in the system of multiple exchange rates the producers pay for foreign-exchange (to import their inputs) at a fraction of the price that they would get from selling their foreign exchange earnings (from exporting their products). The same situation is also true for some manufactured exports. Therefore, the net foreign-exchange earning of non-oil exports is significantly less than the value of these exports indicates. In other words, some of the non-oil exports are no more than 'exports of the oil revenues, repackaged in another form'.[52] Obviously, only a small number of enterprises (such as the Foundation for the Oppressed) have benefited from this profitable arrangement.

The various schemes that the Islamic Republic developed to produce the substantial external financing that it requires, and to make foreign borrowing politically more palatable, entail extensive direct participation of foreign capital in the Iranian economy. External financing, whether borrowing or investments, was, however, deeply objectionable to those in the populist-statist faction who had not been swayed by the tide of pragmatism in the Islamic Republic. They saw it, as was repeatedly stated in editorials and feature articles in *Kayhan*, and in speeches by some members of the Islamic Republic, as the critical step toward the reconstruction of 'the dependent economy of Iran under the Shah'. They believed that 'Our borders must not be opened to dependent capitalism.'[53] This was a slogan of the revolution, whose validity had obviously expired, as Hashemi Rafsanjani explained in his Friday prayer sermon on 12 January 1990. He stated that as long as foreign investment or borrowing was used in productive projects they would not be detrimental to the economy.[54] A symbolically significant move toward normalization of international financial relations with Iran was the Islamic Republic's reception of the World Bank–International Monetary Fund (IMF) mission to Iran in June 1990. This was the first World Bank–IMF mission to Iran since the 1979 revolution, and was followed by subsequent visits by these two international financial agencies.

The move toward external financing has had two important immediate implications. First, it was viewed as a reflection of the failure of the populist-statist faction. Second, it not only necessitated a more cooperative posture on the part of the Islamic Republic, but it also required a clear demonstration of progress toward free market conditions in the domestic economy. In fact, as the 1990 World Bank–IMF mission reported, the Islamic Republic officials 'expressed their determination to move forward with broadly based macroeconomic adjustment, encompassing a strengthened role for the private sector and a step-by-step opening up of the economy'.[55] The accelerated move to return nationalized enterprises to the private sector, the reduction in consumer subsidies, and the liberalization of foreign-exchange controls in 1990–91 were clear indications of the Islamic Republic's determination to move toward the 'macroeconomic adjustment' of the World Bank–IMF type.[56] The World Bank's loan of $250 million in March of 1991 was the first indication that the Islamic Republic was making progress toward 'macroeconomic adjustment'.[57] By May 1994, the World Bank had approved $850 million for various projects in Iran.[58]

Transformation of Iranian Politics: The Dominance of Pragmatism

The death of Ayatollah Khomeini accelerated the growth of the pragmatist trend. His occasional condemnation of 'Satanic states', his frequent praise of the 'oppressed', and emphasis of ideals of the revolution nourished the remaining populist-statists within the Islamic Republic. Without Khomeini, the populist-statist tendencies waned more quickly. Ironically, the remaining elements within the populist-statist faction could rely on little popular support. This faction had been associated for more than a decade with a government that was contemptuous, repressive, bureaucratic and arbitrary. It pursued an adventurous war. It brutally repressed political opposition among the revolutionary forces. It strangulated the cultural existence of many segments of the Iranian population. It failed to fulfil many of its major promises to the peasants, the urban poor and the working class. It nurtured a flourishing culture of clientalism and corruption. For its part, the bourgeoisie, represented by a pragmatist tendency, presented itself as the force of social, cultural and economic rejuvenation. It opposed bureaucratic corruption, arbitrary economic intervention and regulation of the state; and promised the rule of law and reason. Its political platform was peace, economic prosperity, employment, and, no less significant, 'a kinder and gentler nation'. These slogans were appealing, not only to the bourgeoisie and the urban middle class, but also to the mass of urban poor, who had gained little from the Islamic Republic, and which in turn saw them as little more than a reserve army of potential martyrs.

Pragmatists recognized by 1988 the inevitability of the victory of a 'moderate' faction, particularly in its less fundamentalist form, as represented by Mehdi Bazargan and his Freedom Movement of Iran.[59] Hashemi Rafsanjani, the president and leading exponent of the pragmatist ideology, acted until about 1986 as the leader of the populist-statist faction. In 1982 he came under serious attack by bazaar merchants (who distributed his picture with a red-coloured turban) as a socialist mullah. The bazaar merchants were particularly upset about his Friday prayer sermons on economic justice, which summarized Muhammad Baqir Sadr's book on Islamic economics.[60] This attack, supported by the conservative clergy, was so strong that for many weeks Ayatollah Mahdavi Kani replaced Hashemi Rafsanjani as the Imam of Tehran's Friday prayers.

In the early post-revolutionary years, Hashemi Rafsanjani repeatedly voiced the frustration of the majority of the Majles deputies about the conservative jurisprudential interpretations of the Council of Guardians and its opposition to several reform bills passed by the Majles. Opportunism, *realpolitik*, or whatever else may be the cause of Hashemi Rafsanjani's political metamorphosis, the fact remains that by 1990 pragmatism had become the dominant ideology of the Islamic Republic. Hashemi Rafsanjani was elected as the president of the Islamic Republic in July 1989, and was given extended powers as the position of prime minister was eliminated from the constitution at the same time.

The elimination of a number of ardent supporters of the populist-statist ideology from their positions of power in 1989 and 1990, including Ahmad Khomeini (Ayatollah Khomeini's son), Mir Hosein Mosavi (former prime minister), Abdol-Karim Musavi-Ardebili (former head of the Supreme Judicial Council), Mohammad Musavi-Kho'iniha (former prosecutor-general), Ali-Akbar Mohtashami (former minister of the interior) and Behzad Nabavi (former minister of heavy industries), was a manifestation of the dominance of pragmatism in the Islamic Republic. The struggle within the regime was still not over, however; the remaining advocates of the populist-statist ideology were still active. In 1991 they had 70 members in the Majles (from a total of 270 deputies), but they managed to muster a majority on certain issues by forming alliances with other interest groups.[61] They hoped to reorganize for a possible comeback while at the same time restraining Hashemi Rafsanjani from implementing his pragmatic policies of normalization of production in the domestic economy and the complete restoration of international economic ties with Europe and the United States. Occasional speeches in the parliament, the proclamations of Ali Khamene'i, the Leader of the Revolution, and statements by deposed high-ranking officials of the Islamic Republic were all indicators of the continuing struggle within the regime.

Ups and Downs on the Road to Liberalization

The Persian Gulf war was a blessing for Hashemi Rafsanjani's pragmatist faction, 'Ado shavad sabab-e kheyr agar khoda khahad! (A foe ['ado] may bring you grace, God willing). 'Ado came to the rescue at a critical point in the transformation of post-revolutionary politics in Iran and accelerated the Islamic Republic's move toward the establishment of a new economic order. The disruption in the production and export of oil by Iraq and Kuwait caused oil prices to rise. Consequently, Iran's oil revenues increased just when the Islamic Republic seriously needed foreign exchange to carry on its reconstruction programme and pull the economy out of its post-revolutionary decline.[62] Oil production in Iran in 1990 increased to 3.2 million barrels a day from a low of 2.2 million barrels a day in 1986[63] (see also Chapter 6). The price of Iranian light crude oil in the spot market increased from $13 in 1986 to around $20 per barrel in 1990.[64] The oil revenues of Iran in 1990 and 1991 increased to $18 billion and $16 billion, respectively, in spite of a decline in the price of oil in 1991, and remained above $16 billion in 1992 (see Table 4.3). This substantial increase in oil revenues (from $10 billion in 1988) generated the growth of the oil-dependent economy of Iran. Imports increased from $11 billion in 1988 to $24 billion in 1991 (see Table 4.3). Meanwhile, non-oil GDP grew by 8.5 per cent in 1990, 10.4 per cent in 1991 and 7.0 per cent in 1992. The increase in oil revenues and the resulting economic growth created an aura of optimism and enabled the Islamic Republic to muster support for its policy of economic liberalization, and to further weaken the populist elements within the regime.

The liberalization policy of the Islamic Republic included unification of exchange rates, adoption of a floating exchange-rate system, privatization of nationalized enterprises, decontrolling of prices, and elimination of subsidies. The mainstream view of this standard World Bank–IMF prescription was that by allowing competition into the marketplace, and by making prices a true indicator of the scarcity of resources, productivity and profitability would increase, production would expand, consumption growth would be contained, imports would decrease, and exports would increase; as a result the economy would grow, employment would increase and the foreign-exchange gap would be eliminated. To reach this state of economic fitness the economy needs to undergo a painful period of adjustment, which may be likened, metaphorically, to a patient 'sweating out' the fever after having taken medicine. However, if the case is very complicated, a large dose of medicine may cause convulsions and death; on the other hand, if the dosage is reduced a relapse is unavoidable. Such is the story of Iran's experience with the standard liberalization policy.

Iran's multiple exchange-rate policy was an instrument of the Islamic Republic's industrial and social policy. It served two basic aims: first, to run an industrial structure highly dependent on imports; and second, to minimize erosion of the standard of living of the Iranian population in a stagnating (and even declining) economy with a high rate of population growth. The artificially low foreign-exchange price provided Iranian industries with low-cost imported inputs. The manufacturing enterprises were established between the mid-1960s and the mid-1970s when 'cheap' foreign exchange was ever more abundant, thanks to the increasing volume and price of Iranian oil exports.

Since the largest proportion of Iranian imports are industrial inputs, and since there are few domestic substitutes for these imports, Iran's demand for imports (and thus for foreign exchange) has a relatively low elasticity. Therefore only a large devaluation will result in a significant decrease in imports. On the other hand, a devaluation would have only a small effect on exports earnings because the export of crude oil is not affected by exchange-rate changes.[65] Non-oil exports constitute such a small fraction of the total value of exports that only major increases in their earning can have an appreciable effect on Iran's exchange earnings. The issue is exacerbated by the fact that non-oil exports have a large import content. Putting together the demand for, and supply of, foreign exchange to overcome even a small foreign-exchange gap necessitates a large devaluation. This is not to say that a devaluation does not have a positive impact on the size of the foreign-exchange gap: it does; but because of low elasticities both on the inpayment and outpayment side, the foreign-exchange market has a low degree of responsiveness to exchange-rate changes.[66] However, a devaluation large enough to overcome the foreign-exchange gap will have drastic effects on an economy so dependent on imports. For example, a 200 per cent devaluation of the rial may increase by as much as 100 per cent the input cost of an establishment that imports half of its inputs.[67] With little substitution of domestic inputs possible, it is highly improbable that such a large increase in cost could be absorbed by the increase in the efficiency in production, which may result, for example, from privatization of these enterprises. Simply put, many enterprises depending on imported inputs will have to shut down. The widespread price effect of such a devaluation could shock the economy.

The resulting price increase will cause a reduction in demand for imported and high-import-content consumer goods. This impact would be significant only to the extent that government price control on imported goods were effective before the devaluation. The goods that were sold in the black (or free) market would not have an appreciable price increase since their prices would already reflect the scarcity of the foreign exchange.[68] Therefore, whatever decrease there may be in the demand for imported (or import-based) products is due only to the reduced demand by those who managed to receive these products at official prices.

The political implications of a devaluation policy in these circumstances is clear. The privileged industrialists and merchants – who received cheap foreign-exchange quotas – and the wide array of consumers who received goods at official prices would be most directly affected. The first group (including, among others, the Foundation for the Oppressed, other quasi-state enterprises and the cronies of the regime) cannot openly defend their privileged positions and may easily negotiate with the state for other economic privileges. The second group, 'the consumers', will be the losers. They will end up paying for the promise of having a better job (or just a job) somewhere in the economy, by enduring the devastatingly high rate of inflation. Other policies to reduce domestic absorption by measures such as cutting direct government subsidies for essential food items and increasing the cost of government services would have a positive impact toward decreasing the foreign-exchange gap by squeezing 'the consumer' – the base of the Islamic Republic.

The Islamic Republic began a gradual liberalization of the foreign-exchange market in 1990 (see Chapter 7). In 1991 the cabinet issued a communiqué announcing the privatization of nearly 400 enterprises.[69] Meanwhile, the government abandoned much of its control over the price of goods produced by the private sector. These liberalization measures were implemented at a time of rising oil revenues. In March 1993, and with confidence inspired by favourable conditions in the world oil market, the Islamic Republic moved to unify the exchange rates by floating the rial from $1 = IR 70 (used mostly for government orders) and $1 = IR 600 (for favoured enterprises which had received an exchange quota) to a 'float' of $1 = IR 1542. As prices began to rise in response to the sharp devaluation, the oil revenue began to decline. At the same time, a loan crisis, resulting from overdue letters of credit used to finance the large value of imports, which had surfaced in January 1993, became a crucial factor constraining the Islamic Republic's foreign-exchange credit. With a foreign-exchange crunch, the value of the rial continued to fall in the free market. By late May 1994, the exchange rate had dropped to $1 = IR 2850, and consequently the Bank Markazi resumed its control of the foreign-exchange market.[70] Meanwhile, price increases generated a strong opposition. In the parliament this opposition was directed toward the government for raising, or intending to raise, the price of goods and services it provided – such as water, electricity, telephone, mail, airline and train tickets, and most importantly petroleum products. (See Chapter 6). In January 1994, the Majles deputies rejected the government's proposed increases in the price of petroleum products. Immediately, the minister of commerce announced a moratorium on increases in the price of goods provided by the government. In April 1994 a number of deputies introduced a bill which required that any future price increase for goods and services be approved by the Majles.[71] Thus, as the exchange control was restored, a cap on price movements was also restored. Moreover, many subsidies were to continue in the next five-year plan.[72]

Conclusion: The Crisis Continues

Implementation of the economic liberalization policy has had some strong social welfare implications. Realigning the foreign-exchange rate, decontrolling prices and cutting subsidies has given rise to an inflationary spiral that will seriously erode the standard of living of a large segment of the population. Meanwhile, privatization of nationalized enterprises and reduction in the size of government bureaucracy has resulted in an increase in the rate of urban unemployment, which has accentuated the decline in the standard of living. But as prices increase and employment falls, consumption also declines, as only those who can afford the new prices received the goods, without the long queues and the inconveniences of rationing. When production is 'absorbed' at a much higher market price, profits soar. Such a policy changes the distributive shares in an economy, increasing the portion that goes to profitmakers and reducing the income of wage earners. The first serves to increase investment, and the second makes the allocation of real resources from consumption to investment possible. This clearly implies a shift in the political base of the Islamic Republic, which still presents itself as a revolutionary government.

The harsh impact of the liberalization policy on a large segment of the population has intensified both the popular opposition to the regime and the factional conflicts within the Islamic Republic. There is no longer an authoritative political figure comparable to Ayatollah Khomeini, who could contain the internal feuds in the regime and appeal to the masses for their support. It is doubtful that even Ayatollah Khomeini could have made this political turnaround a smooth process, as his power seemed to lie in making crisis a sustainable state of affairs. So far, the Islamic

Republic has been engaged in dispersing its internal opposition while attempting to appease certain crucial groups in the urban economy. In the elections for the Fourth Majles in April 1992, Hashemi Rafsanjani and his allies managed to purge a large number of proponents of the populist-statist policies. In those elections only 79 deputies, of the 270, were re-elected. Those who were considered 'unreformed' were either disqualified by the Council of Guardians or were not elected. Former deputies such as Fazel Harandi, Mohammad Salamati, Mortaza Alviri, Mehdi Karubi, Sadeq Khalkhali, Hadi Khamene'i, Asadollah Bayat, Abolqasem Sarhadizadeh, Atefeh Reja'i and Abbas Duzduzani lost their seats. Most notable among those who lost the elections were Ali Akbar Mohtashami and Mohammad Musavi Kho'iniha, leading figures of the populist-statist faction opposing the pragmatist ideology in the Islamic Republic.[73] Meanwhile, the regime has shown a high degree of flexibility in trying to mitigate the economic impacts of the liberalization policy, even though it contradicts overall policy objectives. It extended a number of salary increases to civil servants, increased the minimum wage rate, and negotiated with striking workers. Most importantly, it retreated from its policies toward exchange-rate unification, decontrolling prices and cutting subsidies. The Islamic Republic seems to be pursuing a gradualist strategy in its liberalization policy.

Any success in this strategy hinges on the state's ability to secure an environment for investment. This implies that the state must demonstrate its commitment to pursuing a consistent policy without frequent retreats and turnarounds. Furthermore, the state must intervene in the market to make it more attractive for capital. The conservative demand for *laissez faire* is only an expression of opposition to those interventions that hinder capital accumulation. In modern capitalist economies the state takes on extensive interventionist policies to facilitate capital accumulation. In a post-revolutionary economy, where many institutions of the market have been weakened and many policies that promote capital accumulation have been condemned and abandoned, the state must intervene to provide safety and security and, above all, a high rate of profit for capital.

The Islamic Republic has already found itself compelled to intervene in the market to stimulate investment; avenues for foreign investment have been more welcoming than in the pre-revolutionary period. The Majles is now considering a bill that proposes to extend to foreign capital further assurances and more attractive investment conditions than the pre-revolutionary foreign-investment law provided.[74] As the chairman of Iran's Chamber of Commerce has stated, with the new exchange rate 'Iran is one of the world's cheapest countries for foreign investment.'[75] The nationalized industries are being offered wholesale to domestic and foreign bidders. Even petroleum and petrochemical industries have been opened up to private investment. Yet, neither foreign nor domestic capital have responded enthusiastically to the invitation. Capitalists sense the limits of economic growth and profitability in Iran. They demand government guarantees of more favourable conditions; an unequivocal commitment to promotion of an unregulated market; and a 'less restrictive' labour law. The state is expected to provide direct inducements for investment. This implies the implementation of measures such as tariffs; monopolistic barriers for protection of the newly established and privatized enterprises by overt means such as licensing of industries; and favourable credit and tax schemes. A major dilemma that the Islamic Republic will encounter is that the large manufacturing enterprises in Iran, because of their high dependence on imported inputs, must have access to 'cheap' foreign exchange in order to operate profitably. Therefore, short of a miraculously large increase in oil revenues, the Islamic Republic will find it necessary to remain in a system of multiple exchange rates, unless it chooses to rely on more transparent subsidies to favoured enterprises. These enticements will, once again, create an exclusive and privileged domain of large modern enterprises.

The crisis continues. The regime's internal opposition presses on for more controlling power. With the riots in Mashhad, Arak, Zahedan, Tabriz and Qazvin, and the open expressions of dissatisfaction by the urban population, public discontent is becoming a more serious concern in the Islamic Republic. Hashemi Rafsanjani and his alliance of pragmatists had hoped to phase in the economic reform quickly enough for its expected fruits to appear before the fermenting of a mass social protest. If that expectation is not realized (and there is no indication that it will be) social protest will intensify – especially among the popular base of the Islamic Republic.[76] With an already heavy foreign debt amounting to between $17 to $20 billion, the duration of this phase of the crisis will depend, more than anything else, on the international oil market. High oil revenues of around $16–18 billion will enable the Islamic Republic to continue in its present state. A major decline in these revenues will, however, invite some abrupt changes in Iran. A complete repudiation of past policies and a full-force effort to maintain the liberalization policy are highly probable outcomes. Thus the Islamic Republic may be tempted to close off the possibilities of public protest available at the moment to its conditional allies. Shifts and shufflings in the position of opposing factions within the regime is the other possibility. This would only prolong the economic crisis. The road taken in the past 16 years has brought the Islamic Republic to a dead end. Its only way to survive is to negate itself.

The theocracy that claimed to be the government of the oppressed has no way other than to crown itself a 'run of the mill' capitalist state. *Enna lellah wa enna 'eleyhe raja'on.*

Notes

1. This is distinct from the recurrent economic fluctuations in capitalist economies.

2. For a review of the post-revolutionary economic crisis in other countries, see, among others, Boorstein, Edward, *The Economic Transformation of Cuba* (New York: Monthly Review Press, 1968); Sweezy, Paul, and Harry Magdoff (eds), *Revolution and Counter-Revolution in Chile* (New York: Monthly Review Press, 1974); and Spalding, Rose J., *The Political Economy of Revolutionary Nicaragua* (Boston: Allen and Unwin, 1987).

3. Skocpol, Theda, *State and Social Revolution* (Cambridge, MA: Harvard University Press, 1979).

4. Keddie, Nikki, *The Roots of Revolution: An Interpretive History of Modern Iran* (New Haven, CT: Yale University Press, 1981), ch 9; Parsa, Misagh, *Social Origin of the Iranian Revolution* (New York: Rutgers University Press, 1989); and Moaddel, Mansoor, *Class Politics, and Ideology in the Iran Revolution* (New York: Columbia University Press, 1993).

5. See Kuran, Timur, 'Economic impact of Islamic fundamentalism', in Martin E. Marty and R. Scott Appleby (eds), *Fundamentalism and the State* (Chicago: University of Chicago Press, 1993); Nomani, Farhad, and Ali Rahnema, *Islamic Economic Systems* (London: Zed Books, 1994); and Behdad, Sohrab, 'Islamic economics: A utopian-scholastic-neoclassical-Keynesian synthesis!', *Research in the History of Economic Thought and Methodology*, vol 9 (1992).

6. Behdad, Sohrab, 'A disputed utopia: Islamic economics in revolutionary Iran', *Comparative Studies in Society and History* 36/4 (October 1994).

7. Behdad, Sohrab, 'Property rights in contemporary Islamic economic thought: A critical perspective', *Review of Social Economy* 47/2 (1989), pp 185–211.

8. On principles of the theocratic government of Iran, see Arjomand, Said Amir, *The Turban for the Crown: The Islamic Revolution in Iran* (Oxford: Oxford University Press, 1988), ch 8.

9. Behdad, Sohrab, 'Winners and losers of the Iranian revolution: A study in income distribution', *International Journal of Middle East Studies* 21/3 (1989), p 340.

10. This resolution is reprinted in Khalili, Akbar, *Gam be Gam ba Enqelab* (Tehran: Soroush, 1981), pp 114–16.

11. For a pre-revolutionary statement of Marxist tendencies, see, for example, Jazani, Birhan, *Capitalism and Revolution in Iran* (London: Zed Press, 1980). The original Persian text was published abroad in 1976.

12. For a summary of these demands, see Cherikha-ye Fada'i-ye Khalq, *Negahi be Mobarezat-e Tabaqeh-ye Kargar (23 Bahman 57–11 Ordibehesht-e 59)* (n.p.: Havadaran-e Cherikha-ye Fada'i-ye Khalq dar Uropa, n.d.); and various issues of *Hambastegi: Khabarnameh-ye Moshtarek-e Sazman-e Melli-ye Daneshgahiyan Iran, Kanun-Nevisandegan-e Iran va Komiteh-ye Defa' az Hoquq-e Zendanian-e Siyasi*, published in December 1978 and January 1979.

13. Here, one example will suffice. The demand for nationalization of banks was included in the long list of revolutionary demands when a large demonstration passed by the main building of the Bank Markazi Iran on Ferdowsi Avenue some weeks before the February uprising. Some personnel of the Bank, who were on strike and staging a 'sit-in' in the Bank, appeared at the windows to express their

solidarity with the demonstrators. The Bank employees shouted: 'Banks must be nationalized!' The demonstrators shouted approval and included the slogan on their list of demands. From then on, nationalization of banks became an integral part of many lists of demands.

14. Bayat, Assef, *Workers and Revolution in Iran* (London: Zed Books, 1987); Rahnema, Saeed, 'Work Councils in Iran: The Illusion of Workers Control', *Economic and Industrial Democracy: An International Journal*, 13/1 (1992).

15. Statistical Centre of Iran, *Statistical Yearbook, 1983* (in Persian, Tehran, 1985), pp 434–35.

16. Statistical Centre of Iran, *Statistical Yearbook, 1979* (in Persian, Tehran, 1981), p 746. The data for value-added or output are not available.

17. Bonyad-e Mostaz'afan, *Gozareshi az Bonyad-e Mostaz'afan* (Tehran: n.p., n.d., c. 1983)

18. See Alerasool, Mahvash, *Freezing Assets: The USA and the Most Effective Economic Sanction* (New York: St. Martin's Press, 1993); and Hufbauer, Gary C., Jeffrey J. Schott, and Kimberly A. Elliot, *Economic Sanctions Reconsidered; History and Current Policy* (Washington DC: Institute for International Economics, 1990), pp 153–62.

19. The earlier estimates of Bank Markazi, in 1977 prices, show a larger decline in the level of economic activities in the 1977–80 period. See Bank Markazi, *A Survey of National Economic Conditions after the Revolution* (in Persian, Tehran, n.d., c. 1984), pp 504–5; and compare with Bank Markazi, *National Accounts of Iran (1974–1987)*, (in Persian, Tehran, 1991), pp 148–9.

20. Behdad, 'Winners and losers of the Iranian revolution', pp 339–43.

21. Khomeini, however, confronted Ayatollah Shariatmadari when Shariatmadari challenged the legitimacy of the Islamic Republic.

22. Behdad, Sohrab, 'The political economy of Islamic planning in Iran', in Hooshang Amirahmadi and Manoucher Parvin (eds), *Post-Revolutionary Iran* (Boulder: Westview Press, 1988), p 111.

23. *Constitution of the Islamic Republic of Iran*, trans. Hamid Algar (Berkeley: Mizan Press, 1980), pp 44–5.

24. Ibid., pp 46–7.

25. The Quran, 4:29. Translation by Abdullah Yusuf Ali, *The Meaning of the Holy Quran, Text, Translation and Commentary* (Brentwood, MD: Amana, 1991).

26. Madani, Seyyed Jalaloddin, *Hoquq-e Asasi dar Jomhuri-ye Eslami*, 7 vols (Tehran: Sorush, 1987–1990), Vol 4, pp 199–203.

27. Since acquiring a deed for any *mawat* land has always meant being subject to various acts of reclamation (making the land *dayer*) such as erecting walls, building roads, etc., nearly all the urban land is technically considered as *dayer* or at most *bayer*. For the text of the Urban Land Law see Edareh-ye Koll-e Qavanin, *Majmu'eh-ye Qavanin Avvalin Dowreh-ye Qanungozari-ye Majles-e Showra-ye Eslami* (Tehran: Chapkaneh-ye Majles, 1985) pp 176–9

28. The rulings of the Council of Guardians are collected in Madani, *Hoquq-e Asasi*, Vol 4, pp 177–457, and Vol 7, pp 211–82.

29. For the text of the law that was approved by the Council of Expediency (discussed below) in November 1991, see Rezazadeh-Malek, Rahim, *Qanun-e Kar (Jadid)* (Tehran: Entesharat-e Ordibehesht, 1991). For the views of the Council of Guardians see Madani, *Hoquq-e Asasi*, Vol 7, pp 261–8.

30. See Behdad, Sohrab, 'Foreign exchange gap, structural constraints, and the

political economy of exchange rate determination in Iran', *International Journal of Middle East Studies* 20 /1 (1988), p 19.

31. Sadr, Muhammad Baqir, *Iqtisaduna* (Beirut: Dar al-Fikr, 1968); and Motahhari, Mortaza, *Barresi-ye Ejmali-ye Mabani-ye Eqtesad-e Eslami* (Tehran: Entesharat-e Hekmat 1982). See Behdad, 'A disputed utopia' for a critique of the debate.

32. One hundred thousand copies of Motahhari's book were published (according to the publisher). This book was considered an unauthorized publication of Motahhari's manuscripts and speeches. In December 1986 and in May 1987 *Kayhan Hava'i* published excerpts of Motahhari's manuscripts on capitalism and the use of machinery. The Council for Overseeing Publication of Martyr Motahhari condemned the publication of these speeches and referred to them as an attempt to settle economic disputes (*Ettela'at*,5 May 1987).

33. This will give rise to 'structural involution', by which I mean a process of change involving elaboration of, and entanglement in, the existing economic structure, without the transformation of the economic structure itself. For a theoretical discussion of the manifestations of structural involution, see Behdad, Sohrab, 'Production and employment in Iran: involution and de-industrialisation theses', in Thierry Coville (ed.), *The Economy of Islamic Iran: Between State and Market* (Louvain: Peeters, 1994).

34. Behdad, 'Winners and losers of the Iranian revolution', pp 339–43.

35. Behdad, 'Production and employment in Iran'.

36. This is the total of all transactions for goods and services, payments for return on capital (interest and profit), and unilateral transfers (including the transfers by Iranian workers abroad, and by foreign workers in Iran).

37. Bank Markazi, *Economic Report and the Balance Sheet*, various issues.

38. Ibid.

39. This figure is from Bank Markazi, *National Accounts (1974–1987)* and *National Accounts (1988–1990)*, and reflects the revisions in the statistics reported in the earlier years in the *Economic Report and Balance Sheet*.

40. Bank Markazi, *Survey of Large Manufacturing Enterprises, 1991* (in Persian, Tehran, 1993), p 17.

41. Bank Markazi, *Economic Report and the Balance Sheet for 1988*, pp. 250–51.

42. Ibid., pp 214–17.

43. For a review of the debate in the course of formulating the plan, see Behdad, 'The political economy of Islamic planning in Iran'; and for an analysis of the First Economic Plan, see Ghasimi, M.R., 'Iranian economy after the revolution: An economic appraisal of the Five Year Plan', *International Journal of Middle East Studies* 24/4 (1992).

44. *Kayhan Hava'i*, 14 August 1991.

45. *Kayhan*, 21 July 1988.

46. The largest among these 'non-profit' giants is the Foundation for the Oppressed, with a $10 billion annual budget in 1992 and unknown assets. See Waldman, Peter, 'Clergy Capitalism', *The Wall Street Journal*, 5 May 1992.

47. Bank Markazi, *National Accounts (1974–1987)*, pp 254–5; and *National Accounts (1988–90)*, p 59.

48. Stated by Ayatollah Montazeri in a meeting with the bazaar leaders. *Kayhan*,18 February 1989.

49. Ghasimi, 'Iranian economy after the revolution', p 609.

50. Plan and Budget organization, *Appendix to the Law for the First Economic, Social and Cultural Plan of the Islamic Republic of Iran, 1989–1993* (in Persian, Tehran, 1988), p II-8.

51. *Kayhan*, 25 April 1992.

52. Ibid.

53. Title of an article in *Kayhan*, 30 August 1988.

54. *Kayhan Hava'i*, 17 January 1990.

55. IMF, 'Islamic Republic of Iran undergoes profound institutional, structural changes', *IMF Survey*, 30 July 1990, p 228.

56. For a critical analysis of the World Bank–IMF-type of macroeconomic adjustments, see Korner, Peter, Gero Maass, Thomas Siebold and Rainer Tetzlaff, *The IMF and the Debt Crisis* (London: Zed Books, 1987).

57. *MEED*, 29 March 1991, p 12.

58. Under pressure from the United States, the executive board of the World Bank rejected $400 million new loans to Iran. See *MEED*, 20 May 1994.

59. Bazargan's 'Hoshdar; Nameh-ye Sargoshadeh be Rahbar-e Enqelab [Ayatollah Khomeini]' in the spring of 1988 and a similar letter to President Khamene'i in August of 1988 contain daring condemnations of Ayatollah Khomeini and other leaders of the Islamic Republic.

60. These sermons are published in five volumes, entitled *Edalat-e ejtema'i: 'masa'el-e eqtesadi'* (Tehran: Public Relations of the Organization for the National Industries of Iran, 1982–84).

61. The estimate is from *MEED*, 25 January 1991, p 20.

62. For an account of the reconstruction programme, see Amirahmadi, Hooshang, *Revolution and Economic Transition: The Iranian Experience* (Albany: SUNY Press, 1990), ch 4.

63. Bank Markazi, *Economic Report and the Balance Sheet for 1990*, p 181.

64. Ibid., p 178; and Bank Markazi, *Economic Report and the Balance Sheet for 1986*, p 164. In July 1986 the price of Iranian light crude had dropped to $8.

65. This is because oil prices are determined in dollars in the international market, and because the volume of Iran's exports of oil depend on international market considerations (determined by the OPEC quota, or on its own), not by the rial cost of production of oil.

66. In technical terms, the condition of stability is not the issue. The reactions of the foreign-exchange market to the recent changes in the exchange rate of Iran show that the condition of stability is met. See Pesaran, Hashem, 'The Iranian foreign exchange policy and the black market for dollars', *International Journal of Middle East Studies* 24/1 (1992); and Lautenschlager, Wolfgang, 'The effects of an overvalued exchange rate on the Iranian economy, 1979–84', *International Journal of Middle East Studies* 18/1 (1986)

67. That assumes that the cost of domestic inputs does not change as the result of devaluation. For data on import dependence of various manufacturing activities, see Behdad, 'Political economy of exchange rate determination in Iran', p 11.

68. Theoretically, the price of products previously sold in the black market may actually fall after the devaluation.

69. Sherkat-e Sarma'igozari, *Gozaresh-e Tahqiqati*, no 24 (1992), p 34.

70. *Kayhan*, 28 May 1994.

71. *Kayhan*, 31 January, 9 March, 27 April and 3 May 1994.

72. Reuter, 'Iran parliament orders curb on subsidy cuts', 8 August 1994.

73. For an analysis of the 1992 elections, see Sabri, Farzin, 'The post-Khomeini era in Iran: The elections of the Fourth Islamic Majlis', *The Middle East Journal* 48/1 (1994).

74. *MEED*, 15 July 1994.

75. IRNA, 'Iran Most Suitable Country for foreign investments', 21 July 1994 (via the electronic network).

76. See also Halliday, Fred, 'An elusive normalization: Western Europe and the Iranian revolution', *The Middle East Journal* 48/2 (1994) for an insightful analysis of the crisis in the Islamic Republic.

5

Continuity and Change in Industrial Policy

Saeed Rahnema

One economic objective of the Islamic Republic has been to establish a strong and 'independent' industrial base. The leaders of the Islamic Republic blamed the deficiencies of Iran's industrial structure on the policies of the Shah's regime, and promised sustained industrial development in order to satisfy growing domestic demands and to increase the country's manufacturing exports. Yet, after a decade and a half the industrial deficiencies have only been aggravated, the industrial structure has deteriorated, and the share of manufacturing in GDP has declined. The revolutionary upheaval, the US-imposed economic embargo, the Iran–Iraq war, and the conflicting policies of the Islamic Republic, have all had disruptive effects on the industrial sector. The virtual withdrawal of the private sector from large industrial firms, because of massive nationalization and confiscation policies, has expanded the areas of control of an inefficient government bureaucracy and the newly formed parastatal/religious foundations.

Iran's modern industrial sector was formed during the decades preceding the 1979 revolution, when Mohammad Reza Shah undertook a major drive toward industrialization. In the absence of a strong entrepreneurial class, the government played a dominant role in directing this industrialization, which relied heavily on multinational corporations (MNCs) for capital and technology. In this chapter I argue that Iran's industrial structure was predominantly domestic-oriented with strong emphasis on the production of consumer goods, and with a weak capital goods sector. Iranian industries relied heavily on imported inputs and had little export capability. These characteristics are typical of the early stages of industrialization, and are partly the result of the objective constraints of a relatively backward socio-economic structure. However, after decades of effort toward industrialization, and despite the expenditure of massive financial and human resources, Iran's industrial sector retained these undeveloped characteristics. I argue that the particular industrial policies introduced by the Shah's regime (and later followed by the Islamic Republic) have been responsible for the perpetuation of the deficiencies of the country's industrial structure. The newly industrializing countries, particularly in Southeast Asia, though possessing more limited resources, were able to develop their industrial structure through the formulation and implementation of vigorous industrial policies.

Industrial Policy and Industrialization before the Revolution

The process of industrialization in pre-revolutionary Iran went through several stages. In each, the state played a significant role. Apart from earlier – in the late ninteenth century – limited efforts toward the establishment of a manufacturing sector, Reza Shah's rule (1925–41) can be considered the starting point of modern industry in Iran.[1] The government established new industries and relied heavily on protectionist policies. Yet, despite serious efforts, the industrial sector remained insignificant. Industries were run inefficiently, investment capital was scarce, and entrepreneurs were reluctant to venture into manufacturing. As a result, the growth of the industrial sector was slow.

In the post-Reza Shah period, indigenous private capital gradually came to influence industrial policy, particularly under the popular nationalist government of Mohammad Mosaddeq (1951–53). This period saw the introduction and partial implementation of the First National Development Plan, initiated in 1949.[2] However, an oil embargo, imposed on Iran following the nationalization of oil industries in 1951, cut the oil revenues severely. The resulting financial pressure on the economy halted the industrialization effort. In this period, no consistent industrial policy was implemented and no major changes in the economic and industrial structures of the country took place.[3] The instability of the regime and the intrigues of foreign powers, including Britain, the United States and the former Soviet Union, against Mosaddeq's nationalist government were fundamental obstacles to the formulation and implementation of an industrial policy.

The third and most important stage in Iran's industrialization began when the Shah returned to power in 1953 through the CIA's coup d'état. This period continued until the downfall of the Shah's regime in the 1979 revolution. In this period a big indigenous industrial–financial capitalist class emerged. The period also witnessed, for the first time, the direct involvement of foreign capital in the non-oil manufacturing sector, through foreign direct investment (FDI) and licensing agreements with MNCs. The US government, through its 'economic agreement' and 'Point IV' mission, and the International Monetary Fund, through its standard 'stabilization programme', also acted as sources of industrial policy for Iran. This period itself can be divided into three distinct phases: the first from 1953 to 1962; the second from 1962 to 1973; and the third from 1973 to 1979.

The first phase represents a continuation of earlier social and economic policies. In these years the Second Development Plan (1955–62), was partially implemented. In addition to infrastructural projects, several major industries were established. While the government intended to undertake major industrial projects directly, the IMF inhibited state involvement in the expansion of manufacturing.[4] An important goal of industrial policy in this phase was to attract foreign capital. In 1955 the Centre for the Attraction and Protection of Foreign Investment, later renamed the Organization for Investment, Economic and Technical Assistance (OIETA), was established. Despite various promotional measures, foreign capital did not during this period show a significant interest in Iran.

The second phase was by far the most important, and major structural changes occurred in Iran's industry and economy through the implementation of the Third and Fourth Development Plans (1962–68 and 1968–72). Industrial policy continued to combine the state's direct investment in the manufacturing sector with encouragement and support for private-sector investment. As a part of its efforts to encourage private investment in manufacturing, the government sold shares in its light-consumer-goods industries. Moreover, it used various promotional measures such as tax credits, grants and loans to encourage the establishment of new industries. New financial institutions were set up to provide medium- and long-term industrial loans and to enter into equity participation with the private sector. The most important of these financial institutions were the Industrial and Mining Development Bank of Iran, privately owned jointly with 19 foreign banks; the government-owned Industrial Credit Bank of Iran; and the Development and Investment Bank of Iran, privately owned jointly with a number of foreign banks.

Another major policy instrument in this phase was the establishment of the state-owned Industrial Development and Renovation Organization (IDRO) in 1967, which became the largest industrial conglomerate in the country. IDRO took over the government's ailing industries, mostly established during the early stages of industrialization under Reza Shah. IDRO's aim was to renovate and make these industries profitable. At the same time, IDRO was charged with setting up large modern heavy industries. It also became the major government partner in joint ventures with foreign corporations. IDRO, through its subsidiary – the Industrial Management Institute – began to provide consultancy and management training for industries. During this phase, as a result of the government's promotional measures, foreign investment and licensing agreements grew rapidly. Between 1962 and 1973, 102 units of FDI in manufacturing projects were registered through OIETA.[5] Most of these projects were joint ventures either with the government or private sector.

The major thrust of Iran's industrial policy in this phase was import substitution. This was to be undertaken sequentially through different

Table 5.1 Value-added of 'Large' Industrial Units According to Activity for Selected Years (IR billion and %)

ISIC subdivisions	1971 IR bn	1971 %	1976 IR bn	1976 %	1979 IR bn	1979 %	1981 IR bn	1981 %	1984 IR bn	1984 %	1986 IR bn	1986 %
31. Food	19.5	27.9	58.5	22.4	55.2	15.5	111.8	14.3	131.0	12.0	156.9	16.6
32. Textiles	13.3	18.8	55.2	21.2	63.6	17.9	152.6	19.6	220.0	21.0	223.9	23.6
33. Wood	1.2	1.7	2.3	0.9	4.1	1.2	7.8	1.0	14.8	1.0	14.4	1.5
34. Paper	2.5	3.5	4.2	1.6	14.2	4.1	18.5	2.4	31.8	3.0	30.0	3.2
35. Chemicals	13.5	19.1	38.8	14.9	72.4	20.4	231.1	29.7	123.0	12.0	124.0	132.1
36. Non-metallic minerals	4.9	5.9	27.2	10.4	50.8	14.2	94.5	12.1	139.0	13.0	131.1	13.8
37. Basic metals	3.1	4.4	6.2	2.4	22.4	5.3	27.7	3.6	76.5	7.0	76.4	8.1
38. Fabricated metals	12.3	17.4	67.8	26.0	71.1	20.1	135.4	17.4	281.0	26.0	189.0	19.9
39. Miscellaneous	0.2	0.2	0.4	0.2	0.3	0.1	0.7	0.01	2.2	0.2	1.9	0.2
Total	70.5	100.0	260.6	100.0	354.2	100.0	779.2	100.0	1066.0	100.0	948.0	100.0

Source: Statistical Centre of Iran, *Data of Large Industries*, Tehran, various issues.

Figure 5.1   Share of Main Activities in Total Value-added in Manufacturing (%)

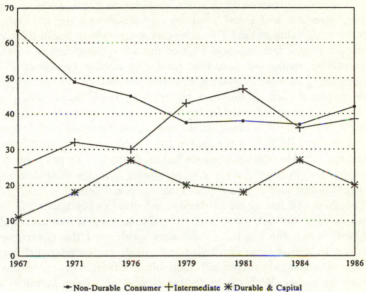

← Non-Durable Consumer + Intermediate ✳ Durable & Capital

Source: Statistical Centre of Iran, *Data of Large Industries*, Tehran, various issues.

stages, from production of consumer goods to intermediate goods and finally to capital goods, and was expected to move to an export-oriented industrialization. During the 1960s, some degree of import substitution took place in several branches of manufacturing.[6]

Along with the growth of consumer goods, the demand for intermediate and capital goods increased. The value of imported steel increased from $65.8 million in 1959 to $305.6 million in 1970; imported aluminium from $2.0 million to $19.6 million; and copper from $5.4 million to $24.6 million. The imports of machinery and CKD (Completely Knocked Down) components increased from $85.8 million to $366.7 million during the same period.[7]

The change in the configuration of the three groups of industries – consumer, intermediate and capital goods – indicates a significant change in the structure of manufacturing in this phase. Throughout the 1960s, firms producing non-durable consumer goods still constituted the majority of large firms, the largest portion of the total value-added, and the largest employment level of all large manufacturing firms. In 1967, 62.8 per cent of the total value-added in manufacturing was in non-durable consumer goods – mainly food, beverages, tobacco, textiles, apparel and wood and leather products. Durable and capital goods such as electrical and non-electrical machinery and transport equipment constituted 10.3 per cent of the manufacturing value-added, while intermediate goods such as paper, rubber, chemicals and metal products constituted 25.6 per cent of the manufacturing value-added.[8] This configuration, however, began to change during the Fourth Development Plan of the late 1960s and early 1970s, as an increasing number of industries producing durable consumer goods, intermediate goods and capital goods were established. These industries made products such as automobiles, tractors, steel, aluminium, petro-chemicals and machine tools. In 1973 the share of non-durable consumer goods in the total value-added of the manufacturing sector had decreased to 47.5 per cent (from 62.8 per cent in 1967), while the share of fabricated metals and durable consumer goods had increased to 20.7 per cent (from 10.3 per cent in 1967).[9] This was no doubt a major contribution to industrial policy in this phase (see Table 5.1 and Figure 5.1).

The third and last phase of Iranian industrial policy under the Shah began in 1973 and coincided with the Fifth Revised Development Plan (1973–78), when the sudden oil bonanza quadrupled the government's revenues. Industrial expansion relied increasingly on multinational corpo-rations, which rapidly expanded their direct investment and licensing agreements in Iran. With the increasing number of foreign investors and the growing economic strength of the country, the government intro-duced a set of restrictions and even eliminated some of the incentives offered to MNCs in the earlier phases of industrialization. Companies that had been set up with a perpetual 50 per cent tax exemption had their exemptions reduced to 25 per cent. Tougher tax regulations were enforced, and foreign ownership of Iranian industries became limited by sector.[10] Yet, despite these limitations, as discussed later, industrial policy remained less concerned with issues such as the local content of industries operating under MNC licences, inter-industry linkages, and limiting MNCs' restrictive practices and promotion of manufacturing exports in the industries under MNCs' licences.

A major aspect of industrial policy during this phase was the spatial division of labour and location of industry. Heavy concentration of industries in Tehran (about 50 per cent of all 'large' manufacturing firms) had created severe congestion and other serious problems. The govern-ment used both coercive measures as well as incentives to decentralize industrial production geographically. Several 'development poles' (*qotb-ha-ye towse'h*) were identified to create the critical mass of capital investment and to generate economies of scale. With this spatial division of labour, Azerbaijan became the site for machine-tool manufacturing, Isfahan for iron and steel, Fars for chemicals, Khuzestan for petrochemicals, and Gilan for electrical products.[11] Around each of these poles, it was expected that downstream industries related to each sector would be developed.

Industrial parks and towns were created in Saveh, Qazvin, Zanjan and other areas.

In terms of industry choices, the industrial policy continued to favour durable consumer and intermediate goods industries. The value-added share of fabricated metals and metal products in the total value-added in large manufacturing industries was increased from 20.7 per cent in 1973 to 26.0 per cent in 1976. Most of these industries were related to durable consumer goods.[12] Non-durable consumer-goods-producing industries also grew at about the same rate as in the previous phase. However, almost no new major capital-goods-producing industries were established, despite the financial ability and the growing demands. Many of the original production plans for the two major capital-goods-producing industries of the country, Mashinsazi-ye Tabriz and Mashinsazi-ye Arak, established with the help of Czechoslovakia and (the former) Soviet Union, were changed and new contracts were signed with Western European and North American companies. In a situation similar to that of consumer durable goods, the production of capital goods in these two complexes and their subsidiaries had a reduced local content. Confident about Iran's massive oil revenue, the Shah's government relied increasingly on imports, without any serious concern for increasing local production capabilities.

In an effort to legitimize the Shah's rule, and to harness the anarchic economic situation during the oil boom, the government introduced a set of policies that affected industrial production. The 'share participation law', through which all companies had to sell 49 per cent of their equities to employees and the public, and legislation against profiteering and price control antagonized many industrialists who began gradually to move part of their capital to non-manufacturing sectors and foreign banks.

The Structure of Iran's Manufacturing Industry

By 1979 Iran's manufacturing had certain weaknesses. The sector constituted about 11 per cent of the GDP (17.5 of the non-oil GDP) in 1977, which, compared with many newly industrializing countries, was a modest share. In South Korea, for example, the share of manufacturing in GDP in the 1950–60 period was 11.5 per cent, and by 1970 this had reached 23.2 per cent.[13] In terms of employment, Iranian manufacturing constituted only 19 per cent of the economically active population.

In 1976 (the year of the last industrial census before the revolution), only about 4 per cent of firms were considered large (with ten or more employees). The majority of the 'large' firms were consumer-goods-producing units. About 36 per cent of these firms manufactured food, beverages, tobacco, textiles, apparel and footwear.[14] Consumer-goods industries such as textile, apparel and footwear manufacturing employed over 27 per cent of the workforce of large industries. This was despite the fact that these industries were responsible for only 14.8 per cent of the total value-added of the large industrial firms. This demonstrates the low productivity of most of the firms in this category.

Although the share of intermediate and capital goods-producing industries – in terms of number of firms, value-added and employment – increased, these industries remained limited in scope, intensity and linkages. The weak and unintegrated nature of the intermediate and capital-goods-producing sectors determined the continued heavy reliance on imported technology, materials and machinery. A striking feature of the large modern manufacturing firms (which accounted for the largest proportion of value-added of the manufacturing sector and were mostly established through foreign direct investment or licensing agreements with MNCs), was the low level of local content and a heavy reliance on imported inputs. Modern industrial technology used in Iranian manufacturing was mostly related to the tail end of the production process and was limited to the assembly of imported CKDs. Nearly all foreign licensing contracts were accompanied by a series of restrictions, which prevented Iranian firms from progressively adding to their local manufacturing capability. This was true of the durable-consumer-goods and the capital-goods-producing industries. As mentioned earlier, the Shah's regime, while imposing a series of limitations on MNCs' operations, did little to convince the MNCs to add to their local content, or to establish capital-goods-producing industries. The result of this policy was that by the revolution 56.7 per cent, on average, of the inputs of Iran's large industries were imported. The figure for fabricated metal was 84.8 per cent and for basic metals 54.6 per cent.[15] As a further example, only 1.9 per cent of machinery and parts used in textile manufacturing was produced locally. In some branches, such as in the production of food and paper products, 100 per cent of the parts and machinery was imported.

By the late 1970s, intermediate and capital goods comprised the largest portion of the country's imports. In fact through each stage of industrial growth, the share of manufacturing imports had grown continuously. Although an initial rise in imports is to be expected in the early stages of import-substitution industrialization, in the later stages such imports should be 'substituted'. Throughout the 1960s and up to 1977, the share of imports in GDP not only did not decline but continually increased. The share of imports to GDP in 1960 was 15.9 per cent. By 1977 this figure had reached 28 per cent.[16] This was the opposite of what was happening in other Third World industrializing countries.[17] In Iran, although a degree of import substitution had taken place, it was predominantly in consumer goods (mostly non-durable). In the case of durable consumer goods, the import of finished products had been substituted mainly by the imported components of such products.

Industrial policy during the Shah's regime paid little attention to the growth of domestic production and technological capabilities of the country; a major indicator of this was the very limited research and development (R&D) activities. Almost none of the large modern industries had any serious R&D programmes, and none of the licensing contracts with MNCs had a provision for such programmes. Neither were there any linkages between industries and technical universities, despite the relatively high standard of academic activities in some universities, particularly the (former) Aryamehr Technological University and the College of Engineering of Tehran University.

The total number of scientists and engineers in Iran was very limited compared with many other Third World countries. For example, in 1974, at the height of industrialization, the total scientific and technical workforce was 217,632 persons. By way of comparison, the figure for South Korea – with a more or less similar population at the time – was 1,650,094 in 1976.[18] Government spending on R&D was minimal and in 1972 it amounted to only IR 3531 million or 0.30 per cent of a GDP of IR 1168 billion. The limited R&D capabilities, along with the reluctance of the MNCs to increase local content and the government's failure to direct MNCs' operations toward increasing indigenous technological capabilities and establishing capital-goods-producing industries, limited the scope of industries and industrial linkages in Iran.

Another major weakness of Iran's industrial structure was the domestic-market orientation of the vast majority of large modern industries and their minimal share in exports. Few promotional measures were directed toward enhancing manufacturing exports. In the early 1970s corporate tax incentives became conditional on export capabilities. If a company could export 15 per cent of its production, it was eligible for a 100 per cent tax exemption.[19] Yet these and other measures were not enforced seriously, particularly after the 1973 oil bonanza.

Although non-oil exports rose continuously from $128.2 million in 1963 to $634.7 million in 1973,[20] the largest proportion of such exports was traditional items such as carpets, leather, cotton, fruits and minerals. While the share of new industrial exports in the total non-oil exports rose from 20.1 per cent in 1973 to about 30 per cent in 1978, the share of manufacturing exports as a whole remained minimal and comprised about 2 per cent of the country's manufacturing output. After the oil boom of 1973 the value of non-oil exports actually dropped from $634.7 million in 1973 to $592.2 million in 1975, and to $539.9 million in 1976. In 1977, it fell to US$ 62.2 million. The importance of manufacturing exports for Iran was not merely in reducing the reliance on oil exports, but more in the potential for establishing world-class industries, characterized by high productivity, technological innovation, and ability to compete in the international market.

Industrial Policy in the Post-Revolutionary Period

As a result of the political transformations, the post-revolutionary period in Iran witnessed successive changes in industrial policy. During most of this period, as a result of the inter-factional conflicts within the Islamic regime, contradictory policies were put into effect. From its inception the populist faction pushed for nationalization of large industries and foreign trade, and state regulation of industries aimed at 'independence', 'self-sufficiency' and 'full employment'. The 'pragmatist' faction pushed for deregulation, denationalization of industries, 'rationalization' of labour processes, and the expansion of foreign capital involvement in Iranian industry. The post-revolutionary period can itself be divided into three distinct phases. The first phase, from February to October 1979, was the short-lived rule of the Provisional Government of Bazargan; the second phase, from 1980 to 1988, spanned the whole period of the Iran–Iraq war; and the third phase, 1988 to the present day, relates to the postwar reconstruction and post-Khomeini era.

In the first phase, in an anarchic atmosphere and in a situation where most owners and managers of large industrial firms had fled the country, foreign contractors too had left, and the major factories were under the control of the workers' and employees' councils (*showra*s), the most important aspect of the new government's industrial policy was to take over the largest private enterprises. For the first time, and for just a short while, blue- and white-collar workers influenced some aspects of industrial policy as a part of their immediate demand for state control of industries.[21]

The Law for Protection and Development of Iranian Industries placed industrial firms into four groups: Group A, heavy and strategic industries; Group B, firms belonging to those closely linked with the previous regime; Group C, bankrupt and debtor firms; and Group D, firms owned and operated by 'legitimate' owners. The first three groups came under the control of the government. A new organization, the National Iranian Industries Organization (NIIO), was established to supervise 464 (later about 700) newly nationalized firms. Other confiscated firms (more than 110 industrial units) came under the control of another newly established organization, the Foundation for the Oppressed (Bonyad-e Mostaz'afin). Apart from shifts in ownership patterns, however, no major change took place in industrial policy in this phase. The provisional government was powerless in the face of the Islamic populists, who were preparing themselves to take over the government, and factory councils that demanded radical changes.

The second phase, the period of war economy, saw successive changes in industrial strategy and conflicting policies. In 1981 the Ministry of Industry and Mines was disbanded and three new ministries were established: the Ministry of Heavy Industries, responsible for the basic, strategic and heavy industries, with IDRO as its operational arm; the Ministry of

Industry, responsible for light consumer and intermediate industries, with NIIO and National Iranian Handicraft Industries (NIHI) as its operational instruments; and the Ministry of Mines and Metals, with several operational arms such as the National Iranian Steel Corporation (NISC) and National Iranian Copper Industries (NICI). (The first two ministries eventually merged in September 1994.) In addition, The Martyr Foundation (Bonyad-e Shahid) came to control several large heavy and light industrial firms which had been confiscated.

The first and the most serious problem for industries in this phase was the shortage of imported materials and components, occasioned by the US embargo against Iran and the sharp decline of oil revenues. The outbreak of war with Iraq in 1980, which began to drain the government's foreign-exchange revenues, further aggravated the situation. The most important aspect of the Islamic government's industrial policy in this phase was the setting of production quotas on different industrial branches to meet the needs of the war economy and to utilize the continually diminishing foreign-exchange resources. For example, the foreign-exchange quota allocated to the industries under the jurisdiction of the Ministry of Industry was decreased from $4000 million in 1983 to $2750 million in 1984, and, after a temporary rise in 1985, dropped sharply to $750 million in 1986 and to $310 million in 1988.[22] The same trend affected the Ministry of Heavy Industries, where the foreign-exchange quota decreased from $2400 million in 1983 to $1600 million in 1986, $230 million in 1987, and $110 million in 1988.[23] This had drastic effects on Iran's heavy industries because of their extremely high reliance (up to 89.4 per cent) on imported materials and components.[24]

A second major problem was the reluctance of the private sector to invest in manufacturing, despite numerous promotional measures introduced by the government. This reflected insecurity resulting from factional conflicts and continuous legislative changes, and the much higher rate of profitability of commercial and real-estate activities.

A third serious problem confronting Iran's industries was the severe shortage of professional managers and skilled technical workers. This shortage was caused partly by the increasing exodus of professional personnel from the country, and partly by the continuous purge of non-conformist (non-Islamic) managers, engineers and other professionals by the Islamic Republic. Diversified sources of policy-making in the shape of different governmental and parastatal/religious institutions also created serious problems for industries.

Nevertheless, most branches of industry grew modestly in this phase in terms of the number of firms, value-added and employment (see Figures 5.1 and 5.2). The total value-added of large manufacturing firms grew from IR 779.2 billion in 1981 to IR 948.0 billion in 1986, and employment in these firms rose from about 486,000 to over 558,000 in the same period.

Figure 5.2   Total Production Index of Heavy and Light Industries 1978–1988

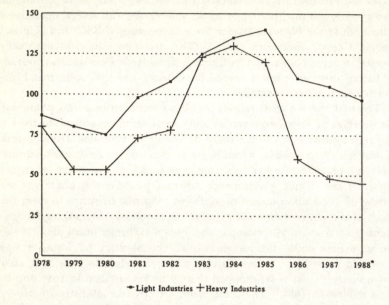

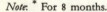
← Light Industries + Heavy Industries

Note: * For 8 months.
Source: Adapted from IDRO, *Data of Heavy Industries;* and NIIO, *Data of Small and Medium Industries,* 1989, Tehran.

Yet in terms of structural configuration the industrial structure deterio-rated. The share of non-durable consumer goods rose from 34.9 per cent in 1981 to 41.7 per cent in 1986, while the share of intermediate goods manufacturing dropped from 47.8 to 38.2 per cent in the same period. Production of durable consumer and capital goods rose slightly from 17.4 per cent in 1981 to 19.9 per cent in 1986, although its share was much below the value-added share of these industries a decade earlier (26.0 per cent in 1976). Although data for firms with ten or more employees are no longer provided separately by the Statistical Centre of Iran,[25] the data for firms with 50 and more employees show that in 1988 the non-durable-consumer-goods industries comprised 42.7 per cent of employment and 43.9 per cent of value-added of large industries.[26]

The data for large firms owned or controlled by the government (those affiliated with IDRO and NIIO) point to a declining production index in most branches of manufacturing. As shown in Figure 5.2, the total pro-duction index of both light and heavy government industries, which had sharply declined during the revolution, continued its downturn to 1980, after which it started to rise. Yet it took until 1982 in the light industries (and 1983 in heavy industries) for the production index to reach the pre-revolutionary (1977) level. This increase in the production index was temporary, and by 1986, with the sharper decline of oil revenues, the index for both groups of industries began to fall. For example, for heavy industries it fell to 47 per cent of the 1977 level. Responding to the immediate needs of the economy, priority was given to industries such as drugs and pharmaceuticals.

Except for armament industries, which were significantly expanded, no new major project for heavy industry was launched in this phase. Several projects unfinished from the time of the Shah, such as the second phase of the expansion of the Esfahan Steel Complex, Mobarakeh Steel and Asfarayen foundry complex, were continued. In car manufacturing the Islamic Republic followed policies similar to the pre-revolutionary period, exemplified by the signing of two major contracts, one with the French company Renault for the production of the Renault 9, 11 and 21, and the other for a $1.5 billion licensing agreement with France's Peugeot for the assembly of 500,000 cars within ten years. Both contracts relied heavily on imported components and an extremely low local input.

A strong emphasis on small industries formed yet another significant aspect of industrial policy during this phase. Favoured particularly by the populist faction, the government introduced new organizational instruments such as the Production and Development Services Centres. Over 700 of these mostly production cooperatives were established in different parts of the country. Although they received handsome credits from the banks, as unintegrated small manufacturing units most were unprofitable enterprises. Another innovative organizational instrument related to small industries was the establishment of the University of the Ministry of Industry, linked to NIHI, to educate students in the manufacture of textiles, wood, ceramics, glass and metals.[27]

Some attention was paid to R&D. The Organization of Scientific and Industrial Research expanded its activities – conducting research, supporting inventors and researchers, establishing a data bank and holding R&D seminars. In addition to its support of nearly 106 research projects with a meagre budget of IR 400 million (roughly $5 million), the organization contemplated more ambitious and questionable projects, such as a 100 per cent locally produced refinery, and the design and production of the 'national Khodrow – a 100 per cent made-in-Iran automobile'. Despite these sporadic efforts, however, R&D remained limited, and according to some indicators even declined compared to the pre-revolutionary period. For example, the total number of scientists/engineers and technicians engaged in R&D activities declined from 5753 in 1972 to 5048 in 1985. Within this category the number of scientists and engineers declined from 4896 to 3194.[28] In 1985 the number of scientists and engineers per million population in Iran was 72. In South Korea the number in 1986 was 1120.[29]

Finally, in response to the severe shortage of foreign exchange in this phase, the government laid a strong emphasis on the export of manufacturing products. It used different incentives to promote exports and, among other things, permitted firms exporting their products to use their earned foreign exchange to purchase imported materials and parts. Non-oil exports grew in the latter part of the 1980s, mainly through cuts in domestic consumption. Since 1986 (when oil revenues dropped sharply) the government placed a stronger emphasis on non-oil exports. The value of exports of industrial goods (manufacturing and raw materials), which had reached its lowest level in 1981 ($13.5 million), climbed in 1987 to $84.5 million. Yet this represented only 7.7 per cent of total exports. Only a small portion was related to manufacturing products.[30]

The third and present phase of industrial policy in Iran relates to the post-Iran–Iraq war and post-Khomeini era. Following the end of the war, industries continued to be plagued with input shortages. Most large factories operated at about 30 per cent capacity.[31] Several policy measures were introduced to resolve the problem. One was the 'buy-back' system through which Iranian manufacturing firms tried to find prospective foreign purchasers who would agree to provide necessary materials and components and in return would buy back the finished products. The plan faced serious problems because of the low productivity, low quality and high prices of the Iranian manufacturing firms.

Numerous and conflicting sources of policy-making; lack of coordination among the three industrial ministries, IDRO, NIIO, and various foundations; and rapidly changing regulations and legislation continued to afflict the industries. At some points there were 11 formal exchange rates alongside a black market for foreign exchange. Aggravating this situation was the policy of strict price control intended to curb inflation. At a time when manufacturing firms faced increasing costs from inputs and production, they were forced to sell their products below cost, and borrow from banks to cover their losses.

Another severe problem for most manufacturing firms was government employment practices. Faced with serious unemployment, particularly after the war, the government forced all government institutions, including state-owned or controlled manufacturing firms, to hire veterans (*razmandegan*), the male members of the martyrs' (*shohada*) families, the disabled (*janbazan*), and released POWs (*azadegan*). This policy, mostly favoured by the populist faction, increased industries' wage costs enormously.

The government continued to be the only major actor in industrial expansion. Despite government encouragements, the private sector hesitated to venture into manufacturing. One notable aspect of this phase was the introduction of the First (post-revolutionary) Development Plan (1989–93), and the formulation of postwar reconstruction policies. The plan set targets for industries, expecting to double the value-added of the manufacturing sector by the end of the plan, and improve the industrial structure by increasing the share of intermediate and capital-goods-producing industries.[32] Priorities for reconstruction were granted to those industries with 'high levels of employment and production'.[33]

The industrial policy of the Rafsanjani administration, both during his first and second (since 1993) presidency, had several new features. Privatization of previously confiscated industries was a central element of this industrial policy. State enterprises were to be sold through the revived Tehran Stock Exchange, or through other means such as sale by tender, or sale of stocks to managers or employees. The postwar reconstruction policies also emphasized the 'participation' of the public in manufacturing investment. The public sector was obligated to sell all its industrial and commercial units, except for the 'important and strategic' industries. Following this policy, the NIIO began in 1990 to sell its small- and medium-sized industries. After a meagre start in 1990 (the sale of IR 10.4 billion – about $7.4 million – worth of shares), the value of shares sold increased to over IR 222.6 billion in 1991. However, the figure dropped sharply to IR 123.9 billion in 1992, and to IR 30.9 billion in the first quarter of 1993. During this process, the management of only 48 companies (of about 700) was transferred to the shareholders.[34] The initial rise in the sale of shares was related to the optimism of the early years of Rafsanjani's first presidency, when the private sector and the public believed that he could effectively contain the populist tendency in the Islamic Republic and would revive the economy. The sluggish economy and political uncertainty contributed to the decline in the sale of shares. Despite all the incentives, as one top official admitted, the private sector remained reluctant to purchase government-controlled industries.[35] Later, in April 1994, a group of senior government officials bought up all the government shares in Iran Vanet, a nationalized plant that assembles Mazda pick-up trucks. This transaction, valued at about $38.6 million, amounted to 13 per cent of all the shares sold on the Tehran Stock Exchange in the previous year.[36]

The second feature of industrial policy in this period was a stronger emphasis on industrial exports. In addition to several promotional measures and the creation of an export support fund, the government moved to establish free-trade zones in the Persian Gulf islands of Kish and Qeshm and later in Sirjan. The Qeshm Free Trade Zone Corporation was authorized to raise $15,000 million from foreign and local sources for financing the development of an industrial zone, including a steel-mill complex, with the help of the Japanese.[37] Export assistance funds provided loans to industries to import needed materials and components, only to be paid back in instalments after exporting the manufactured products.[38] Another measure was a hidden subsidy through which Iranian firms would buy foreign exchange from the government at the lowest official exchange rate at the time ($1 = IR 70, or about one-fifteenth of the market value), to import materials and components and sell the finished products at a low price to the domestic market.[39]

The first plan set the target of non-oil exports at $17.8 billion for its duration, over 50 per cent of which (about $9 billion) was expected to be earned from the export of industrial goods.[40] It was not clear, however, on what basis the planners had arrived at this figure, or how this aim could possibly be achieved. Despite the efforts toward increasing export of industrial goods, and at the cost of depriving local consumers, industrial exports in the year before the implementation of the plan (1988) had reached only $84.5 million. This was less than one-twentieth of the annual industrial export revenue envisaged by the plan. Considering the constraints on industrial growth, ranging from financial and technological problems to the shortages of skilled labour, and the problems of penetrating international markets and meeting quality standards, the plan's target was misleading. The total figure of manufacturing exports for this period has not been published, but the data of small and medium industries of NIIO show that the total dollar value of the exports of these industries during the first four years of the plan (1989–92) reached only $382 million.[41]

Another major shift in industrial policy was the Islamic Republic's acceptance of foreign borrowing and investments. The First Five-Year Plan provided for $27 billion in foreign financing and investment.[42] Despite extensive opposition from the populist faction of the Islamic Republic, the government continued its efforts to attract foreign direct investment. The Ministry of Economy and Finance declared that the Bank Markazi would guarantee repayment of loans to foreign lenders. Moreover, the government increased the ownership ceiling for foreign partners in joint ventures to 49 per cent (as opposed to 35 per cent in the pre-revolutionary period).[43] With the strengthening of the Rafsanjani administration after the 1992 parliamentary election, the government began attracting foreign capital more vigorously. The High Council on Investment even abolished the 49 per cent ceiling and other limitations on foreign investment.[44] Of the anticipated $27 billion in foreign financing, $10 billion was allocated to increasing the output of existing industries, and about $9 billion for new industrial, mining and agricultural projects.[45] The government started borrowing from the World Bank and the IMF. In May 1992, after extensive negotiations, the World Bank approved a $134 million loan for Iran,[46] and later another loan of $150 million.

Promotional measures did attract some foreign companies to Iran. Between 1990 and 1992, a total of 80 foreign companies from 17 different countries (eight Yugoslavian, six South Korean, five Italian, five French, four Japanese, four British, two German, two Swiss, with the Czech Republic, Bahrain, Brazil, Pakistan, Turkey, Dubai, Belgium and the United Arab Emirates, each having one project), started operations in Iran. Yet these were mostly smaller projects, as their total investment for the period 1990–92 was only 37.7 billion rials (about $27 million).[47] With the hope of attracting more capital, the Islamic Republic even lifted the limitation imposed on private investment in 'strategic' industries, including petrochemicals. The head of Iran Petrochemical Industries, emphasizing the need for additional incentives for foreign capital, admitted that 'during the First Five Year Plan, no real foreign direct investment occurred in Iran'.[48]

Following the IMF's recommendations, the Rafsanjani government lifted import barriers and devalued the rial. In March 1993 the rial was devalued and a single floating rate was introduced (see Chapter 7). The Central Bank discontinued the decades-old official rate of 70 rials to the US dollar, and raised the official exchange rate to 1540 and then 1693 rials. The free-market value of the US dollar jumped to 1860 and even exceeded 2800 rials in March 1994. The industries, which for the whole post-revolutionary period had enjoyed a low official rate of exchange, at times over one-twentieth of the market value, were suddenly deprived of this source of subsidy. The sharp increase in the costs of imported materials and components, on which industries were heavily dependent, along with the open-door policy and unrestricted imports, severely affected all industries. For example, in the first half of 1993, compared to the previous year, the production of pick-up trucks fell from 93,980 to 12,782; cars from 22,328 to 18,149, and buses from 4108 to 2829 [49] In April 1994, the Minister of Heavy Industry announced that 84 per cent of the factories under his ministry 'suffer from zero or slow sales'.[50]

The industrial policy of the Rafsanjani government aimed at reviving the industrial sector. Data are not available for the years since 1990; therefore it is not possible to assess accurately the industrial structural changes that have occurred in the third phase of the post-revolutionary period under the Rafsanjani government. Nevertheless, considering the fact that, as a result of the open-door policy, Iranian industries cannot compete with imports and must get their imported inputs at much higher cost, it can be said with certainty that the manufacturing sector deteriorated in this phase.

Conclusion

After a decade and a half, and having experimented with diverse policies, the Islamic Republic has failed to fulfil its objective of creating a dynamic manufacturing sector. During the post-revolutionary period the industrial sector declined, and the share of manufacturing in GDP fell dramatically and is now far below what it was in the early 1970s or even mid-1960s (7.4 per cent in 1990, as compared to 12.5 per cent in 1973 and 11.6 per cent in 1965).[51] The structural deficiencies inherited from the time of the Shah continue to prevail. Iran's manufacturing sector is still dominated by domestic-oriented, consumer-goods-producing industries which have a low local content and rely heavily on imported inputs and technology. Compared to the pre-revolutionary period, the industrial sector now faces far more serious internal and external obstacles. Internally, different sources of policy-making, a bulkier and less professional and more corrupt bureaucracy, a weaker private sector, and a more uncertain and insecure environment have created serious problems for Iranian industries. Externally, in a more globalized economy, Iran has lost many opportunities during and after the revolution. Entering the international market for manufacturing exports is now much more difficult due to the larger number of competitors. Furthermore, with the growing hegemonic power of MNCs, Iran, like many other developing countries, has less and less bargaining power to influence these corporations and orient their activities toward the goals of national development. Iran, like many other Middle Eastern countries, has been excluded from the global pattern of investment clustered around the three major economic blocs of Europe, Southeast Asia and North America.[52]

Despite all the internal and external constraints, Iran, in both the pre- and post-revolutionary periods, has had a great potential for industrialization. Its relatively large market and its significant financial, natural and human resources provide great possibilities for industrial development. Yet the country, both under the Shah and the Islamic Republic, lacked an environment conducive to national development. Such an environment calls for a competent state capable of the design and implementation of a comprehensive industrial-development strategy, and a stable civil society in which the private citizen has a guaranteed sense of social, political and economic security.

Industrial policy is an integral part of the national development strategy. The Shah's industrial policy did not pay serious enough attention to enhancing indigenous production and technological capabilities and linkages by encouraging the establishment of capital-goods-producing industries and R&D. It also failed to emphasize manufacturing exports and to establish export-oriented industries in areas where Iran could acquire a competitive advantage in the global market. The Islamic government, after much toing and froing, ended up following pre-revolutionary strategies and policies, and went even further than the Shah's regime in introducing an open-door policy. From full indiscriminate protection of all industries, the Islamic Republic moved to the other extreme of exposing them all to market mechanisms.

The industrial sector has to fulfil diversified and, at times, conflicting needs such as satisfying local demands for manufactured goods, increasing industrial employment, establishing an indigenous technological base, and enhancing manufacturing exports. The more successful newly industrializing countries, such as those of Southeast Asia, have consciously followed industrial policies that constantly target their industries through promotional and protective measures. These countries have vigorously emphasized the growth of local technological and production capabilities, as well as manufacturing exports. Through the development of a 'vision' for the future, the 'sunset' or declining industries are gradually phased out and replaced, while the 'sunrise' industries are vigorously promoted and supported.[53] The major industrial restructuring and the rapid development of markets in these countries over the past two decades have been the result of consistent policies and comprehensive state intervention in the industrial sector. Through a symbiotic relationship between a professional state bureaucracy and a strong private entrepreneurial sector – itself partly a product of state policies – industrial strategies are designed and implemented in which the state focuses on the overall developmental goals and the private sector concerns itself with productivity and profit.

Iran, particularly under the Islamic Republic, has neither a professional state bureaucracy capable of formulating consistent and comprehensive industrial policies, nor a strong entrepreneurial sector capable of aggressively venturing into manufacturing and seeking new strategies for penetrating the global market. The only feature that Iran shares with the countries of Southeast Asia is its authoritarian system of government, a feature that, ironically, has been a major source of tension and weakness in those societies. With the continuing anarchic situation in Iran, internal strife, conflicting policies, political and economic insecurity, and lack of a professional and effective bureaucracy, it is unlikely that the Islamic Republic will be able to break the cycle of industrial backwardness inherited from the Shah's regime and aggravated in the post-revolutionary period.

Notes

1. See Banani, Amin, *The Modernization of Iran; 1921–1941* (Stanford: Stanford University Press, 1961), p 138; Bharier, Julian, *Economic Development in Iran; 1900–1970* (New York: Oxford University Press, 1971), p 174; and Karshenas, Massoud, *Oil, State and Industrialization in Iran* (Cambridge: Cambridge University Press, 1990).

2. Baldwin, George B., *Planning and Development in Iran* (Baltimore: The Johns Hopkins Press, 1967), pp 24–39.

3. In 1947 there were only 175 'large' manufacturing units with ten or more employees, mainly producing non-durable consumer goods. The Iranian government owned and directly controlled 64 major industries, which accounted for almost 50 per cent of the total workforce of the large industries. Bharier, *Economic Development*, p 181.

4. See Benedick, Richard E., *Industrial Finance in Iran* (Boston: Harvard University Press, 1974), p 29.

5. Rahnema, Saeed, 'Multinationals and Iranian Industry; 1957–1979', *Journal of Developing Areas* 24/3 (1990), p 299.

6. For example, the import of cube and granulated sugar and sweets dropped

from $32.7 million in 1960 to $7.2 million in 1970. The import of processed tea also declined from $26.1 million to $9.3 million in the same period. The import of some completely finished durable items, such as cars, also dropped continuously. The value of imported finished cars dropped from $22.3 million in 1960 to $7.3 million in 1970. Bank Markazi Iran, *Annual Report and the Balance Sheet*, (Tehran, 1970), pp 134–5.

7. Bank Markazi Iran: *Annual Report*, pp 134–5.

8. Looney, Robert E., *The Economic Development of Iran* (New York: Praeger Publishers,1973), p 108; based on the Ministry of Economy, *Annual Industrial Survey* Tehran, 1967.

9. Statistical Centre of Iran, *Survey of Large Manufacturing Establishments* (Tehran, 1976), p 3.

10. Rahnema: 'Multinational', p 295.

11. Business International, *Operating in Iran* (Geneva: BI, 1978), p 23.

12. Statistical Centre of Iran, *Survey of Large Manufacturing Establishments*, p 19.

13. The share of manufacturing in non-oil GDP in Iran in the 1960s was 13.2 per cent. World Bank, *World Tables* (New York: Oxford University Press, 1980), pp 106–7.

14. Statistical Centre of Iran, *Survey of Large Manufacturing Establishments* (Tehran, 1977).

15. Statistical Centre of Iran, *A Survey of Insufficiencies and Dependencies of the Large Industries of the Country* (Tehran, 1980), p 8.

16. World Bank, *World Tables* (New York: Oxford University Press, 1987), pp 106–7.

17. For example, Brazil in its early stages of industrialization managed to decrease the share of imports in GDP from 12 per cent in 1950–52 to 8 per cent in 1964–66 (Ian Little et al., *Industry and Trade in Some Developing Countries* (London: Oxford University Press, 1970, p 63). In South Korea, between 1960 and 1970, the final import content of the Korean fixed-capital formation decreased from 21 to 18 per cent, and the intermediate import content of fixed capital increased from 14 to 19 per cent (Suk Tai Suh, *Import-Substitution and Economic Development in Korea* (Seoul: Korea Development Institute, 1975, pp 257–8).

18. UNESCO, *Statistical Yearbook* (Paris: UNESCO, 1977 and 1980), pp 662 and 756 respectively.

19. For further details, see Business International, *Operating in Iran*, p 113.

20. Bank Markazi Iran, *Annual Report*, p 57.

21. For *showras* (councils) in Iran, see Rahnema, Saeed, 'Work Councils in Iran: The illusions of workers' control', *Economic and Industrial Democracy: An International Journal* 13/1 (1992). For a different view, see Bayat, Assef, *Workers and Revolution in Iran* (London: Zed Books, 1989).

22. *Kayhan*, 5 August 1989.

23. *Kayhan*, 29 July 1989.

24. Ministry of Heavy Industry, *The Comprehensive Plan of Iran's Heavy Industry*, Vol 2, (Tehran, 1986), p 79.

25. The 1988 data on 'large' firms in Iran covered those with 50 or more employees. Since 1990, the Statistical Centre of Iran has not published the data of the annual survey of Iranian industries.

26. Statistical Centre of Iran, *Data of Industrial Firms With 50 and More Employees*

(Tehran, 1988), p 5.

27. *Kayhan*, 11 September 1989.

28. UNESCO, *Statistical Yearbook (1988)*, p 763.

29. Ibid., pp 5–112.

30. Centre for Export Promotion, *Report of Non-Oil Exports* (Tehran, 1988), p 14.

31. *Kayhan*, 8 July 1989.

32. Plan and Budget Organization, *The First Plan of Development*, Vol 2 (Tehran, 1989), pp 5, 6 and 7.

33. *Keyhan*, 10 May 1989.

34. Ministry of Industry, 'A short report of the activities of the Ministry of Industry during the first four years of the First Plan, 1989–1992', (Tehran, 1993), p 12.

35. Deputy Minister of the Plan and Budget Organization, cited in *Iran Times*, 29 January 1993.

36. *Iran Times*, 15 April 1994.

37. *Middle East Economic Digest (MEED)*, 31 August 1990. p 11.

38. *Keyhan*, 27 October 1989.

39. *Iran Times*, 27 October 1989.

40. *Kayhan*, 6 April 1991.

41. Ministry of Industry, 'A short report', pp 10–11.

42. *MEED*, 9 February 1990, p 18.

43. Ibid.

44. *Iran Times*, 15 May 1992.

45. *MEED*, 19 January 1990, p 14.

46. *Iran Times*, 15 May 1992.

47. Data of the Statistics Department of the Central Bank of Iran, cited in *Iran Times*, 4 June 1993.

48. *Iran Times*, 15 October 1993.

49. *Iran Times*, 11 December 1993.

50. *Iran Times*, 15 April 1994.

51. The World Bank, *Trend in Developing Economies* (Washington DC, 1992), p 277.

52. For a brief and succinct argument on this issue, see Doug Henwood, 'Global Economic Integration: The Missing Middle East', *Middle East Report* 184, (September–October 1993).

53. For the significance of the role of the state in the industrialization process of Southeast Asian countries, see, among others, Deyo, Frederic C. (ed.), *The Political Economy of the New Asian Industrialism* (Ithaca: Cornell University Press, 1987).

6

The Oil Sector after the Revolution

Djavad Salehi-Isfahani

Introduction

For a country with 5 per cent of the world's oil and 14 per cent of the natural gas reserves, Iran is not likely to run out of hydrocarbons any time soon. The combined oil and gas reserves of more than 150 billion oil-equivalent barrels will last beyond the year 2070 at current rates of production of nearly two billion barrels per year (or about five million barrels per day). Five times the amount of hydrocarbons that have been extracted since the beginning of Iran's oil industry to date still remain in the ground. Valued at a price of $15 per barrel, for the average Iranian family the oil wealth is worth about a quarter of a million dollars.

Three things intercede between the average person and this great wealth: the oil sector that determines how much oil can be extracted and sold every year; the oil market that determines the value of the oil sold; and the economic system that determines who gets how much of the oil revenues in any given year. In this chapter I consider the first two. I will first discuss the physical side of the sector (reserves and production of oil and gas), and its new institutional setup. I will then focus on government policy, which is not a narrow focus given the fact that the government owns and operates the entire industry, from extraction to refining and marketing.

This deep involvement is a mixed blessing for the government. Access to an easy source of revenue is evenly matched by the blame for everything that goes wrong with the economy. It is natural to compare economic life before and after the revolution, something Iranians do quite often. Explanations of why the economy is so much worse in the 1990s than it was in the 1970s often include oil, but they rarely reduce it to simple arithmetic. Per-capita oil revenues were in 1994 about one-fourth compared with 1973 and one-eighth compared with 1974. In 1994, the real price of oil was less than half what its value was in the mid-1970s and about what it was in 1973 – just before the great price hike. The volume of oil exported was half its 1973 level, while Iran's population is twice as large. Of course, more is involved than just arithmetic, and to understand the differences between the post- and pre-revolutionary oil sector we need to examine the changes in the physical aspects of the industry, domestic demand and the world market.

On the physical side, production capacity cannot be set at will to suit the revenue needs of a given period. Iran's oil fields are getting older and need more investment to yield the same output as before. Nearly $10 billion has been spent since the end of the Iran–Iraq war to repair and improve Iran's production capacity. As a result, production capacity rose by 1.5 million barrels per day (mbd) to 4.2 mbd.

The world market in which Iran now operates is also very different from that of the 1970s, when the price was high and Iran could sell all it wanted. In the 1990s, even if capacity were to permit, increased production by Iran would lower prices on the world market, not only hurting Iran but other OPEC members as well. This introduces a strategic element into Iran's export policy which did not exist before the revolution. These strategic considerations also enter into the untested set of relations that Iran is trying to forge with its Persian Gulf neighbours who also happen to be fellow OPEC members.

At home, there is also a new factor that did not exist in the 1970s: the rising domestic demand for petroleum products. In 1973, Iran produced 5.9 mbd and consumed 250 thousand barrels daily (tbd), compared to the production of 3.4 mbd and consumption of 1.1 mbd in 1993. The share of domestic consumption in total production thus jumped from 4 per cent in 1973 to nearly one-third in 1993. The reasons are the fall in real prices in the domestic market and a larger population. The average real price of domestically consumed oil in 1993 was only a fourth of its value 20 years earlier, while the population had become almost twice as large. Rising domestic appetites for fuel consumption makes exporting more difficult every year.

For the next 10–15 years, during which dependence on oil revenues cannot be reduced, Iran faces some unpleasant dilemmas. On the domestic front there is a clear dilemma: it must curtail consumption of refined products or spend billions of dollars in expanding capacity. The existing policy is to do a bit of both: to increase oil production capacity to five mbd, and to reduce domestic consumption by substituting natural gas for oil. Attempts at using prices to control consumption have so far been limited in extent, mainly because of their political ramifications. So far, the expansion of the gas network has only slowed down the rate of increase in oil consumption. The policy of substituting natural gas for oil is based on the fact that oil and gas are not equally exportable. But oil and gas are connected not just in consumption but also in production. Oil production is increasingly dependent on the reinjection of natural gas for maintenance of reservoir pressure.[1]

The options on the international front are less obvious. There is the presumption that, perhaps through OPEC, Iran can do something to boost its revenues. Should Iran attempt to gain power inside OPEC or help OPEC become more powerful? Should Iran side with the hawks and push for higher prices, or side with the moderates and hope for economic recovery to lift the demand for oil. A bigger share of power in OPEC may be achieved by posting more proved reserves, by having a higher production or excess capacity, as does Saudi Arabia, or by an entirely non-oil means, such as through diplomacy and foreign relations. Compared to the domestic dilemmas, the choices in the international field are less clear cut and the consequences of these choices unknown.

Production and Reserves

Oil

Total oil-in-place, both on- and offshore, is estimated at 382 billion barrels. Proven reserves – the part that is commercially recoverable at current prices – come in two versions, both of which can be described as official. An international version, printed in the current OPEC statistics, puts proven reserves at 92.8 billion barrels.[2] A domestic version, according to the First Five-Year Plan published in 1988, puts proven reserves much lower at 59 billion barrels. The latter figure is a rather conservative estimate. Reserve figures for OPEC countries should be treated with caution. They are influenced by strategic considerations, as they serve to enhance members' bargaining power in the organization. Their reliability is further undermined by the fact that, unlike reserve figures for international oil companies, they do not have any legal basis. For example, the larger numbers place Iran on more or less equal footing with Iraq and Kuwait, which is essential for Iran's role as a big player in OPEC. Additional ambiguities arise because changes in proven reserves are not always due to new discoveries. Proven reserves are defined as that part of reserves worth recovering at current prices, and thus vary directly with the price of oil. Iran has rarely adjusted its figure for proven reserves as prices change; but in response to upward adjustments by Iraq and Kuwait to 100 and 97 billion barrels, respectively, Iran raised its proven reserves figure to 92.8 billion barrels.

Table 6.1 gives the breakdown of reserve figures according to the more conservative estimate of the First Five-Year Plan. Of the total proven reserves of 59 billion barrels 53.4 billion barrels are located onshore, of which 36.4 billion barrels is exploitable with primary recovery and the rest require secondary recovery techniques. Offshore proven reserves are 5.6

Table 6.1 Iran's Oil Reserves

Fields	Oil-in-place	Proved reserves	Primary recovery	Secondary recovery
Onshore	342.8	53.4	36.4	17.0
Offshore	39.0	5.6	4.4	1.2
Total	381.8	59.0	40.8	18.2

Source: The Plan and Budget Organization, *First Five Year Plan* (1990) P IX9.

billion barrels, of which 4.4 billion barrels are recoverable with primary recovery.

Iran's oil production peaked at 6.1 mbd in the mid-1970s. Immediately after the revolution, production fell but capacity remained high. In 1979, buoyed by high oil prices and a current-account surplus, Iran imposed an output ceiling of 4 mbd.[3] Although this ceiling has not yet been broken, it is no longer official policy. Production averaged 3.17 mbd in 1979, due in part to the slow recovery in the oil fields after a four-month strike by the oil workers in the fall of 1978. The Iraqi invasion in 1980 cut production down to 1.5 mbd. There were physical impediments to production created by the war in the oil-producing region of Khuzestan, as well as an increased risk for buyers to which Iran did not react in time. By 1982 Iran was giving price discounts, which helped sales reach 2.2 mbd by the fourth quarter. Thereafter, production picked up gradually despite the war and the severing of ties with foreign contractors and suppliers due to the diplomatic isolation of a country that had survived the hostage crisis of 1980. Between 1982 and 1989 average output was 2.5 mbd.

The end of the war and increased access to foreign technology and capital allowed Iran to embark on an ambitious programme during the First Five-Year Plan. Planned expenditures were 1288.1 billion rials, consisting of $8.35 billion in foreign exchange, valued at 70 rials per dollar, and local expenditures of 755 billion rials. Actual expenditures announced at 4087.9 billion rials[4] exceeded this nominally, but in real terms may have even fallen short, for devaluation during the plan boosted foreign expenditure, and inflation far exceeded the plan's allowance. Since different parts of foreign expenditures have been counted at different dollar rates, without a detailed breakdown of the expenditure data it is hard to assess the plan's fulfilment rate. In terms of output, the plan's target of average production of 3.528 mbd for 1993 was exceeded by nearly 400,000 barrels per day in that year. The overachievement is explained by the fact that after the first plan had gone into effect a new programme to raise capacity to 5 mbd was announced by Oil Minister Aghazadeh. The government appears to have abandoned the 5 mbd target and now claims a sustainable capacity of 4.5 mbd.[5]

Significantly, in contrast to the onshore fields, the plan underachieved its target of 503,000 barrels per day for offshore fields by over 100,000 barrels per day. Foreign-exchange shortages of the last two years have created delays in payment to foreign contractors working in the offshore areas, thus delaying reconstruction of the damaged offshore platforms and other facilities. Onshore reconstruction did not involve foreign contractors and therefore was not beset by the same problem.

The gain of nearly 1.5 mbd in capacity during the first plan will not be repeated in the second plan. There are three reasons for this. First, future gains in capacity will be more costly and therefore come at a slower pace. The next 1.5 mbd will probably cost $15 billion, 50 per cent more than the previous 1.5 mbd. Second, given the current market conditions, an increase in capacity is unlikely to translate into actual production and hence revenue. With the expected re-entry of Iraq, Iran will do well by just maintaining its current export level of 2.5 mbd. Excess capacity, which is thought to be the source of Saudi power, will bring limited OPEC leverage to Iran only at great cost. Third, given the high political cost of raising fuel prices at home, the higher production capacity will inevitably be eaten up by domestic consumption. Under the circumstances, the surest way to control domestic demand is to keep capacity constant and let domestic consumers compete with exports.

The main obstacle to raising Iran's oil production is low pressure in the onshore fields, where currently 90 per cent of the oil comes from. Iran's main oil fields are between 30 and 60 years old, and a serious drop in pressure had been noticed as early as the 1960s when the Consortium was in charge of the oil fields. For reasons of its own, perhaps related to its perception of a short horizon of control of the oil industry in Iran, the Consortium did not undertake any remedial action.[6] In the early 1970s, the National Iranian Oil Company (NIOC) took over the management of the fields and initiated a massive reinjection programme; but little actual reinjection was done, as a result of the revolution and the war. Between 1977 and 1987 total gas injected dropped by three-quarters, from 25.7 million cubic metres (mcm) per day to 6.2 mcm per day.[7] During the war, low reservoir pressure was not the actual constraint on production and reinjection was therefore not a high priority, but soon it became very important. Twelve of Iran's onshore fields require reinjection on a continuous basis. In 1992, reinjection was already taking place in Marun, Gachsaran, Haftkel and Karanj.

The gas needs for the entire programme are quite large, estimated at about 3000 billion cubic metres (bcm) or about 15 per cent of the proven gas reserves. The Second Five-Year Plan calls for an increase in reinjection from 19.7 bcm per year (54 mcm per day) in 1994 to 40.4 bcm per year in 1998. This is to rise to 70 bcm when the entire programme is implemented. Both associated and non-associated gas will have to be used. In 1994, most of the gas was from associated sources, but in the long run a significant proportion would have to come from non-associated sources such as the Pars offshore gas fields. The reinjection programme under implementation will add 2.6 billion barrels to Iran's proven reserves, and account for about 1 mbd of production capacity. The project is expected to cost $800 million, averaging about 30 cents per barrel of oil recovered.[8]

Delay in the development of the offshore gas fields created a shortage of natural gas in 1994 and held up progress on the reinjection programme. Despite this delay, Iran has thus far been able to produce at the level determined by its quota of 3.6 mbd. When output falls temporarily below this level, as it did in the first few months of 1994, the Oil Ministry denies any fall, for such rumours undermine Iran's claim to the second largest quota in OPEC. What is forgotten is that quotas need not be satisfied every single month: depending on prices, Iran may choose to sell more or less during a given period as long as the average for the quarter or the year adds up to the quota.

Natural gas

Iran's gas reserves of 20 trillion cubic metres are about twice as large as its oil reserves in thermal equivalent units.[9] After Russia, this is the largest amount of gas found in a single country. About two-thirds of this amount is non-associated gas, the rest only recoverable in joint production with oil. Nearly half of this total is the result of development after the revolution.

Iran's gas fields are geographically more dispersed than its oil fields. There are 2 gas fields in the north, 15 in the south, and 2 offshore in the Persian Gulf. The oldest onshore field is Khangiran, near Sarakhs in the northeast 700 miles east of Tehran and very close to the border with Turkemanistan. Proven reserves in Khangiran are estimated at 514 bcm. There is also a smaller field in Gorgan, and in 1993 Iran announced the discovery of gas near Bandar Anzali on the Caspian Sea. Exploration in this area continues.

The major fields in the south are the onshore fields of Kangan (314 bcm) and Nar (400 bcm), and the offshore fields of North (1371 bcm) and South Pars (2857 bcm). Kangan is the only other natural gas field besides Sarakhs to have been developed before the revolution; it is linked via a pipeline to the Caspian port city of Astara, from which gas used to flow to the former Soviet Union. The nearby Kangan field is currently operating and expanding. Its gas is used for domestic purposes and reinjection. The mammoth South Pars field, located about 60 miles offshore south of Kangan, is considered an extension of Qatar's north field.

Iran is competing with Qatar both in extraction from this field as well as in marketing. Work on the development of South Pars has been delayed because of the lack of foreign interest. A $1.7 billion project – the largest single project since the revolution – was awarded in 1992 to a consortium of Italian, Japanese and Russian contractors.[10] The contractors were to be paid with production from the fields – in this case, condensates.[11] The deal fell through, however, in 1994 before operations had begun because the Italian export credit agency SACE decided to withdraw its cover.[12] South Pars is expected to produce 10 bcm per year of gas and 2.5 million tonnes of condensates. This gas output could rise to 70 bcm per year upon completion of the project's final, seventh phase. Shell has shown interest in the North Pars field and is currently doing a feasibility study.

Relative to oil, gas production in Iran is underdeveloped. The concession of 1954 and its later revisions did not give the Consortium the incentive to utilize the gas produced as byproduct of oil production for domestic or reinjection purposes. Until recently gas was a byproduct of oil and most of it was flared.[13] Interestingly, while in the past gas production was dependent on the production of oil, in the 1990s the need for reinjection of the oil fields has reversed the dependence: it is now oil production that depends on gas.

Natural gas is used in reinjection, petrochemical feedstock, household and industrial use, and exports. The National Iranian Gas Company is now in charge of the development of the gas fields and the pipeline network. The share of natural gas in providing the country's hydrocarbon energy rose from 10 per cent in 1977 to 31.6 per cent in 1992. In 1992 total production was 43.8 bcm, 39 bcm of which was used for household, commercial, industrial purposes and power generation, and the rest was flared. Putting an end to flaring of associated gas, the most wasteful aspect of oil production in Iran, remains an elusive goal. As early as 1948 Iran had suggested that the Anglo-Iranian Oil Company, the Consortiums's precursor, should channel gas to a domestic network instead of burning it.[14] Flaring now accounts for 40 per cent of all associated gas (32 mcm per day), down from 59 per cent in 1973. The second plan envisages a further reduction to 10.7 per cent.[15]

The programme for domestic use of gas picked up in earnest after the revolution. Since 1983, Iran has embarked on an ambitious investment programme for distribution of natural gas within the country, aiming primarily at large urban centres, electricity production and industrial sites. Power generation, which used most of the natural gas before the revolution, still accounts for the bulk of gas used domestically. In 1990, 55 per cent of all natural gas was used to produce about half of the total electricity generated (see Table 6.2). In 1992, 19 power plants each with a capacity of 6000 megawatts operated using natural gas. The largest gain has been in the household and commercial sectors, where before the revolution use

Table 6.2   Production and Consumption of Natural Gas

	1980	1985	1990	1994
Uses				
Household, commercial and industrial	980	4963	7451	14,418
Power generation	3000	4149	8897	13,213
Petrochemicals	na	na	na	3796
Total uses	3980	9085	16,348	32,594
Sources				
Associated gas	3994	7118	6890	10,220
Northeast	426	2360	4626	9271
Qeshm-Sarkhun	55	398	1256	3723
nar-Kangan	0	0	7870	19,700
Total sources	4475	9478	20,642	46,173

Source: Plan and Budget Organization; figures are projected.

was limited because of its small network. During 1983–93, the number of household and commercial subscribers increased from 50,000 to over 1.4 million in 153 cities; two-thirds of these were connected to the gas network following the end of the war in 1988. Consumption has increased accordingly. Between 1980 and 1990, the overall sale of natural gas to households, commercial and industrial establishments and power stations increased from 3.5 bcm to 16.4 bcm, an annual increase of 15 per cent.

In the First Five-Year Plan, accomplishments in the gas sector have been modest. With the exception of the construction of the gas network, where the plan's goal was achieved 100 per cent, in gas production, refining, pipelines and the number of customers hooked up, only two-thirds of the targets were achieved.[16] Gas production is currently the most critical bottleneck: planned production for 1993 was 171.4 mcm per day, while actual production was only 88 mcm per day. This falls far short of the refining capacity of 112 mcm per day[17] and the reinjection needs of 190 mcm per day.

Before the revolution, Iran exported about 9 bcm of natural gas to the Soviet Union each year. With the decrease in oil production in 1978–79, exports of natural gas declined to half and then stopped completely in 1980. Disputes over the price and increased domestic needs contributed to the decision to stop the sale of gas to the Soviet Union. There was a brief resumption of gas exports in small amounts (2.2 bcm) in 1990–91, but that too stopped after a short while. Since the gas deal with the Soviet

Union was a barter agreement with an implicit price well below the world market, it is unlikely to serve as a model for future deals.[18]

As the second largest owner of natural gas reserves in the world, Iran in the long run will become a natural gas exporter, but it will be another decade before any pipelines are laid. The external market for Iran's natural gas need not be limited to one buyer as it was in the 1970s. The northern neighbours have multiplied, and old potential buyers such as Western European countries and South Asian countries appear more interested in a long-term arrangement. However, the high cost of placing pipelines to these markets and the political complications of running the pipeline through several countries have so far prevented any particular deal going beyond the signing of protocols. Iran is not financially capable of undertaking the entire cost of the infrastructure to transport gas. Western European countries, especially France, who have the capability to finance such a project have shown considerable interest in importing Iran's gas, but face difficulties in routeing the pipeline through third-party countries. India is also interested but suffers from a shortage of capital and logistics – routeing the pipeline through Pakistan is politically infeasible, leaving the Indian Ocean bed as a high-cost alternative. The newly independent nations of Armenia, Azerbaijan and Georgia to the north, and Pakistan to the east also have political and financial disadvantages. In a sense the break-up of the Soviet Union has made the transfer of gas to Western Europe more difficult. In 1975 when similar deals were first discussed, there was only one go-between, the Soviet Union, which has now been replaced by several independent and warring republics. In the medium term, the best uses of natural gas are at home – as reinjection for secondary recovery and domestic consumption.

Institutional Change

On 5 March 1979 the provisional revolutionary government unilaterally cancelled the agreements with the Consortium and abandoned several foreign joint-venture projects. The last agreement with the Consortium, signed in 1973 for a 20–year period, was in effect a sales and service agreement, according to which the Consortium, through its subsidiary the Oil Service Company of Iran (OSCI) produced oil from the Consortium area for NIOC and then purchased it at a discount. The cancellation of the agreement put the Consortium members on the same footing as other buyers of Iranian oil. NIOC also operated four joint ventures in the offshore fields, which were also taken over. For the ten years following the revolution the exploration, production and marketing (in which the NIOC had been involved to some degree before the revolution) became the sole responsibility of an expanded NIOC that was almost entirely dependent on Iranian personnel.[19] The foreign companies concerned were subsequently reimbursed for losses incurred as a result of the takeover of property and the cancellation of contracts.[20] Much of the property operated by OSCI and taken over at the time of the revolution was actually owned by Iran, and therefore did not entail compensation.

The revolution was in fact the last step in a gradual process of increased control by Iran over the fate of its industry. In the 1960s, Iran fought hard to gain some degree of control over production, but was largely unsuccessful. For example, in 1967 the Consortium refused to increase its take from the Iranian fields by 20 per cent despite threats by Premier Hoveyda that, 'We cannot stand by idly while our oil resources are kept unexploited.'[21] In 1972–73, Iran played a key role in OPEC's successful bid for setting the price of oil. Since the 1960s, Iran had been engaged in joint ventures in areas outside the control of the Consortium. In these deals Iran was usually a 50 per cent partner with equal say in all matters, including the level of production. In the 1970s, Iran expanded its de facto control of production to the fields under concession to the Consortium. By 1979, through management of all the refineries and some of the oil fields, NIOC had gained the necessary skills for the takeover.

The revolution brought with it some reorganization in the bureaucratic structure of the oil sector. Until 1980 Iran did not have a separate ministry for oil and gas. The Minister of Finance and Economy represented Iran in OPEC at the ministerial level, but all other matters related to the sector, from long-range planning to day-to-day operations, were handled by the state-owned NIOC. This system was designed by the Shah, who wanted the NIOC chief to report directly to him rather than to the cabinet. NIOC acted more or less as a ministry of hydrocarbons as it also controlled the National Iranian Gas Company (NIGC) and the National Petrochemical Company (NPC). In the mid-1970s infighting led to reorganization, as a result of which NIGC and NPC gained autonomy.[22] In 1980 the Ministry of Petroleum was set up, taking over control of the three corporations dealing with oil, gas and petrochemicals. NIOC remained in control of the development of the oil fields and refining and distribution of oil products, operating through four subsidiaries: the National Iran Offshore Oil Company (NIOOC); the National Iranian Drilling Company (NIDC); the National Iranian Tanker Corporation; the National Refined Product Distribution Company; and Kala, which took over all purchasing orders for the oil industry, the task formerly performed by the Oil Service Company, a Consortium-owned entity.

In March 1992, NIOC was redefined when it was divided into two distinct upstream and downstream divisions. Refining and distribution of products came under the control of a new division. Exploration, production and marketing of crude oil came under another division. The National Iranian Gas is now in charge of development of the gas fields and the pipeline network for domestic use and exports. It has only one subsidiary for exploring the potential for Liquified Natural Gas (LNG) exports. Despite these changes, NIOC is still by far the largest company in Iran. In 1993 it was ranked the fifth largest oil company in the world. It is the oldest oil company in the Middle East, dating back to 1951, with long experience in all aspects of the oil business.

The role of foreign firms in the Iranian oil industry was strengthened once again by the reconstruction and expansion programme that began in 1988. Rather than routine maintenance, projects became much more complex, and foreign technology and capital became essential. In particular, technically complex offshore development projects could no longer rely solely on local skills. Two obstacles slowed down full cooperation with foreign companies. The pressure from the United States on its Western allies not to do business with Iran, especially where transfer of advanced technology was concerned, prevented some viable projects from getting foreign financing. In 1994, the United States prevented the World Bank from going ahead with several projects. The reduction of flaring of associated gases was one of these. Moreover, in Iran there remains considerable sensitivity to the presence of foreign firms in general, and Western firms in the oil industry in particular. Fortuitously, foreign assistance is needed more for offshore projects, to which such contracts have been limited so far, thereby avoiding the large-scale presence of foreign workers in populated areas.

A more intractable problem has arisen in designing contracts with foreign companies. Where the project is well-defined and its returns are not subject to risk, service contracts – in which contractors are paid fixed sums for services rendered – usually work well. So far, Iran has tried to stay close to service contracts and away from equity or participation agreements in which foreign companies become full partners, sharing in the risks and profits of the project. Much of the reconstruction work, such as repairing war-damaged infrastructure in the Persian Gulf, appeared suited to service contracts. However, in practice the delay in payment – especially in 1993 and 1994, when Iran was hit by several foreign-exchange shortages – and delays in completion of projects due to local problems have made contractors wary of service contracts.

Service contracts are even less desirable for large, complex projects with uncertain yields. These projects often need foreign financing and their uncertainties make it difficult to find lenders. Furthermore, large and established foreign firms are often in a better position to take financial risks than a financially strapped country such as Iran. Therefore, it is only efficient to shift some of these risks to the large firms. Equity participation is designed to solve these problems, but, like other oil-exporting countries, Iran cannot take advantage because of the sensitivity to giving any ownership of its oil fields to foreign companies.

In the early 1990s Iran designed a contract in which foreign firms provided the financing and were to be paid later from resulting production. The amount of production allocated in this way depended on the price of the product at the time of payback. This is referred to as *be'i-ye mataqabel*, meaning barter. Payment by future extraction from a specific field entails some risk for the contracting firm, which under normal circumstances would have some control over operations. Perhaps it is the inclusion of these control elements that has prompted the oil media to remark that the new Iranian formula resembles 'equity participation'.[23]

The huge $1.7 billion South Pars natural-gas project involving Italian, Japanese and Russian partners is an important test case for this type of arrangement – in which payment comes in the form of condensates produced from the gas field. The contract appeared to be working until the Italian export credit agency suddenly withdrew its insurance protection and the deal was cancelled. It is not clear whether political pressure from the United States or simple economic calculations led the agency to deny coverage to this project. A possible objection may have been that the value of the condensates, to be determined five to seven years later when the field was ready for exploitation, may not be sufficient to pay for the costs. Parliament is now debating the expansion of the definition of 'the product' from a given project. The new rule would allow the National Iranian Gas Company, for example, to promise refined products supposedly saved from the substitution of natural gas, or oil recovered as a result of the reinjection of that gas into an oil field, to be available as payment for gas projects. This amendment is primarily designed to allow those projects, such as the North Pars field, that do not have an exportable product to take advantage of this formula. It will reduce the risk borne by foreign contractors in so far as there may be uncertainty regarding the amount of condensates in place, but still leaves intact the risks deriving from uncertainty about the amount of gas. The fate of the two largest gas fields in Iran, North and South Pars, on which the hydrocarbon strategy of Iran largely depends, awaits the development of an acceptable formula that would bring foreign capital and technology to Iran.

Domestic Demand for Refined Products

In a curious institutional setup, NIOC's revenues derive solely from its monopoly in the sale of refined products at home, whereas its costs arise from the entire oil operations – from exploration to development to export. To prevent NIOC from arbitrarily charging higher prices to raise more revenue, the price-making power is given to the Supreme Economic Council. This arrangement completely divorces energy prices from economic calculations – one reason why domestic prices of petroleum products do not bear any relation to costs and are essentially political variables. Since no actual subsidy is necessary to keep product prices

Figure 6.1   Prices of Refined Products (current IR/litre)

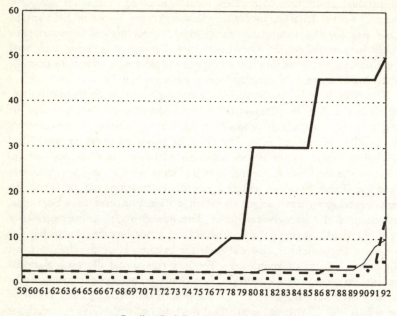

—Gasoil ··Fueloil --Kerosene —Gasoline

Source: Ministry of Oil.

below cost, the economic burden is not as evident as in the case of food subsidies.

Except for gasoline, nominal energy prices have changed very little in the last 30 years; as a result, they have declined in real terms significantly (see Figures 6.1 and 6.2). Price differentials between products have widened since the revolution, reflecting the shift in the social basis of political power.[24] The price of gasoline at 50 rials per litre – up tenfold since 1979 – was five times that of gasoil in 1991, ten times that of fuel oil and over twelve times that of kerosene. Politically, the gasoline price has been the easiest to adjust. It was first increased by 200 per cent in 1980 and then along with other products by 66 per cent in 1987. Despite these increases, even gasoline is very cheap and far below its opportunity cost. In 1994, at 50 rials per litre, the cost of a gallon of gasoline to the Iranian consumer was 10 cents ($1 = 2000 rials), or one-tenth of its price to the US consumer and one-fortieth of that on the European market. Kerosene, gasoil and fuel oil all sell for less than a nickel per gallon, far below their opportunity costs. The cost of the subsidy is estimated at about $5 billion,

Figure 6.2   Real Prices of Refined Products (1959 constant prices)

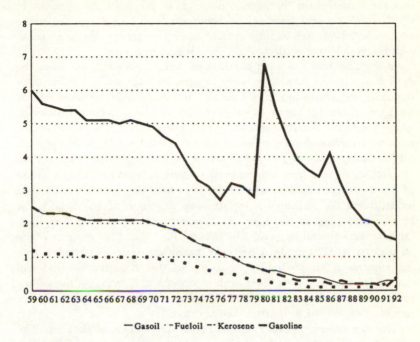

—Gasoil · ‒Fueloil ‒· Kerosene —Gasoline

Source: Ministry of Oil. Prices are deflated using the consumer price index from Bank Markazi, *Econimic Report and Balance Sheet,* various issues.

which far exceeded the $1.2 billion subsidy planned for all other 'essential products' in 1994.[25] Natural gas has also been added recently to the list of subsidized energy products. At 5 rials per cubic metre, natural gas is now cheaper than kerosene.

Energy prices are the main instrument for controlling demand, and where they are burdened with the role of income redistribution or that of a social safety net, control of demand can get out of hand. This is precisely what has happened in Iran. In response to falling real prices, consumption has averaged a 9 per cent increase per year for the past 25 years. For the 15 years before the revolution this rate was 12.6 per cent per year, but fell to 4.8 per cent in the 1980s when economic growth came to a halt and demand was rationed. The war conditions called for large-scale rationing of essential products: refined petroleum products being an important component. When the war ended, rationing was slowly dismantled, but prices did not rise to restrain demand. Demand has continued to increase at about 8 per cent per year, putting pressure on exports. At this rate, any likely increases in capacity will be taken up by domestic demand. In short, without a mechanism to control demand, in the best-case scenario in which Iran's capacity increases by another 1 mbd in the next ten years, exports will be frozen at their current level. If capacity fails to increase, exports would have to decline or rationing be reinstated.

In the past Iran was a net exporter of refined products, but since the destruction of the Abadan refinery in 1980 by Iraqi artillery it has been importing its refined products. Like the subsidies for domestically refined products, those for imported products are also well hidden. Instead of giving a subsidy to NIOC to import fuel, every year NIOC is authorized to swap a certain amount of crude oil for refined products. In 1992–93, NIOC swapped about 280 tbd of crude oil. In September 1993 the oil minister announced that, with the Arak refinery at full capacity (an addition of 60 tbd), there would be no need for imports.[26] However, in March 1994 he protested the parliament's import swap allocation of 190 tbd for the Iranian year 1994 as too low.[27] As a part of the First Five-Year Plan, imports were to end by 1994. The Second Five-Year Plan projects crude oil exports to fall only by 5 per cent during the 1994–98 period. Given the constraints on production, this implies that domestic demand will remain at its present level. Even with an optimistic forecast for the substitution of natural gas for refined oil products, this is only possible if rationing of refined products is reintroduced.

The fuel subsidy has also complicated NIOC's financial situation. The real value of its revenues has declined over the years with the fall in real product prices. By 1991 recurrent expenditures (cost of total oil production, refining and distribution of its domestic component) of NIOC had caught up with its revenues, leaving no savings to finance its ambitious capacity expansion programme. This was an important impetus to the historic decision by the parliament to grant NIOC – and other public firms – the right to borrow abroad to finance its investment programme.

There is serious political resistance to any increase in fuel prices. The November 1993 political crisis in Nigeria that led to a coup over the raising of the costs of petroleum products is only a recent reminder of the extreme sensitivity to any move to adjust long-unchanged prices. Interestingly, the first plan that recognized a rising demand for refined products as an important impediment to the expansion of oil exports, did not list raising prices among its many policy tools to control demand.

The political resistance to raising the price of oil products has increased since the first plan was drafted in 1988. After several years of structural adjustment, which adversely affected personal incomes and caused an upward adjustment in many prices, Iranians seem less willing to take another beating, especially one that appears uncalled for in a country rich in energy resources. The parliament that went along with the 1994 budget recommendations and slashed the essential-products subsidy from $3.4 in

1993 to $1.2 for 1994 rejected all requests for fuel price increases, including gasoline. As an item of consumption for the middle class, most populist governments find gasoline price increases palatable but they reject price increases for kerosene.[28]

The sheer magnitude of the price increases required to effect any meaningful reform is additional reason why prices are unlikely to go high enough to match opportunity cost. As Figure 6.2 suggests, even an increase that would only restore prices to their pre-revolutionary level is very large. Is a price increase an effective way to control demand anyway? Price elasticities estimated for petroleum products, except for kerosene, are non-negligible and indicate that consumption may decline by 30–40 per cent if prices double in real terms.[29]

There are also sound economic reasons for raising energy prices in Iran. Cheap energy has caused a decline in energy efficiency for the past 20 years. In 1989, despite a decline of 12 per cent in real GDP compared to 1977, consumption of petroleum products was up by 78 per cent, even outpacing the rate of growth of population, which was 40 per cent between the same years. During 1972–89, a period of rising world energy prices, energy intensity (defined as the ratio of refined product consumption to GDP) doubled in Iran while in OECD countries it fell by nearly one-quarter. Moreover, Iran was already using more energy per unit of production in 1972 than the average for the OECD; Iran used 5.9 barrels of petroleum products per $1000 of non-oil GDP, compared to four barrels for the OECD.[30]

The expansion of a natural gas network should relieve the demand pressure on non-transportation fuels. Natural gas is priced very low to encourage switching where possible. In 1994, gas prices were 8 rials per cubic metres for domestic and commercial users and 5 rials for industrial users.[31]

External Oil Policy

The Islamic Republic began its experience with oil in exceptional times. The effects of the 1973 price increase had not yet been reflected by the demand for oil. Slack demand during 1977–78 was abruptly reversed by lower production from Iran, first by the oil workers' strike that reduced production to a trickle during the last quarter of 1978, and then by the Iraqi invasion of Iran that reduced production from both countries. The price of oil soared to nearly $40, far higher than its earlier peak of $12, which only six years earlier had been termed the 'oil price revolution'. Panic buying created a feeling, not just in Iran but also in the international oil industry and among many academics, that the upper limit on the price of oil was not set by demand but by OPEC, or more precisely, by the moderates within it – Saudi Arabia, Kuwait and the United Arab Emirates.

This thinking originated from the belief, again widely held at the time, that OPEC not only engineered the 22 December 1973 price increase but also helped prevent it from sliding back down in the years that followed. Even the price increase of 1980, which seemed beyond OPEC's imagination, much less control, was attributed to OPEC. In reality, OPEC was following the spot market, and many countries were even late – sometimes purposefully as in the case of Saudi Arabia – in adjusting their prices to the world level, thus subsidizing particular oil companies who happened to have buying contracts at the time. In 1982, when the first signs of excess supply emerged, OPEC had no experience in controlling members' outputs. OPEC had ridden the high price of the 1970s without any quotas in place or even any discussion of production limits.[32]

The Islamic Republic began its OPEC career with excessive optimism regarding OPEC's significance in the world market, and a belief that the moderates and not the market stood between OPEC and a high price. Predictably, Iran's policy tilted in the direction of the so-called 'hawks' – Libya and Algeria – who tried to keep the price announced by OPEC (not to be confused with the actual market price) as high as possible. Thus Iran abandoned its earlier middle ground and its independent role in OPEC. Iran's OPEC policy had a political motive as well. The division inside OPEC corresponded somewhat closely with the line-up in international politics and the Iran–Iraq war. On the Iraqi side there were many OPEC moderates, whereas on Iran's side there was at least one hawk – Libya. If OPEC's decisions meant anything during this period, and many doubt that it did, Iran's side lost. On paper, Iraq received by far the better treatment: being allowed to produce as it wished, while Iran was allotted meagre quotas.

With hindsight, the heightening of tension within OPEC, to which Iran contributed, was to no one's advantage, as prices eventually collapsed in 1986 because of excess supply that reduced Saudi production from 10 mbd in 1980 to 2.5 mbd in 1985. It is not clear that OPEC could have prevented the price collapse, but it could certainly have prevented the terrible way in which it happened. Saudi Arabia first threatened to cut prices and was ignored; it then switched to the infamous netback pricing policy that ensured Saudi oil was the cheapest in the world.[33] The political division within OPEC helped blur the economic fact of life that, in the face of inability to control members' output, OPEC needed to adjust the price downward without backbiting.

The Islamic Republic's production policy was also affected by a view of OPEC as a price-setting agency. To the extent that the world price was decided in bargaining over price rather than output, Iran's decision to adopt a production ceiling of 4 mbd made sense. From the vantage point of 1979 the quota wars of the late 1980s must have seemed remote. Prices were so high and foreign exchange so abundant that no country was thinking of expanding production, much less doing so while cheating or acting against the interests of fellow OPEC members.[34] In view of Iran's later struggle to increase its quota to 3.6 mbd, the self-imposed production ceiling was counterproductive, in that it considerably weakened the weight of Iran's high output levels of 5 to 6 mbd in the 1970s. Since quotas appear to be influenced by historical production levels, Iran would have been better off emphasizing higher production needs (even if it decided to produce less) rather than conservation. When the price collapsed in 1986, so did the logic of conservation that had been used to criticize the Shah's oil policy.

Sometime after the price collapse of August 1986 and the end of the war in August 1988, Iran quietly decided to abandon its production ceiling and to expand capacity. In 1991 the first statements of a production capacity of 5 mbd were made and Iran began to lobby for a higher quota. It is not clear whether at this time Iran really needed OPEC's blessing to increase capacity and production, but it nevertheless decided to spend some of its radical, anti-Western political capital by moving closer to Saudi Arabia, which was in a position to help Iran gain its OPEC share.[35] This shift paid off quickly; by abandoning its firm stance, Iran received Saudi support for a higher quota. Of course, Iran could have acted as Iraq did and simply increased its production. But doing so would have also cost some political capital, for Iran would have likely received the blame for a weakened OPEC. Iran was already receiving blame for its aggressive marketing strategy in the early 1980s when it used discounting and barter trade to regain lost markets, but at that time it had a good excuse. Being at war, Iran was forced to compensate buyers for the increased uncertainty in supply and higher insurance premiums, which may have also provided cover for other forms of discounting.[36]

In recent years Iran has maintained the middle course and appears to have found its natural place in OPEC as one of the two most important producers in the organization and as a mediator between the hawks and doves. However, Iran's external oil policy is more precisely defined by its rivalry with Saudi Arabia for leadership of OPEC. Ever since the Persian Gulf war took Iraq out of the picture, Iran has moved in to fill the vacuum. While in pure commercial terms Iran is in no position to mount a serious challenge to Saudi Arabia by capturing its market share, it has applied considerable pressure on other fronts. What it lacks in oil reserves and production capacity Iran has tried to make up for by using its independent political stance as a Third World power. Iran has used the Saudi weakness in this respect quite effectively, portraying the Kingdom's oil policies in general, and its decisions in OPEC in particular, as motivated by its subservience to the consuming nations' interests, particularly that of the United States. Iran also appeared to have the initiative in 1994, if only because of its unexpected shifts in rhetoric, depicting Saudi Arabia alternately as friend and foe. For example, to break the deadlock in OPEC's September 1993 negotiations, President Rafsanjani initiated a call to King Fahd of Saudi Arabia, which resulted in a compromise and ended the stalemate in favour of a boost in Iran's quota from 3.4 to 3.6 mbd. But less than six months later the moderate language toward Saudi Arabia that followed this friendly gesture had returned to a war of words. This was in time for the next OPEC meeting of March 1994 in which Iran advocated a drop of 1.4 mbd in the OPEC ceiling (from 24.52 mbd), most of which would presumably have come from Saudi Arabia. In that meeting, Saudi Arabia prevailed and OPEC froze its ceiling for another nine months. The Iranian press was once again on the offensive, accusing Saudi Arabia of maintaining a high output of 8 mbd against its own interests and solely for the purpose of pleasing the United States. Although oil issues at times seem to dominate the relations between Iran and Saudi Arabia, the two countries interact at several other levels, competing for leadership in the Persian Gulf and in the Islamic world.

In commercial terms Iran and Saudi Arabia follow the same strategy, maximizing revenues by selling all they can in a weak market. This is known as the 'market share strategy'. But Iran's and Saudi Arabia's actual positions in the market are quite different. Saudi Arabia exports almost three times as much as Iran. By reducing its exports by half Saudi Arabia can shock the world market because this would reduce world supply by about 4 mbd. A similar act by Iran would only cut supply by 1.3 mbd. In addition, Iran's act would appear more costly to itself and therefore will be seen as not long-lasting, whereas a decision by the Saudis would have serious long-term implications. Although the Saudis have abandoned their role as a swing producer, the sheer size of their exports relative to world supply implies market power (that is, the ability to influence the world price). The asymmetry in the positions of Saudi Arabia and Iran are the result of fundamental differences in their endowments of hydrocarbons. Saudi Arabia has nearly three times the oil reserves of Iran. It makes little sense for Iran to compete in oil production.

The dialogue with Saudi Arabia may well be a sign that Iran realizes the limitations in OPEC power that derive from fundamental incentive problems within any cartel, and that actions taken by Saudi Arabia, more than actions by OPEC, can affect Iran's fortunes. The failure of OPEC to reach its goal of a $21–per-barrel price for oil has brought its role in the world market increasingly into question. As in most cartels, OPEC has little power to overcome free-riding and other incentive problems within its ranks. Individual incentives within OPEC are to raise production when prices rise, while collective interests dictate otherwise. OPEC must not only detect but punish cheaters if it is to give each member the incentive to abide by its quota. So far it has been unable to detect, much less punish, those who produce more than their quotas. More pressure on individual members may result in defection from its ranks, as demonstrated by Ecuador in 1992.

Quite possibly, a decrease of 2 to 3 mbd would increase rather than decrease aggregate member revenues. But reductions of this magnitude have never been achieved except by events beyond OPEC's control, such as wars and revolutions. This may explain why Iran has elected to apply pressure on Saudi Arabia rather than on OPEC members evenly. Rather than getting OPEC to reduce output by 2 to 3 mbd, Iran has argued that Saudi Arabia has an unfairly large OPEC share of 25 per cent and a reduction in Saudi output alone would solve everybody's problem. The difficulty with this approach is that it solves not just Iran's but all other producers' problems as well, and any cost Iran bears to get it would not be recoverable from those who would also benefit from a higher price. The cost paid by Iran in the event that the Saudis agree to reduce their output can come in different forms. Iran may have to forego demands on another contentious issue such as the disputed Persian Gulf islands or war reparations from Iraq, or it may place itself as the target of additional hostility on the part of consuming nations, mainly in the West, who might see the resulting higher prices as yet another piece of evidence in favour of the badly needed 'Iranian threat'.

For its part Saudi Arabia is aware that it may not be able to make up for the loss in output from higher prices, for other producers may raise their output to take advantage of temporarily higher prices. Furthermore, while Iraq's fate is being decided by the United Nations, Saudi Arabia is unlikely to relinquish its output share to Iran or any other OPEC member; it sees itself as keeping a place for the eventual resumption of Iraqi oil exports. The return of Iraq, presumably with 3 mbd, in a few years, will complicate the picture for Iran considerably. In that case, Iran's rivalry with Saudi Arabia may give way to a fight with Iraq for the second-place position. In doing that Iran would lose the advantage it has due to its political posture vis-à-vis Saudi Arabia, for at this time Iraq enjoys no less 'Third World credit' for its opposition to the United States than does Iran.

Conclusion

While oil revenues per capita have declined significantly, Iran's ability to reverse this has diminished. It is difficult to raise oil revenues for two reasons. First, it is very hard to increase the level of crude exports. Iran's production capacity seems to have reached its upper bound at 4.5 mbd. In the last two decades major new discoveries have been in natural gas not oil. While the possibility of exports of natural gas on a large scale are remote at present, increased domestic use may free some capacity for export of crude oil. Natural gas can also potentially 'produce' one million

barrels per day more of oil via reinjection. Unfortunately, development of
the large gas fields in the Persian Gulf require foreign financing and
technology, the attraction of which is not a strong aspect of the Islamic
Republic. The fundamental benefits of these projects for Iran and foreign
firms are obvious, but domestic and international politics have so far
prevented a deal from being struck.

Domestic politics also affect the overall energy picture in yet another
way. Demand for refined petroleum products at home shows no sign of
abating. After several years of threatening to raise prices for domestic
fuel, the government does not seem much closer actually to doing so. As
a result, a barrel of oil is sold at home at one-twentieth of its international
price, and domestic demand continues to put pressure on exports.

Second, there is very little that Iran (or any other country for that
matter except Saudi Arabia) can do to increase the price at which it sells
its crude in the world market. The oil market in the 1990s is a completely
different economic environment for Iran than it was in the 1970s or
1980s. More than ever before, oil prices are influenced by market forces
rather than politics. So far, Iran's attempts either to work inside OPEC or
to engage Saudi Arabia have simply not paid off, at least not in terms of
higher oil prices.

It is doubtful that Iran would gain much from focusing its attention
either on OPEC or Saudi Arabia. Many players in the market are realizing
that OPEC has never had any real power over the price of oil. This may
cause OPEC to return to its pre-1973 position, which would be similar to
other producers' organizations, such as the coffee and copper commodity
agreements, that continue to meet to exchange information but with little
real consequence. Iran will gain more from regional cooperation in the
Persian Gulf than from coordinating oil policies with distant OPEC
members such as Venezuela, Nigeria or Indonesia. This is not to say that
Iran will benefit from abandoning OPEC, for, as OPEC's second largest
and most influential member, Iran's presence in the organization is still
critical for it to function as a clearing house of information for its
members. In the past OPEC has rarely prevented Iran from reaching its
desirable or feasible production level. Capacity rather than quotas have
since 1980 determined Iran's production and every increase in capacity
has been followed by an increase in Iran's quotas. There is no reason to
think that OPEC will restrain Iran's production or exports from now on,
as the quota is close to capacity and the latter is unlikely to increase in
the future.

By refocusing its institutional energy on the Persian Gulf rather than
on Vienna or Riyadh, Iran may integrate its oil and foreign policy. As Iran
expands its oil and gas operations in the Persian Gulf, it may find more
reasons for cooperation as well as confrontation with the moderate Arab
producers of the region. An obvious source of tension is an increasing

amount of oil and gas found near or in the border areas. The potential of jointly owned fields for conflict or cooperation are much more real than the bickering in OPEC over market shares. There are oil fields located in the border areas of Iran and Iraq, and gas fields that span the continental shelves of Iran and Qatar. The huge gas reserves of the South Pars field are generally considered to be an extension of Qatar's North Field; Khouf-e-Salman of Iran is connected to Abu al-Bukhoosh of Qatar. Cooperation to prevent overexhaustion as a result of the 'tragedy of commons' is badly needed in all these cases. Qatar and Iran will soon be competing for the nearby South Asian gas market. Qatar is way ahead of Iran in developing its field, and perhaps will have an easier time coming into agreements for its sale and finding financing for the huge fixed costs of building a pipeline. As a small country, Qatar presents a potential importer connected via an expensive pipeline with less uncertainty in future sales than Iran, a much larger country with a reputation for mixing its economic and political relations.

The Persian Gulf is shallow enough for its entirety to fall within the continental shelf of the countries located on one side or the other. The fate of the three Persian Gulf islands of Abu Musa and the Greater and Lesser Tunb, currently occupied by Iran, has a direct impact on the length of territory that Iran can claim as its continental shelf. For example, the Mubarak oil field, currently on the continental shelf of the United Arab Emirates, is only 25 kilometres south of the Abu Musa island. The oil fields of Abu al-Bukhoosh and Fateh are located only a few kilometres south of the existing international boundary line. Consequently, any re-drawing of borders in the Persian Gulf affects the ownership of large reserves of oil, known and potential, and will be the source of immense tensions in the region.

Notes

1. Oil is generally found in conjunction with gas, which provides the pressure that allows oil to flow to the surface.

2. In 1994 Oil Minister Aghazadeh offered the figure of 90 billion barrels, which is consistent after reserve depletion has been taken into account (see *Middle East Economic Survey* (*MEES*), 10 January 1994, p A10).

3. Between 1978 and 1979, Iranian light crude rose from $12.81 per barrel to $30.

4. Plan and Budget Organization (PBO), *The Performance of the First Five-Year Plan* (in Persian, Tehran, 1994), p iv–1.

5. The last confirmation of this was production of 4.0 mbd during a test week in October 1992, observed by the oil trade journalists. At the time, *MEES* believed that 4.5 mbd was within striking distance (*MEES*, 10 October 1992, p 1).

6. Fesharaki, Fereidun, *Revolution and Energy Policy in Iran* (London: The Economist Intelligence Unit, 1980).

7. The figure for 1977 is from Mossavar-Rahmani, Bijan, *Energy Policy in Iran* (New York: Pergamon Press, 1981), p 78; and the figure for 1987 is from the PBO, *The First Five Year Economic, Social and Cultural Development Plan of the Islamic Republic of Iran,* (in Persian, Tehran, 1990), p ix–2.

8. These calculations may not include the opportunity cost of the gas itself, and therefore may underestimate the true cost. Roughly speaking, for every ten barrels of oil recovered the amount of natural gas injected is equivalent to one barrel of crude, of which about 15 per cent is never recovered. This would add about 23 cents to the cost of each barrel recovered. Even with this addition reinjection is still the least expensive way to increase capacity.

9. One barrel of oil is the thermal equivalent of 159 cubic metres of gas.

10. The consortium included the Italian firms Saipem, a subsidiary of the ENI group, and Techologie Progetti Lavori, Japan's Mitsubishi group and Russia's Machinoimport.

11. Natural gas is costly to trade and is therefore not used as payback. Condensates are the tradable part of the production from the fields and are used instead. The problem arises where there is uncertainty regarding there being enough condensates to compensate the contractors fully, or, as in the case of North Pars, where fields do not have any condensates. The Majles, which has forbidden borrowing for such projects, is now debating allowing refined products, ostensibly 'saved' as a result of the gases from the project to be used as a payback.

12. The reason may be the expectation of some improvement in Iran's foreign-investment law favouring foreign investors (see below).

13. About 40 per cent of the associated gas is still being flared.

14. Elm, Mostafa, *Oil, Power and Principle, Iran's Nationalization and its Aftermath* (Syracuse: Syracuse University Press, 1992), p 53.

15. PBO, *The Bill of The Second Five Year Plan of the Islamic Republic* (in Persian, Tehran, 1993), p iii–4.

16. PBO: *The Performance of the First Five Year Plan.*

17. Ibid., p iv–5.

18. Mossavar-Rahmani, *Energy Policy in Iran,* pp 73–5.

19. The number of foreign personnel was down from over 1500 in 1977 to 115 in 1981 (Razzaqi, Ebrahim, *Eqtesad-e Iran* (Tehran: Nashre-e Ney, 1988), p 504).

20. For example, the last case was that of AMOCO with a claim of $1753 million plus interest, which was settled at $270 million plus interest in 1990. For more information on the settlement of cases before the international tribunal, see Alerassoul, Mahvash, *Freezing Assets: The USA and the Most Effective Economic Sanction* (New York: St Martin's Press, 1993).

21. Stocking, George W., *Middle East Oil* (Nashville: Vanderbilt University Press, 1970), p 140. In the end, the Consortium agreed to a 12 per cent increase.

22. Fesharaki, *Revolution,* p 23.

23. 'Iran blazing trails on new equity deals for Middle East', *Petroleum Intelligence Weekly,* 14 October 1991, p 1.

24. Sterner, Thomas, 'Oil products in Latin America: the politics of energy pricing', *The Energy Journal* 9/2 (1989), pp 25–46.

25. This is not an out-of-pocket expense for the government. It is income foregone based on the export value of the products sold domestically. For more details, see Salehi-Isfahani, Djavad, 'Pricing of petroleum products in Iran,' Oxford Institute

for Energy Studies, mimeo, 1992.

26. *MEES*, 12 September 1993.

27. *Iran Times*, 11 March 1994, p. 15.

28. Sterner, 'Oil products'.

29. Salehi-Isfahani, 'Pricing of petroleum products in Iran'.

30. Ibid.

31. To see how inexpensive this gas is, note that at 8 rials per cubic metre, a barrel of oil would cost 64 cents!

32. For a survey of OPEC and market behaviour during this period, see Cremer, Jacques, and Djavad Salehi-Isfahani, *Models of the Oil Market*, Fundamentals of Pure and Applied Economics, no 44 (Chur, Switzerland: Harwood Academic Publishers, 1991).

33. Iran put the blame for the price collapse squarely on Saudi Arabia, declaring the act as 'treason' and 'declaration of war' (*MEES* 10, October 1988). For a description of the events that led to the price collapse, see Cremer and Salehi-Isfahani, *Models of the Oil Market*, ch 3.

34. This is the argument behind the backward bending supply curve for oil which argues that OPEC was not a cartel before 1982, and thereafter only an unsuccessful one. See Cremer, Jacques, and Djavad Salehi-Isfahani, 'The rise and fall of oil prices: a competitive view', *Annales d'Economie et de Statistique* 15/16 (July–December 1989), pp 427–54.

35. Iran's share in OPEC output in fact declined from around 20 per cent in 1970s to 10 per cent in 1980s. In 1994 its share rose to 15 per cent.

36. Mossavar-Rahmani, Bijan, and Fereidun Fesharaki, 'Oil dependence and mega-projects: return to economic normalcy in Iran?', *MEES*, supplement to 26/19, 21 February 1983, pp 1–11.

7

The Political Economy of
Foreign Exchange Reform

Hossein Farzin

Introduction

With the ending of the Iran–Iraq war, the Islamic Republic embarked on a five-year reconstruction and development plan with the principal objective of bringing the economy back to its normal situation and maintaining a sustained growth path. As a part of this general objective, and to gain access to international capital markets to borrow foreign-exchange resources to reconstruct the economy, the government began a dialogue with the International Monetary Fund (IMF) and the World Bank about an extensive economic reform programme.[1] The principal components of the reform programme included: (1) liberalization of the exchange-rate system and allocation; (2) liberalization of the trade regime and tariffs; (3) decontrolling of domestic prices; (4) privatization of some of the public enterprises; and (5) adoption of a social safety net to protect the vulnerable groups during the reform process.

This chapter examines the reform of the exchange-rate system and its associated safety-net programme, with the prime motive of addressing some of the unresolved political-economy issues.[2] Specifically, it argues that the three-tier multiple-exchange-rate system was not only a major cause of inefficiencies in resource allocation, by intensifying the rent-seeking orientation of the Iranian economy; it also caused growing inequality in the distribution of income and wealth between those (such as the quasi-public foundations and import-licence holders) who had access to, or indirectly benefited from, the subsidized exchange rates and the rest of society. This chapter also addresses the welfare implications of the exchange-rate unification and its implementation problems. At the same time that it argues in favour of a single-step unification and against a gradual one, it calls into question the prudence of the IMF's proposed 'restricted coupon system' as a social safety net, and the assignment of a key role to the quasi-public foundations for protecting the poor and vulnerable groups against the adverse effects of the unification. An alternative approach to the safety net is proposed.

Finally, the chapter examines the March 1993 exchange-rate unification and, by drawing on available early indications, attempts to answer three specific questions: How serious can the initial adverse effects of the unification be and how effective have the government's safety-net policies thus far been? What explains the expedited timing of the unification?, and Did the Central Bank choose an appropriate exchange rate for the unification? The chapter ends with a summary of the main arguments and some concluding remarks.

Undesirable Consequences of the Multiple-Exchange-Rate System

At the centre of the economic reform programme, formulated in consultation with the IMF, is the reform of the foreign-exchange-rate system. Since the Second World War, foreign transactions have taken place within a multiple-exchange-rate system. At one time during the war, the number of exchange rates applicable to imports exceeded seven. But, on the IMF's recommendation, the exchange-rate reforms of January 1991 reduced this number to three rates. These rates were the basic 'official' rate of $1 = IR 70, the 'competitive' rate of $1 = IR 600, and the Central Bank-announced 'floating' rate, which was about $1 = IR 1460 a year before the multiple-exchange-rate system was abandoned. There was only a minor difference between this 'floating' rate, at which commercial banks sold foreign exchange supplied by the Central Bank, and the 'free' rate at which foreign exchange was sold on the open market.

For each exchange rate, there was a pre-announced list of eligible imports. For example, there was a list of 16 'essential' consumer items plus items for development projects and defence needs whose imports were eligible for foreign-exchange allocation at the basic official exchange rate. All government imports were at the basic official exchange rate. Similarly, there was a list of 290 items of mainly raw materials and intermediate inputs that were importable either at the 'competitive' exchange rate or the 'floating' exchange rate, depending on destination and conditions for their use. All other non-banned items were importable only at the floating rate. The official basic rate was applied to about 60 per cent of imports, the floating rate to about 10–15 per cent, and the competitive rate to the rest.

The multiple-exchange-rate regime inflicted several major problems on the economy: (1) it was a principal source of distortion in resource allocation and hence the overall inefficiency of the Iranian economy. As a consequence, it diverted the economy from productive activities and toward rent-seeking, intermediary, non-productive services and operations. (2) It was a notorious source of non-transparency in the trade regime, leading to pervasive corruption, and interest-group advocacies in government economic policies. (3) By enriching the groups with privileged access to importation of goods at the basic official exchange rate on the one hand, and by adding to inflationary pressures (via massive implicit subsidies and growing fiscal deficit) on the other hand, the multiple-exchange-rate system further deepened the inequality in distribution of income and wealth. This nullified the government intention to protect the poor from inflation by rationing goods through the coupon system.

The following observations support the charges of allocative inefficiency, widespread corruption, and aggravation of income and wealth inequality attributed to the pre-reform exchange rate regime.[3]

First, the multiple-exchange-rate system generated a set of implicit (non-budgeted) subsidies and taxes. Since the 'floating' rate is the marginal cost of foreign exchange, importers obtaining allocations at basic or competitive rates received a subsidy. Calculated at the floating rate of $1 = IR 70 prevailing during March– April 1992, the subsidies were as high as ((1460 − 70)/70) × 100 = 1985 per cent on the official rate and ((1460 − 600)/600) × 100 = 143 per cent on the competitive rate. Although almost all allocations of foreign exchange at the subsidized rates were rationed, the larger importers presumably received greater allocations than smaller importers. The multiple-exchange-rate system, therefore, provided a substantial subsidy to larger domestic industries and especially to those with a high import content and hence a low share of value-added in gross output.

Second, in the case of foreign exchange allocations at the 'competitive' exchange rate, there was evidence of 'conditional' allocations to both public and private firms.[4] In the case of manufacturing firms, these conditions had the specific forms of tying exchange allocations to *local content* arrangements, or *buy-back* requirements, or *export sales*. For example, there were reports that several assembling firms normally received foreign-exchange allocations at the competitive rate for only one-half of their foreign-exchange requirements, but could get additional allocations if they persuaded their suppliers to buy back some fraction of the output. In another case, a firm applying for a licence to import heavy machinery was required to obtain guarantees from its foreign supplier to buy back 25 per cent of the value of the initial transaction. The buy-back items were to be supplied not by the same firm but by another in an allied industry.

Third, the multiple-exchange-rate regime was biased against non-oil exports and in favour of domestic import-substituting industries, particularly the public-sector enterprises which had greater access to foreign exchange at the competitive exchange rate than the private firms. This was because access to foreign exchange at concessional rates, as well as the quantitative import restrictions and the local-content and buy-back requirements, all provide heavy protection to domestic import-competing output. This led to misallocation of resources by shifting them away from export-oriented industries to protected public enterprises, with consequent higher consumer prices (or larger subsidy expenditures if the government decided to keep consumer prices in check by subsidizing them) in the latter sectors.

Fourth, there were reports of many cases of allocation of foreign exchange at the basic official rate to private manufacturers for raw material (for example, inputs for producing detergents) and capital equipment (for example, machinery for a new firm producing refractory materials). Similarly, in some cases, foreign exchange at the basic official rate was also allocated for construction materials (for example, steel rods). All these cases defied the government's pre-announced list of essential imports eligible for foreign exchange at the official rate; importers must have in each case purchased foreign exchange at the floating rate which was more than 20 times higher.

Among importers with access to subsidized foreign-exchange rates are some of the 'revolutionary foundations' (or *bonyads*). As charity institutions exempt from taxes and many legal restrictions and only answerable to the Leader, these foundations operate independently of the government, with the apparent objective of improving the welfare of the poor and 'oppressed', and hence alleviate economic and social inequality in society. Some of the foundations own considerable assets and enterprises, and are active in domestic production, foreign trade (mainly imports), banking and credit, and procurement and distribution of goods and services. The most prominent among them is the Foundation for the Oppressed (Bonyad-e-Mostaz'afin).[5] It was set up on the fortune of the Shah (mainly the former Pahlavi Foundation) and other confiscated private businesses and companies. It is economically the most powerful and, institutionally and legally, the most obscure of the foundations. With some 400,000 employees and more than 1500 operations, this *bonyad* has already established itself in agriculture, industry (including steel and auto production), mining, housing development and construction, transportation (land, shipping, and aviation) and tourism (hotels and tourist centres). To appreciate better the heavy weight of Bonyad-e-Mostaz'afin in Iran's economy, it is sufficient to note that in addition to having special access to fuel oil produced by domestic refineries, it has obtained access to crude oil produced by the National Iranian Oil Company for marketing abroad through its London-based company, Bonoil UK. According to the *Petroleum Intelligence Weekly* (*PIW*), Bonyad-e-Mostaz'afin has also held talks with European oil companies, including France's Total, about possible downstream investments.[6]

Welfare Implications of Exchange Unification

Because of the foregoing flaws in the current multiple-exchange-rate regime, both the IMF and the World Bank emphasized the need for an early unification of exchange rates (by March 1994) as a core condition for improving the efficiency of the Iranian economy. By unifying the exchange rates, liberalizing the trade regime and decontrolling prices, the IMF believed that 'the economic reforms would improve the efficiency of the Iranian economy and would contribute to sustained economic growth over the medium and long term'.[7] However, although the long-run benefits of reform cannot be disputed, in the short run, when relative prices change and resources are reallocated, some groups will experience a decline in their real incomes and others will become unemployed as the industries relying on low-price foreign exchange shrink or disappear. The enormity of the short-run implications of the exchange-rate unification for the economic welfare of the Iranian people is best appreciated by noting how completely the present living standard depends on subsidies. Rafsanjani, the president of the Islamic Republic, underscored this dependence in his speech on 6 March 1992,

> We are paying a heavy price for subsidies. Our people receive bread practically free of charge. We buy [wheat] at 15 tomans [IR 150] a kilo, convert it into flour and pass it to the people at one toman a kilo to the bakeries. We buy sugar at 40–50 tomans a kilo from the factory and sell it to the people at between 2.7 and three tomans. We buy cooking oil at 40–50 tomans and sell it to the people at 3–4 tomans a kilo. We supply the farmers with more or less free pesticide and fertilizer. As regards fuel, not only do we supply it freely, but we add a little something extra to it, too. We supply the people with 1.2 million barrels of oil a day free of charge, and our sales do not even cover our delivery charge. This is our people's life style.... This is the existing situation; however, conditions are such that we cannot suddenly terminate these [subsidies], since that would ruin the life of the weak strata. We are progressing through our [five] year plan, by maintaining the people's purchasing power, achieving equilibrium with increases in salaries. This year we raised the wages of employees and we will do likewise next year.[8]

The huge subsidies on consumer goods, as well as those on industrial and agricultural inputs, was partially in the form of preferential exchange rates. So unification of the exchange rate at the floating rate implies a huge jump in the cost of living. The IMF's October 1990 mission estimated that the establishment of a dual exchange rate with an official rate of $1 = IR 800 and a floating rate would raise the cost of living by 70 per cent for the low-income and 40 per cent for the high-income groups.[9] To keep consumers' real purchasing power at its present levels the government must finance and sustain a correspondingly huge jump in subsidy expenditure. IMF's March 1991 mission estimated that following a major devaluation explicit budgetary subsidies to maintain the official prices at their present levels would cost about 4.3 per cent of 1990 GDP. Alternatively, the government should raise wages in proportion to consumer price increases. However, both of these policies would lead to unbearably high inflationary pressures and would further destabilize the economy.

Recognizing the welfare distribution concern of the government, the IMF mission in May 1991 stressed the need for a social safety net to be created to protect the poor and vulnerable groups during the transition. The IMF recommended that the government redesign the existing system of subsidies to make it explicit, less costly and more effective in protecting the poor. More specifically, it recommended that the government reduce the number of subsidized commodities from 11 items to only 6 items (bread, rice, sugar, cheese, vegetable oils and infant formula) while liberalizing other prices fully; and through a scaled-down coupon system, ensure the poor's access to minimum levels of consumption of the six commodities at subsidized prices during the economic reform. This list omitted eggs, butter, meat, detergent and soap. They were considered to be less essential and consumed largely by the non-poor, with negligible shares in the budget of poor households.

Because rigorous identification of poor from non-poor entailed substantial time and effort, the IMF recommended that the coupons could continue to be distributed to every household regardless of income, but by increasing the frequency of coupon distribution from once to four to six times a year, and by using property ownership records, it was hoped that the government would motivate the better-off households to withdraw from the subsidy system.

The IMF estimated that for the 11 subsidized commodities, with unchanged official prices, the budgetary subsidies would amount to 10 per cent of GDP in 1991 if the exchange rate were to be unified at the devalued rate of $1 = IR 1350. But limiting the subsidies to the specified six commodities and reducing coupon quantities to the levels close to actual consumption of the poorest quintal – which for bread, for example, meant a 20 per cent consumption cut – the amount of subsidies would be cut about 40 per cent, thus preventing a potentially large increase in the budget deficit. The IMF maintained that the government could further reduce subsidies substantially by increasing official prices, as this would further motivate the better-off households to leave the subsidy system.

Implementation Problems

That the highly distortive and non-transparent exchange-rate regime should have been terminated by unifying the existing rates at a free-market rate is a reform not in dispute. Of fundamental concern, however, were the twin questions of (1) the pace of the reform, and (2) how to cope with its adverse welfare effects in the short run.

(1) *The pace of unification*

Should the government have adopted a 'gradual' approach and unified the three exchange rates slowly, or should it have adopted the so called 'cold turkey' approach in a single step? The literature on this issue is rather new and has been emerging in response to the need for price reforms in the countries of Eastern Europe and the former Soviet Union.[10] Two factors complicate the choice. First, an exchange-rate unification leads to higher prices. Price rises have on the one hand, an adverse welfare effect and on the other a beneficial effect to the extent that they raise supply. Second, expectations of future exchange-rate devaluations lead to intertemporal speculation in the foreign-exchange market as well as in markets for storable goods.

Under a gradual approach to unification, there will be greater incentive for speculation in the exchange market against the future exchange value of the rial, thus exacerbating the initial imbalance in the foreign-exchange market and further destabilizing it. Increased instability in the exchange market will in turn raise the probability that the government will abandon the unification programme halfway through. At the same time, as van Wijnbergen has shown, under the gradual approach, there will be an increase in hoarding of goods in the early stages of the reform.[11] The intuition behind this proposition is simple. Under a gradual reunification programme, prices in the initial period will be lower, giving rise to expectations of larger capital gains in future when the exchange rate is fully liberalized. More hoarding means, of course, lower supply response to exchange-rate devaluation in the early stages of the programme, which in turn increases the probability that the programme will be abandoned halfway through. Given the high propensity of the Iranian economy toward rent-seeking activities, the adverse hoarding effect of a gradual reform programme was likely to be quite large.

In contrast to the gradual change, with a 'cold turkey' approach, which unifies the various exchange rates in a single step, there will be little incentive for intertemporal speculation in either the exchange market or in the goods market. Under the 'cold turkey' approach, the exchange rate and hence prices are immediately and fully liberalized. Thus, if it is certain that the reform will actually be implemented – that is, if there is no credibility problem with the reform programme – then there will be no prospects of capital gains resulting from the programme, and hence there would be no hoarding. On the other hand, if there is a credibility problem – that is, if there is a strong probability that the unification reform will not be maintained – then the disincentives for hoarding will be even stronger, since the collapse of the reform would mean a return to controlled exchange rates and prices, thus leading to capital losses both on foreign-exchange deposits and on inventories of goods.

Thus, contrary to the 'gradual' approach, which leads to increased hoarding and hence reduced supply response, a 'cold turkey' approach results in dishoarding and much larger supply response and less transitional unemployment. A wise policy would therefore seek to unify the existing exchange rates in a single step. Clearly, the most desirable time for taking this single step would be when the macroeconomic stabilizing policies are fully active and when an effective social safety-net programme has already been prepared to protect the vulnerable, those on a low income and the jobless groups against the pitfalls of the unification.

The policy-makers in Iran and in the IMF opted for a gradual unification of the exchange rates by moving some of the items eligible for imports at the basic official exchange rate to the list of items that can be imported at the competitive rate or floating rate. In line with this policy, the timing of the exchange-rate unification was postponed several times. For example, on 1 December 1992, Rafsanjani declared on Iranian television that the unification of exchange rates would not be included in the budget for the new Iranian year 1372, which started on 21 March 1993, thus postponing the target date of March 1994 as previously set in agreement with the IMF.[12] Furthermore, Rafsanjani noted that 'the result of numerous meetings of the cabinet, the Supreme Economic Council and Majles was the decision to separate the path of exchange-rate unification from reforms aimed at balancing the economy.'[13] Subsequently, the head of the Plan and Budget Committee of the Majles stated that unification of the exchange rates was seen as attainable within three years.[14]

(2) The social safety net

To cope with the adverse welfare effect of exchange-rate unification, especially for the poor and vulnerable groups, the IMF proposed a social-safety-net system consisting of two essential components: a scaled-down coupon system (explained above) and reliance on the existing public and quasi-public institutions (namely, the various revolutionary foundations and organizations) for assisting the poor. For several reasons, however, it is doubtful if the proposed safety net holds much economic merit or is tight enough to protect the poor from loss of welfare during and after reform.

First, even if one takes the IMF's estimates at face value, the scaled-down coupon system would bring a saving of 40 per cent in budgetary subsidies compared to continuation of the present extensive subsidy system in the face of a unification of the exchange rate at $1 = IR 1350. Surely the economic merit of this saving should be weighed against the welfare losses that consumers will incur because of both substantial cuts in their consumption levels of the remaining subsidized commodities and increases in the prices of the other commodities that they buy at market prices. If reliable data on household expenditures were available, it would be a straightforward task to quantify the welfare losses (in terms of compensating variation or equivalent variation) due to the proposed quantity cuts for the subsidized items and price jumps for other goods. However, even without engaging in such calculations, it seems plausible, in view of the essential nature of the subsidized goods and the enormity of price increases for non-subsidized ones, to expect that the welfare losses resulting from the scaled-down coupon system will be huge. Further, the expected reduction in subsidies, which is the main justification for adopting the restricted coupon system, loses its significance when it is noted that upon exchange-rate unification the government's earnings from oil and gas exports (which presently provide about 20 per cent of its total revenue on an actual basis) will increase by more than 20 times.

Second, even if one were to give a zero weight to the loss of welfare by the high-income groups whose cost of living will (according to the IMF) increase by 40 per cent, the restricted coupon system would fall short of even compensating the welfare loss of the low-income households whose cost of living will (according to the IMF) jump by 70 per cent under a dual exchange rate and considerably more upon the unification at the free exchange rate. The IMF report acknowledges this shortcoming, but unrealistically holds the view that 'the real compensation is expected to come through a more efficient allocation of resources in the economy, resulting in greater economic output, higher real wages, and improved income-earning opportunities'.[15] This expectation, even if justified, evades the problem at hand. For it does not indicate how the welfare of the poor should be supported in the transition period; nor does it indicate for how long the poor should endure the loss of welfare before they benefit from the greater economic output expected to result from reform. Even worse, it does not explain what mechanism will ensure that the low-income groups will necessarily be among the beneficiaries of reform.

Third, to see how unrealistic the IMF's expectations are, one needs to note that by the IMF's own estimates, which are based on official statistics, there are about 2 million unemployed workers in Iran, of whom nearly 1.4 million reside in urban areas and 0.6 million in rural areas. These correspond to unemployment rates of 20 per cent and 12 per cent, respectively. As bleak as these official statistics are, they do not reflect the full extent of unemployment since they ignore hundreds of thousands of people who suffer from disguised unemployment, or are underemployed, or have given up looking for work because they believe the prospects of finding a job are so poor. Whatever the actual unemployment rate, to it should be added the additional unemployment that will result from the economic reform. Lacking a regular source of income, the unemployed group will not be able to purchase basic commodities at market prices. Furthermore, only 40,000 or about 2 per cent of the unemployed population currently receives unemployment benefits, and extending the unemployment benefits to the rest is neither financially viable nor economically a sound policy. Although a part of the unemployed population has some skills, it is not certain that their skills will be demanded in the new economic activities emerging in the post-reform era. Still worse is the fate of unemployed labour with no skills. This group, which forms a significant portion of the unemployed population, will be particularly vulnerable both during and after reform, as it will have very little chance of finding a permanent income-earning opportunity – let alone the higher real wages that the IMF optimistically expects.

Fourth, as a supplement to the restricted coupon system, the IMF resorts to non-governmental organizations and foundations (cited earlier) to provide a safety net for vulnerable groups. In fact it goes so far as to recommend that such institutions should play a pivotal role in protecting the poor. For the reasons spelled out below, this recommendation not only falls far short of solving the problem of a social safety net, but in several ways sharply contradicts the reform's own objective of improving the efficiency and transparency of resource allocation in the Iranian economy.

These foundations were themselves the major beneficiaries of the multiple-exchange-rate system; they obtain goods and intermediate inputs at heavily subsidized prices and acquire considerable amount of foreign exchange at highly favourable rates, which is nothing but pure rent. What is perhaps noteworthy in this regard is the complaint of the governor of the Central Bank that some of these foundations have been buying foreign exchange at the official rate and then reselling it on the free market at a huge profit.[16] Noting also that several of the foundations, especially the Komiteh-ye-Emdad, also receive substantial amounts of budgetary and non-budgetary transfers as well as religious taxes, it is clear that the foundations have been drawing massive amounts of resources in the form of implicit and explicit subsidies and transfers. On the other hand, with no governmental discretion over expenses, no shareholders, no public account, and no clear legal status, they have been operating autonomously from the government, and thus have been effectively a law unto themselves. As such, and despite their political importance to the Islamic Republic as the grassroots constituencies of the revolution, it cannot be denied that the foundations have themselves been a major source of distortion and non-transparency in resource allocation and a major financial drag on the Iranian economy.

It follows that the IMF's presumption that the foundations are pure charity institutions operating for the benefit of the poor is simplistic, particularly as this includes the largest and the wealthiest of these religious foundations, the Foundation for the Oppressed. This latter is indeed a giant monopoly with vast control over the Iranian economy. As such, its activities, being strictly driven by the motive of profit-making on non-competitive terms and rent-seeking activities, are neither economically justifiable nor have relevance to the improvement of the well-being of the 'oppressed'. Thus, for example, in stark contrast to its assigned task of building cheap housing for the poor, the foundation has been making huge profits by building mansions that only the very rich can afford. It is ironic, in this regard, that the very same revolutionary foundations that were set up to protect the 'disinherited' and the 'deprived' classes against the 'capitalist exploiters' have themselves turned out to have been selling out to profit.

Further, there lies a more fundamental contradiction in the IMF's recommendation that the foundations be assigned the important task of providing a safety net against the adverse effects of the exchange-rate reform or of economic reform in general. As noted earlier, economic survival of the foundations – and hence hundreds of the industrial enter-prises controlled by them – rests upon their privileged access to foreign exchange at the subsidized rates. So a reform of the exchange rate which aims to apply a unified, market-determined, exchange rate to all foreign-exchange transactions, including those of the foundations, will inevitably hit the economic base of the very same foundations that the IMF recom-mends play the key role in providing a social safety net. What is particularly startling about the IMF's recommendation is that it ignores the fact that in the face of losing their economic privileges and power as a result of exchange unification, the foundations will use their enormous political power to oppose or hamper reform itself.

Productive Employment Opportunity: The Intact Safety Net

Any economic reform inevitably involves loss of welfare to some groups, at least for a time. In the case of exchange-rate unification the most serious adverse effect, besides acceleration of the inflation rate, will be higher unemployment rates resulting from contraction or closure of enter-prises that are intensively dependent on imports and have hitherto been sheltered by subsidized exchange rates. Obviously, for the workers who manage to remain employed (for example, government employees), the consequence of the reform can be a noticeable decline in their real incomes; for those who lose their jobs it is a total loss of purchasing power. Unemployment is not only a personal tragedy for this group; it is also a major economic waste in terms of obsolete skills, lost production and tax revenue, an increase in the costs of welfare and unemployment compensation programmes, in addition to other social costs (such as higher crime rates). Therefore, in protecting low-income groups from the adverse effects of reform no safety net can be more effective, reliable and economically desirable than to provide them with productive employment opportunities.

This implies a number of specific measures that a government should undertake before implementing reform. First and foremost, it should give high priority to investment in human resources. For unskilled workers this means providing education and skills training as a precondition to their taking advantage of new opportunities arising from economic reform. As a transitory measure, some unskilled labour (especially the urban poor) can be employed in public-works programmes, with payment in cash or in kind (for example, food, clothing and shelter for work). For those workers who stand to lose their jobs or earnings because reform will render their skills redundant there will be need for an employment transition programme to retrain (through technical and vocational training schemes) and provide adjustment assistance and employment services. It also follows that the government should encourage the private sector to train and retrain workers by (1) designing and implementing training programmes in cooperation with private enterprises, (2) sharing the costs of these programmes, and (3) offering training allowances and income support for those workers who participate. These programmes should be targeted at disadvantaged and occupationally dislocated workers who are most in need. In the rural areas where the bulk of the poor consists of landless labourers, farmers of smallholdings and the self-employed with small enterprises, the government should assist these groups by providing them with the necessary means of production when viable self-employment projects exist, or employing them in projects such as construction, irrigation, or infrastructural rehabilitation. There are also other poor groups who, for reasons of disability, old age, illness, and the like, cannot work. These groups should be covered by well-targeted social-security schemes, managed by governmental agencies such as the Welfare Organization of the Ministry of Health and Welfare.

Second, contrary to the IMF's recommendation that the non-governmental foundations be made responsible for providing a safety net, and in view of the previous arguments put forward against this recommendation, it is in fact the government which should provide the effective safety net. An important policy implication of this point is that the non-governmental foundations that presently operate autonomously should be integrated into the existing relevant ministries. Among the benefits of this measure would be: substantial savings of resources by avoiding duplication of efforts in assisting the poor and vulnerable groups; minimization of bureaucratic bottlenecks and more transparency in targeting the groups most in need; improvement in the efficiency and transparency of resource allocation; and last, but not least, improvement in fiscal discipline.

The March 1993 Unification: An Early Assessment

On 27 March 1993, the Islamic Republic introduced its exchange-rate reform by officially pegging the rial at $1 = IR 1538, an effective 95.6 per cent devaluation from the (trade-weighted) average rate of $1 = IR 786.3 prior to 21 March 1993. While it is still too early to assess fully the effects of the exchange-rate unification, several important questions arise, which I will attempt to answer: (1) How serious will the initial adverse welfare effects of the unification be and how effective have the government safety-net policies been thus far? (2) What explains the timing of the unification? (3) Was the exchange rate chosen for the unification an appropriate one?

The welfare effects of the unification and the government safety net

It should be noted that, although officially the exchange rates are unified, in practice the unification is not yet complete. This is because the government has earmarked about $3800 million in hard currency for imports of essential goods at the old official rate of $1 = IR 70. Of this amount, which is more than 20 per cent of the estimated export earnings in 1993, about $1200 million is allocated to fuel imports, $1300 million to food, $850 million to defence, $388 million to medicine, and $80 million to students abroad.[17] The primary reason for continuing to employ this dramatically subsidized exchange rate is apparently to attempt to ease the burden of accelerated inflation. However, since the importing of most basic goods has been customarily in the hands of the revolutionary foundations,[18] and in view of the foundations' economic dependence on subsidized exchange rates, it would not be implausible to think of the exemption of $3800 million in imports from the unified exchange rate in part as the government's concession to the foundations in order to secure their political approval of the exchange reform.

In any event, even if one were to accept that the purpose of retaining the old official exchange rate for the earmarked sum has been merely to cushion the burden of increased inflation, one cannot but seriously doubt the effectiveness of the measure. In the case of food, this is seen from simple calculations that show that despite allowing $1200 million for importing essential food items at the old official exchange rate of $1 = IR 70 the exchange-rate unification could, through its inflationary effect on imported food alone, lead to an overall food price increase of between 50 and 85 per cent, implying a decline of between 15 and 25 per cent in the living standards of rural families and between 22 and 38 per cent in the case of urban households.[19] Of course, the unification also raises the prices of domestically produced food and, more importantly, those of non-food items, thus further eroding living standards. For instance, a similar rough calculation for medicine indicates that, even allowing for the $388 million imports at the old official exchange rate, the exchange reform could raise the overall price of imported medicine by 100 per cent.[20] Noting that currently 6.2 per cent of urban families' expenditure is on average spent on health care,[21] the adverse effect of these sharp price increases on living standards becomes apparent. In fact, following the reform, the government soon announced price increases of 60–140 per cent on some medicinal items, and, despite the quick reversal of increases in bread prices which bakers sought in anticipation of higher prices of imported wheat and flour, prices of many household goods were reported in April 1993 to have already risen by 30 per cent since early March.[22]

These rough calculations and the supporting early indications of actual price increases cast serious doubt on the plausibility of the official estimate of a 30 per cent inflation rate for 1993, and gives credibility to expectations that the actual rate may well reach 70 per cent.[23] It is therefore highly doubtful that the government policy of applying the old official exchange rate to earmarked imported amounts of some basic goods has been an effective tool to counteract the inflationary impact of the exchange-rate unification. In view of this and the above argument that the main beneficiaries of such a policy may well be the inefficient import agencies of the revolutionary foundations, one can conclude that a more prudent policy would have been to unify fully the exchange rates and hence eliminate associated price distortions, and to use direct compensatory measures to protect the welfare of the low-income groups.

In fact, as a supplementary measure to offset the negative welfare effect of the exchange-rate unification, the government has intended to allocate IR 324 billion (about 18 per cent of government personnel expenditures) to salary increases for state employees[24] and raise the minimum daily wage rate from IR 2267 to IR 2994 in 1994.[25] But the quantitative impact of these measures is at best only marginal, and their economic wisdom questionable. To see this one should note that according to recent estimates some 4 million people, or nearly one-third of the employed labour force, are currently in state employment.[26] To protect the purchasing power of this population meaningfully against the inflationary effect of the unification would entail a salary-adjustment expenditure many times larger than the allocated amount. Of course, if such a large expenditure were to be allocated, it would be necessary to offset it fully by means of appropriate expenditure cuts elsewhere in the budget so as to minimize its otherwise inflationary impact. The same thing can be said about the minimum wage increase: if a working family earning the minimum daily wage rate of IR 2267 in 1993 (amounting to an annual income of IR 827,455) were to afford the average annual expenditure of an urban family in 1989, estimated officially[27] at IR 2,086,138, its income would need to be raised six-fold[28] compared with the 32 per cent implied by the proposed wage increase.[29] In fact, the real spending power of such a family income (amounting to IR 359,763 in 1989 prices) would be as low as one half of the lowest quintile of the family expenditure distribution in 1989.[30] Taking into account that in 1989 the income of a family with a single earner at the minimum wage rate of IR 1160[31] was about IR 423,400, or nearly one-fifth of the average purchasing power of an urban family in that same year, one can readily see both the depth of inequality in distribution of income and the increasing intensity of poverty in Iran. Not surprisingly, to afford a basic living standard, a noticeable and growing proportion of the working population has had to work two or sometimes three shifts a day at the same time that corruption, especially among state employees, has become widespread.[32]

Bleak as it is, this is not yet the full picture. As early indications suggest, the exchange-rate unification is also going to reduce the number of in-efficient enterprises, especially those in the public sector which have merely been kept in operation because their managers had access to heavily sub-sidized exchange rates.[33] In the absence of a well-prepared programme to cope with its incidence, this otherwise essential and positive restructuring is bound to add substantially to the existing 2 million (or more) un-employed people who are not fortunate enough to earn the minimum wage rate.

The extent of the government's unpreparedness to mitigate the un-employment effect of the reform is best seen from its 1993 budget allocations. Of the 'social affairs' budget,[34] only 2.8 per cent has been allocated to 'technical and vocational training' programmes, and of the 'general affairs' budget, only 1.5 per cent has been allocated to 'manage-ment of labour force', including as little as 0.7 per cent allocated to 'employment and job service' programmes and 0.1 per cent to 'employee and employer relations' programmes. Put together, these programmes are given no more than 1.2 per cent of the total budget. The point can be seen more clearly by noticing that of the nearly IR 10,436 billion addi-tional revenue anticipated to accrue to the government upon valuing oil and gas exports at a devalued exchange rate implicit in the 1993 budget,[35] only 3 per cent has been allocated to programmes that directly pertain to easing unemployment stemming from the exchange-rate devaluation. As suggested above, to ease the incidence of unemployment under the exchange-rate reform the government should have prepared an employ-ment transition programme that deployed such extra revenues to provide skills through technical and vocational training and retraining schemes, employment adjustment assistance, employment services, as well as work for unskilled labour through public-works programmes.

In sum, the above analysis indicates clearly the failure of the government to provide a social safety net against the inflationary and unemployment effects of the exchange-rate reform. Interestingly, one year after the exchange-rate reform of 23 March 1993 this failure was explicitly acknowledged by the Speaker of the Majles, who commented 'I believe we should carry out these reforms, but first we must create the social safety net. Otherwise the vulnerable strata cannot bear the pressure.'[36]

The timing of the unification

Leaving aside the inflationary and unemployment effects of the unification, one is led to ask two closely connected questions: Was the timing of the unification correct, and was the chosen rate of $1 = IR 1538 appropriate? While, for the reasons previously noted, the effort of the government to unify the rates in a single step (except for the earmarked imports at the old official rate) is to be commended, the appropriateness of its timing and the rate chosen are open to debate. In the absence of a hard theory to explain what the equilibrium exchange rate is exactly and how it should be determined, it seems reasonable to suppose that an appropriate exchange rate should reflect the true productive capacity of the Iranian economy relative to those of its trading partners. Provided that macro-economic stabilizing policies are in place and major price distortions are corrected so as to avoid large speculative demands for foreign currencies, such a rate should in principle shadow the free market exchange rate and appreciate or depreciate as the underlying comparative productivity trend rises or declines. Using this rough yardstick and taking into account the country's economic and political environment at the time of unification, as well as the behaviour of the exchange market after the unification, an attempt will be made to shed some light on the two questions posed above.

The exchange-rate unification took place one year sooner than the target date of March 1994 agreed upon with the IMF, and in total contrast to frequent formal indications by key government authorities that in the interest of protecting the poor's welfare it would be gradual. What explains such a change of policy? Admittedly, no one could have predicted the future course of the economy with certainty. Nonetheless, the economic facts prevailing at the time would seriously challenge a claim that the economic conditions were at their best for introducing reform. For one thing, the very high import levels in 1990, 1991 and 1992 (about $65 billion combined) had given rise to expectations of continued high import-demand level in 1993 (budgeted at about $30 billion) on the one hand, and to the accumulation of nearly $30 billion foreign debt by March 1993 on the other. Importantly, about two-thirds of this debt consisted of letters of credit (LC), of which up to $15 billion were to mature in 1993. In fact, by March 1993 about $9 billion was already due for repayment, in addition to repayment arrears of between $3 and $5 billion which had built up since early 1992.[37] Actual foreign-exchange earnings in 1992 (about $17.3 billion) had fallen considerably below the optimistically budgeted amount

Figure 7.1   Exchange-Rate Movements

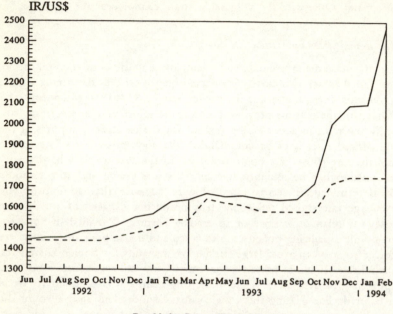

Source: Table 7.1.

Source: Table 7.1.

of nearly \$20 billion, mainly because oil revenues failed to match expec-
tations. Further, by March 1993 Iran's foreign-reserve assets at the Bank
for International Settlements (BIS) had fallen to about \$5.88 billion while
its liabilities had risen to well above \$9.1 billion,[38] thus limiting the amount
of foreign-exchange reserves that the Central Bank could count on to
support the rial after its devaluation.[39] Finally, in spite of the Central
Bank's plan to restrict the growth of liquidity (M2) of the private sector
to about 5.8 per cent in 1992, the actual growth rate was dramatically
higher, 24.7 per cent,[40] thus building up inflationary pressures and adding
to pent-up demands for foreign exchange. Accordingly, early in 1993 the
relevant indicators all pointed to acute shortages of foreign exchange in
the months to come. Not surprisingly, the expectations of foreign-exchange
scarcity were already being reflected in the market through a widening of
the gap between the floating and free-market exchange rates. As can be
seen in Figure 7.1 and the supporting data in Table 7.1, the gap between
the two rates had begun growing rapidly after June 1992 and had reached
a record high by the time unification was announced. Given the prevailing
economic conditions, were the government to postpone the unification

Table 7.1   Trends in Exchange Rates, June 1992–February 1994[a]

	Floating rate	Free-market rate	Free/float rate (%)
June 1992	1439	1443	100.3
July	1439	1453	101.0
August	1439	1455	101.1
September	1439	1485	103.2
October	1439	1490	103.5
November	1459	1515	103.8
December	1479	1555	105.1
January 1993	1497	1570	104.9
February	1542	1630	105.7
March	*1542*	*1640*	*106.4*
April	1643	1670	101.6
May	1625	1655	101.8
June	1613	1660	102.9
July	1584	1645	103.9
August	1584	1640	103.5
September	1584	1645	103.9
October	1584	1720	108.6
November	1720	2007	116.7
December	1750	2095	119.7
January 1994	1750	2100	120.0
February	1750	2470	141.1

Note: [a] End-of-the-month selling rates in Tehran.

Sources: Floating rates from *International Financial Statistics*, IMF, February 1994; and *Iran Focus*, MENAS Associates, London, various issues. Free-market rates are from author's correspondence with Ali Pakpour, Foreign Exchange Bureau, London.

further the gap would have most likely grown so large that reform would have been rendered both economically and politically impracticable.

Besides the dictate of economic conditions, however, what particularly motivated the acceleration of reform was probably the prevailing domestic political conditions. First, with the radicals being reduced to a distinct minority in the new parliament, the opposition to Rafsanjani's economic reform programme was effectively marginalized. Second, and more importantly, with the certainty of his winning a second term as president in the following June 1993 election, and a sensing of the public perception that economic reform was unavoidable, Rafsanjani introduced what was politically the most risky and economically the most painful element of his reform at a time that was politically most opportune.

The chosen exchange rate for unification

This brings us to the question of whether the chosen rate for unification was appropriate. It can hardly be disputed that the true value of the rial is ultimately determined by the fundamental realities about the overall productivity of the Iranian economy. To the extent that these realities form the basis of economic agents' expectations about the future course of the economy, it is reasonable to suppose that the true value of the rial is reflected in its free market exchange rate.[41]

It follows that if the Central Bank's floating rate is set appropriately in the sense of reflecting more or less the rial's true value, it should at the same time satisfy two criteria: (1) the gap between the floating and the free market rates should remain reasonably small, and (2) neither of the two rates should exhibit wild fluctuations over a reasonable period of time. Otherwise, the arbitrage gains will cause the free market rate to diverge from an inappropriately set floating rate for as long as the Central Bank resists adjusting it, thereby making a sharp eventual adjustment inevitable.

With these criteria in mind and not forgetting that it has been a rather short period since the unification, let us look at the behaviour of the two rates as depicted in Figure 7.1. At the time when the official exchange rates were unified, the value of the rial in the free market was already about 6 per cent below the Central Bank's chosen rate of $1 = IR 1538 for unification. Reacting to this, and in a testing of the Central Bank's commitment to its chosen rate, the value of the rial in the free market soon came under pressure, particularly as the difficulties with LC payments loomed large; as over 100,000 pilgrims going on Hajj in May 1993 pushed up the demand for foreign exchange and as a rush for imports emerged in response to the government's announcement that import taxes and duties were to go up in July 1993. By 11 April the free market rate had fallen to an unprecedented low of $1 = IR 1830, nearly 20 per cent below its official value, causing a fear that the market might lose its confidence in the rial and let it fall freely. Following the meeting of a special 'Exchange Market Regulation Committee' chaired by Rafsanjani, on 13 April the Central Bank declared the rial 'fully convertible' and decreed that any importer could open LC and buy foreign exchange without limitations and that banks could sell up to $5000 hard currency to anybody who asks for it without requiring documentation. As the decree did not restrict the frequency of a person's demand, it effectively amounted to no limitation on an individual's demand for foreign currency and particularly benefited the large currency dealers. The next day the Central Bank devalued the floating rate by 6.7 per cent to $1 = IR 1648 and claimed that it had set aside $2 billion in a special fund to support the rial.[42] These moves, backed by commercial banks fully satisfying all customers' demands for foreign exchange, restored the free market's confidence in the rial and in the Central Bank's commitment to defend its value to the extent that for a few days in the third week of April the market rate fell below the floating rate.

As Figure 7.1 shows, the market confidence in the value of the rial lasted for the period May–September 1993, owing principally to the Central Bank's heavy intervention in the exchange market which forced the market rate to shadow the floating rate within a band of less than 1 per cent. Furthermore, during this period both rates remained remarkably stable, showing a very slight increase in the value of the rial (an overall 3.5 per cent according to the floating rate and 1.5 per cent on the free market). As the movements of the exchange rate during this period fully satisfy criteria (1) and (2), one is tempted to conclude that the appropriate exchange rate should have been set somewhere in the range of IR 1625–1584 to the dollar, which after all is not so significantly (about 36 per cent) higher than the Central Bank's chosen rate of $1 = IR 1538.

However, it should be emphasized that the relative stability of the rates over this rather short period was due to the massive intervention by the Central Bank and not the fundamental realities about foreign-exchange availability and obligations. The fundamental realities, which primarily consisted of reduced hard currency earnings due to falling oil prices, the hangover of the short-term debt repayments, reduced expectations about inflows of foreign loans and direct investments, and a high minimum imports requirement, all pointed to an imminent foreign-exchange scarcity, thus raising serious doubt about the Central Bank's ability to sustain its floating rate for long by supplying the market with foreign exchange. Together with expectations of rising domestic inflation rates, this naturally led the market to anticipate a pending fall of the rial and hence triggered a vigorous speculation against it. Not unexpectedly, and despite the Central Bank's resistance to change in its floating rate, the rial's value on the open market fell by nearly 9 per cent in October. Since then the fundamental realities of the economy, as reflected by the foreign-exchange market, have not only forced the value of the rial to fall continually, they have also forced the free market rate to diverge from the floating rate at an increasing speed. At the time of writing, the free market rate had risen to more than 40 per cent higher than the floating rate, and had lost over half its value since the unification date, as compared with a 13.5 per cent devaluation of the floating rate. Accordingly, seen from the long term, the movements of the two rates have so far failed to fulfill criteria (1) and (2), thus casting serious doubt on the appropriateness of the rate chosen by the Central Bank for unification. As the foregoing analysis makes clear, the chosen rate was out of tune with precisely the same adverse economic realities that had in the first place urged the government to expedite the date of unification; and, as such, it grossly overvalued the rial.

Although there is no quick solution to the problem of the imbalance between the demand for and supply of foreign exchange, there are several policy measures that can help to bring stability to foreign-exchange markets. For the near future, the likelihood of a substantial rise in world oil prices or in non-oil exports is remote, and since under the current hostile international economic and political environment the prospects for attracting large flows of foreign capital are poor, there is very little that can be done significantly to raise Iran's hard currency earnings. The best thing that can be done in this respect is perhaps to avoid creating false expectations by making unrealistically optimistic projections. Judging by the projections presented in the budget for 1994, it seems that the government has now learned this lesson from past mistakes.[43]

Inevitably, the policy measures should concentrate on reducing the demand for foreign exchange. An important immediate step in this direction would be a successful rescheduling of the external debt arrears, now standing at about $8 billion. At the time of writing there are indications that these arrears may be rescheduled bilaterally rather than under the Paris Club's multilateral rules. While this would be a positive move, if the debt refinancing is to offer more than merely a breathing space it is important that the payment arrears be converted to medium- and long-term loans on terms that are competitive with those available on international capital markets. A second policy measure would seek to curtail import demand. Although one must recognize the existence of a political limit to a reduction in imports and despite the fact that Iran's imports have been declining considerably since early 1992, there is still room for economizing on official demands for imports. This can be achieved in at least two ways: (1) by resetting the government's development priorities with the aim of eliminating or postponing investment projects with high import intensities and long gestation periods; and, more importantly, (2) by accelerating the privatization programme both through speeding up the direct sale of inefficient state-owned enterprises (mostly controlled by the foundations), and by boosting the activities of the Tehran stock exchange. An accelerated privatization programme has an additional merit: it complements other policy measures, such as a tightening of the money supply and actively conducting open market operations, which should be adopted to control the liquidity and hence the inflationary pressures that have been a major source of disequilibrium in the foreign-exchange market.

With regard to the expected long-term benefits of the exchange rate unification (higher investment, output and employment) it is still too early to judge, although the boost in private-sector activities and noticeable increases in non-oil exports in 1993 may be interpreted as early promising indications.

Summary and Conclusion

This chapter has argued that the multi-rate exchange regime was not only a major source of inefficiency in resource allocation, it also intensified the rent-seeking orientation of the Iranian economy and hence the inequality in distribution of income and wealth between those with access to the subsidized exchange rates (especially the revolutionary foundations and private licence holders) and the rest of society. As such, the wisdom of unifying the multiple exchange rates at a single market-determined rate is unquestionable. What this study has called into question are two important sets of issues: (1) the pace, timing and exchange rate chosen for the unification; and (2) the design, administration and hence the efficacy of the govenment's safety-net policies to deal with the adverse welfare effects of the foreign-exchange reform.

On the first set of issues, the arguments of this chapter have been that: (1) a prudent policy would have unified the exchange rates in a single step as against the gradual approach adopted in effect by the government. (2) The advancing of the reform date from March 1994 (as had been officially agreed with the IMF) to March 1993 was not done because the prevailing macroeconomic conditions were ideal for reform. Rather, it was done because the prevailing political conditions were most opportune. Economic conditions influenced the timing only to the extent that the severely deteriorating prospects for the economy practically eliminated any chance of success with a further-delayed reform. (3) In view of the adverse fundamental realities concerning the Iranian economy in general and its foreign-exchange market in particular, the chosen exchange rate for unification grossly overvalued the rial and therefore is unsustainable.

On the second set of issues, this study has cast serious doubt on the economic merit, effectiveness and consistency of the IMF's proposed safety net by arguing that: (1) it ignores the welfare losses resulting from the scaled-down coupon system and the additional rial revenues accruing to government upon the exchange-rate unification, both of which are likely to be much larger than the percieved savings on subsidies; and (2) the assigning of a key role to the revolutionary foundations to provide a safety net is both ineffective and inconsistent with the objective of reform, because as major beneficiaries of the subsidized exchange rates and politically powerful monopolies unaccountable to government the foundations will use their leverage on both the legislative and executive branches to oppose or hinder reform.

Furthermore, this chapter has demonstrated that neither the govenment's policy of applying the dramatically overvalued, old official exchange rate of $1 = IR 70 to imports of some basic goods, nor its policy of raising the minimum wage rate and salaries of state employees, have been effective tools to counteract the impoverishing inflationary effect of the exchange reform. In addition, the government's failure to design in advance a cohesive employment transition programme to ease the unemployment effect of reform has shown its unpreparedness to deal with the adverse welfare effects of its exchange reform.

The arguments presented here suggest that the Islamic Republic faces a very difficult choice between two fundamental and yet inherently conflicting objectives. These are, on the one hand, to achieve the economic progress needed to satisfy the middle-class and conservative groups; and on the other, to maintain a revolutionary political stance. While economic liberalization, with exchange-rate unification at its core, is an imperative for the former objective, support for the radical constituencies and their affiliated revolutionary foundations is a necessary condition for the latter. The necessity of choosing between the two objectives stems from the fact that the exchange reform will not only face growing discontent in the low- and middle-income groups as welfare gets further eroded by the ensuing higher inflation and unemployment rates. More importantly, it will face severe resistance from radical constituencies and the revolutionary foundations whose economic and hence political survival depends largely on their ability to secure massive explicit and implicit subsidies in the form of concessional exchange rates.[44] The necessity of choosing is underscored by the fact that Iran's foreign-exchange-earning capacity and reserves are inadequate to support the exchange-rate unification and stabilize the foreign-exchange market. This is because of the lack of foreign-exchange resources, which are needed to expand oil and non-oil export capacities. On the other hand, expectations of attracting large inflows of foreign loans and direct investment to support the exchange-rate unification may well prove unjustified, both because of Iran's limited capacity to service large amounts of external debt and, more importantly, its insistence on maintaining a revolutionary political stance. Of course, the Islamic Republic may opt not to choose between the two fundamental objectives; but it is not certain for how long it will be able to pursue both.

Notes

I dedicate this study to the memory of Professor Hossein Pirnia, my first teacher of economics. I would like to thank Sohrab Behdad for helpful comments and suggestions. An earlier draft of this study was presented at a 'Middle East Economic Association' session of the ASSA meetings, Anaheim, Los Angeles, 5–7 January 1993.

1. After the 1979 revolution, both the World Bank and the IMF were regarded by many Iranian political figures as the tools, primarily in the hands of the United States, serving to impose imperialistic goals on the Third World countries. This attitude was radically reversed, perhaps inevitably, after the end of the Iran–Iraq war when the Rafsanjani administration took office. The World Bank has been

approached for development loans, and the IMF for technical consultation in the design of the economic reform programme.

2. As such, the present chapter is not concerned with the determination and estimation of the extent of misalignment of the Iranian rial (IR) from its equilibrium level. Nor is it concerned with the quantitative effects of its devaluation on external trade balances. For an empirical study of the former issues, see Pesaran, M. Hashem, 'The Iranian foreign exchange policy and the black market for dollars', *International Journal of Middle East Studies* 24/1 (1992), pp 101–25; and for an analysis of the latter issue, see Behdad, Sohrab, 'Foreign exchange gap, structural constraints, and the political economy of exchange rate determination in Iran', *International Journal of Middle East Studies* 20/1 (1988), pp 1–21; and Lautenschlager, Wolfgang, 'The effects of an overvalued exchange rate on the Iranian Economy', *International Journal of Middle East Studies* 18/1 (1986), pp 39–52.

3. Obviously, to provide quantitative evidence for the extent of these effects is a complex and challenging task that requires thorough economic research based on hard data and formal economic modelling. Far from that, the observations made here are meant only to give some qualitative support for the consequences cited above.

4. The cases cited here are the observations of a World Bank mission to Iran reported in 'Islamic Republic of Iran: trade policy study', World Bank Aide Memoire, Tehran, March 1992.

5. Other non-governmental revolutionary foundations include: the Martyr's Foundation (Bonyad-e-Shaheed), whose task is to provide support for martyrs' families; the Fifteenth Khordad Foundation (Bonyad-e Panzdah-e Khordad), whose task is to provide specialized services, such as in-kind transfers, educational support and housing services to widows, orphans and victims of the war; the Imam's Assistance Committee (Komiteh-ye Emdad), which is one of the largest foundations and whose duty is to provide a variety of assistance to the very poor, especially in the rural sector; the Organization for Economic Mobilization (Sazman-e Basij-e Eqtesadi), whose main task is the administration of the coupon system; and the Organization for the Construction Crusade (Jahad-e Sazandegi), whose primary task is rural and infrastructural development.

6. *Petroleum Intelligence Weekly*, 30 March 1992, p 3.

7. International Monetary Fund (IMF), 'Islamic Republic of Iran: a social safety net system for the transition', November 1991.

8. *Iran Focus*, April 1992, p 11.

9. The increase in the cost of living of the high-income groups would be less because they already meet a significant portion of their consumption needs through free markets at unsubsidized prices.

10. See, for example, Dornbusch, Rudiger, 'Credibility and stabilization', NBER, Working paper 2790, (Cambridge, MA: National Bureau of Economic Research, 1989) 1989; Alesina, Alex, and Alberto Cukierman, 'The politics of ambiguity', *The Quarterly Journal of Economics* cv/4 (1990), pp 829–51; and van Wijnbergen, Sweder, 'Intertemporal speculation, shortages and the political economy of price reform', *Economic Journal* 102/4 (1992), pp 1395–406.

11. Ibid.

12. *Iran Focus*, December 1992, p 15.

13. Ibid.

14. Ibid.

15. The IMF, 'Islamic republic of Iran', p 31.

16. *Iran Focus,* December 1991, p 9.

17. *The Bill of National Budget for 1993* (in Persian), Part I, Plan and Budget Organization, 1993 ; *MEED,* 9 April 1993, p 19; and *Iran Focus,* April 1993, p 11.

18. The extent of the foundations' control over the imports of basic goods is well noted by a correspondent of *The Economist* in Iran, who reports 'Mr Rafiqdoost [the head of the Foundation for the Oppressed] himself is proud of the fact that the government will often approach him to intervene in economic policy. When lifting its subsidy in chickens, for example, it asked the *Bonyad* to import millions of chickens, to bring down the price. "We have intervened over iron, tea, rice and cooking oil," says Mr. Rafiqdoost' (September 1993, p 54).

19. These estimates are obtained as follows. The percentage increase in the price of imported food is calculated from

$$\Delta p_f / p_f = (1 - \alpha)(E_1/E_o - 1)/[\alpha e_o/E_o + (1 - \alpha)]$$

where p_f is the overall food import price, E_1 is the average floating exchange rate prevailing after unification, E_o and e_o are respectively the exchange rates applicable to imports of essential and non-essential food items before unification, and α and $1 - \alpha$ are the share of these categories in total food imports. Iran's total food imports for 1993 are estimated to be over \$3 billion (source: updated from World Bank, *Trends in Developing Economies,* World Bank, 1993). With \$1.3 billion allocated to essential items (wheat, flour, rice, red meat, sugar, cheese and vegetable oil), one has approximately $\alpha = 0.40$. Assuming that the domestic prices of these essential items continue to be controlled at their pre-reform subsidized levels, only the price of 60 per cent of non-essential food imports will then rise as a result of the devaluation. Assuming conservatively (for E_o) that before the unification, non-essential food items were imported at the competitive rate of \$1 = IR 600 or, even more conservatively, at the weighted average exchange rate of \$1 = IR 786.3 prevailing before 21 March 1993, and using (for E_1) the average floating exchange rate of \$1 = IR1616 over the 27 March–30 December 1993 period, the overall increase in the domestic price of imported food would be about 170 per cent in the former case and 100 per cent in the more conservative case. Further, it is assumed that imported food counts for one-half of the urban diet but only one-third of the rural one. The share of food in family expenditure has been estimated to be the same for both rural and urban families at about 45 per cent for the 1990–93 period (source: updated from data by Statistical Centre of Iran, as reported in *Iran Focus,* September 1993, p 9).

20. Using the formula given in the previous note and assuming that (a) the sum of \$388 million covers about 85 per cent of the total imports of medicine, baby formula, and pharmaceutical raw material in 1993 (that is, $\alpha = 0.85$) whose domestic price will not change from the previous year; and (b) the rest (15 per cent) were imported at the competitive exchange rate (E_o) of \$1 = IR 600 before the unification, one obtains $\Delta p/p = 102$ per cent.

21. *Iran Focus,* 'The Pharmaceutical Industry', April 1993, p 13.

22. *MEED,* 30 April 1993, p 3.

23. See, for example, *Oxford Analytica,* April 1993, p 2.

24. *The Bill of National Budget for 1993* Part IV, Plan and Budget Organization, 1993

(in Persian).

25. *Iran Focus*, March 1993, p 16.

26. *Oxford Analytica*, 8 April 1993, p 3.

27. Statistical Centre of Iran, *Statistical Year Book of 1989*, January 1991.

28. This is based on the official (Central Bank of Iran) estimates of (CPI) inflation rates of 9 per cent in 1990, 17 per cent in 1991, 23 per cent in 1992, and an assumed urban price inflation of 50 per cent for 1993.

29. It is noted that, as with the price of labour, the minimum wage and salaries of government employees should ideally be raised in proportion to respective productivities so as to avoid creating further distortions in the labour market.

30. The lowest quintile family expenditure in 1989 is estimated at IR 725,700 (from IMF, 'Islamic Republic of Iran', p 53, Table 7).

31. Estimated by deflating the minimum wage rate of IR 1667 in 1991 (*Iran Focus* March 1992, p. 16) by the indices of the daily wage of an unskilled construction worker for years 1990 and 1989 (Bank Markazi, *Annual Report*, 1991).

32. Corruption has become so prevalent that, according to *Iran Focus*, (June 1993, p 11), in mid-1993 the parliament (Majles) approved a bill banning government officials from receiving kickbacks on foreign deals, and making them liable to a fine equal to the sum illicitly earned as well as a prison term of between two and five years. The bill also applied to 'commissions' received since early 1979, but relieves officials from prosecution if they promptly transfer any such earnings to the Treasury. The bill, whose effectiveness is much in doubt, becomes law if approved by the Council of Guardians.

33. For example, as reported in *MEED*, 23 April 1993, p 22, in early April 1993, the state-owned Khavar company, which assembles Mercedes trucks, laid off some 1200 workers, some of whom did not receive severance pay. Seeking clarification, the workers were threatened with 'harsh treatment' by the plant's top security officials.

34. The sectors of activities under this budget category include public education, higher education, technical and vocational training, social security and welfare, culture, physical training, youth affairs, and health and medical care.

35. The 1993 budget anticipates revenues from oil and gas exports to be $17.93 billion and IR 15,815.3 billion, thus implying an exchange rate of $1 = IR 882. The corresponding figures in the 1992 budget are respectively $17.2 billion and IR 5149.7 billion, implying an exchange rate of $1 = IR 300. These figures suggest an increase of $17.2 (882 − 300) = IR 10,010.4 billion in government's oil and gas revenues due to valuing oil and gas revenues at a devalued rial in the 1993 budget (*The Bill of National Budget for 1993*; and *Iran Focus*, February 1992, p 10).

36. *MEED*, 25 March 1994, p 13.

37. It has been estimated that the $30 billion outstanding foreign debt includes $5–7 billion LC commitments which were not acted upon and $3–4 billion medium-term project loans (*MEED*, 30 April 1993, pp 2–3).

38. Bank for International Settlements, *International Banking and Financial Market Developments*, 1993.

39. The Minister of Economy and Finance and the Governor of the Central Bank had been reported to have earmarked some $2–3 billion to support the rial (*MEED*, 30 April 1993, p 2). However, in view of Iran's low foreign-exchange reserves relative to its foreign-exchange obligations, this figure seems unrealistic.

40. Bank Markazi, *Annual Report;* Statistical Centre of Iran, *Yearbook 1993;* and IMF, 'Islamic Republic of Iran'.

41. Changes in the overall productivity of the Iranian economy relative to those of its trading partners will eventually lead to changes in its comparative international price levels. The latter will, according to purchasing power parity (PPP) theory, determine the change in the exchange rates of Iran's rial against the currencies of its partners. Interestingly, in a testing of the PPP theory between the Iranian rial and 19 other currencies, Bahmani-Oskooee finds enough econometric evidence to support the theory when he uses the free market exchange rate, but no support when the official exchange rate is used. Bahmani-Oskooee, Mohsen, 'Black market exchange rate versus official exchange rate in testing purchasing power parity: An examination of the Iranian rial', *Applied Economics* 25/4 (1993), pp 465–72.

42. See, for example, *MEED*, 23 April 1993, p 22.

43. The revised projections for oil export revenue is about $10 billion, down from $17 billion projected in the 1993 budget and $14 billion realized revenue (*MEED*, 11 February 1994, p 7).

44. In this connection it is interesting to note that only a few weeks after writing this, on 15 March 1994, the Majles, under pressure from the radical factions, voted to put a halt to the economic reform programme and approved application of the old official exchange rate to $3000 million imports of some essential consumer commodities and defence material (*MEED*, 18 March 1994, p 23, and 25 March 1994, p 12).

PART III

Social Policy and State Legitimacy

8

Regime Legitimacy and High-school Textbooks

Sussan Siavoshi

Introduction

Twentieth-century Iran has witnessed growing state control over civil society. With the exception of a few dramatic but short-lived periods, such as the Second World War and the 1979 revolution, this growth has been continuous. Although the 1979 revolution aimed, among other things, to curb the control of the state over certain private domains, it stopped the process only briefly, and the post-revolutionary state proved to be no less interventionist than its predecessor.

The rise of an overarching state requires the submission of civil society to governmental decisions. The important question is how governments achieve this submission. One avenue available to many, and particularly to autocratic regimes, is the use of force; but mere coercion is hardly enough to ensure the long-term survival of governments. The use of force is not only costly but, as modern history has shown, also unreliable. A preferable strategy is to convince the subject population, or at least a significant portion of it, of the state's right to govern. In other words, the aim of the state is to socialize people into accepting the legitimacy of state domination.[1]

Every society has several agents of political socialization. The educational system, particularly in autocratic states, has often been utilized to create legitimacy for governments. This chapter examines how both the pre- and post-revolutionary states in Iran have used the educational system, or more precisely, high-school social science and humanities textbooks, to acquire legitimacy. The study shows how the two regimes radically differ in certain aspects of their value systems. The radical difference in their professed values and the regimes' attempts to inculcate them in the youth, however, did not mean that the two regimes always succeeded in adhering to their values in practice. For this study I have chosen eight value themes and arranged them in four pairs. Each pair consists of two conflicting values, one associated with the Pahlavi regime and the other with the

Islamic Republic. The pairs are as follows: secularism versus religiousness, economic growth versus economic justice, alliance versus non-alliance, and status quo monarchism versus popular revolutionism. The choice of these categories is justified on the grounds of their overall comprehensiveness. They cover salient cultural, economic, foreign-policy and political concerns of each of the regimes. A careful reading of the social-science and history textbooks confirms the relevance and importance of these themes for each regime.

Secularism versus Religiousness

The Pahlavi regime, as a secular regime, adhered to the idea of separation of religion from politics and encouraged the religious community to confine itself to the private matter of the relationship of the individual with God.[2] In the pre-revolutionary social-science and history textbooks, religion was treated as a private matter, an institution separate from and, with regard to power, inferior to the political institutions. In one sociology textbook it was clearly stated that 'the authority of the government ... is greater and more extensive than any other institutions such as ... religious institution.'[3] Textbooks criticized religious interference in politics. For example, the history book for the third year of high school stated that the unjustified interference of the Zoroastrian clergy in the running of the political affairs of the country was an important reason for the defeat of the Persian empire by the Muslims.[4]

In social and economic matters the analyses of problems and the solutions offered were generally materialistic and secular. Attacks on some traditions and customs such as polygamy, dowry and low age requirement for marriage implied criticism of religion.[5] Not so implicit were statements such as 'the increase in birth rate, which is not a positive phenomenon in the developing countries, is caused by the following factors: beliefs, customs ... and religious values.'[6] Economic development, the pre-revolutionary textbooks contended, required a transformation of social values and institutions. The heroic Third-World leader in the third-year general history book was Kemal Ataturk, the Western-oriented leader of modern Turkey in the 1920s and 1930s, who introduced an aggressive programme for the elimination of many traditional institutions and customs as well as the secularization of politics.[7] Overall, religion appeared to have little relevance to public life in the pre-revolutionary social-science and history textbooks. Secularism was their dominant feature. The Pahlavi regime, under both Reza Shah and Mohammad Reza Shah, aspired to develop Iran along the same lines as the Western countries. Both Shahs viewed secularization of the polity as essential to this goal.[8] The educational reforms, manifested in a dramatic decline in the number of clergy-run educational institutions and changes in educational materials, reflected these goals.

The 1979 revolution, on the other hand, brought religion into politics. The religious leadership of the revolution succeeded in neutralizing the secular forces and in dominating the state apparatus. In striving to maintain legitimacy for their rule, the dominant groups have contended that religion and politics are inseparable and that religious leaders are more suitable than lay people to rule the nation. These ideas have found their place in the educational materials.

In the post-revolutionary textbooks Islam is the focus of attention, and politics is explained in the light of religion. The integration of politics and religion is a theme repeated in every grade in all social-science and history books. The fourth-year *Danesh-e Ejtema'i* (social knowledge) text-book presents a comprehensive argument to demonstrate the necessity of the interference of religion in politics and the difference between the conception of politics in Islam and that in the Western ideologies:

> Another important difference about the conception of politics between Western scholars and Islam is that in the West politics is more related to the worldly issues ... In Islam, however, [politics] is for guiding the human being towards human perfection ... which results in ... his eternal happiness.[9]

The argument starts with the fundamental premiss that power originates not from human beings but from God, and it is the Almighty who has the exclusive right to make laws.[10]

In this textbook, references are made to the works of Muslim phil-osophers and theologians such as Ibn Khaldun, Abul Ala Maududi and Allameh Mirza Mohammad Hosein Na'ini. The role of human beings in politics is limited to the understanding and implementation of the divine laws. The most comprehensive of these laws, demonstrating God's intentions and plans for the creation of an ideal society, have been revealed in Islam through the Prophet Mohammad. As the messenger of God, Mohammad's duties go beyond the mere unveiling of the divine plan for the salvation and happiness of the human race and include implemen-tation of the plan as well. Mohammad's role as both the spiritual and political leader of the society of the faithful (*ommat*), combined with his successes on both counts, empirically proves the assertions regarding the natural union between politics and religion.

To supplement the theoretical aspects with concrete manifestations, textbooks point to two opposing historical forces in the struggle for progress. The opposition is between Shi'ism, in its attempt to establish social justice, and colonial force, which strives to sabotage progress in Muslim societies in order to prolong its domination over these societies.[11] Since true religion creates barriers to any kind of subjugation, the colonial powers deem it necessary to neutralize religion's influence on politics through the introduction in Muslim societies of the Western idea of the separation of politics from religion.[12]

The pervasive theme in all post-revolutionary textbooks is the desirability, indeed the necessity, that religion interfere in politics. Therefore Islamic societies should be led by Islamic jurists and scholars.[13] Such necessity is theological and practical. The eternal felicity requires submission to God's will as manifested in the Islamic laws and as interpreted and implemented by religious leaders.[14] Moreover, the creation of an ideal, just, independent and dignified society in this world is only possible through adherence to Islamic politics as part of this comprehensive religion.[15] The message of the textbooks in the Islamic Republic is that Islam as an ideology does not submit to the artificial separation of religion from social and political issues.

Economic Growth versus Economic Redistribution

Economic development has been one of the most salient issues for both pre- and post-revolutionary governments. However, the two regimes differ in the emphasis placed on economic goals and values in their textbooks. The Pahlavi regime, in its quest for economic development, put its emphasis on economic growth rather than on equity of income distribution.[16] In the pre-revolutionary high-school textbooks, the modernization approach provides the analytical framework for the introduction of economic issues to the students.[17] Starting with Rostow's five developmental stages, the social-science textbooks analyse the causes of underdevelopment in the Third World.[18] In the tradition of modernization theories, the emphasis is on the dichotomy between tradition and modernity and on the need for a movement away from the former toward establishing modern values and institutions. As for the economic aspects of modernization, the model most praised is that of Japan, which according to the textbooks emphasizes industrialization, the necessity of saving, and the utilization of technology and science.[19]

Regarding the issue of economic equity, very little was said in the pre-revolutionary textbooks. For example, the entire 138-page sociology textbook for the third year of high school included only a very brief and non-committal paragraph on global maldistribution of wealth.[20] There was no analysis in any of the social-science or history textbooks of the role of international economic and political systems in creating or perpetuating underdevelopment. Discussion of colonialism, which appeared very rarely, was descriptive and limited mainly to 'old colonialism'. The general history textbook for the third year of high school devoted only two and a half pages to 'neo-colonialism'.[21] These pages, however, were not connected in any systematic way to the rest of the book. In fact, the European countries and the United States were generally portrayed in a positive light. In the case of Iran itself, discussion of welfare programmes and economic justice was limited to praise for the achievements of Mohammad Reza Shah's regime.[22]

It is yet to become clear how significant the problem of economic injustice was in the precipitation and ultimate success of the revolution; however, promises of economic reform were among the main revolutionary slogans. Some tendencies within the Islamic Republic have strongly supported redistributive economic policies. Moreover, a major constituent of the Islamic Republic has been the lower and lower-middle classes, who have demanded redistributive economic policies. It is not surprising, therefore, that the post-revolutionary textbooks concentrate on economic justice.

In contrast to the modernization approach of the pre-revolutionary textbooks, the Islamic Republic has introduced high-school students to the dependency theory of underdevelopment.[23] The general history textbook for the fourth year, for example, starts with a preface on the twentieth century as an era that witnessed the division of the world into the very rich and very poor, and as the century of neocolonialism.[24] The entire textbook is an elaboration on how such a state of affairs became possible. Going back to the seventeenth century, the book describes how technological advancement enabled the Europeans to embark on overseas adventures, plundering wealth and subjugating people in other parts of the world. The book also shows how that process led to a fierce competition, and ultimately to wars for economic and political supremacy, among the Europeans themselves.[25] This analysis is extended to the aftermath of the Second World War, the development of the two superpowers, the continuation of colonialism in its new guise, and the emergence of national liberation movements.

In dealing with the case of Iran, the history books apply the dependency approach and interpret Western penetration as an attempt to find new consumer markets and gain access to cheap raw materials, both of which, according to these books, were essential for the survival of the Western capitalist system.[26]

In contrast to economic growth, economic justice has been the dominant theme of post-revolutionary high-school textbooks. Starting with the premiss that God intended a unitary (*towhidi*) community and that in the Islamic community there is no room for classes, the textbooks advocate equality and cooperation.[27] The Lockean notion of an individual's natural right to private property, implicitly advocated by the pre-revolutionary regime, has been replaced with the Rousseauian concept of the trusteeship of property. Property has been entrusted to the individual and is conditional rather than absolute. If the conditions are not upheld, the property can be taken away from the individual.[28] Moreover, it has been argued that the unalterable goal in an Islamic society is to achieve the

same standard of living for the whole community through a just distribution of means of production and income.[29]

Alliance versus Non-alliance

The outlook of the two regimes on issues of colonialism and neo-
colonialism affected their respective views on Iran's relationship with the
outside world in general and with the West in particular. The Pahlavi
regime saw the outside world as dominated by the 'free world' of capitalism
and the evil force of communism. In such a global context the choice for
countries such as Iran was to ally with one of the two global camps. The
pre-revolutionary regime was fascinated by the cultural and social aspects
of Western civilization. This social and cultural affinity was tied to the
economic interests of the ruling class. These factors were responsible for
the close alliance between Iran and the West.

The pre-revolutionary textbooks were full of praise for the achievements of the West. The general history for third-year high-school students
devoted the section on nineteenth-century sciences and literature exclu-
sively to Western achievements.[30] The Western scientific outlook and
methods were dominant in sociology textbooks. The views of Western
philosophers, sociologists, economists and psychologists such as John Stuart
Mill, August Comte, Émile Durkheim, Adam Smith, Rostow and Sigmund
Freud prevailed in these textbooks.[31] At the political level, Western ideas
and actions such as British liberalism, the French Revolution, the Declaration of Human Rights and the American defence of self-determination
for nations were considered positive developments not only for the West
but also for the Third World. In fact, according to these textbooks, the
above factors and the efforts of Christian priests in advocating the equality
of humankind were the elements that precipitated anti-colonial and
nationalist movements in the Third World.[32]

The pre-revolutionary textbooks praised the role of the United States
as the champion of freedom and as the challenger to the menace of
communism in the context of the Cold War.[33] These textbooks presented
a Manichean view of the global situation, according to which there were
two forces, one representing whatever was good, the other everything that
was evil. The democratic, capitalist West led by the United States represented the good; and the dictatorships of the communist world, led by the
Soviet Union, symbolized the evil.[34] The natural choice for Iran, implied
in the textbooks, was to side with the forces of Western capitalism. Iran's
alliance with the West, evidenced by Iranian participation in defence
organizations such as CENTO, was therefore justified as a rational choice.[35]

Such an alliance, the pre-revolutionary textbooks maintained, was not
a sign of dependence. Instead they asserted that Iran adhered to an
'independent national policy'.[36] Taken verbatim from Mohammad Reza

Shah's, *Towards the Great Civilization*, the policy, as stated in the fourth-year history textbook, called for peaceful coexistence and goodwill in bilateral relations between countries, acceptance of the United Nations as the supreme authority, and adherence to 'positive nationalism', as opposed to the 'negative balance'. Positive nationalism was defined as an approach that attempted to secure maximum independence while avoiding isolation from the rest of the world. 'Negative balance policy', which interestingly enough was not defined in the pre-revolutionary textbooks, refers to the non-aligned approach taken by the Mosaddeq administration between 1951 and 1953. This approach called for Iran's economic and political independence.

The 1979 revolution had a strong anti-imperialist, anti-dependency orientation. The pre-revolutionary East–West categorization was not a meaningful moral–political division to the leader of the revolution. For Ayatollah Khomeini and many members of the revolutionary coalition, East and West were both oppressors. In opposition to both camps of oppressors were a vast number of countries that constituted the oppressed nations of the world. It was with regard to this division that Iran sought to choose sides. The Islamic Republic saw Iran among the oppressed nations. Based on this world-view, the only dignified stand for oppressed countries such as Iran was to be non-aligned or to follow what came to be known as the 'neither East, nor West' policy in economic, political and cultural domains. In fact the Islamic Republic, and the Ayatollah Khomeini as its supreme leader, considered cultural independence as the most important and primary factor in achieving a true non-aligned stand. Considering pre-revolutionary state-run cultural education as detrimental to the cause of independence, a campaign developed to change the content of the textbooks. The result was a sharp break with the past.

The preface to the fourth-year *History of Islam* provides a critical assessment of Islamic studies by Western orientalists, very similar to the ideas presented in Edward Said's *Orientalism*. The aim of this assessment is to call for an indigenous critique of Western orientalism as a way of neutralizing Western distortions.[37] An important change is immediately evident in the sources and authorities referred to in the textbooks. In sociology and social knowledge textbooks, for example, the Western sources have been replaced, for the most part, by their Islamic and Iranian counterparts. Instead of Smith, Mill or Freud, students are introduced to Ibn Khaldun, Na'ini, or Maududi. Introducing the students to cultural, artistic and scientific domains, the post-revolutionary textbooks pay a great deal of attention to non-Western, particularly Islamic and Iranian, achievements. Efforts are made to show how the modern Western development in these areas is indebted to the thriving Islamic civilization of the Middle Ages. Abu Nasr Farabi, Abu Ali Sina, Mohammad Ghazzali, Shahabeddin Sohrevardi, Nasireddin Tusi, Omar Khayyam, Qyiaseddin Kashani, and

Ibn Zohar are among the philosophers, mathematicians and physicians whose contributions to the advancement of civilization are mentioned.[38]

The post-revolutionary textbooks emphasize the positive aspects of tradition, particularly Islamic values. This is in contrast to the pre-revolutionary textbooks that focused on the negative aspects of tradition to emphasize the need for abolishing or weakening them for the sake of economic development. The new textbooks argue that the causes of decline and underdevelopment in countries such as Iran can be found in the Western military, economic, political and particularly cultural campaigns against the Islamic world.[39]

The cultural weapon, according to the textbooks, has greater potency than economic and political tools because it affects the soul of a community. Through humiliation, brainwashing and the spread of consumerism, it is asserted, the imperial powers manipulate the identity of the oppressed nations. Even ideas such as democracy and freedom, which seem to be regarded as universally accepted moral values, are distorted by the West. According to the textbooks, the Western interpretation and practice of democracy and freedom are objectionable. Moreover, neither democracy nor freedom has been instrumental in defeating colonialism, the post-revolutionary textbooks claim.[40] Implicit in these arguments is the idea that Islamic liberation will require a critical view of Western values and institutions.

As for the contemporary political situation, the post-revolutionary textbooks, like their pre-revolutionary counterparts, discuss the phenomenon of the Cold War. However, the post-revolutionary texts offer a different analysis of the competition between East and West. Here the struggle is not between the forces of good and evil, but is instead a competition for domination of the world and suppression of the oppressed nations. The textbooks claim that a good example of such behaviour was manifested in Lebanon, where the United States, through the Eisenhower Doctrine, attempted to suppress Arab nationalist aspirations in the name of protecting the Middle East from communism.[41] As for the Soviet Union, its suppression of the Hungarian and Polish uprisings provide enough evidence to support the theory of competitive domination.[42]

In Iran, recent instances of interference abound. The roles played by the Soviet Union, the British and ultimately the United States do not leave any room for illusions about the benign intentions of the foreign powers. Unlike the pre-revolutionary textbooks, the Islamic Republic's educational materials point to the blatant interference of these powers in instances such as the Azerbaijan event in 1946, the oil nationalization era of 1949–53, and the 1953 CIA coup d'état in Iran.[43] Each one of these events by itself provides enough reason why Iran should seek non-alignment or adhere to the policy of 'neither East, nor West'. The principles of this policy include the negation of domination and oppression, the protection of the geographical integrity of Iran, the striving for the unity of Muslims around the world, non-alignment in Iran's relationship with the colonial powers, support for liberation movements, and peaceful co-existence with the non-belligerent states.[44]

Status Quo Monarchism versus Popular Revolutionism

The Pahlavi regime was both modernist and authoritarian. True to its authoritarian nature, the regime tried to keep civil society out of politics. With the exception of government-sponsored rallies and meetings, the state, through its coercive, economic and cultural means, did its utmost to discourage popular participation in politics. After the 1953 coup d'état Mohammed Reza Shah gradually increased his power and became the sole decision-maker in Iran. He tried hard to portray himself as the paternal monarch who benevolently ruled over his people. He also attempted to represent himself as the true heir to the ancient institution of monarchy that, according to his claim, had brought glory to Iran in its 2500 years of history. In the pre-revolutionary textbooks, the institution of monarchy in Iran was considered a natural phenomenon based on socio-economic laws.[45] 'History has shown that whenever the monarchical institution established itself firmly, the economy, industry, and varieties of art and educational fields have progressed as well.'[46] The textbooks argued that one of the most important reasons for the rise and fall of nations lies in the strength of their leaders. The powerful kings of the Achaemenid, Sasanid, and Pahlavi dynasties were effective leaders.[47] To give the monarchy a legitimacy that could not be questioned, the textbooks asserted that the strength of the king, as the 'navigator of the fate of the country', is based on God's will.[48]

In contrast to their emphasis on powerful kings, the pre-revolutionary textbooks ignored the role of the people in shaping Iran's destiny. This contrast was particularly striking in the description of the reigns of both Reza Shah and Mohammed Reza Shah. The textbooks attributed all the positive accomplishments of that era to these two kings. Cultivating the role of the leaders, full-length pictures of the Pahlavi Shahs adorned many pages of the textbooks.

In addition to the positive role of the kings in bringing prosperity and progress to the nation, the textbooks emphasized the necessity of political stability, both internal and external, in furthering economic development.[49] Political stability was praised for providing a suitable environment for economic growth through the attraction of foreign investment. Stating that Iran enjoyed international respect, the textbooks, quoting from *Towards the Great Civilization*, attributed this respect to Iran's efforts to uphold global order.[50]

As a general rule the pre-revolutionary textbooks gave a sketchy account of revolutionary movements, both in Iran and abroad. Influential reformers and revolutionaries such as Mohammad Mosaddeq and Heydar Khan Amo-Oghlo were ignored. Absent from the general history textbooks were monumental radical events such as the Bolshevik and Chinese revolutions.

Anti-monarchism was probably the glue that bound together many oppositional groups in the 1979 revolutionary movement.[51] Above all, Ayatollah Khomeini's distaste for the institution of the monarchy, revealed in most of his speeches, sealed the fate of the monarchy once the revolution was triumphant. With the establishment of the Islamic Republic, the leader of the revolution aspired to replace the pre-revolutionary system with one that would make Shari'a the law of the land. His directives were reflected in the contents of post-revolutionary high-school educational materials.

Anti-monarchical remarks abound in post-revolutionary textbooks. According to textbooks the most authoritative statements critical of the monarchy come from the Quran.[52] 'In its description of the history of prophets's movements, [the Quran] has portrayed the anti-revolutionary and anti-monotheism of the monarchs. Wherever [the Quran] has hinted at the attempts of the prophets in ... establishing God's sovereignty, [it] has shown the monarchs as the heads of the opposition [to the prophets].'[53] The textbooks assert that the goal of the prophets in guiding and ruling over people, as their austere lives have attested, has not been to provide a luxurious lifestyle for themselves, but to strive for the felicity of human beings, particularly the oppressed classes.[54] In contrast, the goal of the historical absolutist monarchies, which were erected and maintained by exploitation, repression and manipulation of the masses, was to satisfy the appetites of the dictatorial rulers.[55]

The anti-monarchical stand of the the post-revolutionary educational materials does not necessarily rule out the legitimacy of one supreme authority. As the institution of velayat-e faqih (the rule of the just jurist) demonstrates, it is not the number of people in power that is at issue, but the nature of the rule. The rule of Mohammad as the pious faithful subject of God is indeed an ideal political institution. The same can be said about having a pious and knowledgeable religious leader as the political leader in modern times.

Besides the differences between the king and the faqih in terms of the personal characteristics required for leadership, the manner in which they assume their role also differs. In a monarchy, heredity determines who will be the leader; people do not play any role in the process. The faqih, on the other hand, is chosen according to the constitution of the Islamic Republic, by the people through their representatives in the Assembly of Experts. The faqih has many rights but his obligations are immense;[56] and if he does not fulfil them he can be dismissed by the people's representatives. Therefore, the textbooks argue, the Islamic regime is based on dual 'God–popular' sovereignty. Unlike in other regimes, the people are neither totally devoid of power nor free to act contrary to their 'true interests'.[57] Popular participation in the Islamic regime demonstrates itself in the concepts of *showra* (council) and *mashvarat* (consultation). The leader is advised to consult the people on issues for which there are no directives from the Shari'a.[58]

The positive attitude toward revolution in the textbooks concerns the pre-revolutionary history of Iran. In treating revolutionary movements as popular uprisings against the injustices of the elite, however, a great deal of emphasis has been put on the role of religious personalities in guiding and shaping revolutions.[59] As far as outside movements such as the 1917 Russian Revolution are concerned, the popular initiatives have been praised but the outcomes of these movements and their leaderships have been criticized.[60]

It is in the analysis of the global system that revolutionary values find their strongest expression. The status quo power arrangement, regarded as imperialistic, is severely criticized and liberation movements are hailed.[61] The role of the Islamic Republic in challenging the status quo and in revolutionizing the system is outlined in the principles and goals of Iran's foreign policies.[62]

Conclusion

The above study reveals that the pre- and post-revolutionary regimes have used the educational system to convince the youth of their right to rule based on the legitimacy of their institutions and the soundness of their values and policies. The Pahlavi regime is now part of history, but the Islamic Republic is still in place and is still a young state. A look at the developments of the past 16 years demonstrates that the Iranian political system is still in the process of evolving and that its stabilized character is yet to be determined.

The demise of Ayatollah Khomeini, the charismatic and final arbiter, left Iran with a factionalized polity. Since the early 1980s three factions have developed in Iran. The first faction identifies itself with issues such as economic justice, revolutionary populism and non-alignment. The second faction advocates a conservative approach in all areas of life. As such, the conservatives, while adhering strongly to the Islamic institutions and Islamic cultural values, frown upon the early revolutionary ideals. The third faction, headed by Hashemi Rafsanjani, the current president of the Islamic Republic, represents a middle-of-the-road, pragmatic outlook, emphasizing economic growth and better relations with the outside world.

In many ways this last faction has also distanced itself from the revolutionary ideals, if not in its rhetoric, at least in practice.

All the significant developments both in domestic and foreign-policy domains, particularly since 1989, point to the gradual but precarious ascendence of the pragmatists, who are in an uneasy coalition with the conservatives. If the trend of increasing influence of these two factions continues, Iran will witness the emergence of a state that in some very important ways would be similar to the old regime. Economic growth, stability, closer identification with the existing international power structure, and withdrawal of active support for the revolutionary movements will be among the goals pursued by the triumphant factions. Differences between the pre-revolutionary regime and the emerging regime will probably persist in the areas of cultural values and the role of the religious leadership in politics. What will be the impact of these developments on the content of educational materials? The logical answer points away from revolutionary ideals and toward the fostering of values and attitudes that accommodate the goals of the victorious power group.

A Note on the Impact of Socialization

The primary focus of this study was the input of the socialization process. The next step should involve a study of the output (the impact on the attitudes and behaviour of the youth) of this socialization attempt. Although it has not been the intent of this chapter to address this important issue, a preliminary assertion could be made here. The 1979 revolution, in which university and high-school students were among the most active participants, demonstrated the failure of the Pahlavi regime to foster its values among the youth. The generation of politically active students who were exposed to the pre-revolutionary educational materials developed attitudes that were antithetical to the attitude wished for by the regime. The slogans used by the young revolutionary activists attest to this fact.

Although not as evident as it was in the pre-revolutionary case, the post-revolutionary students have shown signs of resistance to certain ideals promoted in the first decade of post-revolutionary educational materials. Those university student organizations that support the ideal of the revolution have repeatedly warned against the lack of revolutionary commitment on the part of the students and the necessity for combatting this negative trend.[63] Those who hold political power also voice their concern about socialization of the young. In many major public addresses, explicit and implicit admissions of failure to inculcate 'Islamic values', particularly in the cultural sphere, have been expressed by the elite. However, a comprehensive and thorough study of the attitudes of the post-revolutionary students will be needed before any definitive statement can be made about the success or failure of the Islamic Republic in socializing its youth.

Notes

1. The importance of socialization and its relation to the stability and strength of the state has been stressed by social theorists throughout history and is not just a modern concern. See Plato's *Republic*, translated by Allan Bloom (NY: Basic Books, 1968) Books II and III. For a modern treatment of the issue, see Max Weber, 'Legitimacy, politics and the state', in William Connolly (ed.), *Legitimacy and the State* (Oxford: Blackwell, 1984), pp 32–62. For a more contemporary treatment of the relation between socialization and state legitimacy, see David Easton and Jack Dennis, *Children in the Political System: Origins of Political Legitimacy* (Chicago: University of Chicago Press, 1980).

2. See Akhavi, Shahrough, *Religion and Politics in Contemporary Iran: Clergy–State Relations in the Pahlavi Period* (Albany: Suny Press 1980), pp 23–4.

3. *Sociology*, General Secondary Education, Fourth Year, in Persian (Tehran, 1978), p 84.

4. *History*, Secondary Education, Third Year, in Persian (Tehran, 1977), p 82.

5. Ibid., pp 29–31; and *Sociology*, General Education, Third Year, in Persian (Tehran, 1977), pp 56–7.

6. Ibid., pp 57–8.

7. *General History*, High School Education, Third Year, in Persian (Tehran, 1977), p 11.

8. Akhavi, *Religion and Politics*, pp 23–59 and 91–158.

9. *Social Knowledge*, Secondary Education, Fourth Year, in Persian (Tehran, 1982), p 14.

10. *Social Knowledge*, High School Education, Fourth Year, in Persian (Tehran, 1989), pp 59–60.

11. In all post-revolutionary Iranian history textbooks, the theme of revolutionary struggles on the part of religious figures and communities in countering injustice, corruption, colonialism and despotism is quite dominant.

12. See also *Social Knowledge*, High School Education, Second Year, in Persian (Tehran, 1989), pp 87–97.

13. See *Social Knowledge*, Fourth Year, pp 59–60.

14. Ibid., p 14.

15. Ibid., pp 14, 17 and 24.

16. See Looney, Robert, *Economic Origins of the Iranian Revolution* (New York: Pergamon Press, 1982), pp 12–25; and Katouzian, Homa, *The Political Economy of Modern Iran*, (New York: New York University Press, 1981), pp 255–73.

17. *Sociology*, High School Education, Second Year (Tehran, 1978).

18. *Sociology*, High School Education, Fourth Year (Tehran, 1978), pp 1–10.

19. Ibid., p 13.

20. *Sociology*, High School Education, Third Year, (Tehran, 1978), p 61.

21. *General History*, High School Education, Third Year, in Persian (Tehran, 1977)

pp 65–98.

22. For example, see *History*, High School Education, Fourth Year (Tehran, 1978), pp 31–41.

23. For a review of works on dependency, see Palma Gabriel, 'Dependency and development: A critical overview', *World Development* 6/7–8 (1978), pp 881–924.

24. *General History: A Look at World History in the Twentieth Century*, High School Education, Fourth Year, in Persian (Tehran, 1989), preface.

25. Ibid., parts I–XI, pp 1–75.

26. *The Contemporary History of Iran*, High School Education, Third Year, in Persian (Tehran, 1989).

27. See *Social Knowledge*, Fourth Year, pp 56–8; and *Social Knowledge*, High School Education, First Year (1989), pp 102–18.

28. Ibid., pp 57–8.

29. Ibid., p 59.

30. *General History*, High School Education, Third Year (Tehran, 1977), pp 99–105.

31. See *Sociology*, High School Education, Second, Third and Fourth Years.

32. *General History*, High School Education, Third Year (Tehran, 1977), pp 88–9.

33. Ibid., p 26.

34. Ibid., p 32.

35. Ibid., p 60.

36. *History*, High School Education, Fourth Year (Tehran, 1978), pp 24–30.

37. *The Contemporary History of Iran*, High School Education, Third Year (Tehran, 1989), pp 157–82.

38. See *History of Civilization and Culture*, High School Education, Second Year (Tehran, 1989), pp 116–47; and *History: Introduction to the Islamic Civilization and Culture*, High School Education, Second Year (Tehran, 1982), pp 81–168.

39. *History of Civilization*, Second Year, pp 153–62; and *Social Knowledge*, Fourth Year, pp 120–25.

40. *Social Knowledge*, Fourth Year, pp 44–7.

41. *General History*, Fourth Year, pp 96–7.

42. Ibid., p 95.

43. *The Contemporary History of Iran*, pp 157–182.

44. *Social Knowledge*, Fourth Year, pp 92–94.

45. *History*, Fourth Year, 1978, p 98.

46. Ibid., p 109.

47. Ibid., p 6.

48. Ibid., p 9.

49. Ibid., 1978, pp 42–5.

50. Ibid., pp 24–30.

51. See Bazargan, Mehdi, *Enqelab-e Iran dar Do Harekat* (Iran's Revolution in Two Motions) (Tehran, 1984). According to Bazargan, among the plurality of revolutionary slogans and banners, about 38 per cent targeted the monarchical system, p 37.

52. *History in Islam*, High School Education, Fourth-Year (Tehran, 1982), pp 48–9.

53. Ibid., p 48.

54. Ibid., pp 49–50.

55. Ibid., p 52.

56. *Social Knowledge*, Fourth Year, pp 63–70.

57. *Social Knowledge*, First Year, pp 27–29.

58. *Social Knowledge*, Fourth Year, pp 79–87.

59. *The Contemporary History of Iran.*

60. *General History*, Fourth Year, pp 26–32.

61. Ibid.

62. *Social Knowledge*, Fourth Year, pp 88–109.

63. For a sample of these statements, see *Daneshgah-e Enqelab*, January, February and March 1990.

9

Health Policy and Medical Education

Asghar Rastegar

Introduction

One of the tragic consequences of economic and social underdevelopment in any country is inadequate health care for the population. It is therefore not surprising that a major priority of all governments in developing societies has been to provide their citizens with sufficient health care. The structure of the health-care system in Iran before the revolution was characterized by many of the inequities prevalent in developing societies, such as a shortage of trained health-care workers, poor distribution of resources, antiquated facilities, and a lack of emphasis on preventive care. In this chapter I analyse the policies of the Iranian government in the post-revolutionary period which deal with the shortage of trained health-care personnel, and examine the social and educational ramifications of these policies. To provide a comparative basis of analysis, I will also briefly review the pre-revolutionary policies and practices. The Iranian health-care system during the pre-revolutionary period had clearly failed to address the needs of the population. The high infant mortality of rate of 103–130 deaths per thousand live births, compared to 14–30 per thousand in industrialized countries, a high proportion of deaths among children (accounting for one-half of all deaths, often from easily preventable or treatable diseases), a life expectancy of only 50 years – compared to 70 years in developed economies – and the poor distribution of health-care resources, are some of the manifestations of this tragic failure (see Table 9.1).

Prior to the revolution, the Iranian health-care system was a mixed, private/public one, financed by private payers, social-service insurance and government subsidies. Private and insured care was available only in the cities, mainly to upper- and middle-income households. The majority of Iranians, however, had to depend on the free care provided by poorly staffed government clinics and hospitals.

Table 9.1   Health Status of the Population Before the Revolution: Selected Statistics

Life expectancy (years)	50
Infant mortality (per 1000)	
Urban	103
Village	131
Deaths among children under five (as % of total deaths)	50
Physicians (per 1000 population)	
Tehran	1.3
Zanjan	0.06
Proportion of specialists in Tehran (%)	66
Cost/month per family (rials)	
Middle class	20,000
Peasants	560

Source: Adapted from the Royal Organization for Social Services (ROSS), *New Path to Health: Report of the Committee to Investigate the Health and Therapeutic Issues in Iran*, Vol 1 (Tehran: ROSS, 1972); A.M. Razi, 'Health and Medical Education', *Amuzesh va Farhang* no 2 (1980), pp 23–32; *Iran Times*, 29 December 1990.

Medical schools produced a small throughput of physicians, no more than 700 a year. Medical students were primarily from middle- and upper-income families. A study at Pahlavi (now Shiraz) University Medical School shows that the chance of entering medical school was 300 and 100 times greater for the children of military and professional families than for those of workers and farmers.[1] In 1979, there were approximately 15,000 physicians in Iran, which is reflected in the ratio of 0.4 physician per 1000 population, compared to 1.5 to 2.5 in most industrialized countries (see Table 9.2). In addition to the general shortage of physicians, there was a significantly poor distribution of physicians in the provinces, and between urban and rural areas. For example, as shown in Table 9.1, the number of physicians per 1000 people was 1.3 in Tehran province and 0.06 in Zanjan province. Similar shortages existed among other health-care workers, including nurses, dentists and pharmacists.

In the post-revolutionary period many health-care workers, especially physicians, migrated abroad for economic and political reasons. The exact number of physicians who left Iran is not known. However, based on

Table 9.2   Trends in Health-care Resources in Iran 1978–1992

	Total population	Beds	Physicians	Specialists	MD graduates /year	Health-care workers
1978	36,000,000	56,000 (1.5)	15,000 (0.41)	7000 (0.19)	700	39,065 (1.1)
1988	53,000,000	77,000 (1.4)	21,500 (0.34)	11,000 (0.21)	734	89,832 (1.7)
1992	57,000,000	91,000 (1.6)	24,500 (0.43)	16,000 (0.28)	1,962	106,176 (1.9)

Note: Figures in parenthesis are per 1000 population.

Source: Adapted from Ministry of Health, Treatment and Education, *Progress Report*, in Persian (Tehran, June 1993).

personal information, I estimate the number to be about 4000. The migration of physicians occurred primarily among specialists, many of whom had received part of their training abroad. Faced with an acute shortage of health-care workers, especially physicians, the Islamic Republic adopted a two-pronged approach. First, it politicized and centralized the educational process to keep universities under the control of the government. Second, it pursued a policy to increase the number and class size of medical schools, and schools for training allied health professionals. These policies had an immediate impact on higher education in general, and on the training of health-care workers and physicians in particular.

Politicization of the Educational Process

Following the Iranian Revolution – for about 15 months before the onslaught of the Cultural Revolution – Iranian universities enjoyed an autonomy not previously seen in the history of these institutions. This autonomy resulted in both chaos and creativity. In most universities, student-based political groups, often associated with national political organizations, engaged in activities unrelated to the mission of a university. On the other hand, this autonomy led to the development of creative curricula and teaching methods, in an attempt to bridge the gap between the university and society.

Medical schools, as educational service institutions, were in the forefront of these events.[2] Many committed faculty and students hoped that these efforts would result in the development of creative educational models to

Table 9.3   Trends in Educational Workforce and Resources in Health Care

	Health-care students	Medical students	Faculty	Student–faculty ratio	Medical schools	Cost/student (1977 rials)
1978	22,000 (0.61)	5100 (0.14)	2500	9:1	8	345,000
1988	45,000 (0.94)	11,000 (0.21)	3625	12:1	19	43,000
1992	100,000 (1.70)	32,000 (0.56)	6000	17:1	30	n.a.

Note: Figures in parenthesis are per 1000 population.

Source: Adapted from Ministry of Health, Treatment and Education, *Progress Report*, in Persian (Tehran, June 1993); Ministry of Higher Education, *Evaluation of Activities in Higher Education*, in Persian (Tehran, March 1989), p 73.

deal with the shortage and poor distribution of health-care resources while improving their quality. A critical aspect of the new proposals was the development of a community-based educational curriculum governed by a decentralized and democratic administrative structure at the university level.

In the spring of 1980, the Islamic Republic waged the Cultural Revolution initially to close and then to remould the system of higher education in Iran. Ironically, the Islamic Republic attempted to neutralize the universities as centres of opposition and political activity by politicizing all aspects of university life to the smallest detail. This resulted in a high degree of centralization of authority at the institutional and national level – much greater than in the previous regime – in which a level of organizational and local autonomy was allowed as long as it did not threaten the authority of the central government.

The Islamic Republic developed a single curriculum for all the medical schools, regardless of their strengths and weaknesses, or their long-term missions. This new uniform curriculum was nothing but traditional lecture-based pedagogy, depending heavily on memorization of frequently outdated facts and data. The rapid increase in the number of medical schools, as well as of students in each institution, without appropriate increases in resources (shown in Table 9.3), resulted in a curriculum with little or no laboratory experience during the preclinical years. The educational content was not changed significantly except for the addition of several required courses in Islamic law and culture.

The student-selection process, however, was radically changed to allow for assessment of students' loyalty to the Islamic Republic. In addition, more than one-half of the places were earmarked for the 'revolutionary foundations'. Although this policy allowed the admission of some candidates from lower social classes and underserved regions of the country, no attempt was made to prepare these students for a university education. This resulted in a marked discrepancy in educational achievement among students, and a tendency among the faculty to adjust academic standards to the lowest common denominator.

The independent process of faculty selection and promotion within the university system was a serious challenge to the government. In the immediate post-revolutionary period, only a small number of faculty were dismissed or imprisoned on political grounds. The departure of faculty in large numbers, however, began after the Cultural Revolution. In the first post-revolutionary year, the faculty members, who had mostly supported the revolution, remained in their universities hoping to strengthen the democratic structure of their institutions. The Cultural Revolution, however, resulted in the closure of all institutions of higher learning and the dismissal of faculty members who were thought to be disloyal to the Islamic Republic. During this period many professors who had no political affiliation also left to find more secure positions in Iran or abroad. Although statistics for the whole country are not available, at Shiraz University Medical School approximately 10 of 173 full-time faculty resigned from the university during the 14 months before the Cultural Revolution. However, by 1982 only 67 of the original faculty members remained. Many of these professors have since departed.[3] This trend was, more or less, true of other universities and of other disciplines. For example, by 1982, at Tehran University, of the 2000 faculty members at the time of the revolution, only 750 faculty still remained.[4]

The process of faculty selection and retention, previously handled at the institutional level, was shifted to a centralized committee in Tehran, called the Komiteh-ye Gozinesh (selection committee), which was not accountable to the academic community. The deliberations of this committee were secret and no recourse was available to faculty members who felt unjustly dismissed or demoted. The reward system was also heavily politicized, and faculty promotions, which were previously based primarily on academic merit, came to rely heavily on the administration. This was done at a time when all administrative positions were given to politically loyal and trusted individuals. Favouritism also extended to the granting of sabbatical leave, permission to participate in international meetings, and other perks associated with academic positions. In a clear manner, the Islamic government actively rewarded loyalty over competence and creativity. These circumstances have resulted in the rise of a new elite group which often proves poorly prepared to manage the affairs of institutions of higher learning.

In summary, the centralization of the decision-making process resulted in the politicization of all aspects of university life, even down to the smallest detail, allowing for heavy-handed political control of these institutions by the government. The departure of many highly qualified faculty and the selection of new faculty and students, primarily on the basis of political ideology and loyalty rather than academic competence and achievement, have resulted in an educational environment that stifles creativity, diversity and debate – so critical to the soul of a progressive educational system – at the expense of political expediency.

Mass Production of Health-care Workers

The government of the Islamic Republic, while attempting to enforce its rule over the universities, was aware of the severe shortage of health-care workers. This shortage was aggravated by the Cultural Revolution, which kept all institutions of higher learning closed for two years. During this time, the number of new graduates decreased, while many highly skilled health-care workers, especially physicians, were leaving Iran. The Iran–Iraq war, with its tens of thousands of casualties, put an additional strain on health-care resources.

The government responded to this challenge by expanding existing medical schools and creating some new ones.[5] As shown in Table 9.3, since the revolution, the number of medical schools has more than trebled, rising from 8 in 1978 to 19 in 1988, and to 30 in 1992. The number of medical students and other health-care workers has increased significantly in both absolute and relative terms. Between 1978 and 1992, the total number of students in health fields increased from 22,000 to 100,000, a 4.5-fold increase. During the same period, the number of medical students increased more than 6-fold, from 5100 to 32,000. These data should be interpreted in the light of the dramatic increase in the population since the revolution. In relative terms, the number of medical and health-care students has increased from 0.14 and 0.61 per thousand population respectively in 1978 to 0.57 and 1.7 in 1992 (see Table 9.3). The continuing rise in the number of graduates will undoubtedly have a significant impact on the ratio of health-care workers to population in the coming decade.[6] The annual number of medical-school graduates per 1000 population in Iran will soon surpass that of the USA by 50 per cent (0.1 in Iran as opposed to 0.06 in the USA), a country with a relative overabundance of physicians.

As shown in Table 9.3, the overall number of university faculty in the health-care field has increased from 2500 in 1978, to 3625 in 1988, and to 6000 in 1992. A large proportion of this increase is, however, the outcome of the restructuring of the Ministry of Health (discussed below). This restructuring has resulted in the inclusion of clinical practitioners as faculty members in medical schools. The vast majority of faculty members, however, hold the junior ranks of instructor (41 per cent) and assistant professor (48 per cent) with only 11 per cent holding the ranks of associate and full professor.[7] Shiraz University Medical School, losing as it did the majority of its senior faculty with valuable expertise in both general practice and specialized medicine, is by no means unique among Iranian universities. It is estimated that only half of the university faculty have doctoral degrees in their field. In addition, due to the marked increase in the number of students, the student/faculty ratio in the health-care field has increased from 9:1 to 17:1 (compared to the international standard of 7:1) (see Table 9.3).

The above data reflect the situation in the well-established state-run universities, which are generally better supported and staffed. The newly created Azad University (Open University), which is financially dependent on students' tuition fees (and is therefore essentially a private institution) has a student/faculty ratio of 62:1. Considering the fact that two-thirds of the faculty at Azad University are part time, the true ratio is significantly higher. It should be noted that despite major resource limitations, Azad University accepted more new students in all fields in 1990 than all the well-established state-run universities put together (70,000 compared with 56,000).

University salaries have decreased in real terms (1977 rates) by 70 per cent: from 90,000 rials per month before the revolution to 25,000 devalued rials in 1989.[8] Although salaries for full-time faculty were increased in 1991, this did not significantly change the marked decrease in their buying power. For example, a three-bedroom apartment in northern Tehran with a rent of 50,000 rials in 1978 now rents for 600,000 to 800,000 rials, a 12- to 16-fold increase, while the full-time salary for a medical-school faculty member has only increased about four-fold, from 90,000 to 400,000 rials. This decline in the real salary of professors has resulted in a major shift in the commitment of the faculty from teaching and research to private practice to make up for lost income. For example, the faculty at Shiraz University Medical School each now work six to eight hours per day in direct patient care outside their full-time university schedule, compared to six to eight hours per week in the pre-revolutionary period. This has detracted from their ability to carry out teaching and research activities. If we take into account the decrease in faculty teaching and research time, the actual professor–student ratio is significantly higher than 17:1. Each professor offers much less than full attention to her/his students.

Resource deficiencies are not limited to just faculty; there is also a significant shortfall in available space. There is consequently less than one hospital bed per student in most medical schools in Iran compared to five in most developed countries. Given the marked increase in the number of students and the decrease in overall resources, it is therefore not surprising that the cost of educating each university student has decreased sharply from 345,000 to 43,000 devalued rials per year (1977 rates), an 88 per cent decrease[9] (see Table 9.3).

There is at present no reliable way to measure the quality of medical students leaving Iranian medical schools. My own observation after many visits to these schools is that they continue to produce a small number of highly competent physicians who often, through their own effort, maintain a level of competency comparable to the best in the world, but that the mean quality has declined significantly. It follows, therefore, that upon graduation the average student is poorly prepared to face the changing and challenging world of patient care, community health service and research.

In 1985, the Majles passed a law that shifted the responsibility for medical education from the Ministry of Higher Education to the Ministry of Health, renaming it the Ministry of Health, Treatment and Medical Education. The stated purpose of this change was to allow better co-ordination of medical schools. This move also significantly expanded the number of faculty and training sites by making the resources of the Ministry of Health available to medical schools. The overall impact of this policy is difficult to assess at this time. On the one hand, many of the new faculty members (mostly general practitioners) recruited from the Ministry of Health do not have the appropriate training to act as educators in their field. On the other hand, the policy has allowed the utilization of hospitals belonging to the Ministry of Health as training sites. In addition, it has allowed better coordination of the assignment of recent graduates to deprived areas. However, this reorganization has raised a more complex issue regarding the role of medical schools in tackling the day-to-day deficiencies in the health-care system. Some argue that the main goals of a university are the development of an environment for the dissemination of knowledge through education, the creation of new knowledge through research, and the provision of limited and well-defined services. If universities are saddled with enormous service obligations, other missions will be overwhelmed by the immediate service needs. This would force the universities to become, at best, expensive trade schools, not serving the long-term needs of society.

The present policy has succeeded in increasing the number of physicians and other health-care workers in Iran from 15,000 in 1978 to 24,500 in 1992. However, due to the marked increase in population, the number of physicians per 1000 population has not changed significantly (0.41 increasing to 0.43). The situation is better for other health-care workers, where the number per 1000 population has increased from 1.1 to 1.9 in the same period (see Table 9.2). The Islamic Republic has been significantly more successful than the Shah's regime in enforcing the social-service commitment which obligates medical graduates to spend three to five years in rural or other underserved areas. This has been associated with a significant increase in the number of 'Khaneh Behdasht' (Houses of Health), from 1800 in 1985 to 12,000 in 1992, and of regional medical clinics from 2420 to 3619 in the same period.[10]

Medical Education and the Health-care System

The provision of health care in such a vast and populous developing country as Iran is an enormous task. There is no doubt that medical schools should be active partners in this venture by providing a reasonable amount of care as well as developing new methods of tackling problems related to specific diseases or to the general health of the population. However, the present focus on the delivery of health-care rather than on education, coupled with a severe shortage of resources, has resulted in the deterioration of the quality of higher education to a point where it has even alarmed the present university administrators. The chancellor of Tehran University recently observed that 'university education has deteriorated to the level of high-school education.'[11] This concern is echoed by other educators.[12]

The basic structure of health-care services in Iran has not changed in a fundamental way since the revolution. The concept of nationalized health care, popular briefly after the revolution, never gained support among the policy-makers. The government introduced certain reforms to shift resources to the underserved areas – for example, by expanding the number of free health clinics and requiring of compulsory service in these areas by recent medical-school graduates.[13] However, the overall mixed public–private structure of funding has not changed and the majority of Iranians remain uninsured, seeking care only when absolutely necessary.

Given the interrelationship of health-care education and the quality and quantity of health-care services, the educational policies of the government will have a direct impact on the health-care of the people. There is no doubt that the health of a society is affected much more by economic and social developments than by preventive or curative means. However, society has an obligation to provide each individual with compassionate care given by competent professionals. In addition, physicians, through their ability to prescribe medications and procedures, are responsible for incurring the largest portion of health-care costs. The present educational system, while attracting some talented high-school graduates, is producing a large number of poorly educated physicians who will not only have a major impact on people's lives but also on health care for many years to come. Undoubtedly, the eventual increase in the number of physicians in Iran will allow greater access to the health-care system. However, as the experience of other Middle Eastern countries has shown, unless such an increase is part of a well-defined and integrated policy to deal with the health of society, it does not lead to improvement in the quality of care and often comes at great cost.[14]

An alternative approach to this complex problem would have been to develop a health-care network staffed by individuals (physicians and non-physicians) with varying levels of sophistication, backed by major teaching hospitals in metropolitan areas.[15] This approach would have required developing medical schools with innovative community-based curricula to train a large number of physicians and other health-care workers to provide preventive and primary care to the population. In addition, several medical schools would have been assigned the task of training specialists, providing sophisticated tertiary care and educating future faculty. However, the Iranian government decided to choose the present path to deal with this issue. Clearly the shortage of health-care workers was a pressing problem left over from the previous regime. This shortage had resulted in the importation of many poorly trained physicians from other Third World countries. It was argued that their replacement by poorly trained Iranian physicians was at least an improvement over the existing situation. There were, however, at least three other important reasons for choosing this policy: (1) the lack of a carefully debated health and educational policy to be implemented following the revolution; (2) the Islamic Republic was seen to respond to the ambitions of the Iranian middle and lower classes, who saw education – especially medical education – as a road to social mobility and security, and therefore would welcome this expansion; and (3) curtailment of the power and prestige of Iranian physicians, who are generally reluctant to accept interference by the Islamic Republic in the practical aspects of their profession.

Conclusion

In summary, the educational policy of the Islamic Republic, first and foremost, reflected its desire to consolidate its control over all institutions of higher learning, including medical schools. This has resulted in the centralization as well as the politicization of the educational process, stifling creativity and diversity. At the same time, the dramatic expansion in the number of Iranian medical schools and the strict enforcement of mandatory service in the underserved areas has succeeded in increasing the access to physicians, especially in rural and previously underserved areas of the country. However, this expansion, which occurred without a concomitant expansion of resources, has created trade schools that train a large number of professional 'prescription writers'. This group will undoubtedly consume enormous resources without improving the health of society. Unless an integrated policy is developed to train appropriately and to utilize future generations of health-care workers in Iran, the present policies will profoundly affect the quality of their education as well as the health-care services provided for decades to come.

Notes

1. Farabi, A.R., and M. Sina, 'A Report on Curricular Changes at the Shiraz University School of Medicine,' *Amuzesh va Farhang* 4 (1980), p 52.

2. Ibid., pp 47–66.

3. *Iran Times*, 29 December 1990.

4. Ibid.

5. Ministry of Health, Treatment and Education, *Progress Report*, in Persian (Tehran, June 1993); and *Evaluation of the Activities in Higher Education in Iran 1979–1988*, in Persian (Tehran, March 1989), p 18.

6. Ronaghy, H.A., and H.J. Simone, 'Effects of the Islamic Revolution in Iran on Medical Education: The Shiraz University School of Medicine', *American Journal of Public Health* 73/12, 1983.

7. *Iran Times*, 11 May 1990.

8. Ministry of Higher Education, *Evaluation of the Activities in Higher Education*, p 18.

9. Ministry of Higher Education, *Programmes of the Section on Higher Education and Research*, Vol 1 (Tehran, May 1989), p 30.

10. Ministry of Higher Education, *Evaluation of the Activities in Higher Education*, p 73.

11. Ministry of Higher Education, *Programs of the Section on Higher Education and Research*, p 24.

12. *Iran Times*, 15 June 1990.

13. Statistical Centre of Iran, *Statistical Yearbook 1988* (Tehran, 1989) pp 71–92.

14. Stork, J., 'Political aspect of health', *Middle East Report*, 161, 1989, pp 4–10.

15. Ronaghi, H.A., et al., 'The front line health worker: selection, training and performance', *American Journal of Public Health* 66, 1976, pp 273–7.

10

The Politics of Nationality and Ethnic Diversity

Shahrzad Mojab and Amir Hassanpour

The revolution of 1978–79 was the most popular political struggle in modern Iranian history. It drew the majority of the population, especially in urban areas, into political activism for the overthrow of a monarchical dictatorship. However, the participants in this revolution did not have a common goal. Visions of a future Iran were diverse, ranging from an Islamic regime to a democratic and socialist state. Activists among the non-Persian peoples, especially in Kurdistan, Turkman Sahra, Baluchistan and Khuzistan, sought a secular, democratic, federal state allowing extensive autonomy in administration, language, culture and economy. In Kurdistan, for example, there was no demand to establish an Islamic state.

Not surprisingly, when the monarchy was overthrown in February 1979, the Islamic regime was not in full control of the country. Tehran was unable to exercise power over the nationalities, the privately owned mass media, or the universities where a situation of dual power prevailed. Moreover, a considerable number of political parties – old and new, religious and secular, liberal and left – had come into the open to seek a role in the post-monarchist state. Under these circumstances, the Islamic Republic tried to extend its control over these autonomous entities while striving to Islamize the vast state machinery inherited from the Pahlavi monarchy. This chapter deals with the problems of the Islamic regime in integrating non-Persian peoples into the Islamic state. It will focus on the Kurds, who have posed the most serious challenge to the Islamic state.

The National and Ethnic Diversity of Iran

The population of Iran is diverse in terms of national, ethnic, linguistic and religious formations. Roughly half of the population are Persians who inhabit the central regions of Iran, especially the provinces of Tehran, Esfahan, Fars and most parts of Khorasan. The rest are Azerbaijani Turks or Azeris (24 per cent), Kurds (9 per cent), Baluchis (3 per cent), Arabs

(2.5 per cent) and Turkmans (1.5 per cent), who live in their ancestral territories in western, southeastern and northeastern regions.[1] Other ethnic peoples include Armenians, Assyrians and Jews who are dispersed throughout the country. They are distinguished from other non-Persian peoples by a lack of ancestral territories.[2]

An important feature of the nationalities system is that each nationality is a part of a larger nation separated by international borders. Thus, the Turkmans are part of the Turkman nation, most of whom live in the neighbouring republic of Turkmanstan. The same is true of the Arabs, Baluchis, Kurds and Azerbaijanis. While there are independent Azerbaijan and Arab states, the Kurds and Baluchis do not have a state of their own. Thus, the social, cultural, linguistic and political life of each nationality is shaped, to varying degrees, by developments in neighbouring countries. Under these conditions, the question of nationalities is rarely an 'internal problem' of the Iranian state.

Another feature that further complicates the nationalities question is their division along religious lines. The Persians and the Azeris are Shi'is while the Baluchis, Turkmans and the majority of the Kurds are Sunnis. The majority of Zoroastrians are Persians, while the Arabs are both Shi'is and Sunnis. The Armenian and Assyrian peoples are Christians. Socioeconomic and cultural differences are also significant. The Persians and the Azeris are more urbanized, while the Turkmans and Baluchis are more rural and, to some extent, have retained their tribal relations.

Before World War I, much of the Near and Middle East was under the rule of the Ottoman Empire and Iran. By the latter part of the nineteenth century, a process of national awareness was evolving among the various peoples of the Middle East. The Arabs, Turks, Persians, Kurds, Pashtuns and others were undergoing social, economic, cultural and linguistic transformations that were in many ways similar to the formation of nations in post-Renaissance Western Europe. Contrary to widespread opinion, the evolution of nationalism among these peoples was not due to the 'influence' of Western nationalism. Although such influence cannot be denied, the evolution of nations[3] is a historical process rooted in the complex internal development of each society. This process (as distinguished from 'nation-building' in the sense of 'state-building') usually entails the emergence of new social forces such as an urban middle class or bourgeoisie, and involves detribalization, the rise of capitalist relations, and so on. For instance, nationalism in Kurdistan emerged in the sixteenth to seventeenth centuries without the influence of the West.[4]

The literature on Iran generally ignores the multinational, multilinguistic and multicultural composition of the country. The dominant image of Iran is a more or less homogeneous society with one national language, Persian, and one religion, Shi'i Islam. Iranian governments brand the nationalist movements of non-Persian peoples simply as 'foreign intrigue'.

Until the mid nineteenth century, the loosely organized Iranian and Ottoman states were not capable of constraining the autonomous life of their 'subject' peoples, most of whom, whether Muslim or Christian, lived under their own rulers. The 'King of the Kings' was usually content with extracting, from lesser kings, a designated amount of tax and military support. Although he was able to put together a sizeable army to punish the unruly or to conquer other lands, the king or sultan could not maintain the force outside the capital for an extended period of time. Thus, this system of self-rule owed more to the inability of the imperial state to centralize political power than adherence to such notions as *omma* or *milla*. In fact, the Safavid state pursued centralization policies, but only the Qajars (1779–1925) were able, during the latter part of the nineteenth century, to eliminate the autonomous entities. In spite of centralization of power, the Qajar state remained a loosely integrated political structure. The Constitutional Revolution (1906–11) succeeded in producing a constitution based on European models of constitutional monarchy. The first constitution (1906) depicted Iran as a nation-state with one official language, Persian, and a centralized political structure. Although the Constitutional Revolution was brutally suppressed in 1911, the formation of a nation-state based on the Persian language and national identity remained on the agenda. Even before the fall of the fledgling Qajar dynasty, the prime minister issued a decree in 1923 proscribing the use of non-Persian languages, Turkish and Kurdish, in the schools of Azerbaijan and Kurdistan.[5]

The Nationalities: The Legacy of the Pahlavi State

The Pahlavi monarchy (1925–79) combined extreme violence with extensive propaganda in order to build the nation-state of Iran – one nation, one language, and one centralized, secular state. Under Reza Shah (1925–41), individuals who spoke in Kurdish were arrested and punished.[6] Ideologically, the Pahlavi state propagated racist and national chauvinistic myths in the state-controlled media, in educational institutions (all state owned), and in government organs. 'Iranians' were declared to be of 'pure' or 'genuine Aryan race' (*nezhad-e asil-e arya'i*), boasting a 2500-year old civilization. Empirical power was the cornerstone of this ancient civilization, which was said to have extended from Egypt to India. The pre-Islamic past associated with Persian culture and its Zoroastrian religion was glorified, while the post-Islamic culture, rooted in Arabic language and traditions, was vilified. Turkish and Arab domination over Iran in the remote past was declared the main historical obstacle to the continuity of the glorious Persian empire.

This racist ideology denied the national, linguistic and cultural diversity of Iran. Turkish, Kurdish and other languages were branded 'local dialects' of Persian. The culture (for example, dance, costume, music and food) of non-Persian peoples was also labelled a 'local' (*mahalli*) or 'tribal' (*'asha'er'i*) variety of the 'Iranian' – that is, Persian – culture. The state machinery, especially the educational system and the media, was used to Persianize non-Persians. In 1935, Reza Shah's regime replaced the word 'Persia' with 'Iran' in official documents (for example, diplomatic correspondence in European languages, passports, stamps), and informed other governments of the change. However, this measure was not motivated by respect for non-Persian peoples. To the contrary, in a country where non-Persians were forcibly assimilated into the Persian entity, 'Iranian' and 'Persian' could not be but full synonyms.

The construction of a nation-state in a multinational country where the dominant nation constituted no more than 50 per cent of the population could not be achieved without the destruction of the ethnic and linguistic identity of non-Persian peoples. The Pahlavi state, especially under Reza Shah, conducted genocide, ethnocide and linguicide in order to Persianize the non-Persians.[7] Reza Shah's army conducted many operations in order to integrate the nationalities, and to suppress the tribal and nomadic ways of life. Migrating tribes were forcibly sedentarized and their resistance was brutally suppressed. Much of Western and Iranian historiography celebrates these acts of violence as a much needed 'modernization' programme.[8] Ethnocide, the destruction of the culture of a group or people, was an integral part of the nation-building programme. The music, literature, dance and traditional life of non-Persian peoples were suppressed.[9] Linguicide,[10] the killing of a language by peaceful or violent measures, was one of the pillars of the nation-state.[11] Far from succeeding in de-ethnicizing the nationalities, repression fanned the flames of nationalism, especially in Azerbaijan and Kurdistan. After Reza Shah's abdication, despotism was moderated between 1941 and 1953, but his nation-building policies were pursued until the fall of the dynasty.

Under the Soviet occupation of northern Iran, the Azerbaijanis and Kurds established their autonomous governments in 1946. According to many observers, the Azerbaijan government achieved in one year what the Pahlavi regime failed to do in 20 years. Agrarian land was divided among the peasants in hundreds of villages; important steps were taken in urban development; factories, hospitals, health clinics and orphanages were established; women acquired suffrage rights for the first time in Iranian history; the first provincial university was established in Tabriz; the Turkish language was used in schools, publishing, radio and government offices; Turkish national culture, especially music, theatre and literature, flourished; ethnic, linguistic and religious minorities were granted equal rights; a labour law allowed workers to benefit from collective bargaining rights, minimum wage and maximum hours of work. In Kurdistan, too, similar reforms were undertaken, albeit on a more limited scale. Supported by the United States and Britain, the Iranian army succeeded in overthrowing the two autonomist regimes largely because, under Soviet pressure, the leadership of the two republics did not resist the demoralized and ineffective Iranian army. The Iranian army and gendarmerie, acting like an occupation army, brutally repressed the people.[12] The central government celebrated its victory by, among other things, book-burning ceremonies in Tabriz and publicly executing the arrested leaders throughout Azerbaijan and Kurdistan. Tehran announced the fall of the Azerbaijan government with a national holiday, officially celebrated until the fall of the Pahlavi dynasty. As in the past, any manifestation of Turkish or Kurdish identity was treated as 'secessionism'. Soon, however, political developments in neighbouring countries encouraged Kurdish nationalism and turned Kurdistan into a hotbed of crisis.

In late 1949, the exiled Kurdish leader Mustafa Barzani invited the Kurds, while a guest on Radio Baku, to rise up against Tehran, Ankara and Baghdad. Tehran, Washington and London responded nervously to what they considered a new Soviet aggression. The Shah allocated a budget for development projects in Kurdistan and launched local broadcasting in Kurdish. Later, when Radio Cairo launched a Kurdish programme in 1957, Iran responded by extending its broadcasting in Kurdish. In 1958, the Iraqi monarchy was overthrown, and Radio Baghdad joined Radio Cairo in encouraging Kurdish nationalism. Under these conditions, Tehran began publishing a weekly Kurdish newspaper, *Kurdistan*, in 1959 and allowed limited publishing in this language. Later, the state radio began broadcasting in Turkish and other languages.

The Kurdish autonomist movement in Iraq (1961–75) was another factor that shaped Tehran's policy. Although relations between Baghdad and Tehran were strained, Iran was worried about the failure of the Iraqi state to suppress the movement. The formation of liberated areas in Iraqi Kurdistan was potentially dangerous to the Iranian government because it gave Iranian Kurds considerable advantage for activism. By the mid-1960s, Tehran was able to minimize the threat by giving minimal support to Barzani who, in turn, forbade Iranian Kurds from any action against the Iranian state. However, a group split from the Kurdistan Democratic Party (KDP) did not follow Barzani and, forced to leave Iraqi Kurdistan, came into direct confrontation with Iran's armed forces. In spite of the co-operation of Barzani in repressing this faction of KDP, it took the Shah 18 months to suppress the armed uprising of 1967–68.

By the early 1970s Iran and the United States were actively involved in helping the Kurds of Iraq against a hostile Iraqi government. The two states encouraged Barzani to resist Baghdad, which had offered an autonomy plan in 1970 to be implemented in four years. In 1974, Baghdad announced its intention to create an autonomous region and, at the same time, declared war on the Barzani-led autonomist movement. The

United States and the Shah helped Barzani to resist the Iraqi army offensive. However, a year later when Tehran and Baghdad settled their differences, American and Iranian support was withdrawn. Left in the lurch, Barzani gave up, encouraging some two hundred thousand *peshmargas* (guerrillas), political activists and their families to take refuge in Iran. During these years, propaganda wars between Iraq and Iran were extensive and Tehran expanded its broadcasting in Kurdish and Arabic. Moreover, the government arranged for the offering of two courses in the Kurdish language at the Tehran University's department of linguistics. However, none of these measures indicated any change in the Persianization policy of the state. They all fell within the pragmatic or 'safety valve' policy of the Shah.[13] In fact, during the entire rule of the Pahlavi dynasty, the possession of Kurdish, Turkish or Baluchi publications, gramophone records, or even a handwritten poem, was proof of 'secessionism' of political prisoners.

The non-Persian peoples got the lion's share of poverty, illiteracy and underdevelopment. According to one study of ethnic inequality in Iran, the Shah's 'modernization' policies of the 1960s and 1970s increased socio-economic inequality between the Persians and non-Persian peoples.[14] There is evidence that suggests that, in the latter part of the 1970s, the Shah was contemplating a major relocation of Kurds from areas bordering Iraq into the hinterland.[15] The country in general and border areas in particular were heavily militarized. State control over the villages was extensive. Besides the gendarmerie, members of the army's Health Corps, Literacy Corps and Extension Corps either resided in or frequented the villages. It was official policy not to assign Kurds to the Kurdistan Corps, thereby helping the Persianization process. A similar policy was implemented among other nationalities. Other government organs such as 'House of Equity' and 'Culture House' were also established. However, these policies failed to solve the national question. In fact, nationalism among non-Persian peoples continued to grow, and the Kurds and other nationalities actively participated in the anti-monarchist revolution.

The Islamic Republic

In the last months before the fall of the monarchy and soon after the formation of the Islamic Republic, demands for autonomy were clearly expressed in demonstrations, resolutions, conferences and the petitions submitted to authorities in Tehran and published in the press. In spite of their diversity, the demands had much in common. Autonomous peoples in Kurdistan, Turkman Sahra, Baluchistan or Khuzistan would exercise power in their own social, cultural, linguistic and economic affairs, while the federal government would be responsible for foreign policy and economic, financial and defence issues on the national level.

Kurdistan offered the most serious challenge to the consolidation of the Islamic state. While the Islamic Republic was able to suppress the autonomous movement in Turkman Sahra, Khuzistan and Baluchistan, it was virtually powerless in much of Kurdistan, especially in Mahabad, the centre of Kurdish nationalism, where the military garrison had fallen into Kurdish hands. During the revolution, gendarmerie and police posts had been disarmed by the people and activists of political organizations including the Kurdistan Democratic Party (KDP) and the Revolutionary Organization of the Toilers of Kurdistan, better known in its abbreviated Kurdish name, Komala. The main locus of state power was the military garrisons in Baneh, Sanandaj, Saqqez and other Kurdish cities. In government offices, the staff were mostly Kurds who supported KDP, Komala and other pro-autonomist left organizations such as Fada'iyan, Rah-e Kargar, Paykar, Ranjbaran and the Union of Iranian Communists. During the last months of the revolution, a number of 'councils' had been established to run the affairs of the cities. In the absence of an effective government presence, political parties exercised a great deal of political power. Many party members and other individuals carried firearms, and the government's call for disarming went unheeded. Kurdish cultural and linguistic activities were flourishing; the government was not able to exercise full power over the state-owned radio and television network in Kurdistan.

The leadership of the anti-monarchist revolution in Kurdistan was mostly secular, and independent of Tehran. However, by the end of the revolution, two religious leaders had emerged: one, Sheikh Ezzadin Hoseini in Mahabad, and the other, Ahmad Moftizadeh in Sanandaj. The former, a cleric with a history of nationalist struggle, was a radical who called for the formation of a democratic, secular and federated state. The latter, a religious but non-clerical person, believed that the rights of the Kurds would be honoured under the Islamic regime. While Moftizadeh enjoyed popularity among some people in Sanandaj (the bazaaris and traditionally minded older generation), the majority of the Kurds throughout Kurdistan (except the Shi'i regions of Kermanshah) supported Sheikh Ezzadin. Moftizadeh cooperated with the Islamic Republic and the opponents of autonomy, and Sheikh Ezzadin leaned towards left groups such as Komala.

Kurdish society and politics had changed considerably since the experience of the Kurdish Republic of 1946 which had been led by the only Kurdish political organization of the time, the Kurdistan Democratic Party. By 1979, however, a vast array of political organizations and groups introduced considerable diversity into Kurdish political life, and thus there was no unified vision of autonomy. The KDP continued to demand 'democracy for Iran and autonomy for Kurdistan'. The party's policy was to lead all social classes, groups and individuals who could be rallied to the nationalist cause. Komala, however, envisioned a popular democratic regime and a socialist future for Iran in which the labouring masses of Kurdistan could exercise power free of national oppression. The practice of the two parties was equally different. While Komala organized the peasants and workers, the KDP opposed the formation of peasant unions and other acts of 'class struggle'. The party openly criticized Komala and other left-wing groups for privileging class struggle over national struggle. Such differences laid the foundation for future confrontations between the two sides.

Although the Islamic regime was not homogeneous ideologically and politically, its various factions (liberal, radical, conservative; clerical and non-clerical) pursued more or less similar approaches to the autonomist movements. They did not distinguish between the underdeveloped areas of Kurdistan or Baluchistan and the more developed central provinces such as Esfahan and Tehran. Like Persian nationalists, Islamic leaders did not admit the existence of national oppression. As Khomeini had remarked, there was no difference between the 'provinces', all had been *equally* oppressed. Thus there was no distinction between Persians and non-Persians; they were all Muslims, and had suffered equally under the previous regime. This view would, inevitably, reject demands for autonomy, and equate it with 'secessionism'.[16]

Although Khomeini and other authorities in Tehran initially tried to distance themselves from the leaders of the *ancien régime* by avoiding the charge of secessionism, they soon followed suit. When a border gendarmerie post was attacked by the Kurds, the vice-premier warned that: 'We do not approve of the independence of Kurdistan in any way. It is the policy of the state not to allow the secession of any part and territory of Iran's land and such an event will be forestalled with unfettered power.'[17] A government delegation dispatched to Mahabad was presented with an 'eight-point declaration' drafted by Kurdish representatives who had met in Mahabad. The demands included Kurdish support for the 'Iranian revolution', an end to national oppression and the realization of the right of self-determination within a federated Iranian state, participation in the government by labouring classes, the administration of the garrisons by revolutionary councils, punishment of officers involved in the killings and the formation of a people's army, acceptance of Sheikh Ezzadin as negotiator with the government, and, finally, the expulsion from Iran of the leaders of the Barzani group (the Provisional Leadership of the Kurdistan Democratic Party of Iraq). The vice-premier argued that the Provisional Revolutionary Government of premier Bazargan was not in a position to handle the demand for autonomy, which was to be dealt with by a constituent assembly.[18]

A month later, in a conflict between Safdari, Khomeini's representative in Sanandaj, and the people of the city, the army garrison intervened on the side of the former. On the eve of the new year, Nowruz, Phantom jet fighters from Tehran and helicopters from Kermanshah attacked the city and inflicted heavy casualties.[19] A few days later, after much bloodshed and while a high-ranking delegation (including, among others, Ayatollah Taleqani, Beheshti, Hashemi Rafsanjani, Abolhasan Bani-Sadr) was negotiating a settlement in Sanandaj, jet fighters reappeared and engaged in manoeuvring. Kurdish delegates strongly protested the action. Repercussions on the national level were also significant. Left-wing organizations protested the use of force by General Qarani, who was a participant in the 1953 CIA-staged coup. They argued that the American-trained royal army was still in power, and called for its dismantling. Although the prime minister praised Qarani, he had to dismiss him.[20]

The events in Sanandaj were to be shown as a testing ground for all sides in the conflict. The new rulers, including Ayatollah Khomeini, were not content with less than direct and full control of Kurdistan and the rest of the country. Although Tehran was challenged by a strong secular Kurdish nationalist movement, Khomeini did not choose to extend his rule by appointing the then fairly popular Moftizadeh, a Sunni, as his representative in the predominantly Sunni Kurdistan province. Although Moftizadeh was considered an ally of the government, Khomeini chose as his representative Safdari, a Shi'i, who had no supporters. He had managed to establish a *komiteh* with the help of the army. The Nowruz conflict broke out when Safdari and his protégés fired at a protesting crowd and killed two demonstrators. The result was a humiliating defeat for Khomeini; Safdari had to escape Sanandaj, leaving behind the bodies of his *komiteh* members shot by townspeople in revenge. The events also undermined the status of Moftizadeh, who was the only prominent person in Kurdistan advocating Kurdish rights within the framework of the Islamic state. During the uprising in February 1979, Moftizadeh prevented the people of Sanandaj from disarming the garrison, arguing that it had declared allegiance to the Islamic Republic. Now that the garrison had moved against the people, the left and secular groups – which had called for the replacement of the Iranian army by a people's army – gained more credibility.

Failing to set up a Shi'i Islamic foothold in Kurdistan, the Islamic regime appealed to whatever alternatives were available to weaken the radical and secular forces that led the autonomist movement of Kurdistan. For example, as early as 26 February 1979, the state radio and television network interviewed Sheikh Osman Naqshbandi as the 'representative of the Kurdish people'. This led to a strong protest from the Kurds, who rejected him as a stooge of the Shah's regime and a SAVAK agent. Another ally of the central government that proved more effective was Qiyada-ye Movaqqat (QM, the Provisionary Leadership) of the Kurdistan Democratic Party of Iraq, the remnants of Mustafa Barzani's group who had cooperated with the Shah against the Kurdish autonomist movement in Iran since the mid-1960s. Stationed in Karaj near Tehran, the Barzani-led QM commanded armed groups who had established bases in Kurdistan, especially in Hawraman, Oshnaviyeh and other regions. The Barzanis closely cooperated with Moftizadeh. It must be noted that one of the major demands of the Kurds submitted to the government in March was the expulsion of the QM leadership from Iran.

In spite of their disappointment with the new regime, Kurdish leaders sought a peaceful negotiation. In late March, a KDP delegation headed by Dr Abdulrahman Qasemlu visited Ayatollah Khomeini in Qom and premier Bazargan in Tehran, although no concrete promises were made. In May, the interior minister invited a delegation of clergymen from Kurdistan, including Sheikh Ezzadin. Khomeini met with the delegation, and relegated the handling of all demands to the forthcoming constitution. He did not commit himself to acceptance of nationalities, and emphasized that the demands of the people everywhere must be met. He invited the leaders to unite against the counterrevolution. A member of the delegation was unhappy about declaring Twelver Imam Shi'ism, rather than Islam, the official religion of Iran in the draft of the constitution. Khomeini regarded this as a minor problem that could be worked out.[21] The state radio and television did not cover the visit, which led to protests throughout Kurdistan.[22] The Kurds saw this as another example of unfavourable intentions.

While Kurdistan was not hospitable to Islamic activism (even the Mojahedin-e khalq did not try to expand their activities to Kurdistan), political organizations as well as the societies (jam'iyat)[23] which had appeared in every Kurdish city, conducted their political and cultural activities free from the suppression of the Islamic Republic. By midsummer 1979, numerous peasant unions had been formed throughout Kurdistan. Sheikh Ezzadin endorsed peasant struggles against the landlords who had armed, attacked the peasants and demanded the return of lands they had lost during the Shah's land reform programmes of the 1960s. Initiatives were diverse, including the establishment of educational institutions, native-tongue publications, theatrical and musical performances and other cultural activities. For instance, committees were established for the publication of Kurdish textbooks to be used in Kurdish language instruction during the forthcoming academic year. Another project was the establishment of a Kurdistan University, aided by the National Organization of Iranian Academics (Sazman-e Melli-ye Daneshgahiyan-e Iran), a secular group formed during the revolution.[24]

Cultural activities were, however, overshadowed by political events. Much of Kurdistan boycotted Khomeini's April 1979 referendum, in which voters were required to say 'Yes' or 'No' to the establishment of an Islamic Republic. Although no ballot boxes were put up anywhere in Mahabad, Bukan and Sardasht and those in Saqqez were set on fire, the government released bogus figures for the result of the elections in these and other

Kurdish cities. According to the figures, Kurdistan, like the rest of Iran, had overwhelmingly approved the Islamic Republic. Kurds were startled by this fabrication. The number of voters in Kurdistan, as reported in the referendum results, exceeded the actual size of the voting population.[25]

By early July 1979 the government more actively pursued the establishment of a military presence in Kurdistan in order to put an end to the state of dual power there. Moftizadeh and the Barzanis were cooperating to reinstate the gendarmerie posts and the formation of *pasdar* ('Revolutionary Guards' established by the Islamic leaders to protect them from army coups d'état or other adversaries) headquarters in Kurdish cities. A *pasdar* unit was installed in Marivan after two Khomeini clerical emissaries from Tehran had visited its garrison. The *pasdars* attacked a protesting crowd and killed three people. In a counterattack, seven *pasdars* were killed and the rest were arrested by the armed townspeople. The government sent reinforcements by air and, in spite of negotiations, Tehran relied on military power to bring the city under government control. As a result, the majority of the population left for the nearby woods. People throughout Kurdistan rallied to support the people of Marivan. Thousands of people marched from Sanandaj and other cities to Marivan. Tanks and armoured vehicles dispatched from Kermanshah to Marivan were stopped by protesting Kurds in Kamyaran, although some of the troops were later able to reach Marivan. The government insisted on control of the city by the army and *pasdar* forces. Meanwhile, the state radio and television conducted a propaganda campaign against the autonomist movement, accusing Kurdish leaders of being secessionists and 'agents of foreign powers and SAVAK'. Sheikh Ezzadin became a special target of these attacks. The anti-Kurdish campaign led to widespread demonstrations protesting government provocations. Also, the army and *pasdars* established checkpoints on the entrances of roads leading to Kurdistan and arrested many Kurds.

While the crisis was continuing in Marivan, another crisis developed in Paweh, where Moftizadeh supporters began a sit-in demanding the dispatch of *pasdars* for the control of the town. *Pasdars* were soon flown in by helicopters and occupied some buildings. Thousands of townspeople protested the invasion and asked for their withdrawal, demanding non-interference by outsiders (that is, the Qiyada-ye Movaqqat), and the election of a council to administer the affairs of the city. The demands were not met and fighting broke out in mid-August. After three days of house-to-house fighting, Khomeini ordered the army on 18 August 1979 to bring the battle to an end. Jets and helicopter gunships joined in and captured the city after high casualties on both sides; the troops immediately executed 11 people.

Soon after the conquest of Paweh, Khomeini declared himself commander-in-chief of the armed forces and ordered the army, air force, and even the navy, to attack Kurdistan on 19 August. Formally declaring war, Khomeini charged that the KDP had laid siege to military garrisons, and that women were taken hostage in a Sanandaj mosque. In less than two hours after the announcement, F-4 fighters broke the sound barrier over Sanandaj and the air force built 'an air bridge' to the city, landing troops every hour. The governor of the Kurdistan province, however, said that no women or children had been taken hostage, and that the city was calm and the news of disturbance was 'a complete fabrication'.[26] The army captured Sanandaj, and in about two weeks entered all the Kurdish cities to the north. Behaving as an occupying force, the Islamic army's conquest was followed by summary executions in each city.

The August offensive was staged on the opening day of the Assembly of Experts, which was charged with preparing the final draft of the constitution. Khomeini and other state officials had previously advised the Kurds to wait for a constitutional solution to their grievances. However, as a result of the offensive, elected Kurdish delegates, including Dr Qasimlou, were not able to attend the assembly. In fact, the government declared Qasimlou and Sheikh Ezzadin 'corrupt' persons, to be executed. In order to stifle opposition to the offensive in Kurdistan and to reduce the controversy over the constitution, the government closed down 22 newspapers and magazines and expelled several foreign correspondents.

The offensive backfired, however. The declaration of war occurred on the anniversary of the CIA-staged coup of 1953, which had brought the Shah back to power. The day had been declared a national holiday and celebrated by the Shah's regime. It was also a few days before the feast of Fetr, which is celebrated at the end of the holy month of Ramadan. Resentment against Khomeini was deep-seated; the Kurds viewed him as 'worse than the Shah', and he was considered personally responsible for bringing 'blood and tears' to the two feasts of Nowruz and Fetr.

During the four months of war, the government was unable to consolidate its authority beyond establishing its military presence in the towns and a few military outposts in the countryside. Government offices and educational institutions were purged of suspected pro-autonomy individuals. Other suspects not in government pay were also deported. About one-quarter of the population of the cities had left the urban areas. Still resistance was active and widespread. People protested the executions, deportations and the continuing repression. The environment in Kurdistan was so hostile to the government that even Moftizadeh had to leave his native town of Sanandaj.

By early November, government forces were defeated, some of them withdrawing to the garrisons. Under circumstances of continuing political crisis as a result of hostage-taking in the US embassy in Tehran and the subsequent toppling of the provisional government of Bazargan, the government sent a delegation to meet Kurdish leaders; a cease-fire was declared after Khomeini issued a conciliatory message.

The constitution was drafted in an undemocratic manner, excluding the participation of the Kurds as well as those opposed to the formation of a theocratic state.[27] Much like the 1906 constitution, the Islamic document depicts Iran as a nation-state, with one official language and one official religion. Like its monarchical predecessor, the Islamic regime recognizes three minority religious groups, Christians (Armenians and Assyrians), Jews and Zoroastrians, who are represented in the parliament, and are guaranteed religious freedom according to the constitution. In practice, however, these minorities are repressed. Although both constitutions include provisions for a degree of regional governance through elected local councils, in practice both states refused to implement these stipulations. In fact, according to Article 103 of the Islamic Constitution, governors from the highest rank (province) to the lowest (rural areas) are appointed from the centre. Thus, contrary to the promises made by Khomeini and other top-ranking officials, who had relegated Kurdish autonomist demands to the adoption of a constitution, the document forestalled any democratic approach to the national, ethnic and linguistic diversity of Iran. Instead of a federated state incorporating autonomous peoples and provinces, the constitution stipulated the formation of a centralized, theocratic state. Faced with ongoing political crises, the Islamic regime under Khomeini moved toward increasing concentration of power through purges, and by bringing to perfection the theory and practice of the theocratic state.

After the cease-fire in Kurdistan, Tehran refused to enter into serious negotiations with Kurdish representatives, who had formed a Kurdish People's Representation composed of KDP, Komala, Sheikh Ezzadin and Fada'iyan. The government did not recognize the legitimacy of political organizations involved in the autonomist movement. During the limited contacts between the two sides, government negotiators used divide-and-rule tactics,[28] and at the same time increased their support for the adversaries of the autonomist movement such as Moftizadeh and the QM. While Sheikh Ezzadin and Komala sought a united stance among the members of the Kurdish People's Representation, the KDP pursued a policy of negotiating separately with the government. This policy was aimed at proposing a more limited autonomy acceptable to the government and isolating the left-wing organizations and their agenda. However, the mood in Kurdistan was defiant. For example, when the *pasdars* in Sanandaj opened fire on passers-by and killed several people, all the shopkeepers began an unlimited strike. Public anger developed into a major political struggle involving the entire population of the city and even people from the neighbouring villages and other Kurdish cities. The government suffered another humiliating defeat when it was forced to withdraw all the *pasdars* from Sanandaj, the only time this has happened anywhere in Iran.

By mid-winter 1980, it was obvious that the government was looking for a military solution. Plans were also underway for a final offensive on the campuses of the universities, where left-wing students and faculty had maintained considerable power and were exposing the government's repression of the Kurds.[29] The second military offensive against Kurdistan started in mid-April 1980 when a large army column was dispatched from Hamadan and Kermanshah to Sanandaj. The people of Sanandaj stopped the army from entering the town, and fighting continued for 28 days. Using heavy arms and the support of the air force, the garrisons of Sanandaj, Saqqez, Baneh and Marivan shelled the cities continuously in April and May, and inflicted heavy casualties on the civilian population. Three months after the conquest of southern Kurdistan, the army attacked Mahabad, Sardasht and other key locations in the north (in the province of West Azerbaijan). During these operations, the *pasdars* conducted several massacres in villages near Mahabad and Naghadeh.

By the time the army had occupied Kurdistan in the last month of the summer, the Iraq–Iran war broke out. During this long and destructive war, military operations in Kurdistan continued ceaselessly. Iraqi aggression provided the government with the opportunity and justification for intensifying the militarization of Kurdistan, especially along the Iran–Iraq border. Tehran extended its military presence from the cities to the villages by constructing an extensive network of military roads and numerous military outposts throughout Kurdistan. As in the past, the regime showed extreme brutality in punishing the civilian population for assisting the *peshmarga* forces. Every defeat of the armed forces was met by mass execution of political prisoners or others. In addition to this reprehensible tactic, the army imposed a strict economic blockade on villages that had supported the *peshmargas*. By late 1984, most of the countryside was under government control. Having lost all the liberated areas, the leadership of the political organizations and their *peshmargas* moved to Iraqi Kurdistan, where, aided by Iraq, they were able to maintain their armed presence and conduct guerrilla operations in both the cities and villages.

By 1985 the Islamic regime had won the battle militarily, although its control was not effective everywhere. However, the regime has lost the ideological and political war against Kurdish nationalism. There is little support for the Islamic state, its ideology and politics.

In order to win the hearts and minds of the nationalities, the Islamic Republic has offered a number of concessions including material rewards. In Kurdistan, for example, investment has been made in the electrification of some villages and the construction of roads and bridges in rural areas, and urban development projects such as the expansion of streets and the construction of parks. It must be noted, however, that most of these projects have military significance, and they are dwarfed by the colossal network of army and gendarmerie outposts built throughout the region. Another example of the concessions is the offering of limited quotas in institutions of higher education to high-school graduates. During the 1993–94 academic year, for example, 500 university places were assigned to students from 'deprived regions' (*manateq-e mahrum*). The regions included the provinces of Ilam, Kermanshah, Bushehr, Chahar Mahal and Bakhtiari, Sistan and Baluchistan, Kurdistan, etc.[30] Moreover, universities or branches of higher-education institutions, including the Free Islamic University, have been established in many cities.

The battle in the realm of ideas has been no less intensive than the war waged by the military. Although Kurdish political parties were driven across the border into Iraqi Kurdistan, their voice continues to be heard on a daily basis through a network of clandestine radio stations. The regime has, as a result, expanded its broadcasting, both radio and television, in order to neutralize these opposing voices. In 1992, Kurdish ranked second among the languages used in external broadcasting originating from Tehran (1825 hours per year). This is in addition to 1863 hours (Kurdish and Persian) broadcast on radio stations from the Kurdistan province.[31] The government has also allowed, within the framework of state censorship of communist and anti-Islamic ideas, considerable freedom of publishing in Kurdish and Azarbaijani Turkish. In 1994, two state-sponsored magazines were published in Kurdish. Also, a government-funded centre for Kurdish publishing has been operating in Urmia since the 1980s. Moreover, in the early 1990s, several bookstores and publishers were engaged in Kurdish publishing. Books imported from Iraq were also available in the market. Individuals used Kurdish in private correspondence, on invitation cards or on other occasions. It must be noted that all of these concessions were first offered, albeit on a more limited scale, during the last years of the Pahlavi monarchy.

Much like the Pahlavi regime, the Islamic state has consistently violated the right to an education in the native tongue. According to Article 19 of the Islamic constitution, 'all people of Iran, whatever the ethnic group or tribe to which they belong, enjoy equal rights; and colour, race, language, and the like, do not bestow any privilege.' This equality is, however, fictional. In real life, linguistic power in Iran is not distributed equally. The Persians alone enjoy the right to a native-tongue education. According to Article 15:

The official and common language and script of the people of Iran is Persian. Official documents, correspondence and statements, as well as textbooks, shall be written in this language and script. However, the use of local and ethnic languages in the press and mass media is allowed. The teaching of ethnic literature in the school, together with Persian language instruction, is also permitted.[32]

However, the teaching of 'ethnic literature' has not materialized yet. Although the teaching of a literature does not necessarily involve the use of the language of that literature, the Islamic regime's refusal to implement the stipulation of Article 15 indicates, among other things, its strong Persian nationalist ideology. Apparently the government realizes that the use of a dominated language in teaching contributes to its survival and enhancement.

It is interesting to note that although the Turkish nationalist movement in Azerbaijan has not been as active as the Kurdish movement, the government has adopted a more liberal policy on teaching in Turkish. For example, a BA-level programme in Azeri language and literature has been established in Tabriz University. Moreover, preparations were being made in 1993 for limited teaching of Turkish in primary schools. In publishing, too, the state-controlled *Kayhan* newspaper has launched a Turkish daily paper. It is obvious that this policy is motivated by developments in northern Azerbaijan in the wake of the disintegration of the Soviet Union. Much to the annoyance of the Islamic Republic, the fall of the USSR did not bring northern Azerbaijan (the Azerbaijan Republic) back to the motherland Iran or to the 'embrace' of Islam. In the north, Turkish has been the official language of the republic for seven decades. The Islamic Republic cannot buy influence there while the south is deprived of a basic right such as native-tongue education. In fact, far from succeeding in exporting Islam to the north, the government is preoccupied with protecting Iran's Azeri population from the nationalism of the north. A bill introduced in the Iranian parliament in 1993 authorizes the division of Eastern Azerbaijan province into two provinces.[33] Some Azerbaijanis regard this as an attempt to diminish the authority of Tabriz, a traditional centre of Turkish nationalism. In contrast to Azerbaijan, where Tehran feels threatened by Azeri nationalism, Baluchistan seems to pose less of a weak link. Although sporadic unrest is not uncommon, Tehran's control is more effective on both sides of the Iran–Pakistan border. As a result, concessions to Baluch nationalism are minimal.

The founder of the Islamic Republic, Ayatollah Khomeini, repeatedly attacked nationalism as an enemy of Islam, and a product of Western colonialism which was designed to destroy Islam and its rule. He argued that Islam was superior to nationalism in both practice and theory. He claimed that Islam eliminates racial and ethnic inequalities and treats all human beings equally.[34] This study has, however, demonstrated that *in practice* the Islamic state has been no less nationalist than the Pahlavi state. Also, Islam, as an ideological and political construct, has failed to establish itself as an alternative to nationalism among the non-Persian, Muslim peoples of Iran.

Although the emergence of the theocratic state in Iran encouraged Islamic activism in many countries, it has failed to become an alternative to Kurdish nationalism, which remains secular. Moftizadeh's Sunni alternative also failed, to the extent that public opinion branded him a *jash* ('little donkey', meaning collaborator with the enemy). Soon after consolidating its power in Kurdistan, the Islamic government discarded Moftizadeh, arrested him, and decided to uproot any effort, Islamic or otherwise, for Kurdish self-rule in Iran. Two secretary-generals of the Kurdistan Democratic Party, Dr Qasemlu and Dr Sadeq Sharafkandi, were assassinated, the former during negotiations with the Islamic Republic. Even lower echelon members of the KDP and other political organizations are targets of assassination in Europe and elsewhere. Their bases and camps inside Iraqi Kurdistan are attacked regularly. The Kurdish clergy poses a serious problem for the regime. The two apostles of Kurdish nationalism, Ahmadi Khani (1651–1706) and Haji Qadiri Koyi (1817–1897) were mullahs but their nationalism was secular. Kurdish mosque schools have been one of the breeding grounds of national literature and nationalist thinking. Since the Islamic regime is unable to replace the clergy, the policy has been to win them over, and to train a new generation of loyal clerics. Aiming to weaken secular nationalism, the government's cultural policy promotes the religious element in Kurdish literature and culture. Thus, Kurdish literary figures with Islamic and Sufi tendencies (for example, Mewlewi Tawgozi) are celebrated at conferences, anniversaries and other occasions. Although Tehran has set up Kurdish Islamic parties for the Kurds in Iraq, these pro-Iranian groups do not enjoy any popularity.[35]

Conclusions

Fifteen years after the establishment of the Islamic Republic, the nationalities question has turned into a crisis that the government seems unable to solve. By 1994, military rule has become less effective in Kurdistan, where the countryside is under the control of the *peshmargas* in the evenings, and guerrilla operations are conducted inside the cities. In mid-May 1994, the Iranian press announced a government decision to place land mines in 226 passes in border areas in Western Azerbaijan, Kurdistan and Kermanshahan provinces in order to prevent the entry and exit of 'saboteurs and armed groups'.

Politically, the demand for autonomy is losing ground to an agenda for independence, at least among political activists. Although the two Kurdistan Democratic Parties (there was a split in 1988) still uphold the slogan 'Democracy for Iran, Autonomy for Kurdistan', and Komala seeks self-rule within a socialist Iranian state, the drive toward independence has found organizational form. A Party for the Independence of Kurdistan was formed in 1986 in the Kurdish diaspora. According to this organization, five decades of struggle for autonomy have proved the failure of the autonomy dictum: no Iranian government, secular or religious, allows any degree of self-rule.[36] Sheikh Ezzadin, like many Kurdish leaders seeking autonomy, has also expressed his preference for the right to self-determination including an independent state, although he does not rule out extensive autonomy within a democratic Iranian state.[37]

Further deepening the crisis of the Islamic state in its dealings with Kurdish national demands is the continuing struggle of the Kurds for sovereignty in Turkey and Iraq. Threatened by the prospect of the formation of a Kurdish state or even an autonomous Kurdistan in neighbouring countries, Tehran has been collaborating with Turkey and Syria to abort the state-building efforts of the Kurds in Iraq. However, the ongoing economic and political crisis in the region and on the international level further contributes to the rivalries and conflicts among the countries that rule over Kurdistan.

The demand of the non-Persian people of Iran for self-rule is a democratic pursuit that is incompatible with the despotism of the Iranian state, whether monarchical or theocratic. The Kurds were incorporated into the Iranian state not through dialogue, referenda or other forms of voluntary association but, rather, by the sheer use of force. It would be reasonable to conclude that the Islamic state, much like the Pahlavi regime, has contributed to the deepening and broadening of the nationalist movement by unleashing unbridled terror against the Kurdish people.

The experience of Iranian nationalities under the Islamic Republic rejects the view that Islam and Islamic states tolerate or promote communal or ethnic pluralism.[38] The alleged 'communal pluralism' of the older *khilāfa* (caliphate) and Ottoman states was due to the fact that, as loosely integrated feudal systems, they were unable to form a centralized power structure. Moreover, the histories of these states are characterized by the repression of non-dominant religious (Christians, Jews, 'heretic' Muslim communities) and ethnic (Kurds, Albanians, and so on) formations, which were brought under control by conquest and coercion. In contrast to the older states, modern Islamic powers such as the Islamic Republic are in a position to form a centralized state structure. It must be emphasized, however, that the conceptualization of a state or a revolution as 'Islamic' is inappropriate. Islam and its various interpretations have been advocated by diverse social classes and groups ranging from the feudal nobility of the past to sections of the modern urban bourgeoisie. Failing to account for the social bases of the Islamic state, many studies of the Islamic Republic have assigned religion an autonomous role, turning it into a historical phenomenon unfettered by economy, social class, ethnicity, nationality and other social forces.

The study of the question of national diversity in Iran after the revolution shows that, although Islamic leaders forcefully reject nationalism as a Western conspiracy, the Islamic Republic's approach to ethnic and national diversity of Iran has not deviated from the Persian national chauvinism of the Pahlavi state. It is equally significant that, far from being an isolated case of injustice to the minorities, the approach of the Islamic Republic to national and ethnic diversity is fully consistent with the overall policy of repressing democracy throughout Iran.

Notes

1. None of the Iranian governments has provided statistical information on the national and ethnic composition of the country. The only official data available are 'population according to language' figures released after the 1956 census (see Echo of Iran, *Iran Almanac and Book of Facts*, 5th edn (Tehran, 1976), p 357). The percentages cited here depend on data based on the 1956 census and the information from the ten-volume *Farhang-i Jughrafya'i-ye Iran* (Geographical Dictionary of Iran), which was compiled and published by the Iranian Army in the early 1950s. The data from this dictionary were culled by a Soviet researcher, G.M. Petrov (cited in S.M. Aliyev, 'The problem of nationalities in Iran', *Central Asian Review*, xiv/1 (1966), pp 62–70).

2. The ancient Assyrian and Armenian states ruled over parts of the present territories of northwest Iran. Also, some Armenian populations were transferred by the Safavids from Julfa to a new location near Esfahan where they now live.

3. Like other social-science concepts, the terms used in this chapter are ambiguous. The main term, 'nation' (*mellat*), is defined here as a people, sharing a common language (or dialects of a common language), inhabiting a fixed territory, with common customs and traditions, which may have become sufficiently conscious to take on the aspect of law, and who recognize common interests and a common need for a single sovereign (Roger Scruton, *A Dictionary of Political Thought* (London: Macmillan, 1982), p 312). According to this definition, the Koreans are a single nation divided between two states. Until their separation in 1992, the Czechs and Slovaks were two nations living within the jurisdiction of a single state. A 'nation-state' is a state organized for the government of a single nation (see, among others, Scruton, *A Dictionary*, p 313). In this sense, countries such as Iran, Turkey and Iraq are not nation-states, although this term is often imprecisely applied to these centralized, 'modern' states. Thus, the term 'nation', as used here, is not a synonym for the notion 'country'. Nations can be with or without a state. In the absence of a more adequate concept, the term 'nationality' is used in this chapter to refer to non-Persian peoples such as the Kurds, Azeri Turks, Baluchis, and so forth. Thus, 'nationality' is used synonymously with 'non-state nation'.

4. See, for example, Hassanpour, Amir, 'The Kurdish experience', *Middle East Report*, 24/4, consecutive no. 189 (1994), pp 1–7, 23.

5. See the text of the circular issued by the education office of Azerbaijan and addressed to schools in the province in Hassanpour, Amir, *Nationalism and Language in Kurdistan, 1918–1985* (San Francisco: Mellen Research University Press, 1992), pp 126–7.

6. See Hemin [Mohammad Amin Sheikholeslami], 'Sereta' (Introduction) in Qizilji, Hasan, *Pekenini Geda*, 'The Beggar's Laughing' (Binkey Peshawa Publications, 1972), p 6.

7. For a definition of genocide, see the text of the United Nations Genocide Convention of 1948, in Kuper, Leo, *International Action Against Genocide* (London:

Minority Rights Group), Report No. 53, revised 1984 edn. For information on the suppression of the Kurds and Lurs, see the memoirs of a political prisoner in 1928–42 Tehran, in Avanesian, Ardashir, *Yaddashtha-ye Zendan (Salha-ye 1928–42)* (Memoirs of Prison, 1928–42) (Stockholm: Tudeh Publishing Centre, 1979), pp 61–2.

8. See, among others, Wilber, Donald, *Riza Shah Pahlavi: The Resurrection and Reconstruction of Iran* (New York: Exposition Press, 1975); for a different perspective, see Amin, Camron, 'Under the shadow of Riza Shah: Modern and traditional perceptions of the subjugation of Iranian Kurdistan', paper presented at the Annual Conference of Middle Eastern Studies Association, 1992.

9. See, for example, Hemin, 'Sereta', p 6.

10. Linguicide is 'the extermination of languages, an analogous concept to genocide' (Skuttnab-Kangas, Tove, and Robert Phillipson, 'Linguicide', in *The Encyclopedia of Language and Linguistics* (Oxford: Pergamon Press, 1994), Vol 4, p 2211).

11. For a brief survey of the Pahlavi state's policy on Kurdish language, see Hassanpour, *Nationalism*, pp 125–30.

12. Hassanpour, Amir, 'The nationalist movements in Azerbaijan and Kurdistan, 1941–46,' in John Foran (ed.), *A Century of Revolution: Social Movements in Iranian History* (University of Minnesota Press, forthcoming).

13. Hassanpour, *Nationalism*, pp 125–30.

14. Aghajanian, Akbar, 'Ethnic inequality in Iran: An overview', *International Journal of Middle East Studies*, 15/2 (1983), pp 211–24. See also Amirahmadi, Hooshang, 'A theory of ethnic collective movements and its application to Iran', *Ethnic and Racial Studies*, 10/4 (1987), pp 363–71.

15. Hassanpour, *Nationalism*, pp 287–8.

16. The more liberal or democratic individuals such as Ayatollah Taleqani admitted the existence of economic disparities and cultural and linguistic differences. Taleqani, however, did not go beyond recommending administrative measures as stipulated by the 1906 constitution and its amendments which allowed limited local self-administration (see, for example, his last remarks before his death in 1979 quoted in Rahsepar, Hamid, 'Melliyat-ha va faje'eye Kordestan', *Ketab-e Mehrab*, no 3, (Tehran: Entesharat-e Sabz, n.d.), p 114. Others like Mostafa Chamran, who advocated Islamic 'internationalism', took part in leading the 1979 government offensive against the Kurds (see Chamran, Mostafa, *Kordestan* (Tehran: Bonyad-e Shahid Chamran, 1985)). Like Chamran, other centres of power such as the Islamic Republican Party viewed the autonomist movement as a secessionist threat and pushed for a military solution (for an insider's information, see Goftgou ba Ostad 'Ali-ye Tehrani, *Ketab-e Mehrab*, no. 3 (Tehran: Entesharat-e Sabz, n.d.), pp 161–71 (interview dated Esfand 1959, February-March 1980). The first president of the Islamic Republic, Abolhasan Bani-Sadr, himself was a leader of the second government offensive against Kurdistan. After his removal from power, he wrote in exile that he had supported administrative self-rule, which would have removed from the scene the few 'small groups which had turned the [demand for] autonomy into a means for hostility against the Islamic Republic' (Bani-Sadr, Abolhasan, *Khiyanat be Omid*, p 369.

17. *Ayandegan*, 20 February 1979.

18. *Ayandegan*, 1 March 1979.

19. The total loss of Kurdish life was 215 dead and 420 wounded, much more than the number of casualties in Sanandaj during the revolution. The figures in-

clude casualties resulting from shelling of the city from the nearby garrison (*Ayandegan*, 27 March 1979).

20. *Ayandegan*, 28 March 1979.

21. *Ayandegan*, 21 May 1979.

22. *Paykar*, no. 4, 21 May 1979.

23. These societies were formed by the activists from a number of left-wing, Marxist-Leninist and Maoist organizations and groups; they engaged in activities such as providing relief aid, organizing demonstrations and setting up worker and peasant unions.

24. Designed to serve the needs of Kurdistan, the university's medium of instruction would be Kurdish and Persian. The university was in the process of announcing the admission of students when the Islamic army's offensive against the Kurdish autonomist movement destroyed the project (see Mojab, Shahrzad, *The State and University: The Islamic Cultural Revolution in the Institutions of Higher Education of Iran, 1980–87*, Ph.D. dissertation, University of Illinois at Urbana-Champaign, 1991, pp 144–5).

25. For a comparison of the referendum results with the 1976 census figures, see *Ayandegan*, 4 April 1979.

26. Press reports: *Ettela'at* and *Daily Telegraph*, 20 and 21 August 1979.

27. On the drafting of the constitution, see Bakhash, Shaul, *The Reign of Ayatollahs: Iran and the Islamic Revolution* (New York: Basic Books), pp 71–91.

28. A delegation representing the Kurdish people, composed of KDP, Komala, Sheikh Ezzadin and Fada'iyan, was formed to negotiate with the government's 'good-will' delegation. The Kurdish delegation presented a list of 26 demands, which were rejected, and later replaced by eight demands. The government then negotiated with the KDP and Fada'iyan and President Bani-Sadr announced that the government was willing to negotiate on the basis of six points, which he refused to call 'autonomy' (*khodmokhtai*), preferring a new term *khodgardani* 'self-management'. Outraged by the play on words, public opinion in Kurdistan called this *sargardani* 'vagrancy'.

29. On the struggle for control of the universities, see Mojab, *The State*.

30. Vezarat-e Farhang va Amuzash-e 'Ali, Sazman-e Sanjesh-e Amuzesh-e Keshvar, *Rahnema-ye Entekhab-e Reshteh-ha-ye Tahsili*, no 2, 1372 (1993–94), Tehran, p 6.

31. Statistical Centre of Iran, *Salnameh-ye Amari-ye Keshvar, 1371/Iran Statistical Yearbook 1371 [March 1992–March 1993]*, (Tehran, 1993–94), pp 172, 174.

32. *Constitutions of the Countries of the World, Iran* (Dobbs Ferry, NY: Oceana Publications, 1980), pp 22–3.

33. *Kayhan Havai*, 20 January 1993, p 25.

34. Khomeini's views on nationalism are quoted in *Dar Jost-o-ju-ye Rah az Kalam-e Imam* (*Daftar-e Yazdahom*), *Melligara'i* (Tehran: Amir Kabir, 1983).

35. Iran succeeded in forming these Islamic groups with the support of the Kurdistan Democratic Party of Iraq and the Patriotic Union of Kurdistan; the two parties were allied with Iran during the Iraq–Iran War. In the 1992 elections for a Kurdish parliament in Iraqi Kurdistan, the Islamic parties did not get the minimum 7 per cent of the votes in order to be represented in parliament. However, under conditions of extreme economic hardship, Iranian money has been buying more influence, especially in the border areas inside Iraqi Kurdistan.

36. See *Ala* (Banner), no 1 (1986), organ of the United Democratic Front of Kurdistan which later changed into the Party for Independence of Kurdistan (*Ala*, 7, no. 5, 1993).

37. See interview with Sheikh Ezzadin in *Berbang* 9, no. 62 (Stockholm, 1990), pp 59–65.

38. See, for example, Safi, Louay, 'Nationalism and the multinational state', *The American Journal of Islamic Social Sciences*, 9/3 (1992), pp 338–50.

11

Public Life and Women's Resistance

Haideh Moghissi

This chapter tries to throw some light on the lives of women in the Islamic Republic of Iran, particularly in the post-Khomeini period. It examines the changes in the Islamization policies of the Iranian government over the past 15 years, and studies their effects on the conditions of life and work of the female population of Iran. Rather than taking them as self-evident, this chapter will analyse the processes through which these developments have taken their form. In so doing, this study will examine the driving forces behind these changes and will point to their material consequences for the lives of the female population.

The increasing attention paid to women and issues of women's concern, as epitomized by the official statements and Friday sermons, the formation of numerous women-centred councils, the commissions and bureaux, the generous funding of various Islamic women's groups, the dispatching of many delegations of ideologically and politically trusted women to international conferences and events, are remarkable developments in 'religion soaked' Iran. The removal of the ban placed on certain fields of post-secondary education for women, the success and popularity of new female writers, the advent of several women film-makers, and the increasing appearance of a vocal group of women in public domains, some from the ranks of Muslim women, are consistent with the regime's change of tactic in the treatment of the female population.

If they are not seen in context we run the risk, as have some apologists of the Islamic government and uninformed observers, of taking these developments as signs of the enlightenment of conservative Islamists, the metamorphosis of the clerics in favour of women's rights, and even the compatibility of traditional Islamic values with women's rights and autonomy.[1] These developments, I will argue, are the conspicuous evidence of, on the one hand, the sharp impact of 'the irresistible forces of social change', something the Islamic Republic has been unable to contain, and, on the other, the entanglement of Islamists in political, economic and socio-cultural contradictions. The Islamic Republic is facing challenges that are impossible to meet. These challenges arise from the conflict between the disposition of the Islamists to keep women segregated and the demands of running a capitalist economy. That is, the prerequisite of a market economy is the incorporation of women into market activities, the use of their labour and a reliance on their purchasing power. This requires sexual desegregation, unregulated interaction between the sexes and the formal, legal equality of women.

For conservative Islamists, who consider gender hierarchy and inequality as having divine origin and immune from human intervention, resolving this conflict without making ideological compromises seems an impossible mission. The conflict in the area of women's rights and gender relations transpires in contradictory and increasingly incoherent policies of the state. The clerical state is struggling to find a way, without opening the locked gates of Shari'a to the modern world, to accommodate the increasing demands of women and to respond to their social needs. The tactical changes or compromises in the way the clerical state oversees the rights and wrongs of women's social life, which have allowed the reappearance of women into public domains from which they were barred after the revolution, should be seen in this light. Several interrelated factors and mechanisms, which will be analysed shortly, have facilitated a change of tactics on the part of the Islamists in dealing with women and women's issues. Two main arguments inform this analysis. The first is that the most remarkable stimulus to the state's change of tactics has come from women themselves. Through their resistance women have responded to the conflicts arising from the incompatibility of their day-to-day experience in a relatively modern economy with a religious ideological, legal and political system that tries to genderize and sexually segregate every aspect of social relations. This response comes both from the 'subversive' secular women who try to survive the strict religious rules and regulations through their remarkable resilience and cunning manoeuvring, and from a rising reformist Muslim female elite that is trying to impose a more progressive reading of the Islamic Shari'a on the Islamic Republic. Women have succeeded not only in skilfully manoeuvring within rigid legal and cultural boundaries and prohibitions, but also imposing some compromises on the Islamic state.

Judged by the extent of women's deprivation and the harsh treatment that they are subjected to for defying Islamic codes of conduct, the use of the words 'failure and success' appear paradoxical if they are not contexualized. What the Islamists have failed to achieve is the reshaping of the images of women according to Islamic Shari'a; and they have been unable to silence women and make them accept their lot without resistance. Women have succeeded in placing their plight at the centre of politics in Iran and as a major issue of conflict in political discourse and ideological mobilization. This is an unprecedented development in Iranian history.

Second, the new developments should not cloud the fact that no fundamental compromises have been made by the Islamists in those areas of women's legal and personal status that may threaten to erode what the clergy consider as men's God-given rights and authority over women. For this reason, the condition of women's lives has generally deteriorated in the last decade and a half across all classes; and women's autonomy, personal liberties, cultural expression and freedom of movement have been seriously set back under Islamic rule. For example, women's access to employment and income has been further restricted. The most important illustration of this fact is the dramatic decline in the rate of female labour-force participation from 13.8 per cent in 1976 to 8.9 per cent of the total 'working' population in 1986 – a 34 per cent drop.[2] The problem has been acknowledged by government officials. For example, Shahla Habibi, the president's advisor on women's affairs, has identified 'the propagation of a culture of domesticity and house-wifery for women after the revolution' as one of the causes of the decline in the rate of participation of women in the labour market.[3] Mohammad Yazdi, the Chief Justice of the Islamic Republic, has also conceded the decline in the 'quantity' (*sic*) of women's employment, which in his opinion has been compensated by improvement in the 'quality' of their work. He is alluding to the increase in the percentage share of women in civil-service employment, and the decline in the number of working-class women in the industrial sector.[4] Other government officials who more closely monitor the status of women in the workforce, however, are less positive. A member of the Women's Cultural and Social Council (WCSC, Showra-ye Farhangi va Ejtema'i-e Banovan), which was created in 1988 to review and coordinate the government's activities and to provide policy proposals on issues of concern to women, for example, believes that even with the improvement in the 'quality' of women's work, declining employment opportunities for women means that 'before long we will witness a gradual elimination of women from social activities altogether'.[5]

Women now constitute 33 per cent of the students in institutions of higher education. An increasing number of them, however, are unable to find employment once they leave university. The state-sponsored women's magazine *Zan-e Ruz*, quoting the Employment Committee of the WCSC, reported the large number of unemployed educated women and complained of the 'masculinization of new employments'. For many government organizations, ministries and private agencies, the report alleged, 'only one consideration determines their decision and that is gender of the candidate and not her/his qualifications, expertise, consciousness and work commitment.'[6]

The government's educational policy has also increasingly restricted areas of specialization in universities open to female students. By 1985, women were banned from 91 areas of specialization offered by Iranian institutions of higher education.[7] According to official statistics, in the academic year 1990–91, female students were banned from 28.57 per cent of subfields in the humanities, 55.55 per cent of mathematical science, 23.05 per cent of applied science and 5.26 per cent of the arts' subfields.[8]

Pressed by the demands of persistent young women who are resisting the segregation of knowledge and educational opportunities and the push by Muslim women, whose loyalty to the principles of the Islamic state is not in question, the High Planning Council of the Ministry of Culture and Higher Education removed the ban. It allowed, at least on paper, the admittance of female students into all fields of higher education.[9] Nonetheless, unmarried female students are still banned from using government funds to continue their education abroad. A Bill to remove the ban was repeatedly defeated in the Majles. The last time that the Bill was debated, in the summer of 1993, the deputies articulated their opposition by referring to the 'dangers' involved in sending female students to the West, in that they may get 'infected by Western promiscuous values'. Ali Akbar Hoseini, a Tehran deputy, stated that women 'are easily corruptible' and that they might get infected by AIDS and 'bring it back to the country'.[10]

Although female enrolment and attainment in education has not suffered a dramatic setback, 'a serious attempt has been made by the Islamic Republic to segregate the academic pursuits as well as the future professions of women.'[11] The breakdown of specializations within the field of medicine points to a division of labour and sex segregation according to Islamic values. For example, in 1990–91, close to 50 per cent of medical students were women, while specialization in obstetrics-gynaecology was restricted solely to female students.[12]

The official statistics on the increased rate of divorce, often discussed in the Majles,[13] and the alarming increase in the number of suicides and self-burning, indicate both women's suffering and discontent and their protest. According to the Director General of Iran's Forensic Medicine, in 1990 a total of 50 women died in Tehran as a result of self-burning. The figure reported for the first six months of 1991 was 40 deaths.[14] No significant change is apparent in the state's extensive use of ideological apparatuses for promoting traditional Islamic values in the area of women's rights and gender relations, nor its use of physical coercion against subversive women. In fact, the harassment and persecution of Iranian women reached an all-time high in the summer of 1993, when a teenage girl was shot dead by police in a telephone booth in Tehran for defying the *hejab* code.[15]

All this attests to the complex realities and contradictions of sexual politics in Iran. It is also testimony to the inconsistent and incongruous political character of the 'moderate' Islamists in the post-Khomeini era: that is, the staunch proponents of economic liberalization are not necessarily supporters of cultural and political liberalization. The defeat of their open-door economic policy has only led them to resist more rigorously any move toward flexibility on public morality and personal liberties, particularly as they pertain to women's status and sexuality.

Defying the Guardians of Shari'a

To understand better the complex dynamics of Islamic sexual politics in Iran, it is necessary to look back at the early days of the 1979 revolution. The first official policies of the Islamists against women's rights and autonomy were mandatory *hejab*, abolition of the Family Protection Act, and the banning of women from judiciary professions. These formed the cornerstones of women's oppression in the immediate post-revolutionary years. These policies brought into the open the conflict between the newly established Islamic state and the middle-class secular women and other opposition forces.

The close links between family 'honour' and national pride, and between men's control over women and the nation's control over its 'natural resources' in populist Shi'i ideology, along with deep-seated hostility toward 'emancipated' women, made women the main target for reasserting Islamic identity and the cultural continuity disrupted by the developments of the previous decades. De-womanization of public life, particularly the removal of unveiled women from the streets, educational institutions, offices and factories was a top priority for the clerics. Ayatollah Khomeini's call for the reveiling of women, less than a month after the Shah's downfall, on 8 March 1979, was one of the first 'revolutionary' actions of the post-revolutionary state.[16]

Women responded to the Ayatollah by forceful anti-veil demonstrations. In a sense, they posed the first and most effective challenge, not only to the new government but to Ayatollah Khomeini himself (whose authority and righteousness until then had not been contested). Women's courage, will and ingenuity in organizing demonstrations, sit-ins and work stoppages in ministries, hospitals and schools – despite hostile conditions and direct confrontation with the Hezbollah gangs – astounded everyone and led to the government's temporary retreat. A number of new political and professional organizations formed in defence of women's rights. In the absence of a democratic political culture and an organized and autonomous women's movement, and because of the lack of active support for protesting women on the part of the left and other oppositional movements, discussed elsewhere,[17] the women's insurrection could not fend off the assaults of the new regime against women's legal and social rights.

In the summer of 1980, after the consolidation of Islamic forces in the government and with the elimination of semi-open political opposition, the wearing of the Islamic veil was declared mandatory for women in the workplace and in educational institutions. Eventually it became mandatory for all women. Clearly defined sex roles and sex-segregated policies and relations were established in every aspect of social life. And the clerical state, through a well-organized and forcefully implemented Islamization programme, launched its offensive against secular middle-class women, who, according to Ayatollah Khomeini, 'have been corrupted by the Shah's regime'.[18]

The Muslim ideologues and policy-makers, however, learned important lessons from the women's insurrection. First, the Islamists became conscious, albeit grudgingly, of the impact on women's lives of several decades of economic and social modernization in the pre-revolutionary period. The lives of many middle-class women, their self-images, and their expectations have been transformed in ways not favourable to the enactment of Islamic law and social order. The militancy shown by women against Ayatollah Khomeini's pronouncement on the Islamic dress code, *hejab*, was the direct result of the material and ideological changes they had experienced in the pre-revolutionary period. Women themselves were probably not conscious of this fact until the opportunities that the structural changes of previous decades had produced were threatened and eventually suppressed by the new regime. They had simply taken for granted the access to public education, technical training, paid work, a degree of choice regarding marriage partner, and the relative freedom of movement and personal liberties that they had enjoyed – albeit within the limits of a patriarchal, male-centred culture, and a repressive and corrupt political system.

Second, more pragmatic clergy and their functionaries realized, although hesitantly, that they could not convert and win the support of the female population through state violence alone. Legislation, the regular use of a police force or the Hezbollah gangs and other means of intimidation alone could not accomplish much. Women could be forced to observe the Islamic dress code, *hejab*, but they could never be trusted as the new Muslim women who are to symbolize the transformation of Iran into an Islamic society. After all, everyone, including the Islamists, knew very well that wearing the veil or a head scarf was not a matter of choice or ideological transformation for many women. Many street demonstrations against 'improperly' veiled women (*bad-hejabi*), the existence of serious threats and actual arrest – even torture and public lashings for *bad-hejab* women – and coercive enforcement of *hejab* by special squads and morality police continue to show that the *hejab* is not accepted by many Iranian women.

The Islamists, therefore, have realized that in order to re-create a traditional Muslim value system with regard to women's rights, to remodel the image of Muslim women in people's minds and to reshape the consciousness of the young female population, a more carefully designed resocialization and desecularization policy, including the creation of an Islamic role model, is required. Islamists have concluded that coercion must be complemented with ideological indoctrination.

The project for ideological indoctrination, however, relies heavily on crude, unimaginative and doomed-to-fail methods, such as mandatory prayer and religious instruction at all levels of schooling, beginning with kindergarten; Quranic recital competitions at schools; a series of seminars, lectures and speeches on the *hejab*, Islamic values and morality. The Islamic Republic has resorted to other methods of ideological indoctrination for inculcating Islamic male-defined feminine values and morality. The invention and promotion of the celebration of puberty (*jashn-e taklif*) for nine-year-old girls – who according to Islamic Shari'a have reached legal maturity and are thus able to marry – is a case in point. The idea is to prepare girls for their entry into womanhood with its obligations and responsibilities, as defined and prescribed by the clerics.

The permissible boundary for the adoption of non-traditional concepts and practices, and their reintroduction into society under the cloak of Islam was stretched further after Ayatollah Khomeini's death, to target the new generation of females who were being raised under Islamic rule. For example, an Islamic Women's Day was initially adopted to challenge and undermine International Women's Day (which was celebrated by the left after the revolution) and to mobilize Muslim women in support of the Islamic state and the values it represents. Every year on this day a select number of women usually meet with the Leader of the Islamic Revolution, to be lectured on male-identified moral values and to be praised for their submissive loyalty. In the last few years, however, the celebration has included several other events, including an Islamic fashion show, organized by the newly established Women's Bureau of the Office of the President. In the 1993 ceremony, three hundred 'Islamic' outfits were displayed – all designed under the government dress codes and given Islamic/Arabic names that suggested desirable Islamic values for women, such as Chastity (*effat*), Honour (*sharaf*), Self-possession (*metanat*) and so on.

Despite all these efforts, the Islamic Republic has not achieved any measurable success in the ideological transformation of the female population. The most obvious illustration of this failure to instil traditional Islamic values is the constant conflict over the *hejab* between the state and the secular young middle-class women who refuse to succumb to the Islamic and male-defined moral codes. Hence, an extensive effort has been made to mobilize a group of Muslim women into public life in support of the state. They are attempting to be a new role model for the resisting women. The social and political activites of this group, who have gradually formed a new Muslim feminine elite, also pose a pressing political concern for the regime. The criticisms and unfavourable reports in the

Western media and voiced by the Iranian opposition abroad about the violation of women's rights and the misogynist and male-centred policies of the Islamic state are counterbalanced.

Ashraf Grami, the editor of *Zan-e Ruz*, echoed this concern after her return from a trip abroad. As the first and only woman reporter to accompany the Chief Justice and his delegation in a state visit to several African countries in the summer of 1991, Grami wrote:

> The presence of committed and expert women in delegations sent abroad for political, economic, scientific and cultural purposes can counter-balance the negative propaganda of the world [media] and present to the world the progress and freedoms that the Muslim women in Iran have achieved. It will enrich the export of the Islamic Revolution.... Including women in the delegations sent abroad is a more effective means of propaganda for the Islamic government than hours of lecturing on the unconstrained presence of women in various social activities.[19]

The presence of a Muslim feminine elite is meant to be a message that women can enter the world reserved for men provided they succumb to the state's ideology and value system and respect the boundaries. The tactical changes in the Islamization policies vis-à-vis women, particularly in the post-Khomeini era, are best understood against this background.

A Differential Gender Politics

Women, whose presence in public life has increasingly been noticeable since the mid-1980s, cannot be seen as an undifferentiated whole, with no regard for their actual individual and collective differences and complexities. Based on their socio-cultural experience and their ideological perspectives and affiliations, women in Iran form three distinct groups: conservative Muslims, reformist Muslims and secular women.

The activities of these three distinct groups, their achievements and failures, and their treatment by the state expose the scope and peculiarities of gender politics in the Islamic Republic. The policy of the state in dealing with issues of concern to women and with the female population has been fastidious and selective. That is, conservative Muslim women, committed to male-defined and Islamic values and prescriptions, are the main beneficiaries of the new developments and of financial and ideological support from the state. Indeed, what could be more indicative of an Islamicized society than the presence of Muslim women, active in public and professional life, who are committed to the project of revitalizing Islamic values concerning sexual relations?

The task of representing the ideologically transformed Iranian Muslim woman, and conveying the cultural messages of the clerical state, is the responsibility of the conservative and non-questioning group of Muslim women. Almost all the women in this group who hold well-paid and high-ranking positions in educational and public health institutions, ministries and the Majles are linked to powerful male elites through blood or marriage. A number of them have served the revolution by being the survivor of a martyr, and almost all support the religious leaders of the state and the state's policies for women. Among these women are Ayatollah Khomeini's daughter, Farideh Mostafavi, and his daughter-in-law, Fatemeh Tabataba'i, who jointly run the Society of Women of the Islamic Republic (Jami'at-e Zanan-e Jomhuri-e Eslami), and President Rafsanjani's daughters, Faezeh, deputy to the director of Iran's Olympic Committee, and Fatemeh, head of the Board of Trustees of the Society for Kidney Patients. Others include Maryam Khazali, daughter of Ayatollah Khazali, a prominent member of the powerful Council of Guardians and the deputy director of the Women's Cultural and Social Council; female members of the parliament in the third Majles[20] such as Gohar-ul-Sharieh Dastgheib, Ategheh Raja'i and Marzieh Dabbagh; most women who represent ministries and various government agencies in the Women's Cultural and Social Council, and others involved with the Pasdaran Corps, and the Society for Islamic Propaganda (Howzeh-ye Tablighat-e Eslami).

Essentialist Islamic arguments, which are built around the physical, psychological and sexual differences between men and women – inevitably translated into different obligations and rights for women and men – have much appeal for these women. Many like Marzieh Mohamedian, a member of the Women's Cultural and Social Council, believe that 'the differences between the sexes are not cultural or social constructs, but are the effects of nature, such as women being a weaker sex, thus unfit to do certain jobs.'[21] Some demonstrate a deep conviction that a woman's inferiority leads to a lack of leadership qualities and judgement. The legal advisor to the president's Women's Bureau, Malekeh Yazdi, for example, is an ardent supporter of men's unilateral right to divorce. Following the views of her father, the Chief Justice, she believes, 'if women had the right to divorce, since they are more emotional and act unthinkingly, many families would be destroyed.'[22] The activities of the majority of these women are focused on consolidation of the Islamic regime, export of the revolution, and the uprooting of 'social vices', symbolized by Westernized (*gharbzadehi*) intellectuals, the dominance of western cultural values and particularly *bad-hejabi*.[23] The conservative women, however, do not seem to have much success, at least not with the female population inside Iran, who are increasingly turning elsewhere for role models.

Some of these conservative women, to varing degrees, have gone through political transformations or have adopted new tactics. Maryam Behruzi, for example, was a parliamentary candidate of the Fada'ian-e Islam in the first and second Majles. She often spoke in favour of excluding women from the judicial profession and against *bad-hejabi*. In one of her first trips abroad, along with her colleague Marzieh Dabbagh, she bluntly stated her support for the Islamic punishment of 'subversive women' (those who were improperly dressed), the execution of prostitutes, and preventing women from serving as judges.[24] In the third Majles, however, Behruzi, speaking in favour of women, called for amendments to the Family Law and recommended lifting the ban on sending female students abroad for more education. Moreover, she participated in the 1992 elections for the fourth Majles as a candidate of the 'moderates' and won a comfortable victory. This change of politics might be the result of a changing political alliance. However, with the growing involvement of the Muslim female elite in social and political life and the increased frequency of their trips abroad, the possibility of their gradually awakening to the unbridgeable gap between the socio-economic realities of women's lives and the religious prescriptions and prohibitions cannot be discarded.

This also means that among the new feminine elite are both women with very rigid traditional views, and those with more liberal views on women's rights under Islam. The latter, less dogmatic, Muslim women attempt, without questioning the principles of the Islamic Shari'a or the legitimacy of the Islamic state, to reshuffle traditional attitudes and dogmas in the hope of finding ways of meeting the modern world. In fact, more and more voices of dissatisfaction and protest against sex-based values, practices and policies of the clerical state can be heard from Muslim women. They represent a growing disenchantment with the Islamic government, whose discrimination against women in family law, education and employment they understand as being contrary to the Quran and Mohammad's teachings. They are also critical of other Muslim women who enjoy the state's support and generous funding, but do nothing except organize redundant seminars and congresses and go on state visits to foreign countries.

The influence of modern Islamic thinkers, particularly Ali Shariati, can be traced in the ideological and practical activities of these women. Among them are Azam Taleqani, a daughter of the late Ayatollah Taleqani and leader of the Society of Women of Islamic Revolution (SWIR); Zahra Rahnavard, wife of the former prime minister Amir-Hosein Musavi; and Ashraf Gerami and other women whose views are voiced by *Zan-e Ruz*, as well as contributors to the new women's quarterly *Farzaneh*, and particularly Shahla Sherkat, Mehrangiz Kar and their colleagues at *Zanan*.[25]

Following Shariati, the reformist Muslim women elites represent both a defence of Islamic law and tradition and a different interpretation to that provided by the clergy. They never question or challenge the Islamic laws per se. Instead, they criticize the 'customs' that mask outdated traditions and conservative interpretations of the Quran. By manoeuvring within the cultural, religious and political limits of Islamic traditions, they try to hold onto some degree of autonomy vis-à-vis the policies and practices of the state. Many, following the example of Taleqani, are critical of the orthodox believers who scrupulously follow religious orders in praying and fasting but treat their wives like slaves.[26] Others, like Rahnevard, believe the Islamic government has already lost the war on *hejab* and that reactionary conservatism has blocked women's progress in the Islamic Republic.[27] Ideological disagreement between reformist women and state functionaries writing in state-affiliated newspapers over the possibilities and limits of women's rights under the Islamic order occasionally comes into the open. Such was the case when *Zanan* responded in harsh terms to the accusations by the conservative *Resalat*[28] that *Zanan*'s support of women's social activities and rights represented a 'creeping cultural invasion' and was therefore 'suspect'.[29]

Despite ideological and political differences, and personality clashes and power struggles between the two groups of Muslim female elites, both groups express similar views on certain important issues. The battle to win back the legal rights provisioned in the Shah's Family Protection Act is a case in point. Both groups pushed for new legislation, albeit in different terms and with varying degrees of persistence. The conservative clergy, using the power of the Council of Guardians, actively opposed any reforms in the family law. The new family law that was passed in the Majles in 1990 became a subject of dispute between the Majles and the Council until it was ratified by the Expediency Council in December 1992.[30]

When Hashemi Rafsanjani, in the winter of 1990, talked of the undeniable sexual urges of youth and encouraged young men who could not afford permanent marriages to enter into temporary marriages (*mut'a*) for sexual gratification,[31] his Friday sermon caused a commotion. Both conservative and reformist women were disturbed and alarmed by Rafsanjani's statements. The Society of Women of the Islamic Republic in an editorial in its journal *Neda* spoke of the dangers of temporary marriage for family stability. Encouraging the practice of *mut'a*, it wrote, 'would increase capriciousness ... and draw the youth's attention from more important issues such as the presence of foreign powers in the Persian Gulf, etc'.[32] *Zan-e Ruz*, for its part, also criticized Rafsanjani for supporting the institution of *mut'a*, which, for many people, is nothing but a means of access to sexual pleasure without taking on any responsibilities.[33]

The third group of women active in public life are the secular educated women from the modern middle class. The desperate need for expert and skilled workers has helped these women – particularly at a time when many of their male counterparts left the country – to hold onto their positions or to assume positions of authority in professional and scientific fields. Women are also needed to fill the 'feminine' jobs in schools, hospitals and the state bureaucracy. The policy of the state towards secular women and the women's responses to it, however, are fundamentally different from the two first groups.

Evidence suggests that little change has occurred in the state's policy towards women who have shown no sign of ideological transformation or submission. De-womanization of public life, or at least the removal of this group of women from the public eye, is still the unstated goal of the clerics, the rhetoric of Rafsanjani and his associates favouring the extension of women's social activities notwithstanding. Further restriction of women's access to employment and income, mentioned earlier, speak to the hidden agenda of Islamists for ousting secular, subversive women. The presence of these women is tolerated in government institutions until they can be replaced by newly trained Muslim men and women. The strong resistance of women working in government institutions, who try to hold onto their jobs despite the pressures, and the practical difficulty of returning these women to the home, should not cloud this reality.

More subtle exclusionary practices are also at work to discourage women professionals, researchers and scientists from pursuing their work. Female archaeologists are banned from excavating activities and are transferred to in-house curatorial assignments. Female students in the field are in fact excluded from university courses in excavation.[34] Female botanists and herbalists are also excluded from field research and have to work on plants that have been collected by men with no expertise. Other female researchers have complained that, even when collecting information relevant to the female population, the jobs of data collection and field research are usually assigned to men. In isolated cases where women succeed in overcoming the barriers and biases and join a research team, they have to face insults and humiliation such as not being admitted into hotels along with their research group or being forced to use back doors in order not to be seen by other guests.[35] Central to the survival strategy of these women, however, has been the refusal to give up their profession, sometimes just to make the point that they exist. A female lawyer, Mehrangiz Kar, has remarked that:

> [I]n a sex-divided society which devalues women and the law sanctions the male-centred culture by disqualifying women from the bench, female lawyers have a particularly hard time to practice their profession and often feel their presence in the court to be residuary. Yet, they hope that the new judges and religious jurors will get used to seeing more women who have been educated and active in pre-revolutionary Iran and will not try to push them out of the society into domesticity.[36]

The most obvious sign of women's resistance to the overtly misogynist educational and employment policies has been their refusal to respect and submit to gender boundaries – defined and administered by the religious fanatics – mostly through their defiance of the *hejab* code. As the symbol of the reassertion of Islamic identity and purification of society from Western culture, *hejab* is the focal point of state propaganda. It is the main vehicle for imposing political and moral authority. Not surprisingly, the most consistent sign of women's challenge to the Islamic state and its policies is seen in defiance of the *hejab* code, despite continued surveillance of women and harsh punishment of those who are considered improperly veiled. Women are undermining state authority in exactly the area it uses to assert Islamic identity and clerical authority, that is, women's sexuality, their sexual and moral conduct and physical appearance.

Women have further developed their aptitudes and skills by assenting their identity and their place in social and cultural life. They are reclaiming the social space taken, but not held successfully, by the Islamists. This represents the defeat of Islamic fundamentalism in its battle to reclaim a long-passed moment in history characterized by clearly defined gender relations and sexual segregation. In July 1993 the Tehran vice squads detained 802 women and men for violating the Islamic dress code;[37] officials lamented the fact that 80 per cent of those detained were under the age of 20 – the generation that grew up under the Islamic regime but obviously has not been won over to 'Islamic values'. Consequently, the extent of the changes in the politics of the Islamic Republic in general vis-à-vis the female population should not be exaggerated; neither should the real character of the changes be obscured.

Understanding the political dynamics of the Islamic Republic is of crucial importance here. The Rafsanjani government has shown remarkable adaptability to the dictates of present socio-economic conditions. But his government has been willing to reach compromises with the conservatives on issues of sexual politics, in the hope of neutralizing their resistance on the more 'important' economic and foreign-policy matters. For this reason, despite strong signals sent by the government to convince potential investors, creditors and Iranian experts in the West of its liberalized policies, it has not abandoned its segregationist and misogynist policies. After about a year of discussion, in the winter of 1992 Tehran finally instituted segregation by gender on its buses. Women now have to sit at the back – behind a metal grille – and men sit at the front.[38] The attempts to impose 'Islamic morality' on women have gone further: the policing of women's looks and smiles in public is the new campaign launched by the police in order to stop women from smiling at men – for a woman's smile 'might arouse satanic lust'.[39]

Conclusion

In almost all Islamic countries the main battle of the 1990s, as Fatima Mernissi has astutely observed, seems to be the 'battle over the civil codes, which women challenge as contrary to the Universal Declaration of Human Rights, and which the authoritarian states defend as sacred'.[40] From Afghanistan to Algeria, no authoritarian Islamic state and/or movement has been spared the political and moral challenge posed by women to sexual oppression and hypocrisy and to gendered hierarchy and power.

Iranian women are waging a quiet but resolute battle against the Islamic state to assert some control over their lives. They have been struggling to push back the offensive of the Islamists, inch by inch, to recapture the spheres of public life that were lost immediately after the revolution. The outcome of this battle is of crucial importance to women in other Muslim societies in which Islamic states are being modelled on Iran. The Islamic Republic seems self-consciously aware of this fact. The formation of numerous policy-oriented commissions and endless seminars dealing with the status of women in the Islamic Republic of Iran are examples of the challenges that the government faces in meeting the modern world without compromising its traditional sacred laws and values. The resurfacing of deep-seated cultural and political contradictions and demands pressure the state to make adjustments in its reading of the Shari'a.

The overall political and economic crises of the state; the regime's failure to deliver its promised earthly rewards to the dispossessed; the pressing demands of the poor and the impoverished lower middle classes; and the growing antagonistic socio-cultural contradictions embedded in Islamic rule make it impossible for the Islamic Republic to meet the challenges arising from its gender politics. The growing clashes between the Morality Police and bystanders in the streets of Iran's major cities over the arrest of violators of the Islamic dress codes is an expression of the increasing disenchantment of the people with the Islamic Republic. The Republic's goal has been to purify the body and soul of the female population of non-Islamic values and choices.

The politics of gender is the 'Achilles heel' of the clerical state. This is the dilemma of a theocratic state that must initiate legal and social change without itself changing. The Islamic character and its claims to the sacred, which gave the state its legitimacy, are now acting as a delegitimizing force in the face of deepening socio-economic crises and contradictions. The clerical state has no remedies for this dilemma but its own self-negation.

Despite extensive use of ideological pressures and physical coercion against secular, independent, educated and non-compliant women, this segment of the female population has remained the most effective opposition to the patriarchal-Islamic social and cultural structures of the country. What is even more disparaging to the Islamic state is that voices of discontent emanate from the most unlikely source: the Muslim feminine elite – whose public life, university education and official position are predominantly the product of the Islamic regime. These women, who were essentially mobilized to support Islamization policies and well-defined sexual roles and who may be the main beneficiaries of the Islamic state, are increasingly demanding a change in the gender status quo. Their claim for rights is seen as a potent democratic challenge to Islamic fundamentalism. What these women have yet to recognize is that attempts to acquire women's individual rights and self-autonomy in a religion that is so concerned with sexual ethics and total submission to the rules and codes of conduct set by divine law might be wishful thinking and a battle already lost.

The emergence of a Shi'i reformist feminine elite in support of women's rights and their conflict with policies of the state, whose ideology these women embrace, manifests the dilemma faced by the Islamic government in dealing with women. It reconfirms the fact that gender oppression and the deteriorating status of women are not issues imported from outside and attributed just to cultural imperialism. They are the inevitable results of the dual structure and internal contradictions of a society long integrated into the world capitalist market, but whose politicians try vainly to keep social and human relations, and relations between the sexes, intact.

It is reasonable to assume that there is a limit to the state's tolerance of disagreement and criticism from its own allies. The reformist Muslim women are allowed to campaign for women's rights so long as they do not pass what Rafsanjani has identified as 'the red line'. The fact that the overwhelming majority of women involved in formal and institutional politics are still fundamentalists from a more orthodox, conservative and uncompromising faction of the ruling clergy is an indicator of the limits to freedom of expression on the issue of women's rights in Iran. It seems reasonable to expect that with the intensity of these contradictions and crises the bounds of the state's tolerance will be restricted further and the use of coercion will overtake ideological indoctrination and propaganda. The recruitment of 300,000 militia (*Basiji*) to push back the 'West's cultural invasion', and plans for the training and recruitment of another 300,000 as 'agents of ordering good and preventing evil',[41] signal the state's vision of future development. It also demonstrates the state's plans to concentrate its efforts on dealing with mounting socio-cultural and politico-economic contradictions. This is despite the fact that the evidence shows a failure on the part of attempts to organize the conservative Islamic state to reassert cultural identity in a society that has little in common with the Muslim communities of the seventh century, or to rely on force for resolving socio-cultural contradictions.

Notes

1. See for example, Ramazani, Nesta, 'Women in Iran: The Revolutionary Ebb and Flow', *The Middle East Journal*, 47/ 3 (Summer 1993).

2. Statistical Centre of Iran, *Summary of Population Census* (Tehran, 1986). See also Mehran, Golnar, 'The Application of Women's Empowerment Criteria in the

Educational System of Iran', in *Farzaneh: Journal of Women's Studies and Research*, Tehran: Centre For Women's Studies and Research, 1/2–3 (Winter and Spring 1994).

3. See *Iran Times*, 30 July 1993.

4. See *Payam-e Hajar*, 6 August 1993.

5. See *Iran Times*, 7 March 1991.

6. *Zan-e Ruz*, 23 November 1991.

7. Qahraman, Sahar, 'Siyasat-e Hokumat-e Islami Piramun-e Dastyabi-e Zanan be Amuzesh-e 'Ali' *Nimeh-ye Digar*, 7 (Summer 1988).

8. *Iran Times*, 30 December 1993.

9. *Zan-e Ruz*, 3 December 1993.

10. *Zan-e Ruz*, 5 September 1993.

11. Mehran, Golnar, 'The Creation of the New Muslim Women: Female Education in the Islamic Republic of Iran', *Convergence* (International Council for Adult Education), XXIV/4 (1991). See also Caesium-pour, Shahla, 'Educational and Vocational Activities of Iranian Women: Progress or Regress?', *Farzaneh: Journal of Women's Studies and Research*, Tehran: Centre For Women's Studies and Research, 1/1 (Fall 1993).

12. *Zan-e Ruz*, 22 September 1991.

13. The increase in the rate of divorce has been the subject of debates in the Majles. Some deputies have spoken of a 200 per cent increase in the divorce rate in Tehran in the last decade. See *Zan-e Ruz*, 15 December 1989.

14. *Zan-e Ruz*, 1 March 1992.

15. *Iran Times*, 11 September 1993.

16. *Kayhan*, 7 March 1979.

17. See Moghissi, Haideh, 'Women in the Resistance Movement in Iran', in Haleh Afshar (ed.), *Women in the Middle East: Perceptions, Realities and Struggle for Liberation* (London: Women's Studies at York/Macmillan Series, 1993); Moghissi, Haideh, *Populism and Feminism in Iran: Women's Struggle in a Male-Defined Revolutionary Movement*, (London: MacMillan, 1994)

18. Ayatollah Khomeini's speech on the occasion of [Islamic] Women's Day, 16 May 1979, reprinted in the Ministry of Culture and Islamic Guidance, *Sima-ye Zan Dar Kalam-e Emam Khomeini* (Images of Women in Imam Khomeini's Speeches), (Tehran, 1988), pp 66 and 97.

19. *Zan-e Ruz*, 9, 15 June 1991.

20. Four women served in the third Majles. Female candidates, however, made a strong showing in the Majles election and nine women were elected, four of whom, for the first time, were elected from outside Tehran. *Iran Times*, 17 April 1992, and 29 May 1992.

21. *Zan-e Ruz*, 29 January 1989.

22. See *Zan-e Ruz*, 3 July 1993.

23. The article of the Society of Women of the Islamic Republic was sent to *Zan-e Ruz* following the statement made by Ali Khamene'i on the cultural invasion of the enemies of the Islamic Republic *(Zan-e Ruz*, 1 September 1991).

24. Hakim, Rahana, 'We want to be our own servants, and our own masters', *The Herald* (Karachi) August 1985.

25. The Editorial Board of *Farzaneh* inludes Muslim women such as Mahbubeh Ommi and Monir Gorji, who cannot be identified as reformist or liberal Muslim women committed to women's rights issues. Monir Gorji, for example, the only

female member of the post-revolutionary Majles-e Khobregan (the Assembly of Experts which produced the Constitution of the Islamic Republic), considered that to talk as a woman and for women was blasphemy. See 'An Interview with the only female member of Majles-e Khobregan' *Zanan Dar Mobarezeh* (Women in Struggle), Tehran, October 1979.

26. *Zan-e Ruz*, 22 January 1989.

27. *Iran Times*, 7 March 1991.

28. On the political affiliation of Iranian newspapers, see the Middle East Watch Report *Guardians of Thought: Limits on Freedom of Expression in Iran* (NewYork, Washington, Los Angeles, London, 1993), pp 39–49.

29. *Zanan*, 2/9 (January–February 1993). See also *Zanan's* protest against the portrayal of immigrant Iranian women by *Kayhan Havai'i*, in *Zanan*, 2/14 (October/ November 1993).

30. *Zan-e Ruz*, 28 November 1992. According to the new law, divorce is subject to court approval with both partners having the right to institute divorce proceedings. The new law also requires the presence of women as legal advisors in Special Family Courts, 'whenever that is possible'. In cases where the husband's decision to divorce his wife is not justified and without an acceptable excuse, 'he has to pay the woman for her years of labour in the man's home'. The new law has kept silent about polygamy and temporary marriage. The divorced wife is still not entitled to any alimony beyond the three months and ten days waiting period that she has to observe before remarrying.

31. *Iran Times*, 7 December 1990.

32. *Neda*, Society of Women of the Islamic Republic, 1/3 (Autumn 1990).

33. *Zan-e Ruz*, 8 December 1990.

34. *Zan-e Ruz*, 7 November 1992.

35. Ibid.

36. See *Adineh*, 90, 91 (March 1994).

37. *Iran Times*, 2 July 1993.

38. *Iran Times*, 4 December, 1992.

39. *Iran Times*, 17 June 1994.

40. Mernissi, Fatima, *Islam and Democracy: Fear of the Modern World* (New York: Addison-Wesley, 1992), p 157.

41. *Iran Times*, 28 October 1993.

Appendix

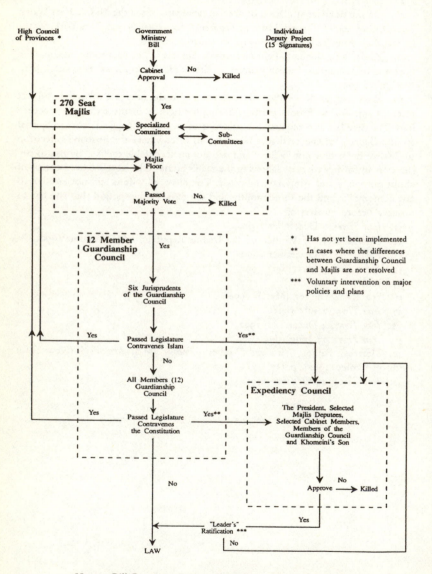

How a Bill Becomes Law in the Islamic Republic of Iran

Bibliography

English Sources

Abrahamian, Ervand, *Radical Islam: The Iranian Mojahedin* (London: I.B. Tauris, 1989).
———— *Iran Between Two Revolutions* (Princeton, NJ: Princeton University Press, 1981).
Afzal-ur-Rahman, *Economic Doctrines of Islam* (Lahore: Islamic Publications, 1980).
Aghajanian, Akbar, 'Ethnic inequality in Iran: An overview', *International Journal of Middle East Studies* 15/2 (1983).
Ajami, Ismail, 'Land Reform and modernization of the farming structure in Iran', *Oxford Agrarian Studies* 11 (1973).
Akhavi, Shahrough, *Religion and Politics in Contemporary Iran: Clergy–State Relations in the Pahlavi Period* (Albany: Suny Press 1980).
Al-'Azm, Sadiq Jalal, 'Orientalism and Orientalism in reverse', in John Rothschild (ed.), *Forbidden Agendas: Intolerance and Defiance in the Middle East* (London: Al-Saqi Books, 1984).
Al-i Ahmad, Jalal, *Occidentosis; A Plague from the West*, trans. R. Campbell (Berkeley: Mizan Press, 1984).
Alerasool, Mahvash, *Freezing Assets: The USA and the Most Effective Economic Sanction* (New York: St. Martin's Press, 1993).
Alesina, Alberta, and Alex Cukierman, 'The politics of ambiguity', *Quarterly Journal of Economics* cv/4 (1990), pp 829–51.
Algar, Hamid, *The Roots of the Islamic Revolution* (Markham, Ontario: The Open Press, 1983).
Ali, Abdullah Yusuf, *The Meaning of the Holy Quran, Text, Translation and Commentary* (Brentwood, MD: Amana, 1991).
Aliyev, S.M., 'The problem of nationalities in Iran', *Central Asian Review* xiv/1 (1966).
Amin, Camron, 'Under the shadow of Riza Shah: Modern and traditional perceptions of the subjugation of Iranian Kurdistan', paper presented at the Annual Conference of Middle East Studies Association (1992).
Amini, Ali, 'An interview with Dr Ali Amini on land reform in Iran', conducted by Hormoz Hekmat (Paris, 1986), Ahmad Ashraf's personal file.
Amirahmadi, Hooshang, 'A theory of ethnic collective movements and its application to Iran', *Ethnic and Racial Studies* 10/4 (1987).

———— *Revolution and Economic Transition: The Iranian Experience* (Albany: SUNY Press, 1990).

Arjomand, Said Amir, *The Turban for the Crown: The Islamic Revolution in Iran* (Oxford: Oxford University Press, 1988).

Ashraf, Ahmad, 'Chamber of commerce, industries, and mines of Persia', *Encyclopaedia Iranica* V (1992).

———— 'State and agrarian relations before and after the Iranian Revolution, 1960–1990', in Farhad Kazemi and John Waterbury (eds), *Peasant Politics in the Modern Middle East* (Gainsville: Florida International University Press, 1991).

———— 'Theocracy and charisma: New men of power in Iran', *International Journal of Politics, Culture and Society* 4/1 (1990).

———— 'Bazar iii. Socio-economic and political role of the bazar', *Encyclopaedia Iranica* IV (1990).

Ashraf, Ahmad and Ali Banuazizi, 'Class system vi. Classes in the Pahlavi period', *Encyclopaedia Iranica* V (1992).

————'The state, classes, and modes of mobilization in the Iranian Revolution', in *International Journal of State, Culture and Society* 1/3 (1985).

———— 'Policies and strategies of land reform in Iran' in Inayatullah (ed.), *Land Reform: Some Asian Experiences* (Kuala Lumpur: APDAC, 1980).

Bahmani-Oskooee, Mohsen, 'Black market exchange rate versus official exchange rates in testing purchasing power parity: An examination of the Iranian rial', *Applied Economics* 25/4 (1993).

Bakhash, Shaul, 'The politics of land, law, and social justice in Iran', *Middle East Journal* XXXXIII/2 (1989).

———— *Reign of the Ayatollahs: Iran and the Islamic Revolution* (New York: Basic Books, 1984).

Baldwin, George B., *Planning and Development in Iran* (Baltimore: Johns Hopkins Press, 1967), pp 24–39.

Banani, Amin, *The Modernization of Iran; 1921–1941* (Stanford: Stanford University Press, 1961).

Bayat, Assef, *Workers and Revolution in Iran* (London: Zed Books, 1987).

Behdad, Sohrab, 'A disputed utopia: Islamic economics in revolutionary Iran', *Comparative Studies in Society and History* 36/4 (October 1994).

———— 'Production and employment in Iran: Involution and de-industrialisation theses', in Thierry Coville (ed.), *The Economy of Islamic Iran: Between State and Market* (Louvain, Belgium: Peeters, 1994).

———— 'Islamic economics: A utopian-scholastic-neoclassical-Keynesian synthesis!', *Research in the History of Economic Thought and Methodology*, vol 9 (1992).

———— 'Winners and losers of the Iranian revolution: A study in income distribution', *International Journal of Middle East Studies* 21/3 (1989).

———— 'Property rights in contemporary Islamic economic thought: A critical perspective', *Review of Social Economy* 47/2 (1989).

———— 'Foreign exchange gap, structural constraints, and the political economy of exchange rate determination in Iran', *International Journal of Middle East Studies* 20/1 (1988).

———— 'The political economy of Islamic planning in Iran', in Hooshang Amirahmadi and Manoucher Parvin (eds), *Post-Revolutionary Iran* (Boulder: Westview Press, 1988).

Benedick, Richard E., *Industrial Finance in Iran* (Boston: Harvard University Press, 1974).

Bharier, Julian, Economic Development in Iran; 1900–1970 (New York: Oxford University Press, 1971).

Bill, James, *The Eagle and the Lion: The Tragedy of American-Iranian Relations* (New-haven: Yale University Press, 1988).

——— *The Politics of Iran: Groups, Classes and Modernization* (Columbus: Merrill, 1972).

Boorstein, Edward, *The Economic Transformation of Cuba* (New York: Monthly Review Press, 1968).

Browne, Edward G., *The Literary History of Persia* (New York: Charles Scribner's Sons, 1902).

Business International, *Operating in Iran* (Geneva, 1978).

Caesium-pour, Shahla, 'Educational and vocational activities of Iranian women: Progress or regress?', *Farzaneh: Journal of Women's Studies and Research*, Tehran: Centre for Women's Studies and Research, 1/1 (1993).

Cameron, A.J., *Hazrat Abu Dharr al-Ghifari* (Lahore: Islamic Publishers, 1982).

Center for Export Promotion, *Report of Non-Oil Exports* (Tehran: 1988).

Constitution of the Islamic Republic of Iran, trans. Hamid Algar (Berkeley: Mizan Press, 1980).

Constitutions of the Countries of the World, Iran (Dobbs Ferry, NY: Oceana Publications, 1980).

Cottam, Richard, *Iran and the United States: A Cold War Case Study* (Pittsburgh: Pittsburgh University Press, 1988).

Cremer, Jacques, and Djavad Salehi-Isfahani, *Models of the Oil Market, Fundamentals of Pure and Applied Economics*, no 44 (Chur, Switzerland: Harwood Academic Publishers, 1991).

——— 'The rise and fall of oil prices: A competitive view', *Annales d'Economie et de Statistique* 15/16 (1989).

Cudsi, Alexander S., and Ali E. Hillal Dessouki (eds), *Islam and Power* (Baltimore: Johns Hopkins University Press 1981).

'Current political attitudes in an Iranian village', *Iranian Studies* 16/1–2 (1983).

Deyo, Frederic C. (ed.), *The Political Economy of the New Asian Industrialism* (Ithaca: Cornell University Press, 1987).

Dornbusch, Rudiger, 'Credibility and stabilization', National Bureau of Economic Research Working Paper 2790 (1989).

Dowlat, Manizheh, Bernard Hourcade and Odil Puech, 'Les paysans et la revolution Iranienne', *Peuples Mediterranéens* 19 (January–March 1980).

Easton, David, and Jack Dennis, *Children in the Political System: Origins of Political Legitimacy* (Chicago:University of Chicago Press, 1980).

Elm, Mostafa, *Oil, Power and Principle, Iran's Nationalization and its Aftermath* (Syracuse: Syracuse University Press, 1992).

Enayat, Hamid, *Modern Islamic Political Thought* (London: Macmillan, 1982).

——— 'The politics of Iranology', *Iranian Studies* VI/1 (1973)

Esposito, John L., *The Islamic Threat: Myth or Reality?* (New York: Oxford University Press, 1992).

Fesharaki, Fereidun, *Revolution and Energy Policy in Iran* (London: The Economist Intelligence Unit, 1980).

Fragner, Bert, 'Social and internal economic affairs', in Peter Jackson and Lawrence Lockhart (eds), *The Cambridge History of Iran* Vol 6 (Cambridge: Cambridge University Press, 1986).

Ghasimi, M.R., 'Iranian economy after the revolution: An economic appraisal of the Five Year Plan', *International Journal of Middle East Studies* 24/4 (1992).

Hagen, Everett E., *On the Theory of Social Change* (Homewood, IL: Dorsey Press, 1962).

Hakim, Rahana, 'We want to be our own servants, and our own masters', *The Herald* (Karachi, August 1985).

Hakimian, Hassan, 'Industrialization and the standard of living of the working class in Iran, 1960–79', *Development and Change* 19 (1988).

Halliday, Fred, 'An elusive normalization: Western Europe and the Iranian Revolution', *The Middle East Journal* 48/2 (1994).

—— *Iran: Dictatorship and Development* (Harmondsworth: Penguin, 1979).

Haqshenas, Torab, 'Communism iii. In Persia after 1953', *Encyclopaedia Iranica* VI (1993).

Hassanpour, Amir, 'The Kurdish experience', *Middle East Report* 24/4 (1994).

—— 'The nationalist movements in Azerbaijan and Kurdistan, 1941–46', in John Foran (ed.), *A Century of Revolution: Social Movements in Iranian History* (Minnesota: University of Minnesota Press, 1994).

—— *Nationalism and Language in Kurdistan, 1918–1985* (San Francisco: Mellen Research University Press, 1992).

Henwood, Doug, 'Global Economic Integration: The Missing Middle East', *Middle East Report* 184 (September–October 1993).

Herz, Martin, 'Some intangible factors in Iranian politics' from American Embassy, Tehran to Department of State, Washington (A-702, 15 June 1964).

Hooglund, Eric, *Land and Revolution in Iran* (Austin: University of Texas Press, 1982).

—— 'Rural participation in the Revolution', *MERIP Reports* 87 (May 1980).

—— 'Khwushnishin population of Iran', *Iranian Studies* (August 1973).

Hourani, Albert, *Islam in European Thought* (Cambridge: Cambridge University Press, 1991).

Hufbauer, Gary C., Jeffrey J. Schott and Kimberly A. Elliot, *Economic Sanctions Reconsidered; History and Current Policy* (Washington, DC: Institute for International Economics, 1990).

Hughes, T., 'Land reform in Iran, implications for the Shah's White Revolution', research memorandum, US Department of State, Director of Intelligence and Research (8 February 1965).

Humphrey, Hubert, *Alliance for Progress: A Firsthand Report From Latin America* (Washington, DC: The Sidney Hillman Lectures, 1963).

Huntington, Samuel, *Political Order in Changing Societies* (New Haven: Yale University Press, 1968).

Ibn Taymiya, Ahmad, *The Institution of the Hisbah* (Leicester: The Islamic Foundation, 1983).

International Monetary Fund, 'Islamic Republic of Iran undergoes profound institutional, structural changes', *IMF Survey* (30 July 1990).

—— 'Islamic Republic of Iran: A social safety net system for the transition' (November, 1991).

'Iran blazing trails on new equity deals for Middle East', *Petroleum Intelligence Weekly*

14 (October 1991).

Issawi, Charles (ed.), *The Economic History of Iran* (Chicago: University of Chicago Press, 1971).

Islahi, Abdul Azim, *Economic Concepts of Ibn Taimiyah* (Leicester: The Islamic Foundation, 1988).

Jazani, Bizhan, *Capitalism and Revolution in Iran* (London: Zed Press, 1982).

Karshenas, Massoud, *Oil, State and Industrialization in Iran* (Cambridge: Cambridge University Press, 1990).

Katouzian, Homa, *The Political Economy of Modern Iran* (New York: New York University Press, 1981).

Kazemi, Farhad, *Poverty and Revolution in Iran* (New York: State University of New York Press, 1980).

Kazemi, Farhad and Ervand Abrahamian, 'The non-revolutionary peasantry of modern Iran', *Iranian Studies* xi (1978).

Keddie, Nikki, *The Roots of Revolution: An Interpretive History of Modern Iran* (New Haven, CT: Yale University Press, 1981).

—— 'Stratification, social control and capitalism in Iranian villages before and after Land Reform', in Richard Antoun (ed.), *Rural Politics and Social Change in the Middle East* (Bloomington: Indiana University Press, 1972).

Korner, Peter , Gero Maass, Thomas Siebold and Rainer Tetzlaff, *The IMF and the Debt Crisis* (London: Zed Books, 1987).

Kuper, Leo, *International Action Against Genocide* (London: Minority Rights Group, Report No. 53, revised 1984 edn).

Kuran, Timur, 'Economic impact of Islamic fundamentalism', in Martin E. Marty and R. Scott Appleby (eds), *Fundamentalism and the State* (Chicago: University of Chicago Press, 1993).

Lambton, Ann K.S., *The Persian Land Reform, 1962–1966* (Oxford: Clarendon Press, 1969).

—— *Landlord and Peasant in Persia* (London: Oxford University Press, 1953).

Lautenschlager, Wofgang, 'The effects of an overvalued exchange rate on the Iranian economy, 1979–84', *International Journal of Middle East Studies* 18/1 (1986)

Lerner, Daniel, *Passing of Traditional Society: Modernizing the Middle East* (Glencoe, IL: Free Press, 1958).

Little, Ian, et al., *Industry and Trade in Some Developing Countries* (London: Oxford University Press, 1970).

Looney, Robert E., *The Economic Development of Iran* (New York: Praeger Publishers, 1973).

—— *Economic Origins of the Iranian Revolution* (New York: Pergamon Press, 1982).

MacLachlan, Keith, *The Neglected Garden: The Politics and Ecology of Agriculture in Iran* (London: I.B. Tauris, 1988).

Mahdavi, Hossein, 'The coming crisis in Iran', *Foreign Affairs* 44 (October 1965).

Majd, Mohammad Qoli, 'The political economy of land reform in Iran', in *Land Use Policy* (January 1991).

Mashkour, M.J., *Dictionary of Islamic Sects* (Mashhad: Astan-e Qods-e Razavi, 1989).

Matin-Asgari, Afshin, 'Confederation of Iranian students', *Encyclopaedia Iranica* VI (1993).

McClelland, David, *The Achieving Society* (Princeton: D. Van Nostrand, 1961).

Mehran, Golnar, 'The application of women's empowerment criteria in the

Educational System of Iran', in *Farzaneh: Journal of Women's Studies and Research*, Tehran: Centre For Women's Studies and Research 1/2–3 (Winter and Spring 1994).

—— 'The creation of the new Muslim women: Female education in the Islamic Republic of Iran', *Convergence* (International Council for Adult Education), XXIV/4 (1991).

Mernissi, Fatima, *Islam and Democracy: Fear of the Modern World* (New York: Addison-Wesley, 1992).

Middle East Watch Report, *Guardians of Thought: Limits on Freedom of Expression in Iran* (New York, Washington, Los Angeles, London, 1993).

Moaddel, Mansoor, *Class, Politics, and Ideology in the Iran Revolution* (New York: Columbia University Press, 1993).

Moghadam, Fatemeh, 'Property rights and Islamic revolution in Iran', in Haleh Esfandiari and A.L. Udovich (eds), *The Economic Dimensions of Middle Eastern History: Essays in Honor of Charles Issawi* (Princeton, NJ: Darwin Press, 1990).

—— 'An historical interpretation of the Iranian Revolution', *Cambridge Journal of Economics* 12 (1988) pp 401–18.

—— 'An evaluation of the productive performance of agribusinesses: an Iranian case study', *Economic Development and Cultural Change* XXXIII/4 (1985).

Moghadam, Val, 'Against Eurocentrism and nativism', *Socialism and Democracy*, vol 9 (1989).

Moghissi, Haideh, *Populism and Feminism in Iran: Women's Struggle in a Male-Defined Revolutionary Movement* (London: MacMillan, 1994).

—— 'Women in the resistance movement in Iran', in Haleh Afshar (ed.), *Women in the Middle East: Perceptions, Realities and Struggle for Liberation* (London: Women's Studies at York/Macmillan Series, 1993).

Mojab, Shahrzad, *The State and University: The Islamic Cultural Revolution in the Institutions of Higher Education of Iran, 1980–87* (Ph.D. dissertation, University of Illinois at Urbana-Champaign, 1991).

Monteil, Vincent, 'The decolonization of the writing of history', in Immanuel Wallerstein (ed.), *Social Change; The Colonial Situation* (New York: John Wiley, 1966; originally published in French in *Preuves* no 142, 1962).

Mossavar-Rahmani, Bijan, and Fereidun Fesharaki, 'Oil dependence and mega-projects: return to economic normalcy in Iran?' *MEES*, supplement to 26/19 (21 February 1983).

Motahhari, Mortaza, *Social and Historical Change: An Islamic Perspective* (Berkeley: Mizan Press, 1986).

Najmabadi, Afsaneh, *Land Reform and Social Change in Iran* (Salt Lake City: Utah University Press, 1987).

Nehru, Jawaharlal, *The Discovery of India* (New York: The John Day Company, 1946).

Ness, Gayl D., *The Sociology of Economic Development; A Reader* (New York: Harper & Row, 1970).

Nomani, Farhad, and Ali Rahnema, *Islamic Economic Systems* (London: Zed Books, 1994).

Nowshirvani, Vahid, 'The beginnings of commercialized agriculture in Iran', in A.L. Udovitch (ed.), *The Islamic Middle East, 700–1900: Studies in Economic and Social History* (Princeton, NJ: Darwin Press, 1981).

Nowshirvani, Vahid, and Ahmad Ashraf, 'Iran's rentier state and the development of its entrepreneurial elite: 1950s–1970s', paper prepared for the Conference on Middle Classes and Entrepreneurial Elites of the Middle East (Berkeley, 9–12 May 1991).

Okazaki, Shoko, *The Development of Large-Scale Farming in Iran: The Case of the Province of Gorgan* (Tokyo: The Institute of Asian Economic Affairs, 1968).

Packenham, Robert, *Liberal America and the Thirld World* (Princeton, NJ: University Press, 1973).

Pahlavi, Mohammad Reza, *Answer to History* (New York: Stein and Day, 1980).

Palma, Gabriel, 'Dependency and development: A critical overview', *World Development* 6/7–8 (1978).

Parsa, Misagh, *Social Origin of the Iranian Revolution* (New York: Rutgers University Press, 1989).

Pesaran, Hashem, 'The Iranian foreign exchange policy and the black market for dollars', *International Journal of Middle East Studies* 24/1 (1992).

Plato, *Republic*, trans. Allan Bloom (New York: Basic Books, 1968).

Rahnema, Ali, and Farhad Nomani, *The Secular Miracle: Religion, Politics and Economic Policy in Iran* (London: Zed Books, 1990).

Rahnema, Saeed, 'Work Councils in Iran: The illusion of workers control', *Economic and Industrial Democracy: An International Journal* 13/1 (1992).

——— 'Multinationals and Iranian Industry; 1957–1979', *Journal of Developing Areas* 24/3 (1990).

Ramazani, Nesta, 'Women in Iran: The revolutionary ebb and flow', *The Middle East Journal* 47/3 (1993).

Robbins, Bruce, 'The east is a career: Edward Said and the logics of professionalism', in Michael Sprinker (ed.), *Edward Said: A Critical Reader* (Oxford: Blackwell, 1992).

Rodinson, Maxime, *Europe and the Mystique of Islam* (Seattle: University of Washington Press, 1991).

——— *Islam and Capitalism* (Austin: University of Texas Press, 1978).

Rouleau, Eric, 'Khomeini's Iran', *Foreign Affairs* 59 (1980).

Roxborough, Ian, *Theories of Underdevelopment* (London: Macmillan, 1979).

Safi, Louay, 'Nationalism and the multinational state', *The American Journal of Islamic Social Sciences* 9/3 (1992).

Said, Edward W., *Culture and Imperialism* (New York: Alfred A. Knopf, 1994).

——— 'Orientalism reconsidered', in S.K. Farsoun (ed.), *Arab Society: Continuity and Change* (London: Croom Helm, 1985).

——— *Covering Islam* (New York: Pantheon Books, 1981).

——— *Orientalism* (New York: Pantheon Books, 1978).

Salehi-Isfahani, Djavad, 'The political economy of credit subsidy in Iran, 1973–1978', *International Journal of Middle East Studies* 21/3 (1989).

Schwab, Raymond, *The Oriental Renaissance: Europe's Rediscovery of India and the East, 1680–1880* (New York: Columbia University Press, 1984; first French publication, 1950).

Scruton, Roger, *A Dictionary of Political Thought* (London: Macmillan, 1982).

Shayegan, Darius, *Cultural Schizophrenia: Islamic Societies Confronting the West* (London: al-Saqi Books, 1992).

Skocpol, Theda, *State and Social Revolution* (Cambridge, MA: Harvard University Press, 1979).

Skuttnab-Kangas, Tove and Robert Phillipson, 'Linguicide', in *The Encyclopedia of Language and Linguistics* (Oxford: Pergamon Press, 1994).

Spalding, Rose J., *The Political Economy of Revolutionary Nicaragua* (Boston: Allen and Unwin, 1987).

Sterner, Thomas, 'Oil products in Latin America: The politics of energy pricing', *The Energy Journal*, 9/2 (1989).

Stocking, George W., *Middle East Oil* (Nashville: Vanderbilt University Press, 1970).

Suk Tai Suh, *Import-Substitution and Economic Development in Korea* (Seoul: Korea Development Institute, 1975).

Sweezy, Paul, and Harry Magdoff (eds), *Revolution and Counter-Revolution in Chile* (New York: Monthly Review Press, 1974).

Tabari, Azar, 'Land, politics, and capital accumulation,' *MERIP Reports* (March–April 1983).

Tibi, Bassam, *The Crisis of Modern Islam: A Preindustrial Culture in the Scientific Technological Age* (Salt Lake City: University of Utah Press, 1988).

UNESCO, *Statistical Yearbook* (Paris, 1977 and 1980).

van Wijnbergen, Sweder, 'Intertemporal speculation, shortages and the political economy of price reform', *Economic Journal* 102/4 (1992).

Warne, William, *Mission for Peace: Point 4 in Iran* (Indianapolis: Merrill, 1956).

Warriner, Doreen, *Land Reform in Principle and Practice* (Oxford: Clarendon Press, 1969).

Weber, Max, 'Legitimacy, politics and the state', in William Connolly (ed.), *Legitimacy and the State* (Oxford: Blackwell, 1984).

Wilber, Donald, 'Memorandum of conversation: Dr Hasan Arsanjani, Minister of Agriculture', (10 November 1962), Ahmad Ashraf's personal file.

Wilber, Donald, *Riza Shah Pahlavi: The Resurrection and Reconstruction of Iran* (New York: Exposition Press, 1975).

World Bank, *Trend in Developing Economies* (Washington, DC, 1992).

World Bank, *World Tables* (New York: Oxford University Press), various years.

Zonis, Marvin, *The Political Elite of Iran* (Princeton, NJ: Princeton University Press, 1971).

Persian Sources

Abolhasani, Ali, *Shahid Motahhari; Efshagar-e Towte'eh* (Tehran: Daftar-e Entesharat-e Eslami, 1984).

Adamiyat, Fereydun, *Ideolozhi-ye Nehzat-e Mashrotiyat-e Iran* (Tehran: Payam, 1976).

Al-e Ahmad, Jalal , *Dar Khedmat va Khiyanat-e Rowshanfekran* (Tehran: n.pub., 1958).

Arsanjani, Hasan, *Mosahebeha-ye Radiyo'i-ye Doktor Arsanjani* (Tehran: Vezarat-e Keshavarzi, 1962).

Ashuri, Daryush, 'Iranshenasi chist?', *Barresi-ye Ketab* (1971).

Avanesian, Ardashir, *Yaddashtha-ye Zendan (Salha-ye 1928–42)* (Stockholm: Tudeh Publishing Centre, 1979).

'Azadi-e Tafakor', *Howzeh* 27 (August/September 1988).

Azimi, Hosein, 'Towzi'-e zamin va daramad dar astana-ye eslahat-e arzi', in *Ketab-e Agah: Masa'el-e Arzi va Dehqani* (Tehran: 1982).

Badamchian, A., and A. Bana'i, *Hey'at-ha-ye Mo'talefeh-e Eslami* (Tehran: Entesharat-e Owj, 1983).

Bank Markazi, *Barresi-ye Tahavvolat-e Eqtesadi-ye Keshvar Ba'd az Enqelab* (Tehran, n.d., circa 1984).

Bastani-Parizi, M.E., *Siyasat va Eqtesad-e 'Asr-e Safavi* (Tehran: Safialishah, 1978).

Bazargan, Mehdi, *Enqelab-e Iran dar Do Harekat* (Tehran: 1984).

―――― *Bazyabi-ye Arzesh-ha* (Tehran: n.pub., 1983).

―――― *Moshkelat va Masa'el-e Avvalin Sal-e Enqelab* (Tehran: n.pub., 1983).

―――― Kar Dar Islam (Houston: Book Distribution Center, 1978).

Bonyad-e Mostaz'afan, *Gozareshi az Bonyad-e Mostaz'afan* (Tehran: n.pub, n.d., circa 1983).

Chamran, Mostafa, *Kordestan* (Tehran: Bonyad-e Shahid Chamran, 1985).

Dana, F.R., *Amperializm va Forupashi-ye Keshavarzi dar Iran* (Tehran: Naqsh-e Jahan, 1979).

Edareh-ye Koll-e Qavanin, *Majmu'eh-ye Qavanin Avvalin Dowreh-ye Qanungozari-ye Majles-e Showra-ye Eslami* (Tehran: Chapkaneh-ye Majles, 1985).

Enjavi-Shirazi, Abolqasem, "Ellat-e vojodi-ye esteshraq va mostashreq', *Negin* 8/85 (1972).

'Eslam va avamel-e jenah-bandi', *Pasdar-e Eslam* 24 (November/December 1983).

'Fiqh va Eqtesad-e Eslami-ye Salem', *Howzeh* 25 (March/April 1988).

'Goft-o-gu ba Ostad 'Ali Tehrani', *Ketab-e Mehrab* no. 3 (Tehran: Entesharat-e Sabz, n.d., circa 1980)

Hambastegi: Khabarnameh-ye Moshtarek-e Sazman-e Melli-ye Daneshgahiyan-e Iran, Kanun-e Nevisandegan-e Iran va Komiteh-ye Defa' az Hoquq-e Zendanian-e Siyasi (December 1978 and January 1979).

Jalili, Abolhasan, 'Sharqshenasi va jahan-e emruz', *'Olum-e Ejtema'i* I/2 (1968).

Jenati, 'Taqrib-e manabe' va mabani-ye fiqh-e ejtehadi beyn mazaheb-e Eslami', *Taqrib Beyn-e Mazaheb-e Eslami* 1 (September/October 1980).

Keshavarz, Hoshang, *Barrasi-ye Eqtesadi va Ejtema'i-ye Sherkat-e Sahami-ye Zera'i-ye Reza Pahlavi* (Tehran: Institute for Social Research, 1970).

Keyhan, Mehdi, *Haftad Sal-e Jonbesh-e Sandika'i dar Iran* (Tehran: 1980).

Khalili, Akbar, *Gam be Gam ba Enqelab* (Tehran: Soroush, 1981).

Khomeini, Ruhollah, *Velayat-e Faqih, Hokumat-e Eslami* (Tehran: 1978).

―――― Sahifeh-ye Nur (Tehran: Markaz-e Madarek-e Farhanghi-ye Enqelab-e Eslami, 1983–1990).

―――― 'Payam-e Hazrat-e Emam', *Pasdar-e Eslam* 84 (November/December 1988).

―――― *Dar Jost-o-ju-ye Rah az Kalam Imam (Daftar-e Yazdahum), Melligara'i* (Tehran: Amir Kabir, 1983).

Khorasani, M., Va'ezzadeh, *Majmu'eh-ye Maqalat-e Farsi-ye Avvalin Majma'-e Eqtesad-e Eslami* (Tehran: Entesharat-e Astan-e Qods-e Razavi, 1990).

Khoshneiyat, Sayyed Hosein, *Sayyed Mojtaba Navab-Safavi* (Tehran: Entesharat-e Manshoor-e Baradari, 1981).

Khosrovi, Khosrow, *Barrasi-ye Amari-ye Vaz'iyyat-e Arzi-ye Iran dar Shesh Ostan* (Tehran: Markaz-e Nashr-e Daneshgahi, 1988).

―――― *Jame'ehshenasi-ye Roosta'i dar Iran* (Tehran: Tehran University Press, 1972).

Madani, Sayyed Jalaledin, *Tarikh-e Siyasi-e Mo'aser-e Iran* (Qom: Daftar-e Entesharat-e Eslami, 1983).

―――― *Hoquq-e Asasi dar Jomhuri-ye Eslami*, 7 vols (Tehran: Sorush 1987–1990).

Mahdavi, Hosein, 'Tahavvolat-e si saleh-ye yek deh dar dasht-e Qazvin', *Ketab-e Agah: Masa'el-e Arzi va Dehqani* (Tehran: 1982).

'Mavaze'-e Emam dar barabar-e Monafeqin', *Pasdar-e Eslam* (July/August 1982).

Momeni, Baqer, *Eslahat-e Arzi va Jang-e Tabaqati dar Iran* (Tehran: Entesharat-e Peyvand, 1980).

Motahhari, Mortaza, *Nazari be Nezam-e Eqtesadi-ye Eslam* (Tehran: Entesharat-e Sadra, 1989).

―――― *Naqdi bar Marxism* (Tehran: Entesharat-e Sadra, 1984).

―――― *Barresi-ye Ejmali-ye Mabani-ye Eqtesad-e Eslami* (Tehran: Entesharat-e Hekmat, 1982).

―――― *Bist Goftar* (Tehran: Sherkat-e Offset, 1982).

―――― *Jame'eh va Tarikh* (Tehran: Entesharat-e Sadr, n.d.).

―――― *Nehzat-ha-ye Eslami dar Sad Saleh Akhir* (Tehran: Entesharat-e Sadra, n.d.).

―――― *Piramun-e Enqelab-e Eslami* (Tehran: Entesharat-e Sadra, n.d.).

―――― *'Adl-e Elahi* (Tehran: Entesharat-e Sadra, n.d.).

Mowlana Jalaloddin Romi, *Masnavi*, edited by R.A. Nicholson (1925).

Nasafat, Mortaza, *Sanjesh-e Afkar-e Daneshjuyan-e Keshvar* (Tehran: Institute for Psychological Research, 1975).

Nehzat-e Azadi-ye Iran, *Tafsil va Tahlil-e Velayat-e Motlaqeh-ye Faqih* (Tehran: Nehzat-e Azadi, Iran, 1988).

Nika'in, Amir, *Rusta-ye Iran dar entezar-e tahavvol* (Tehran: Hezb-e Tudeh-ye Iran, 1981).

Qahraman, Babak, 'Dow yaddasht', *Ketab-e Agah: Masa'el-e Arzi va Dehqani* (Tehran: 1982).

Qahraman, Sahar, 'Siyasat-e hokumat-e Eslami piramun-e dastyabi-ye zanan be amuzesh-e 'ali' *Nimeh-ye Digar* 7 (1988).

al-Qurdawi, Yusuf, *Al-hal al-Islami, Farida wa Darura* (Beirut, 1974).

Rafsanjani, Ali Akbar Hashemi, *Edalat-e Ejtema'i: 'Masa'el-e eqtesadi'* (Tehran: Public Relations of the Organization for the National Industries of Iran, 1982–84).

―――― *Enqelab ya Be'that-e Jadid* (Qom: n.pub., 1980).

Rahsepar, Hamid, 'Melliyat-ha va faje'eh-ye Kordestan', *Ketab-e Mehrab*, no 3 (Tehran: Entesharat-e Sabz, n.d.)

Razzaqi, Ebrahim, *Eqtesad-e Iran* (Tehran: Nashr-e Ney, 1988).

Rezazadeh-Malek, Rahim, *Qanun-e Kar* (Jadid) (Tehran: Entesharat-e Ordibehesht, 1991).

Rohani, Sayyed Hamid, *Barrasi va Tahlili az Nahzat-e Emam Khomeini dar Iran* (Qom: Entesharat-e Dar al-Fikr, 1979).

Sadr, Muhammad Baqir, *Iqtisaduna* (Beirut: Dar al-Fikr, 1968).

Sazman-e Cherikha-ye Fada'i-ye Khalq, *Negahi be Mobarezat-e Tabaqeh-ye Kargar (23 Bahman 57–11 Ordibehesht-e 59)* (n.pl.: Havadaran-e Cherikha-ye Fada'i-ye Khalq dar Uropa, n.d.).

Sazman-e Cherikha-ye Fedai'i-ye Khalq-e Iran, Jonbesh-e Khalq va Tabaqeh-ye Kargar (reprinted by CISNU, West Berlin, 1978).

―――― *Darbareh-ye Eslahat-e Arzi va Natayej-e Mostaqim-e an* (Tehran: clandestine, 1975).

Shaji'i, Zahra, *Namayendegan-e Majles-e Showra-ye Melli dar 21 dowreh-ye qanungozari* (Tehran: Mo'asasseh-ye Motale'at-e Ejtema'i, 1965).

Shariati, Ali, *Khod Sazi-ye Enqelabi* (Tehran: Hosseiniyeh Ershad, 1977).

―――― *Mazhab 'Aleh-ye Mazhab.* (n.pub., n.d.).

―――― *Tarikh-e Adyan* (n.pub., n.d.).

Sherkat-e Sarmayehgozari, *Gozaresh-e Tahqiqati* no 24 (1992).

Sodagar, M., *Barrasi-ye Eslahat-e Arzi, 1340–1350* (Tehran: Pazand, 1979).

Vezarat-e Farhang va Amuzesh-e 'Ali, Sazmane Sanjesh-e Amuzesh-e Keshvar, *Rahnema-ye Entekhab-e Reshteh-ha-ye Tahsili*, no 2 (Tehran: 1994).

Vezarat-e Farhang va Ershad-e Eslami, *Sima-ye Zan Dar Kalam-e Emam Khomeini* (Tehran: 1988).

Official Iranian Statistical Sources

Bank Markazi Iran, *Gozaresh Eqtesadi va Taraznameh* (Economic Report and Balance Sheet) various issues (Tehran).

――――― *Hesabha-ye Melli Iran (1338–56)* (National Accounts of Iran, 1959–1977) (Tehran: 1981)

――――― *Hesabha-ye Melli Iran (1353–66)* (National Accounts of Iran, 1974–1987) (Tehran: 1991)

――――― *Hesabha-ye Melli Iran (1366–69)* (National Accounts of Iran, 1987–1990) (Tehran: 1992)

――――― *Natayej-e Barresi-ye Kargaha-ye Bozorg-e San'ati-ye Keshvar* (Survey of Large Manufacturing Enterprises) various issues.

Markaz-e Amar-e Iran (Statistical Center of Iran), *Amar-e Kargaha-ye Bozorg San'ati* (Survey of Large Manufacturing Establishments) various years.

――――― *Salnameh-ye Amari-ye Keshvar* (Statistical Yearbook), various years.

――――― *Avvalin Sarshomari-ye Keshavarzi-ye Keshvar* (First National Census of Agriculture) (Tehran: 1962).

――――― *Bayan-e Amari-ye Tahavvolat-e Eqtesadi va Ejtema'i-ye Iran dar Dowran-e Por-eftekhar-e Dudman-e Pahlavi* (Statistical Representation of Economic and Social Progress Under the Glorious Reign of the Pahlavi Dynasty) (Tehran: 1976).

――――― *Barresi-ye Naresa'iha va Vabastegiha-ye Kargaha-ye Bozorg-e San'ati-ye Keshvar* (A Survey of Insufficiencies and Dependencies of the Large Industries of the Country) (Tehran: 1980).

――――― *Sarshomari-ye Nofus va Maskan* (National Census of Population and Housing, November 1976, Total Country) (Tehran: 1981).

――――― *Amar-e Kargaha-ye San'at Dara-ye Panjah Nafar Karkon va Bishtar* (Survey of Manufacturing Establishments with 50 or More Workers) (Tehran: 1988).

Ministry of Economy, *Annual Industrial Survey* (Tehran: 1967).

Sazman-e Barnameh va Budjeh (Plan and Budget Organization), *Budjeh-ye Koll-e Keshvar 1358* (The Budget, 1379) (Tehran: 1979).

――――― *Peyvast: Qanun-e Barnameh-ye Avval-e Towse'eh-ye Eqtesadi, Ejtema'i va Farhangi-ye Jomhuri-ye Eslami* (The First Five Year Economic, Social and Cultural Development Plan of the Islamic Republic of Iran) (Tehran: 1990).

――――― *Layehe-ye Barnameh-ye Dovvom-e Jomhuri-ye Eslami-ye Iran* (The Bill of The Second Five Year Plan of the Islamic Republic of Iran) (Tehran: 1993).

Notes on the Contributors

Ahmad Ashraf teaches sociology and Near Eastern studies at New York University and is an editor of *Encyclopedia Iranica* (Columbia University, New York). He taught at Tehran University (1966–80) and served as Director of the Bureau for Social Research and Planning, Plan and Budget Organization of Iran (1972–82).

Sohrab Behdad teaches economics at Denison University, Ohio, and is Chair of the Department of Economics. He was a member of the Faculty of Economics at Tehran University (1973–83), and is currently President of the Middle East Economic Association (MEEA).

Hossein Farzin has taught economics at Georgetown University, Washington, and has taught at the American University, Washington, and Queen's College, Oxford. He also served as a consultant to the World Bank.

Amir Hassanpour teaches communication studies at Concordia University, Montreal. He has taught at the University of Windsor, Ontario, and was a guest researcher at Upsala University, Sweden.

Fatemeh E. Moghadam teaches economics at Hofstra University, New York. She has taught at Tehran University and Melli University, Tehran, and has worked for the Central Bank of Iran and the Plan and Budget Organization. She is currently the Executive Secretary of the MEEA.

Haideh Moghissi teaches sociology at Atkinson College, York University, Toronto, and has taught at Queen's University, Ontario, and Trent University. She was a Fellow in the Department of Middle East and Islamic

Studies, University of Toronto, and has served as a Senior Archivist of Iran National Archives (1973–84).

Shahrzad Mojab teaches in the Department of Applied Social Sciences at Concordia University, Montreal, and has taught at Windsor University, Ontario.

Farhad Nomani teaches in the Department of International Economics, American University of Paris. He was a member of the Faculty of Economics, Tehran University (1971–83), and was a member of the Editorial Board of the journal *Tahqiqat-e Eqtesadi* (Journal of Economic Research), Tehran University.

Ali Rahnema teaches in the Department of International Economics at the American University of Paris.

Saeed Rahnema teaches in the School of Policy Studies at Queen's University, Ontario, and has taught at the University of Science and Technology, Tehran. He was a senior member of the Industrial Management Institute in Tehran (1971–82) and UNDP. He is currently the editor of *MEEA Newsletter*.

Asghar Rastegar teaches at Yale University School of Medicine, and is Associate Chairman of the Department of Internal Medicine. He was Director of the Residency Training Program, Department of Medicine, University of Colorado. He has served as Associate Dean of Academic Affairs and chairman of the Executive Committee of the Department of Medicine, Shiraz University, Iran (1973–81).

Djavad Salehi-Isfahani teaches economics at Virginia Polytechnic Institute and State University and is Director of Undergraduate Studies in the Department of Economics. He was a Senior Associate member of St Antony's College, Oxford, and a Visiting Fellow at Oxford Institute for Energy Studies.

Sussan Siavoshi teaches political science at Trinity University, San Antonio, Texas. She was a visiting scholar in the Near Eastern Center of the University of California at Los Angeles.

Index

output ceiling, 153; price of, 118, 170 (collapse of, 166, 167; increase of, 48, 166, 194; setting of, 159); production of, 152–5; refined products, demand for, 161–5; reserves, 150; revenues from, 6, 109, 135, 190 (boosting of, 152; decline of, 109, 139, 169; dependence on, 151; growth of, 33, 37, 118, 120, 123; per capita, 150); sale of, 8; volume of exports, 151

oil fields, 48; Abu al-Bukhoosh, 171; Fateh, 171; investment in, 151

oil policy, external, 165–9

oil sector, after the Revolution, 150–73

Oil Service Company, 159

Oil Service Company of Iran (OSCO), 158, 159

omma, 2, 12, 66, 205, 231

open-door policy, 145; defeat of, 255

oppressed peoples, 60, 71, 76, 77, 85, 99, 116, 177; rule of, 105; solidarity with, 73

oppressors (*mostakberin*), 60, 76, 78

Organization for Investment, Economic and Technical Assistance (OIETA), 131

Organization of Petroleum Exporting Countries (OPEC), 48, 151, 152, 154, 155, 159, 165, 166, 168, 169, 170, 171; quotas, 168; role of, 168

Organization of Scientific and Industrial Research, 141

Organization of the People's Mojahedin, 77, 87

orientalism, 3, 4, 5; critique of, 209; reversed, 5

Orientalism, 3, 209

orientalists (*mostashreqin*), 3

orienteurs, 4

Orientitis (*sharqzadegi*), 7

Ottoman Empire, 230, 231, 246

Pahlavi Foundation, 177

Pahlavi regime, 53, 60, 79, 85, 203, 206, 208, 211, 213, 214, 229, 243, 247; collapse of, 40; nationality policies of, 231–4

Pakistan, 9, 158, 244

Paris Club, 194

parliament, 10; representation of minorities, 241; women members of, 259 *see also* Majles *and* elections

Parsons, Talcott, 5

Party for the Independence of Kurdistan, 245

Party of Islamic Nations (*Hezb-e Mellal Eslami*), 82

pasdar see Revolutionary Guards

Pashtuns, 230

pasture, 56; nationalization of, 58

patronage, 34, 38, 39

peasantization of nomads, 52

peasantry, 11, 21, 22, 25, 28, 29, 30, 37, 56, 58, 59, 85, 100, 103, 117; anti-revolutionary, 30; ascendancy over proletariat, 22; land ownership rights, 50, 55, 61; lower, 31; middle, 23, 25, 29, 31; non-revolutionary, 23; pauperization of, 21, 30; revolutionary, 23, 25, 30; suppression of, 26; unions, 236, 238

Persian language, 231, 243

Persianization of society, 232, 234

Persians, 229, 230

peshmargas, 234, 242, 245

petrochemicals, 133, 156

petroleum, price rise of, 121

Peugeot company, 141

physicians: imported from poorer countries, 227; migration abroad, 219, 220; numbers of, 219, 220, 225, 226

pilgrimage: and demand for foreign exchange, 192; duty of, 66, 77

pipelines, 155; building of, 158, 171; domestic, 159

Pipes, Daniel, 3

Point IV Mission of US, 130

political stability, 45–64

politics, Western view of, 205

polygamy, 204

population, growth of, 31

populist-statist position, 112, 116, 118, 122, 143; failure of, 116

pragmatism, 138; dominance of, 116–18; rise of, 109–16

prayer, mandatory, 257

prices: administrative, 67; control of, 67, 109, 120; decontrolling of, 121; distortions of, 187; increase of, 120, 121; market, 67; of energy, 163 (rising, 170); of fuel, increases rejected, 165; reform of, 180; used to control consumption, 151

primary texts, meaning of (*ta'wil*), 69

private property, 45, 61, 73; limits of, 98; rights, 105, 207

privatization, 118, 121, 143, 174, 194

Production and Development Services Centres, 141

productive employment, 184–5